STOCKS
for FUN and PROFIT

~ Adventures of an Amateur Investor ~
Herman VanGenderen

Tellwell Talent
www.tellwell.ca

ISBN
978-1-77302-861-3 (Hardcover)
978-1-77302-862-0 (Paperback)
978-1-77302-860-6 (eBook)

CONTENTS

Herman VanGenderen
Author

INTRODUCTION

The School of Hard Knocks

The book *STOCKS for FUN and PROFIT, Adventures of an Amateur Investor,* is based on a boutique monthly investment newsletter I started in 2014. My mission is to simplify and demystify stock investing for the hard-working middle class and busy professionals who wish to take control of their financial future, build wealth over time with above-average returns and do so with minimal time and effort, as they build their own careers in their chosen profession (like myself). Using my own thought processes and actual investments to demonstrate success, the book focuses on the real rather than the theoretical. It aims to teach by demonstrating success over time and provides actual portfolios including all the warts, the workhorses and the star stocks that make up every real portfolio. While time may change the content of the portfolio, it should not radically change the structure. My focus is on bottom line portfolio performance rather than the component individual stocks. Thus the book provides actionable guidance for readers and because this stuff can get boring, it does so by integrating a little bit of humour along the way.

WHY STOCKS? With all the volatility why would anyone invest in stocks? The answer is very simple. Investing in common stocks has, over the long-term, proven to be a highly profitable investing medium, especially in light of today's almost non-existent interest rates. If this is true, why do most people fail so miserably at investing in stocks? It has been documented that Canadian and US-based stock indexes, over the long-term, have returned over **9% per year**. The average mutual fund has returned about **7% per year**, and the average person in the average mutual fund has achieved a return of less than **4% per year**. How could that happen? I will attempt to explain on the following page. This information is not intended to be a criticism of mutual funds as they are an important part of the investment universe, but the book focuses on stocks and to a lesser extent exchange traded funds (ETFs).

Using the major US stock index of the S&P 500, I looked back 91 years to 1926. Each year the market can do one of four things: It can be **1) down significantly 2) down some 3) up some, or 4) up significantly.** I arbitrarily picked 12.5% as the break point between up or down **some,** and up or down **significantly.** Most would agree that an increase of 12.5%, especially in light of the current very low interest rate environment, would be an excellent year. _Before proceeding please guess the number of years (total of 91) that falls into each of the four categories._ Please keep in mind that these 91 years includes the great depression, Second World War, '70s inflation era, the October crash of 1987 and in more recent years, the 2000 tech bubble and financial crisis of 2007-2009. The book will occasionally integrate an exercise like this to aid the learning process.

About myself: I was born on a small dairy farm to Dutch immigrant parents and grew up in a large family with very modest means. My enthusiasm for farming led to a degree in agriculture, which was 100% paid for by myself without loans, government or parental assistance. I spent my entire 35-year professional career in agricultural sales and management, almost entirely with one organization, for which I led the effort to build a $150M business from virtually zero. I took early retirement from direct employment to start my own business as an agent for this same company. Throughout my career I was an active investor in both real estate and stocks building portfolios in both. My Registered Retirement Savings Plan (RRSP) has a 24-year record with 11.7% compound annual growth rate (CAGR) and my Tax-Free Savings Account (TFSA) has an 18.0% CAGR since this program commenced in 2009. I have achieved similar results in my wife's accounts, but expect the exceptional performance of the TFSA accounts to moderate in time. These results would be the envy of many financial professionals. The newsletter, and thus this book, integrates the learnings from 35 years of amateur investing and life adventures to demonstrate how readers can achieve similar results.

I have taken three required investment courses for a professional designation, but do not have such a designation as it also requires three years of financial industry work experience, which I do not have. What I have is 35 years of investing experience learning from the ultimate educational institution, the School of Hard Knocks. My first decade of stock investing was less than successful as described in the second chapter. These unsuccessful experiences are shared by many investors leading many to give up. With my stubborn and too dumb to quit attitude, I persisted to achieve the success mentioned above. **This book will provide readers a simplified approach through this investing School of Hard Knocks with fewer knocks and greater success.** My objective is to have readers complete the book with a shared enthusiasm for stock investing and an understanding of why STOCKS are both FUN and PROFITABLE.

And now for the answers to the excercise above:

As a successful investor and great believer in the ability of common stocks to outperform other investments, the results were even surprising to me. The breakdown is as follows:

1. **Down significantly**: 7/91 individual years representing **8%** of the years.

2. **Down some**: 17/91 individual years representing **19%** of the years.

3. **Up some**: 21/91 individual years representing **23%** of the years.

4. **Up significantly**: 46/91 individual years representing **50%** of the years.

The great surprise to me (and probably to you as well) is that in half of the past 91 years the market has been up significantly as defined by a gain of greater than 12.5%. **This is VEGAS in reverse with the odds clearly stacked in our favour. If we stick to a simple disciplined strategy, we will certainly WIN at the stock investment game and have lots of fun along the way.**

Why do so many fail? There has been a lot of research into why most professionally managed mutual funds fail to match, let alone beat the market. My interpretation of many articles and books I have read indicate two key reasons are: **1)** Fund managers don't get fired "following the crowd" but do get fired if they "stick their neck out" and get it wrong, and **2)** Fees, which incidentally are usually 1- 2.5% per year. The reason that individual investors do even worse than mutual funds is they put more money in after markets have risen when it is supposedly safe, and they take it out after markets have fallen when it is supposedly dangerous. One of the most important traits for success is the ability to swim against this tide by not pulling out after a market decline.

Format for the book: The inaugural issue of the monthly newsletter was June 1st, 2014, coinciding with a peak in the Canadian market, and after a significant run-up in the American market. During the two and a half years of newsletters included in this book, the Canadian market experienced a full bear market as defined by a decline of over 20%. The American market experienced two large corrections as defined by declines of greater than 10%. This was a difficult stretch in the stock market and a tough time to start a market letter, especially a Canadian-based one. As you read the early chapters in the book, you will experience my approach to these tough times. The early performance is not pretty but serves to illustrate the importance of not panicking, swimming against the tide, taking advantage of others panic and using these periodic difficult times as launch pads for future success. Tough times always give way to better times and represent great opportunities to build portfolios at reasonable valuations. A key component of long-term investing success is the ability to work through dark periods, and in a counter intuitive way the 2014 to 2016 Canadian bear market fortuitously provided crucial investment lessons to aid the readers' learning experience.

Each chapter of the book will be one month's edition of the newsletter, as close as possible to the original version with minor editing. This way the reader can experience as close as possible the fluctuations and emotions experienced through these challenging times and my response to them. With the value of hindsight and reflection, we will also periodically include new comments and learnings at the end of some chapters under the subtitle: "Looking Back." It is important to keep these comments in context because as the saying goes, "hindsight is 20/20," but it is also important to learn from both mistakes and sound decisions. There were three portfolios built during this time frame: a TFSA, an RRSP and a non-registered regular account. The TFSA and RRSP are model accounts based on our personal accounts but tracked as if they are actual accounts. I used model accounts as it would have been unrealistic to expect a new reader or newsletter subscriber to start with portfolios the size of our own after twenty plus years of building. As it is, each of these models was built much faster than would likely occur in real life but should serve to demonstrate how to build a great portfolio over time.

The non-registered account is an actual account set up specifically for the newsletter. It is 100% real. This is where the rubber really hits the road. I have read many newsletters and books over the years, and I do not recall any that were based on what the writer was actually doing as they were doing it. Clearly in book format this is difficult due to time delay, but each chapter is dated for historical reference. Over time, as the book ages, the individual stocks in the portfolios will slowly change but the structure of how they were assembled into a high performance portfolio will not. I emphasize portfolio over individual stock as it is, but as time passes the individual stocks selected should be de-emphasized in favour of how they were selected and constructed into a portfolio.

The second half of the book begins a discussion on the simple use of options in non-registered accounts to enhance performance and specifically in this case, to build the US side of the portfolio without converting a lot of Canadian dollars to US dollars at unattractive exchange rates. Options are not recommended until readers become very comfortable with their stock investing success. Once again, I demonstrate with my own live examples how I use options in conjunction with a stock portfolio.

I design my portfolios to take the best advantage of how taxes are applied to each of the three main types of Canadian portfolios, TFSA, RRSP and non-registered. I am by no means a tax expert and questions about each individual's tax situation should be discussed with your own tax adviser or accountant. Actually I am very much a generalist and don't really consider myself an expert on anything. I am just a regular guy who happens to have found a knack at being successful at a few things, including investments. **You don't have to be an expert.** In fact, being a smaller amateur can be advantageous because overanalysis often prevents action and overconfidence can motivate excessive risk-taking. It may also be wise to remember one of JFK's famous quips about "never relying solely on experts."

While this book is designed to help those who wish to take full control of their financial future by investing online, I realize this is not the answer for everyone. For those who wish to work with a financial adviser, the book will be very useful at building your knowledge base and provides extensive background information for your discussions with such an adviser. It will equip readers to ask more intelligent questions and prepare you to not always accept everything at face value. You will be in a more knowledgeable position to evaluate whether the adviser is really working for you rather than their commission check. In this regard Chapter 9 is critical as it illustrates a simple way to accurately measure and benchmark portfolio performance. This may seem like a simple exercise, and it is, but it is also one which is often done incorrectly.

I would like to forewarn readers the book contains a fair level of detail. Please don't confuse detail with complexity as they are different. The math used and explained is fairly straightforward. While I have integrated some humour this is not meant to be an entertaining novel. It is meant to be book that helps educate and motivate investing success. As such, a significant level of detail was required. If you can laugh at numbers it will be humorous.

And lastly a note to American readers who may have come across this Canadian book: While the book refers to our tax-advantaged programs, the US also has retirement accounts and, of course, non-registered accounts are the same with the exception of different taxation impacts. Building high-performance portfolios follows the same principles on both sides of the border. I have been heavily weighted to US stocks over the past decade as our dollar flirted with parity to the US dollar over this time frame. Our RRSPs and non-registered accounts were over 60% based on US equities. During the time frame of the book I tilted slightly back towards Canadian equities with the decline of the Canadian currency relative to the US. Most investors have a home country bias, and it is extremely unusual for a Canadian investor to have such a heavy weighting in the US. The reasons for that are explained in the book. As home country bias also afflicts American investors, the book will provide you with significant international commentary and the necessary knowledge to escape your own home country bias. You might also appreciate the simple way I work with exchange rates to enhance performance.

I ended each newsletter and will begin this book with the following disclaimer and disclosure:

The information presented has been obtained from sources believed to be reliable, and You1st Enterprises Ltd. endeavours to present all information as accurately as possible. However, complete accuracy cannot be guaranteed. Opinions expressed reflect personal judgment and are subject to change without notice. The publisher and its agents or employees shall not be held liable for any loss or damage that arises from negligence, misrepresentation or any act of omission of the publisher or its agents or employees. Trade in stocks and options carries substantial risk. Anyone considering such strategies recognizes this risk and must carefully consider their investments needs and their need to consult with financial and tax professionals. The writer is not a financial professional, but rather a successful amateur. Writings should not be considered as advice, but rather in the context of what I have done to be successful. Future returns cannot be guaranteed. All investments mentioned were owned by my wife or me on the date stated on the monthly issue, as described. We also often owned more shares and held options on many of the stocks mentioned in other personal accounts. Options are not suggested until an investor has significant stock investing experience and is very comfortable with their stock investing success. This report may not be reproduced or redistributed in whole or in part without the permission of You1st Enterprises Ltd.

With that, let's begin the fun and exciting journey towards building your financial security.

Thanks for purchasing the book. I truly hope you find the read enjoyable and educational.

Sincerely,
Herman VanGenderen

You1st **Enterprises Ltd.** where *"Your Success Is Our Quest"*

ISSUE #1: JUNE 1, 2014

Ancient Chinese Proverb:
"Journey of 1000 Miles Begins with a Single Step"

Welcome to the inaugural issue of *STOCKS for FUN and PROFIT* and congratulations on taking that first critical step in your own journey. I titled this issue with the ancient Chinese proverb because the first thing I would like to instill on subscribers is how little things (steps) compounded over long periods add up to big things.

Exercise: If you took a penny (I know they are out of circulation, but we still know what they are) and doubled it each day of the month, how much money would you end up with at the end of the month? I will integrate the answer below but please calculate on your own, as the process of calculating the answer was illuminating to me and I think it will be to you.

I hope this exercise has illustrated a couple things about longer-term investment success. **First, you can start with a small amount and grow it over time and, second, little differences compounded over long periods make big differences**. Computerization and low-fee accounts have made small trades possible and economical. You no longer need to trade even lots of 100 shares, referred to as board lots. This is different than when I started putting stocks into my RRSP in 1993. My records from that long ago aren't perfect but are reasonable for illustration purposes. One of my first stock purchases was Bank of Nova Scotia. I bought 100 shares at about $22.375 for a cost of $2237.50. This was a small trade back then. I would have paid full brokerage of about 3% or even more because the trade was small. Since then BNS has split 2:1 twice so I now own 400 shares. They are worth $69.63 for a total value of $27,852. They currently pay 64 cents quarterly or 3.7% dividend. Looking back at my low fee brokerage account website they were paying a .07 cent per share quarterly dividend then, which is the equivalent of 28 cents split adjusted or 5.0%. **Bottom line**: Over the 21-22 years their value has gone up by more than 10 times and their dividend has gone up in very similar fashion. I have full confidence that their past trajectory will continue such that in about 2034-2039 (twenty to twenty-five years) these shares will have a value of around 10 times their current value or $278,520 and they will be paying a dividend of 3.5-4.0% of the future value. The dividend is a bonus over and above share value growth and can be reinvested in more shares of the same company or other companies. A 3.7% dividend today is more than you can get on government bonds or Guaranteed Investment Certificates (GICs) and dividends increase over time with many companies. While this was a very small trade in 1992/93, today we can economically make much smaller trades. In our children's very small accounts our share purchases are usually around $1000. We don't worry about buying even lots of 100 shares. We just figure out how much money we have to invest, pick the stock and figure out how many shares we can afford. If it is 16 or 38 or whatever, it doesn't matter. The cost is $9.99 per trade so even on a $1000 buy it's just a 1% fee. This is way less than what I paid in 1993 and an insignificant cost if we are buying companies we want to hold for a long time. The often quoted Warren Buffett (arguably the world's best investor) says that his favourite holding period is forever.

With this first edition, I would like to start with my Tax-Free Savings Account (TFSA) securities and strategy. I used the BNS example from my Registered Retirement Savings Plan (RRSP) to give a real world example of the compounding exercise. I hope you all did this exercise on your own, but if not the answer is: If our month was February we would have **$1,342,177**. If it was a 30-day month we would have **$5,368,709** and if it was a 31-day month, we would have **$10,737,418**. For those of you who did not do the exercise, you will probably do it now as you will find the answer to be somewhat unbelievable. What a difference three days makes!

Before we go to my TFSA let's summarize some of the lessons and some of my philosophies illustrated above:

1. You can start with small amounts.

2. Little differences compound over long periods to make big differences.

3. Our favourite holding period is forever.

4. A forever holding period reduces our own workload managing the account.

5. I like stocks that pay dividends, especially in conservative registered accounts. Long-term research has illustrated that dividends represent a big part of overall stock market returns. In the BNS example above since my purchase in 1993, I have accumulated about $9500 in total dividends over and above the $25,614 of capital appreciation. Total return of about $35,114 to date on the $2237 invested.

6. Starting early in life is important, but starting is of utmost importance.

I know looking forward 20 or even 10 years seems like an eternity but think about it: Looking back it doesn't seem that long ago, does it?

Now for my TFSA holdings (values as of May 30th, 2014 with Canadian stocks in Canadian currency and international stocks in USD):

Company	Market	Industry	Ticker	Date Purchased	Purchase Price	Current Price	Current Dividend
Rogers Communication	Canadian	Telecom	RCI.B	Mar 4/14	$ 43.01	$ 43.82	4.18%
Teck Resources Ltd.	Canadian	Mining	TCK.B	Mar 4/14	$ 24.77	$ 24.17	3.72%
Ensco PLC	UK-US ADR	Oil and Gas Serv.	ESV	Jan 6/14	$ 56.45	$ 52.66	5.70%
Glaxo Smithkline	UK-US ADR	Health	GSK	Jan 15/13	$ 43.93	$ 53.94	4.74%
Innvest REIT	Canadian	Hotel Reit	INN.UN	Jan 5/12	$ 4.28	$ 5.16	7.74%
Ship Finance Intl.Ltd.	Bermuda-US ADR	Transportation	SFL	Jan 5/12	$ 9.59	$ 18.52	8.86%
AT&T	US	Telecom	T	Jan 4/11	$ 29.78	$ 35.47	5.19%
Toronto Dominion Bank	Canadian	Bank	TD	Feb 2/09	$ 19.52	$ 53.76	3.50%
Innvest REIT	Canadian	Hotel Reit	INN.UN	Feb 2/09	$ 3.09	$ 5.16	7.74%
							5.45%

Number of key portfolio points:

1. **High dividends**: If each position was equally weighted the yield would be 5.45%. I believe strongly in the purchase of dividend paying companies especially in tax-advantaged accounts, where the dividends accumulate tax-free.

2. **Invest early**: Purchases are made early in the year allowing more time for the money to work.

3. **Diversification:** Despite TFSAs being relatively small accounts at this time ($31,000 total current accumulated deposits, $5000 for 2009, 2010, 2011, 2012 and $5500 for 2013 and 2014) I have managed to create a fairly diversified portfolio with company representation from many key sectors, and including international companies. Over the next few years I will continue to add different industry groups.

4. **Low portfolio turnover**: I did not sell losing positions to make this look positive. I have only sold two positions to date in this portfolio: 1) Shaw Communications purchased January 5, 2010 for $20.80 and sold October 7, 2013 for $24.67. (I got tired of reading about the excessive executive compensation) and 2) BP PLC purchased October 7, 2013 at $42.16 and sold March 3, 2014 at $49.62 when Russia invaded Crimea as one-third of BP production is in Russia. I still like BP as an investment, but the Russian element brings too high a risk for a conservative portfolio. Low portfolio turnover is a key to success, reducing workload and stress managing.

5. **Withholding taxes:** This is one of the little things that can compound over time to make a big difference. I have not purchased any US equities in a TFSA since I had the illumination that we should avoid with-holding taxes when possible. The US government keeps 15% of dividends paid by US companies held in TFSAs, Registered Education Savings Plans (RESPs) and non-registered accounts. However, there is a tax treaty such that they do not have US withholding taxes on RRSP accounts. Thus US dividend companies, like AT&T, are great companies to have in an RRSP where there is no withholding tax, but not a TFSA or RESP. There is no withholding tax on dividends paid by UK companies or from Bermuda where Ship Finance is domiciled, even though you buy these on US exchanges.

6. **Adding to positions:** There are times one of the best strategies is to add to current positions. My first position in Innvest was small as it was the first year for TFSAs. I split between TD and Innvest for some diversification. I added to Innvest in 2012 to increase the size of the position to be in line with others.

7. **Current TFSA value:** $53,000 plus. CAGR (Compound Annual Growth Rate) of over 20% to December 31st, 2013.

8. **Currencies:** The Canadian stock values above are in Canadian dollars. The international stocks are in US dollars. I have picked up some return based on a declining Canadian dollar. That's the idea of international diversification, which I will get into more in future editions. Many international companies trade on US exchanges just like US companies, with what are called American Depository Receipts (ADRs). A UK or Bermuda-US ADR indicates a UK or Bermuda-based company purchased on a US exchange in American dollars (USD).

9. **What to do if starting today:** Below is the model TFSA portfolio we will base future results on, which is based on my TFSA portfolio above. Rogers, Teck and Ensco are new additions to my TFSA, although I have owned Ensco and Teck much longer in other portfolios. I think they all represent a very good entry point at their current price. GlaxoSmithKline, Ship Finance and TD have moved up pretty nicely since I bought, but still represent a fair valuation at these prices and I still like them. Innvest is a higher risk company as it is smaller but I have owned it in other accounts for many years. It keeps paying out its very nice dividend. I believe tourism is making a comeback. Despite the flood, tourism was actually up in Calgary in 2013.

10. **Model TFSA Portfolio:**

Company	# Shares	Cost	Approx Exchange	Cost In CAD	Annual Dividend in CAD	Price/Cash Flow	Price/Earnings	Price/Book
Rogers Communications	100	$ 43.82		$ 4,392	$ 183.00	6.3	14	4.8
Teck Reources Ltd	200	$ 24.17		$ 4,844	$ 180.00	6.9	19.6	0.7
Ensco PLC	100	$ 52.66	1.09	$ 5,750	$ 329.00	6.0	8.8	1.0
Glaxo Smithkline	100	$ 53.94	1.09	$ 5,890	$ 279.04	11.9	15.3	11.2
Ship Finance Int.	180	$ 18.52	1.09	$ 3,644	$ 321.77	9.3	13.1	1.6
TD Bank	100	$ 53.76		$ 5,386	$ 188.00	12.7	14.4	2.0
Innvest REIT	210	$ 5.16		$ 1,094	$ 84.00	14.2	n/a	3.4
				$ 31,000	$ 1,564.81			

The model is based on $31,000 maximum total contribution to a TFSA. **The dividend yield works out to 5.0%,** which is a better return than bonds or GICs. I added a $10.00 fee on each trade as the low fee brokerage charge. As subscribers may act on this at different times and different prices, you may have to juggle the number of shares. I still prefer even board lots of 100 shares but they are not necessary. No harm in going with 90 or 110, etc. Price/Cash Flow, Price/Earnings, Price/Book are all metrics I use to determine value. I will explain better in the next newsletter. There are various ways these ratios are calculated, and if you look at different websites you may find different values. They are approximate.

While past success in my TFSA has been excellent, there is no intent to imply similar results going forward. I certainly don't know the short-term future direction of the market nor each individual security.

Please get started: You may ask, as many are, whether this is a good time since the market has been so strong. Doubt may creep in. Nobody knows the short-term future direction of the market. Pundits are saying that the "EASY MONEY HAS BEEN MADE," but in 2009 they were **NOT** saying, "The easy money will be made in the next five years." There was panic everywhere. I have been expecting a correction for a year and it hasn't happened. Because I know I can't predict the short-term market direction and stayed fully invested, I have made excellent returns across all portfolios. Short-term we may go down but you will collect the dividends as the companies pay them. Short-term we may also go up, and long-term the market has always gone up. **Think long-term.**

Looking Back: I fortunately included the comment and warning regarding past and future potential performance of the TFSA. A CAGR of over 20% was unsustainable and wanted to make sure subscribers knew not to expect continuation of this level of performance. One key attribute to look for in evaluating services (financial or otherwise) is the extent to which claims are made and how realistic they are. Best to avoid hype and the promise of sensational returns. As the saying goes, "If it sounds too good to be true, it probably is." That said, I stick by my ending comments about starting and emphasize regularly the difficulty in predicting short-term market direction. It just so happened that the market and especially anything resource-related entered a deep, prolonged decline shortly after this issue was published.

One of my biggest learnings in the approach I took with the newsletter was regarding lump sum vs. periodic investing. Theory suggests that if one has a lump sum to invest, it is generally more profitable to make those investments all at once. That makes sense as the market goes up a lot more than it goes down. However, it does not take into account emotional and psychological factors if one makes the lump sum investment just prior to a market decline, as occurred here in the newsletter. A brand new stock investor could have been soured on the stock market for a long time. My actual TFSA had evolved over five years compared to the newsletter TFSA model, lump sum approach. I would not suggest using the lump sum approach and strongly prefer making periodic investments, building the portfolio over time.

There are a lot of charts in the book that you might have a tendency to glance over but please watch the evolution of the portfolios over time, as they are instructive.

Current TFSA maximum: At the time of book publication in 2017, the cumulative TFSA max was $52,000. Younger readers will need to calculate their personal maximum based on when they turned 18.

Exchange rate clarification: Canadian/US dollar exchange rates are referred to extensively throughout the book. There are two ways to do it: 1) Mention the number of US dollars or cents it takes to buy a Canadian dollar or 2) Mention the number of Canadian dollars it takes to buy a US dollar. If it takes 80 US cents to buy a Canadian dollar, then it takes $1.25 Canadian to buy a US dollar as 1.00/0.80 = 1.25. My charts and most mentions use the number of Canadian dollars required to buy a US dollar. The stock price in USD times the exchange = the value in CAD. (Example: 100 shares of a US or international company x 10.00/share x 1.25 exchange = $1250 CAD value or cost). There are, however, a few times when the other approach is used.

Taking Control, Ownership and Responsibility

Welcome to the second issue of *STOCKS for FUN and PROFIT*. In this issue I would like to delve more into the valuation metrics I use to make stock selections and describe each of the companies that are in my TFSA covered in Issue #1. Once again, I hope to make this simple and understandable in an effort to make the newsletter educational as well as help with stock selections. This does not need to be rocket science, and in my books keeping it simple leads to better success.

First, please indulge me as I go back into my stock investing history in an effort to help subscribers accelerate through the Investment School of Hard Knocks with less knocks by avoiding some personally experienced mistakes. In Issue #1 there was reference to one of my first RRSP stock selections in the early 1990s being the Bank of Nova Scotia. My experience actually goes all the way back to the early 1980s. One reason for covering this ancient history is that when trial ballooning the newsletter concept with friends I heard similar concerns, which cause many to give up on the market entirely.

(Disclosure: My memory isn't perfect, and there has been significant time and glasses of wine between then and now. I am trying to reflect the details as accurately, illustratively and briefly as possible. There were actually more twists and turns than what I will describe.)

The first stock I owned was Ralston Purina, the company I worked for immediately after university. We were able to participate in the company stock purchase program. After changing employers in 1982 I sold the shares without much thought. That was **Hard Knock #1** as they went on to do very well in the bull market afterwards. Sometime after that, about 1984, I contacted a brokerage company and they connected me with a broker.

He was a new broker, which I learned is the normal process. New small clients get new brokers. Many of these new brokers don't make it as it's a tough business. If you have significant assets you may get a more senior broker, but not someone like me with my couple grand. Starting out I didn't do any research on my own, just took his recommendations and bought what he suggested then sold when he suggested we sell. After all he was in the business, and I was working hard at my own job. This approach wasn't working out so well, even in the bull market of the 1980s so chalk up **Hard Knock #2.** Then along came October 1987, when stock markets around the world dropped in the range of 20% in a day. This was the biggest single day crash since the Great Depression. I'm not sure how much money I had in the market at the time but remember "losing" $5000 that day. That was a lot of money to me at the time (it still is) and this just about shook me entirely out of the market for **Hard Knock #3**, as stocks went on a thirteen year bull run after this infamous day. I focused much more on real estate for investment purposes. While real estate investing has been productive and certainly educational, it also entails a lot of work.

After the crash I decided to change brokers as I hadn't completely given up. (Too dumb to quit?) Besides, look at the numbers, I told myself, there has to be a way to make money at this. I remember looking at the newspaper stock charts. There was a big difference between the yearly high and yearly low on many stocks and I figured that someone was making money. The broker defended himself by pointing out some "successful trades," but I replied that overall the money had not grown. Therein lies a very important lesson. **It's not the individual buy and sell that creates profit; it's how the portfolio grows over time.** Many investors and advisers feel that you only create a profit or loss when you sell and complete the circle. I wholeheartedly disagree. While it may be true from a tax standpoint in a non-registered account, to me this is the wrong way to look at it. In my books it's the overall growth of the portfolio that represents success or failure. Please refer back to the Bank of Nova Scotia example in Issue #1. I have profited handsomely even though the shares have not been sold. I believe many of the market old wives tales, like "sell in May and go away," were started to help brokerages create artificial turnover, which enhances their profitability but not ours.

Back to the history: The new broker was also a junior broker. He looked at the portfolio I transferred to him and his immediate reaction was, "This is all junk...we need to sell most of this stuff, take the losses and move on," which we did for **Hard Knock #4.** After selling the "junk" it promptly rebounded. By this time I was starting to think that I needed to do more learning on my own. While digging through old files in preparation for the newsletter I ran across a handwritten sheet of paper from this era where I had written some advice to myself. Number one on the advice list was **Avoid Broker's Advice.**

The second broker didn't succeed in the firm and my account was then handed to another broker at the same company. It was with this third broker that I transferred my RRSP funds into a stock account. Together, we picked four stocks (including BNS) and four mutual funds. Over time the stocks did so much better than the mutual funds that I quit using mutual funds and focused on stock selection. He must have been good broker as he got promoted and the account was reassigned again. Now to my fourth broker. I didn't care for the new guy but stuck with him because was getting a little tired of all the changes. The fourth broker then changed companies, which often happens in the business. He called, as they all do when they change companies, and tried to get me to follow him to his new company. I stayed with the brokerage and had my account assigned to yet another broker, my fifth, which was actually a team of two who had more seniority. It was the mid to late 1990s when this occurred. I actually maintain this relationship on RRSP/RESP accounts to this day. The main reason is that if something happens to me, my wife will need help and, second, they are good guys and I am loyal. In the 1990s, the Internet was in its infancy and stock investing was still largely in the domain of full service brokers. Early in the relationship with this team they called regularly trying to get me to buy this or sell that, but in keeping with the Personal Advice Note #1 I rarely acted on these suggestions and, if so, only after I had done a little of my own thinking. After a couple of years they got tired of calling me with suggestions and mostly leave it to me to contact them.

Similar experiences to those outlined above cause many to abandon stock investing entirely or to move to supposedly safer mutual funds. One of the key lessons coming out of my first decade of relatively unsuccessful stock market investing, which really helped performance afterwards, was **taking control and full responsibility/ownership of each decision, myself.** No blaming the broker, the newspaper article, the weather, the book or anything else. Even if the broker called and made a suggestion which I took, I made the final decision. This helps minimize the never-ending sport of second guessing. I hope this newsletter, along with Internet investing, helps empower subscribers to similarly take more control of their investing welfare.

Valuation Metrics

How do I go about making stock selections?

1. First, I try to get some sector diversification into each portfolio. With all the government programs couples who fully participate may have, like we do, six to seven portfolios. Two TFSAs, two RRSPs, one RESP and two regular (non-registered) accounts. While diversification is especially important across all the accounts, I also try to have enough diversification in each account for safety reasons. "Don't put all your eggs in one basket" is great investment advice.

2. There are a number of sectors, including financials, utilities, oil and gas, technology, mining (materials), consumer, industrial and health care. Each sector also has sub-sectors.

3. As investing is quite faddish, certain sectors can be currently in favour while others are out of favour. Then after a year or two things switch around. I tend to start with the out of favour sectors as they usually represent better VALUE, and over time I try to build the portfolio such that most sectors are included.

4. I then try to pick companies which currently represent the best value within that sector. There are lots of factors to look at but make decisions largely based on 1) Cash Flow Yield 2) Earnings Yield 3) Dividend Yield, and 4) Price Times Book Value.

Cash Flow Yield is my primary criteria. I have inverted the ratio from what is used in the industry (price to cash flow ratio) as I believe it is more easily understood this way and equates with per cent interest rate, which everyone understands. A 10% cash flow yield means that the company had 10 cents of cash flow for each dollar of stock value, just like 10% interest means you earn 10 cents for each dollar invested. My focus on cash flow came from experience with real estate. There are certain non-cash costs a business has, the main one being depreciation. Cash flow strips out those non-cash costs so you can see how much cash the company generated as a per cent of the current stock price. In real estate (as in farming) taxable profits can be reduced and often eliminated with depreciation. A business can actually be very healthy without making taxable profits. When times get tough it is cash flow that will keep a company solvent.

Earnings Yield is my second most important criteria, but most investors/advisers rank it most important and it is by far the most watched value metric. I am also inverting the ratio from what is commonly used (that being price earnings ratio), so it is also more understandable. A 6% earnings yield means that the company made 6 cents profit for each dollar of stock price, just like 6% interest means you earn 6 cents for each dollar invested, whether that is a bond or GIC (if only...right!).

Dividend Yield is how much the company actually pays to shareholders each year, which you will get deposited in your account.

Price Times Book Value is a ratio of how many dollars the stock is trading for, compared to value of all the assets minus liabilities of the company. Book value is theoretically how much cash the company would have left over if it sold all its assets piecemeal and paid off its debt.

Over time I will build on these valuation metrics but wanted to highlight the key ones and what they mean.

TFSA Model

For illustrative purposes I have now taken the model TFSA portfolio chart from Issue #1, added dividend yield and changed the valuation ratios from what is commonly used in the industry to what I described above to illustrate how it all fits together. I have left the pricing as it was on June 1st as this represents the start point and is how we will measure the portfolio success over time. I will update quarterly to new pricing.

Company	# Shares	Cost	Approx Exchange	Cost In CAD	Annual Dividend in CAD	Dividend Yield	Earnings Yield	Cash Flow Yield	Price Times Book
Rogers Communications	100	$ 43.82		$ 4,392	$ 183.00	4.2%	7.1%	15.9%	4.8
Teck Reources Ltd	200	$ 24.17		$ 4,844	$ 180.00	3.7%	5.1%	14.5%	0.7
Ensco PLC	100	$ 52.66	1.09	$ 5,750	$ 329.00	5.7%	11.4%	16.7%	1.0
Glaxo Smithkline	100	$ 53.94	1.09	$ 5,890	$ 279.04	4.7%	6.5%	8.4%	11.2
Ship Finance Int.	180	$ 18.52	1.09	$ 3,644	$ 321.77	8.9%	7.6%	10.8%	1.6
TD Bank	100	$ 53.76		$ 5,386	$ 188.00	3.5%	6.9%	7.9%	2.0
Innvest REIT	210	$ 5.16		$ 1,094	$ 84.00	7.7%	0.0%	7.0%	3.4
				$ 31,000	$ 1,564.81	5.5%	6.4%	11.6%	3.5

Observations:

1. In general, cash flow yield is higher than earnings yield, which is more than dividends. I did a numerical (not weighted) average of all the companies. Innvest is losing money but still operating with decent cash flow. Please note previous comments on real estate. As a trust it pays out most cash flows as dividends. Last year it paid more. This is not sustainable. Either cash flow must go up or the dividend will be cut.

It lost significant money in the Calgary flood last year so I hope its cash flow grows this year. It is higher risk and thus a smaller position in portfolio.

2. Investments compete with each other. Given the level of earnings yield compared to current bond or GIC yields, stocks still look fairly priced to me. Should interest rates move up and/or earnings yield drop (either by earnings dropping or stocks getting more expensive) to such as point that earnings yield was below interest rates, I would be much more concerned with a potential big market drop. I cannot predict short-term direction (and in my opinion neither can anybody else) but will watch for earnings yield dropping below interest rates.

3. There are lots of variations in valuations, especially across sectors. For example, pharmaceuticals like GSK will have very high price times book. It doesn't take a lot of bricks and mortar to make drugs. If I did such a chart within a sector like drug companies, you would see more consistency.

Description of the companies and why I own each one:

Rogers Communications: New to me as an investment but everyone knows its name. With $12B in sales it is a major telecom, cable provider and media company. It also owns the Toronto Blue Jays and 37.5% of Maple Leaf Sports (Disclosure: I am a Habs fan but trying not to be biased against Rogers because of this). We own Telus and Bell in other portfolios, but Rogers looks like it has the best current valuation in the Canadian telecom sector. The new CEO is promising to reboot growth. The other factor I really like is it recently signed a twelve-year exclusive agreement with the NHL for broadcast rights of all NHL games, all formats of broadcasting, across Canada. I don't know what broadcasting will look like in twelve years but one thing is certain: Canadians will be watching hockey and paying something to Rogers for the privilege.

Teck Resources: With $9B in sales, Teck is one of the largest Canadian mining operations focused on copper, zinc, steelmaking coal and oil sands. It also mines lead, silver, molybdenum, specialty metals and fertilizers. Mining has been hard hit the last couple of years and is currently very out of favour. It sells at just 0.7 times book, or just 70% of its theoretical breakup value. While declining for the last two years it still has very good cash flow, earnings and dividend yields. The commodity business can be a roller coaster but mining will recover at some point. When it does, Teck should also recover.

Ensco PLC: With $5B in annual sales and based out of the UK (no dividend withholding taxes), Ensco is one of the world's largest ocean oil drillers. Oil is not going away anytime soon. When looking at its valuation, you will notice it has the highest cash flow and earnings yields of all the picks. It has a very modern drilling fleet, being the second newest fleet of all ocean drillers. Seadrill, which is my wife's TFSA, has the newest. Ocean drillers in general are selling at great valuations. I believe there is still a hangover effect from the BP Gulf of Mexico disaster, and lately there has been concern that the large increase in US shale oil production will reduce the need for ocean drilling. Shale oil, like most new sources of oil, is not cheap to get. I also have a new article in front of me that says 2013 world oil production went up by 557,000 bpd (barrels per day) and US went up by 1.1M bpd—meaning the world outside the US went down by 554,000 bpd. It also said world oil demand went up by 1.4M bpd. Even with the big increase in US shale production, demand went up more than supply. I am clearly not an oil expert but like it when investor concerns drive valuations to these levels.

GlaxoSmithKline has $26B in annual sales. There is very limited choice for Canadian-based health care companies, so we must look abroad for this sector. UK-based companies are ideal for TFSAs due to zero withholding tax on dividends. GlaxoSmithKline fits the bill. As with most pharma companies, generics have taken a bite out of profitability and the regulatory environment makes it increasingly difficult to get new products to market. However, the world population is aging and these companies bring products to market that enhance the quality and duration of life. It makes prescription medicines, vaccines and consumer health care products. A couple of its consumer brands are Sensodyne and Aquafresh toothpastes, Breathe Right nasal strips, Nicorette and Tums for your tummy. Interestingly Pfizer just tried and failed to buy AstraZeneca, another UK-based pharma of similar size, in order to set up their world headquarters in the UK for lower tax rates than the US.

Ship Finance International: With $300M in annual sales it is not a large company but it is a large owner, operator and lessor of ocean vessels including twenty-four oil tankers, twelve dry bulk carriers, eleven container vessels, two car carriers and four drilling rigs plus supply vessels. Guaranteed, you have purchased items delivered to Canada by an SFL ship. It is based out of Bermuda and plays a large amount of its cash flow out in dividends. It's pricier than I like right now but still reasonable and is a good choice for TFSA as the dividends are not taxed. It should benefit from an expanding global economy.

TD Bank: With $23B in sales it is one of Canada's big five banks. It is large in Canada and growing in the US. The Boston Bruins play from the TD Gardens. TD has a little higher valuation at this time than other Canadian banks with just 6.9% earnings yield, but it usually seems to be a little higher. I bank at TD. I started banking at Canada Trust during my university years. You might recall the "8 to 8, 6 days straight" commercials. TD bought Canada Trust a long time ago. It was a very unusual and successful acquisition as the acquiring company (TD) actually adopted the customer focused culture of the acquired company (Canada Trust). Acquiring companies normally force the acquired to adopt their culture, often leading to culture clash and a less successful integration of the businesses. I recall an article from some time ago that at a bank convention, prior to the financial crisis, numerous bank speakers talked about their "financial engineering strategies" to increase their share price. TD's CEO was the only speaker who talked about their growth strategy of focusing on the customer experience and customer satisfaction. What a unique perspective!!! (Sorry, just a little cynicism.) I also happen to believe that the most successful companies for long-term shareholder value are those that focus on their customers.

Innvest REIT (Real Estate Investment Trust) has $600M in annual sales. It owns 119 hotels across Canada and 50% of Choice Hotels Canada Inc. Its hotels carry many common brands including Comfort Inn, Delta, Hilton, Holiday Inn, Radisson, Sheraton, and Quality Suites. It owns the Fairmont Palliser in Calgary and the Fairmont Hotel Macdonald in Edmonton as well as the Delta London Armouries. As a real estate trust, it pays out most of its cash flow as dividends. There appears to be resurgence in tourism as the economy improves, but hotels are very sensitive to the economic environment and suffer during recessions. It is higher risk and thus a smaller part of the model portfolio.

I hope these descriptions give you a sense of what you may be investing in. If you buy shares you own part of the company. That's one of the FUN and interesting aspects of investing. When you walk into your bank branch or hotel you can think to yourself "I own part of this place" and take some pride in the ownership.

With this issue I attempted to lay a basic but solid foundation of knowledge regarding financial metrics for stock evaluation to complement the stock selections. The next issue (chapter in the book) will delve into my wife's TFSA picks. Until then, **have fun investing.**

Looking Back: On July 1st, 2014, oil was hovering around $100 a barrel, but was about to fall over a cliff that would take it down to $26.00 by early 2016. I'm not sure if the report I had just read was inaccurate or if the surge occurred just afterwards but it doesn't matter. Mistakes happen in this business and it's mostly how we respond to them that determines overall success. Copper was about $3.20/lb. and was set to fall to $2.00. Other commodities experienced similar fates, although none of this was known at the time. Smaller portfolios such as this can be heavily influenced by one or two company positions. Both Ensco and Teck performed unceremonious face plants, taking the portfolio with them. NOT FUN but reality and something a successful stock investor needs to accept as a periodic occurrence. You will witness my response and how the portfolio reacted throughout the book.

One thing to be cautious about when reading the "Looking Back" section is what is referred to as "hindsight bias" or "hindsight vision is 20/20." Hindsight bias is basically occurring when one thinks something like "I knew that was going to happen, so why didn't I act on that knowledge...shucks." The fact of the matter is one never knows for sure something is going to happen and perpetually kicking oneself for not acting is a difficult urge to control but usually counterproductive. It is best to accept what happened, learn from it and move forward.

I have recently severed our relationship with the broker mentioned, with accounts moved to our low-fee Internet brokerage. Our oldest son has proven to be adept at stock investing and can now take over management of our accounts should something happen to me. I sure hope that doesn't come to pass!

Buy Value...Rarely Sell

Investing is a journey. Each subscriber has different experiences, background and financial resources. With each newsletter I hope to help educate and provide stock selection suggestions that will help you meet your individual needs and goals. Each company stock in our model portfolios is owned by myself or my immediate family. In other words we "put our money where our mouth is." While I cannot cater advice individually, subscribers can take some comfort in the fact that our own financial well-being also relies on the stock selections presented.

In this issue we will go through my wife's (Lillian's) TFSA. We will once again show the companies she owns, what she paid and design a model portfolio for $31,000 based on her portfolio. I have started the newsletter series with TFSAs as it is an excellent program for saving and investing. It is also a great place to start with stock investing, as dividends and capital gains are tax-free. Before we get to the meat and potatoes though, let's have some discussion on my primary investment strategy of **Buy Value...Rarely Sell.**

Everyone has heard of and would like to follow the **Buy Low...Sell High** strategy. This often becomes **Buy High...Sell Low** as buying low and selling high is easy to say but very difficult to do. Some recent information illustrated the point. Between 1994 and 2013 the S&P 500 returned 9.2% annually and bonds returned 5.7%. However, the average investor achieved a paltry 2.5%. There was no explanation as to the discrepancy, but one can surmise that many investors bailed out during the two big stock bear markets, which occurred during this time frame, thus investors bought high and sold low. When thinking about how to accurately and succinctly describe my approach, **Buy Value...Rarely Sell** fits perfectly.

Perhaps inheriting my last name has helped in this regard. It doesn't matter whether buying stocks, an auto, shoes or groceries, I tend to look for items ON SALE. **What defines VALUE?** Sounds like a simple question but like beauty, value is in the eye of the beholder. If one asked 10 different people there would probably be 10 different answers with some common threads amongst them. To me it means buying something at a lower price than I was willing to pay in the first place. Example: when recently shopping for a few gym clothing items (after being goaded by the kids... I now have three fashion critics), I found a couple of gym T-shirts that fit, matched the gym shorts and, **bonus**, were marked down by over 50%. I would have bought them anyway, so the markdown created extra value. They satisfied my needs and were priced lower than originally thought.

Similarly, in the stock market world, value can be defined as finding a stock that fits the portfolio and is reasonably priced, or on sale after a correction, using the metrics outlined in Issue #2. It isn't always the best company (How do you really know?), nor the best industry (Again, how do you know long-term?). Value could also be defined as a great company at a good price, or a good company at a fair price or just a fair company at a bargain price. It's difficult to know ahead of time whether a company is great, good or fair, and companies can move up and down that scale simply with a management change or other significant event. Finding value usually means avoiding the current "hot" companies/sectors and hunting for those companies and industries out of favour while still maintaining good portfolio diversification.

That explains the "Buy Value" part but what about the "Rarely Sell"? There have been studies showing portfolios with lower turnover often have better results than those with higher turnover. Is it not uncommon for a mutual fund to have 100% turnover per year. Portfolio managers, like individual investors, often get impatient if the price doesn't rise quickly. Patience is key. One of the reasons for focusing on dividend paying companies is that it's easier to practice patience when receiving dividends. Along with the Bank of Nova Scotia (Issue #1) one of the other companies I bought in the '90s was Noranda. You might remember the name. It's difficult to remember all the details but remember that it was paying about a 4-5% dividend. I held it for a long time without any increase in price, being content to collect the dividend. Then in very short period of time it started to move up and eventually got bought out at a significant premium. I found the slips in some old files in the furnace room. I held it for eleven years, collected the very nice dividend each quarter, and sold at about three times the purchase price. Not quite as good as BNS but pretty darn good. Most of the capital gain was achieved in the last couple years of ownership. That's how the market often works.

However, there are times to sell. Selling is mentally tougher and can be more emotional than buying. Each year from February to April, as most companies report their fiscal year-ends, I go through the financials and identify those companies that are candidates to sell during the upcoming year. This is usually based on valuation concerns or if tweaking the overall mix. As well, if cash is needed for any reason and an opportune time occurs, I have pre-thought the selling decisions taking out some of those emotions. Improved selling is a goal, especially with cyclical stocks like mining. Hopefully that explains the rationale for "Rarely Sell." So let's now move to the meat and potatoes. Are you hungry?

Lillian's TFSA holdings with values as of July 25, 2014:

Company	Market	Industry	Ticker	Date Purchased	Purchase Price	Current Price	Current Dividend
Seadrill	Bermuda-US ADR	Oil and Gas Serv.	SDRL	Apr 11/14	$ 32.98	$ 37.49	10.70%
Rogers Communication	Canadian	Telecom	RCI.B	Jan 6/14	$ 47.09	$ 42.46	4.31%
HSBC Holdings PLC	UK-US ADR	Bank	HSBC	Jan 6/14	$ 54.51	$ 52.82	4.54%
HSBC Holdings PLC	UK-US ADR	Bank	HSBC	June 28/13	$ 51.85	$ 52.82	4.54%
Vodafone Grp PLC	UK-US ADR	Telecom	VOD	Jan 25/13	$ 26.94	$ 34.16	5.34%
Sunlife Financial	Canadian	Insurance	SLF	Jan 6/12	$ 19.56	$ 41.40	3.48%
Husky Energy	Canadian	Oil and Gas	HSE	Jan 5/12	$ 24.51	$ 33.72	3.56%
Husky Energy	Canadian	Oil and Gas	HSE	Mar 23/11	$ 29.27	$ 33.72	3.56%
Hospitality Prop Trust	US	Hotel Reit	HPT	Jan 4/11	$ 23.39	$ 29.64	6.61%
ATCO	Canadian	Utility	ACO.X	Jan 11/10	$ 23.04	$ 50.56	1.70%
ATCO	Canadian	Utility	ACO.X	Feb 18/09	$ 17.60	$ 50.56	1.70%
							5.03%

Notes:

1. The overall dividend yield is once again approximately 5%.

2. Three times we have added to existing positions.

3. Vodafone is UK-based (no withholding taxes on dividends) but has undergone a major restructure as it has recently sold its large share in Verizon Wireless to Verizon. We had originally bought 250 shares at $26.94 and received $1342 cash plus 65 shares of Verizon in the reorganization. Selling the Verizon shares raised another $3402. This $4744 (plus whatever other dividend cash had accumulated) became the initial purchase of Seadrill. We were left with 136 shares of Vodafone. This was one of the more complicated restructures (buyouts) experienced, but a very profitable one. That's the FUN part.

4. During its five and a half years of existence we have only sold three positions in the portfolio. We bought Riocan REIT (shopping centres) for $12.09 in 2009 and sold it for $24.70 in 2011. We didn't sell it because it doubled, but only because of cash flow yield concerns and in light of more shopping going online. We bought CML HealthCare in 2010 for $14.25 and sold in 2013 for $10.59, after it was bought out by another company. CML paid about 8%-10% dividend so the position, calculating dividends, was almost breakeven. I refer to this as a **Successful Failure**. The price of CML tanked, hitting a low of $5- $6 when its then recently purchased US division went south (ha, ha). We held on because of the high dividend, its very positive cash flows and my **Rarely Sell** strategy, allowing us to nearly break even. The third sale was Verizon as explained above. These sales represent a modest 10% portfolio turnover per year.

5. The current portfolio is valued at over $55,000 representing a very nice 20% plus CAGR (compound annual growth rate) to December 31st, 2013. It is unrealistic to expect this kind of growth rate in the future, but it's been a nice start, although I'm ticked because she is now beating me by a couple of grand ☺.

6. What to do if starting today? Based on a $31,000 maximum contribution, my suggested TFSA would look something like:

MODEL Portfolio:

Company	# Shares	Price	Approx Exchange	Cost In CAD	Annual Dividend in CAD	Dividend Yield	Earnings Yield	Cash Flow Yield	Price Times Book
Seadrill	130	$ 37.49	1.09	$ 5,312	$ 561.60	10.7%	9.0%	10.9%	2.3
HSBC Holdings PLC	100	$ 52.82	1.09	$ 5,757	$ 259.20	4.5%	7.6%	15.1%	1.1
Vodaphone	150	$ 34.16	1.09	$ 5,585	$ 294.84	5.3%	21.2%	29.4%	0.7
ATCO	100	$ 50.56		$ 5,066	$ 86.00	1.7%	7.3%	22.2%	2.0
Husky Energy	150	$ 33.72		$ 5,068	$ 180.00	3.6%	5.7%	14.9%	1.7
Sunlife Financial	100	$ 41.40		$ 4,150	$ 144.00	3.5%	6.7%	2.5%	1.4
				$ 30,938	$ 1,525.64	4.9%	9.6%	15.8%	1.5
Cash				$ 62	4.90%				
Total				$ 31,000					

Notes on the model:

1. The average dividend yield is 4.9%, similar to Model #1.

2. There are two stocks in Lillian's TFSA that are not in the model. Rogers Communications was in Model #1 as well as Hospitality Property Trust, due to the US withholding tax issue.

3. If you look at both TFSAs together there is a pretty good mix of companies, both international and Canadian, but certainly a leaning towards oil & gas, financial and telecom.

4. Cash flow yield is not a good metric for financials and I even hesitate to include the number. It is best to focus on earnings yield and price times book with financial companies. Both Sunlife and HSBC look reasonable using these two metrics.

5. Vodafone, as mentioned, has had a major reorganization. The earnings and cash flow yields will drop significantly this year. Consensus estimate is for an earnings yield of 5.8% in 2014/15. Consensus estimates of cash flow are not done.

6. All the stocks mentioned are appropriate for RRSP or non-registered accounts as well. If TFSAs are your only stock investments, it would make sense to include US stocks in the TFSA mix. We don't as we have lots of US exposure in other accounts. I will begin highlighting US companies in the next issue.

7. Best efforts are made to be accurate, but the numbers are constantly changing and errors are possible.

Following are brief descriptions of the companies:

Seadrill: As the name implies, SDRL is a major ocean drilling company with $5-6B in annual sales. It is based in Bermuda, such that there are no withholding taxes on the generous dividends. It has the newest fleet of all ocean drillers. As mentioned last month with Ensco, ocean drillers have declined lately making them look like great value plays, although Seadrill has risen nicely since we purchased it three months ago. This was a case of a great fit at a discount. Just after getting the cash and Verizon shares from Vodafone, we looked at Seadrill and noticed it had declined from the low $40s to the low $30s. Great: Just like the T-shirts, something that fit my TFSA criteria and was on sale.

HSBC Holdings PLC: You probably know the name, especially if you fly. Almost every airport seems to have the ad, "HSBC: The World's Local Bank." Based in the UK, the name actually stands for Hong Kong and Shanghai Banking Corporation, which gives an indication of where a lot of its history and business is located. Unlike Canadian banks, most large worldwide banks have not yet fully recovered from the financial crisis. HSBC trades at just over book value (Canadian banks are trading at 2-2.5 times book) and less than 60% of its pre-crisis peak. Annual sales are in $70B range.

Vodafone: Based in the UK, VOD is a very large telecom company operating in about thirty different countries with 411 million customers. It does business throughout Europe, Africa and India. I hesitated to include VOD in the model because the sale of its share of Verizon Wireless makes it very difficult to decipher the financials, but VOD has recently dropped by almost 20%. Hard to resist the sale price.

The overall tendency of investors is to invest in companies they are familiar with in their home country, but these international companies provide great international exposure that is very difficult to get with Canadian companies.

ATCO: While I think of ATCO as an electric utility it is much more. It has interests in electrical production and transmission, natural gas storage, processing and transportation, and its well-known ATCO structures division. It has some international diversification with interests in the US and Australia. While the dividend is small relative to other utilities, it has increased them twenty years in a row. ATCO is not a fast growing company but seems to be very consistent and has annual sales close to $5B.

Husky Energy: Another well-known name, Husky is an integrated oil and gas company with $23B in annual sales. "Integrated" means it produces, refines and retails, providing more stability than pure production companies. If the price of oil declines, they can make up some of that loss in refining or retail. Husky is one of the largest ethanol producers in the country. It has two major new growth projects: the Sunrise oil sands project coming on stream in late 2014 and the Liwan natural gas project in the South China Sea. Liwan is in partnership with Chinese company CNOOC and started producing in March. Husky is majority owned by Hong Kong's Li-Ki-Shing, the richest guy in Asia. This should be beneficial negotiating with their Chinese customers.

Sunlife Financial: With about $15B in annual sales Sunlife is a large Canadian wealth management, health and life insurance, and employee benefits manager with international exposure. While its share price has doubled in the last couple of years, it has still not fully recovered from the financial crisis. Its share price peaked at $55.00 in 2007/08. Prior to the crisis it steadily grew dividends but since 2008 it has simply maintained them, which is actually pretty good for a financial company. Improving profitability should lead to renewed dividend growth. Increasing interest rates, if and when they occur, should help financial companies increase profitability. They can be looked on as somewhat of an interest rate hedge.

General market comment: North American markets are at all-time highs. Overall, in my opinion (and there are those that would disagree), valuations are still reasonable. Earnings yield of the average company on the Toronto Stock Exchange (TSX) is 4.8%. The average on the US market (S&P 500) is 5.4%. The Nasdaq exchange, which is dominated by tech companies is, however, just 2.8% and thus may be fully valued. There are always companies in any index, regardless of index level, that represent better value with higher earnings yield as the model illustrates. As long as earning yields are significantly above interest yields (as with the TSX and S&P, but not the Nasdaq), there are reasonable valuations to be found. Certainly stocks are not nearly as cheap as three or four years ago and the potential for large gains like we have experienced in the recent past are less likely. As mentioned previously I cannot predict the short-term direction of the market and don't think anyone can with regularity. There is a lot of market chatter about an expected correction. However, the more talk about a correction, the less likely it is to happen. It has been surprising that we have not seen any significant sell-off with all the current geo-political issues. The mid-east situation is same old same old, but the Russia/Ukraine situation is a little unnerving. My encouragement, especially for those new to stock investing, is to proceed with prudence. "Don't go for broke unless you want to get there." That said, it's great to get started, learn and be able to capitalize should we get a pullback in valuations. Long-term, well-selected company stocks will prosper.

Next issue (chapter) will begin the discussion on RRSPs. Until then, **have fun investing.**

Looking Back: Once again, I am happy with the fact I warned subscribers that 20% CAGR was unsustainable and they should move forward with "prudence." However, there is always a reason or excuse to avoid going into stocks. When markets are high we worry they are about a fall. When they are low, we worry about them going lower and the world as we know it coming to an end. I have no regrets in encouraging a cautious approach as one enters the market in order to gain experience. As with all things, confidence and knowledge comes with experience.

Seadrill, however, is a different matter. Despite looking cheap at the time, the oil price collapse took it down to below $1.00 and its very survival as a company is still in question. Having two oil stocks in the portfolio had a deleterious effect on its overall performance. I have now implemented a new portfolio balancing process to try to avoid being this overweight in any sector. At least I'm not too overweight and the gym clothes I bought still fit!

The Rule of 72

In this issue we will begin the discussion on RRSPs, but first a brief summary of the three main tax-advantaged accounts, then an absolutely critical investment lesson and then onto the RRSP. I believe strongly in taking advantage of all government tax-sheltered investment programs due to the beneficial compounding effects from higher rates of return when they are not taxed. My personal priority for the three programs are: 1) TFSA, 2) RRSP, and 3) RESP, although others may prioritize differently under different circumstances. We have maxed out each program ourselves for reasons that I hope become clear with this issue.

1. **TFSA:** While contributions are not tax-deductible, neither are withdrawals. Funds can be withdrawn anytime but this is best avoided except in real emergencies. Funds can be put back in but only in the calendar year following the withdrawal or later. Contribution room is never lost and is now maxed at $31,000 ($5000 for 2009,10,11,12 and $5500 for 2013 and 2014). The Feds have promised to increase the contribution room to $10,000/year upon balancing the budget. The highest income spouse can make the contributions for both partners, creating some income splitting. We always make our contributions early in the year rather than late in the year, thus providing almost an extra year of tax-free returns. That's one of those little things that add up over time. The TFSA is a great, flexible and simple program.

2. **RRSP:** Contributions are tax-deductible, creating an immediate benefit. All returns accumulate tax-free but withdrawals are taxed. Withdrawals can be made but are taxed immediately making it somewhat punitive to take an emergency withdrawal. The benefit of this "penalty" is that it should motivate keeping the funds in the program until their designated use of retirement. The maximum contribution is

determined each year after completion of your income taxes. The tax assessment highlights your eligible contribution limit. I am always surprised that most wait to the last minute to make their contribution, as once again, the earlier it is done the more time the money can work for you.

3. **RESP:** This program doesn't fit everyone and is somewhat complex. The basic premise is to save for your children's post-secondary education. We have always contributed the minimum amount needed to get the maximum government matching funds but are now in the process of withdrawing.

The financial institution used for the accounts or your accountant will be able to answer specific questions on the programs. My purpose here is to **motivate savings, to understand the importance and advantages of the tax-free investing and to help with stock selection for the programs.** Our funds are almost exclusively in stocks for all three programs. However, for those more conservative, the RESP is the best place for interest bearing investments due to the limited timeline involved.

What is the RULE of 72? It is a very simple but very important mathematical rule to help understand how money compounds over time. **72 divided by the annual rate of return = years to double the money.** For instance a 12% return/year would take 72/12 = 6 years to double the money. If the return is 9%, then it would take eight years to double. If the return is 6% then it takes 12 years to double, and if the return is 2% (like today's interest) it will take 36 years to double. It is a very simple method to approximate the result of compounding.

Example 1 — Importance of time and per cent return:

a. If someone the age of twenty puts $5500 into their TFSA, invests in stocks and averages 12% return, what would they have in the account at age 62? Answer: 62 minus 20 equals 42 years of time. The time for a double is the **rule of 72**/12 equals 6 years to double. 42 years of time/6 years for a double = 7 doubles. $5500 x 2 x 2 x 2 x 2 x 2 x 2 x 2 = $704,000. If the next year at age 21, they added another $5500, when they turn 62 it would be: 41 years/6 years = 6.83 doubles. $5500 x 2 x 2 x 2 x 2 x 2 x 2 x 1.83 = another $644,160. Total of the two years of investments would be = **$1,348,160.** Would that be FUN and EXCITING?

b. If someone at age 20 puts $5500 into a TFSA invested in GICs at 2% return, how much would they have at age 62? Time to double would be **Rule of 72**/2 = 36 years. 42 years of time/36 years to double = 1.17 doubles. The amount they would have is = $5500 x 2 x 1.17 = $12,870. If they added another $5500 the next year it would become: 41 years/36 years to double = 1.14 doubles. $5500 x 2 x 1.14 = $12,540. Total for the two years of investments would be **$25,410.** Not near as much FUN and definitely boring.

The advantage of the interest bearing account is the growth will be a straight line. The stock investments will be a very jagged line with lots of ups and downs. However, it's the end result that we are after. The negative side of stocks is the volatility that investors need to accept. One of the purposes of this newsletter is to help subscribers "gut it out" when the inevitable downturns occur.

Skeptics would ask if 12% is realistic or even possible in stock accounts. While it may be on the high side of average, I have achieved 11.6% over 21 years in my RRSP. I believe 9-12% is achievable as 9% is the average of the markets over a very long period of time and have achieved almost 12% myself. Admittedly it's the upper end of the target. The above scenarios a) and b) are why I am such an advocate for investing in stocks.

Example 2 — Importance of tax-free returns:

One reason people don't participate or max out their RRSP contributions is the fear of tax effects upon withdrawing funds at retirement. Let's use the **Rule of 72** to look at a couple of scenarios relative to how the money compounds inside and outside an RRSP. Please recognize this is for illustrative purposes as it's impossible to cover all individual scenarios.

a. How much money would a person have after 24 years of investing if they put $10,000 into an RRSP and achieved 12% return? As we have seen above it would take six years to double, therefore in 24 years they would achieve four doubles. $10,000 x 2 x 2 x 2 x 2 = $160,000.

b. How much would they have putting that $10,000 into a non-registered account and paying 20% income tax on the earnings or growth? The 20% tax rate would effectively take 12% overall return down to 9.6%. The Rule of 72/9.6 = 7.5 years to double, rather than six when no tax is paid. 24 years/7.5 = 3.2 doubles. Therefore in 24 years they would achieve $10,000 x 2 x 2 x 2 x 1.2 = $96,000. This example again illustrates the long-term impact of what might be perceived as a small difference in return (12 vs. 9.6), leading to a big difference in final outcome of $160,000 vs. $96,000. Even if this investor had to pay 40% tax withdrawing the money, which isn't likely, the outcome would be the same as paying 20% tax along the way. Also if the investor using the RRSP has a 30% marginal tax rate they would get an immediate (at tax time) $3000 refund. If that $3000 was invested at the 9.6% outside an RRSP, it would be another $28,800. In all likelihood a retired person has a lower tax rate than when working, so the above represents an almost worst case scenario for the RRSP and it's still way ahead of investing outside an RRSP. Another great advantage to stock investing in an RRSP vs. a taxable account is reduced paperwork and reporting for annual tax purposes. And I'm not a big fan of paperwork...are you?

The **two keys** to investment returns are **TIME and PER CENT**. Being in a tax-sheltered account enhances the per cent returns. Another key observation is with compounding over time, the difference between per cent returns is much greater than the numerical difference in the annual rate of return. The difference between for example 6% and 3% is much greater than two times the return. Go ahead and calculate for yourself the difference between 6% and 3% on $10,000 compounded over 30 years. The **Rule of 72** can also be used to approximate and easily calculate different business scenarios. How big will your farm be if you grow 10% per year for the next 21 years? If the current yield of canola is 35 bu./acre what will it be in 24 years if we increase the yield 3% per year? If inflation is 2% what will a $100 item cost in 36 years?

RRSP Stock Selection

In the next issue I will start building an RRSP model portfolio based on our own holdings, but first I would like to go through stock selection rationale.

1. **Focus on US companies:**

   a. **Withholding tax:** Issue #1 discussed the 15% US government withholding tax on dividends paid by US companies in regular accounts, TFSAs and RESPs but not RRSPs. Therefore, it is best to focus the TFSA on Canada and other countries that don't have a withholding tax, and focus the RRSP on US companies if you have both TFSAs and RRSPs.

   b. **Exchange rate:** For about 40 of the past 50 years the Canadian dollar has been at a significant discount to the US dollar but for the past 10 years it has been close to parity, mostly between 90 cents and $1.05. I don't know where the exchange rate is going but figure that par is not the normal situation. Anytime our dollar is over 90 cents USD is a good time to invest in US companies.

   c. **Currency diversification:** Most of us have the vast majority of our assets in Canadian dollars. Our real estate, whether that be a house, farm, cottage or condo, is mostly, if not all, located in Canada and thus valued in Canadian dollars. The US buck is still the world's reserve currency, and investing is US companies is an easy way to get US dollar exposure.

   d. **Retirement travel:** The RRSP is a retirement fund and when people retire they like to travel. Having US currency exposure provides a great hedge on future foreign travel costs, especially to the US.

2. **Focus on conservative, dividend-paying companies:**

   a. **Target returns:** As we have seen, 9-12% annual returns provide exceptional long-term results. If a company pays a 4% dividend, then we only need to get another 5-8% from capital appreciation. There is no need to chase high-flying, super-growth stocks to get the end result we want. That's the cardinal error often made as those kinds of stocks often lead to disappointment.

   b. **Dividend growth:** It's also best to buy shares of companies that grow their dividends over time. If a company doubled its dividend in the past 10 years it is likely to do so again in the next 10 years.

   c. **Valuation metrics:** As described in Issue #2.

   d. **Avoid losers or zeros:** If you have five companies that have a 12% return in a year, the average return is 12%. Having those five companies with a 12% return and just one that is -12% brings the average return down to 8%. In this business we are guaranteed to make mistakes, at least short-term, but sticking with more conservative companies reduces the probability of making big mistakes. Worse yet is having a company go bankrupt or go to zero. One of the questions I ask myself when making a purchase is "What's the chance this company could go broke?"

3. **Low turnover:** Following the above guidelines reduces the need to turn over stocks, reducing investing workload. The last company I sold in Lillian's RRSP was November 2012, and the last one in my RRSP was October 2013 and was subject to a buyout.

For those of you anxious to get a few more stock picks, here are four we own which will go into the model RRSP. Two were mentioned previously as they are in our TFSAs as well, those being AT&T (ticker T) and

Hospitality Property Trust (ticker HPT). The other two for now are HCP Inc. (ticker HCP), which is my most recent RRSP purchase, and Power Corporation (ticker POW), three US companies and one Canadian. AT&T is a giant telecommunications company. HPT is a hotel real estate investment trust and HCP is a medical property real estate investment trust, investing in all types of medical facilities. POW is a large Canadian insurance company.

Clarification: There is nothing wrong with US companies going into your TFSA, except for the withholding tax issue. If TFSAs are going to be your only stock investments, then it makes sense to have 20-30% American companies in the portfolio and the ones mentioned above are great candidates. If you have both TFSAs and RRSPs, then it makes sense to avoid the withholding tax. Hope that makes sense to you. I'm not sure I always make sense!

Looking Back: The maximum TFSA contribution mentioned was as of the date of the newsletter. The Canadian dollar reverted to its more normal relationship to the US dollar below 90 cents, shortly after writing this issue. I have nothing further to add, just to re-emphasize the importance of the Rule of 72. **I hate rules but this is a good one!**

Answers to questions: 1) 7.6x 2) 70 bu./acre 3) $200. Hope you got them all correct.

ISSUE #5: OCTOBER 1, 2014

LUCK vs. SKILL

While in the process of writing this issue I had the pleasure of a new subscriber calling me with some very nice comments on the content of the first four issues. He mentioned the key points that I have been striving for, saying they were understandable, educational and he enjoyed the small amount of humour. It was great hearing his comments. Financial stuff can be a little dry, so I am doing my best to keep it light and lively. In this issue I would like to do a quarterly review of our model TFSA portfolios and start building an RRSP portfolio, but first would like to discuss **luck vs. skill**.

The process in being a successful investor entails both an element of luck and skill. One of the keys is recognizing which is which, *which* is easier said than done. If we can learn to make this distinction, then we can continually try to improve the skill aspect. It's very difficult improving on the luck aspect! Many investors actually focus more on trying to improve their luck by focusing on short-term gyrations of either the market or their stock picks. This luck vs. skill conundrum plays out in real life as well. There are many times when we mistakenly attribute a successful outcome to our own skill when in fact luck was the main driver. On the other hand, we rarely attribute a successful outcome to luck when it really was our hard work or skill. In other words, we frail human beings tend to congratulate ourselves when we are skillful as well as when we are just lucky. The converse is also true in that we often blame a bad outcome on bad luck rather than our own potential failing or lack of skill.

There are two books I read some time ago related to this topic: *Fooled by Randomness* by Nassim Taleb and *The Drunkards Walk: How Randomness Rules our Lives* by Leonard Mlodinow. Both are very good reads.

Let me try to illustrate with a couple of personal examples:

1. I have been a sales professional (so I like to think, anyway...others may beg to differ) and sales manager all my working career. Sales are subject to both the elements of luck and skill just like investing. Way back in the 1980s, in my first year as a sales manager, I earned a significant sales bonus. The company had some great products at the time and market size was increasing. The sales environment could not have been more favourable. I recall a discussion with my boss at the time where I said something like, "I almost feel guilty cashing this check as I had very little to do with the success we had. It was my first year and our products really drove the results." His response to me was, "Don't feel guilty. What you said may have merit but there will be years you will work your behind (he used another word) off and won't make much bonus because conditions turned against us. Cash the cheque and enjoy it." How true those words turned out to be. That year was the very top of our market, as we sailed into some very strong headwinds that lasted almost two decades. One of the real challenges in any organization is recognizing who has the skills vs. who is lucky. The lucky ones tend to disappear during more challenging times when their luck runs out.

2. I bought my first house in 1983 at the ripe old age of 25, which was significantly younger than most first-time home buyers. Mortgage interest rates were about 13-14% at the time, making the investment look risky. However, in four years the house sold for well over double the purchase price. At the time of purchase I was obviously hoping to make a wise investment, but to suggest that I was expecting this end result would be a gross overstatement. Thus it was more luck than skill. Real estate will be a topic of discussion at some future date.

3. If you read carefully the date of purchase, cost and current value of the stocks held in our two TFSA portfolios, you might have noticed that those shares held for a significant period were all up in value while the more recent purchases were either up or down. I would submit that longer-term results are more driven by skill with a little luck while short-term are driven more by luck. It is only after a long period of time that we can evaluate whether a purchase decision was a good, mediocre or a bad choice.

If the third wealthiest person in the world, Warren Buffett, and one who made his fortune managing money says it is impossible to predict short-term market direction then who am I to argue, whereas many do by focusing so much on short-term trading. **If a stock goes up immediately after we buy we are NOT geniuses, just lucky. Likewise, if a stock goes down immediately after we buy, we should not kick ourselves as we are NOT dummies, but rather may have experienced a little of bad luck.**

One of the dumbest market "old wives' tales" is to sell a stock immediately if it loses 10% from where it was purchased. Some even take this a step further and suggest that we should sell any stock, any time it drops 10% from its recent high. The supposed rationale is that this will prevent any big losses. In my books it will also prevent any big gains. A 10% drop in the market as a whole is not a big change while a 10% change in a specific stock can occur, and often does, in one day due to some good or bad news. Trading every time there is a 10% change would drive me crazy. Selling after a 10% drop is something I believe is motivated by the fact that the industry makes money on transactions. The more transactions, the more money they (not you) make.

I read another recent article reiterating something previously written about. This article reported that between 1989 and 2008 the S&P averaged 8.4% annual gains. The average mutual fund returned 5.5%, and the average investor in those mutual funds gained 1.9% annually. If that's all the average investor is making, then a case can be made for bonds but why would investors do so poorly? Fees make up the biggest part of the gap between the S&P index and mutual funds. As for individual investors my guess is that investors started with or switched to lucky funds (those with good recent performance) from unlucky funds (those with poor recent performance) just as the lucky ones had their luck run out. Whether it is stocks or mutual funds the underlying tendency, but often wrong approach, is to go with the hot hand.

A great analogy would be to compare the game of chess to monopoly or backgammon. Chess is 100% skill, no question. Monopoly, or backgammon, has elements of both skill and luck. In a multiple game best of seven series the most skilled player is likely to win, but in any individual game would have a hard time winning if the less skilled player got a lucky streak and landed on Free Parking five times in a row. The more games played (similar to a longer investment period), the more likely the most skilled player comes out on top.

Now let's have a look at how the model TFSA portfolios are doing to date, based on a September 30 close.

Quarterly TFSA Portfolio Update

TFSA MODEL # 1	Began: June 1st, 2014												
Company	# Shares	Purchase Price	Cost In CAD	Current Value in CAD	Share Price Change	Dividends Collected in Cdn-June/14	Dividends July/14	Dividends Aug/14	Dividends Sept/14	Dividends Since Inception	Total Return	Date Added
Ensco PLC	100	$ 52.66	$ 5,750	$ 4,630	$ (1,120)	$ 79.31			$ 81.60	$ 160.91	-16.7%	May 30/14
Glaxo Smithkline	100	$ 53.94	$ 5,890	$ 5,152	$ (738)					$ -	-12.5%	May 30/14
Ship Finance Int.	180	$ 18.52	$ 3,644	$ 3,413	$ (231)		$ 77.38			$ 77.38	-4.2%	May 30/14
TD Bank	100	$ 53.76	$ 5,386	$ 5,527	$ 141		$ 47.00			$ 47.00	3.5%	May 30/14
Innvest REIT	210	$ 5.16	$ 1,094	$ 1,115	$ 21		$ 6.99	$ 6.99	$ 6.99	$ 20.97	3.8%	May 30/14
Rogers Communications	100	$ 43.82	$ 4,392	$ 4,192	$ (200)		$ 45.75			$ 45.75	-3.5%	May 30/14
Teck Reources Ltd	200	$ 24.17	$ 4,844	$ 4,242	$ (602)		$ 90.00			$ 90.00	-10.6%	May 30/14
			$ 31,000	$ 28,271	$ (2,729)	$ 79.31	$ 267.12	$ 6.99	$ 88.59	$ 442.01	-7.4%	
Cash				$ 442								
Total				$ 28,713								
TFSA MODEL # 2	Began: July 26, 2014											
Seadrill	130	$ 37.49	$ 5,312	$ 3,899	$ (1,413)				$ 140.46	$ 140.46	-24.0%	July 25/14
HSBC Holdings PLC	100	$ 52.82	$ 5,757	$ 5,702	$ (55)					$ -	-1.0%	July 25/14
Vodaphone	150	$ 34.16	$ 5,585	$ 5,529	$ (56)					$ -	-1.0%	July 25/14
ATCO	100	$ 50.56	$ 5,066	$ 4,540	$ (526)				$ 21.50	$ 21.50	-10.0%	July 25/14
Husky Energy	150	$ 33.72	$ 5,068	$ 4,611	$ (457)					$ -	-9.0%	July 25/14
Sunlife Financial	100	$ 41.40	$ 4,150	$ 4,060	$ (90)					$ -	-2.2%	July 25/14
			$ 30,938	$ 28,341	$ (2,597)					$ 161.96	-7.9%	
Cash			$ 62	$ 224								
Total			$ 31,000	$ 28,565								

The portfolios are down, with the main culprit being commodities, especially the ocean drillers. September has been a little tough on the Canadian market, with the TSX down 4.3% and resources down about 10% during the month. GSK and ATCO reported weaker quarterly results and have also declined. Another bit of bad luck was going on holidays on July 27th, thus having built TFSA Model #2 based on July 25th closing prices, rather than the usual month-end date. There was small market decline immediately afterwards. Overall, there is nothing particularly unusual about these fluctuations and I'm certainly NOT currently selling any of the stocks in these portfolios. The Canadian dollar has declined, which has been one positive for the value in

Canadian dollars. **The good news is new subscribers or those who have not yet acted can purchase these portfolios cheaper and get more shares than in the model.**

Quarterly RRSP Portfolio Update

The last issue set the tone for strategies regarding RRSP investing. I have gone through all the companies that we own, trying to select the best companies for a model RRSP portfolio. In total we have forty-five positions, which may be over-diversification, but many of these companies overlap other portfolios. However, our RRSP model will not overlap with companies in the TFSA model portfolios. Over the next four issues we will build the model RRSP portfolio to include about twenty companies and be $100-125,000 in size. Subscribers may have larger or smaller portfolios or may just be starting out. The model should provide enough options for subscribers to select and design for their own needs. Building the model over four months helps spread out purchases so they are not all made on the same date, which is a good way to hedge short-term market fluctuations. I have once again added $10.00 to the cost of each position for transaction costs.

Model RRSP Portfolio							Annual				
Company	Ticker	Date Added	# Shares	Price	Approx Exchange	Cost In CAD	Dividend in CAD	Dividend Yield	Earnings Yield	Cash Flow Yield	Price Times Book
US Companies											
Verizon	VZ	Sept 30/14	100	$ 49.99	1.12	$ 5,609	$ 246.40	4.4%	9.5%	19.6%	3.7
HCP Inc	HCP	Sept 30/14	100	$ 39.71	1.12	$ 4,458	$ 244.16	5.4%	5.0%	7.1%	1.7
Hospitality Prop. Trust	HPT	Sept 30/14	150	$ 26.85	1.12	$ 4,521	$ 329.28	7.2%	3.1%	10.9%	1.3
Canadian Companies											
Bank of Nova Scotia	BNS	Sept30/14	100	$ 69.27		$ 6,937	$ 264.00	3.8%	8.4%	9.1%	1.9
Power Corp	POW	Sept30/14	200	$ 31.08		$ 6,226	$ 232.00	3.7%	7.2%	11.6%	1.3
						$ 27,751	$ 1,315.84				

Company Descriptions

Verizon Communications: The last newsletter mentioned AT&T, but going through the financials, Verizon looks like a slightly better valuation at this time. We own both. With $120B in sales it is slightly smaller than AT&T but still huge. The valuation of these two American majors currently looks more attractive than their Canadian counterparts and fits the US focus of our RRSPs. In the last 10 years VZ has increased its dividend by 37%. It is a slow dividend grower with a high current yield. I originally bought VZ in 2006 at a cost of $31.09 and an exchange rate of 1.16. With more and more communications going wireless over the Internet, VZ should be able to slowly and steadily increase profitability. This is a large turtle not a hare.

HCP Inc. is a medical facility Real Estate Investment Trust. REITs have a different corporate structure in that they are designed to pay the majority of their operating cash flows to shareholders via dividends. The companies themselves do not pay income taxes, passing the tax liability to shareholders. However, as the RRSP is a tax-free vehicle, holding REITs inside the RRSP eliminates that tax burden. HCP owns a large and diversified portfolio of senior housing, life sciences, medical office and hospital properties across the US. It has over $2B in annual sales. Health care is a play on aging demographics. As the population ages we have more use for medical facilities. REITs generally have high current dividends but slow dividend growth. HCP has, however, grown its dividend by 30% in the last 10 years. We recently purchased HCP in June 2014 at $40.20 with a 1.10 exchange rate.

Hospitality Property Trust is a hotel property REIT with $1.6B in annual sales. I spent a lot of time in hotels over my career and figured with their daily rate they must be making good money. Actually, it is a tough business which cycles with the economy. Many hotel REITs quit paying dividends through the 2001-2002 recession and again in the 2008-2009 Great Recession. HPT held its dividend through the 2001 and 2002 period and only suspended it for a very short period in 2009, re-implementing a lower dividend in 2010. From 1995 to 2008 HPT increased its dividend from 24 cents quarterly to 77 cents (over 300%), but since 2010 it has only increased from 45 to the current 49 cents. It is still trading well below its high price of $50.00 per share in 2006. Tourism is making a comeback from the Great Recession and aging demographics should help as we travel more and stay in nicer hotels as we age. HPT owns 291 hotels in the US and Canada. It does not operate the hotels but leases them to the operating companies including Marriot, Intercontinental, Hyatt, Carlson and Wyndham. It also owns 185 travel centres operated by Travel Centres of America. I originally purchased HPT in 2008 at $31.83 with a 1.03 exchange rate. It has not increased in value but with REITs that is secondary to the dividend.

Bank of Nova Scotia: With $19B in annual sales BNS is Canada's most international bank. It operates in eighty countries and derives almost as much income from global banking as it does from Canadian banking. It has a strong presence in the Caribbean, Central and South America. I recall being surprised going to a bank machine in Mexico and it being a BNS machine. It also operates in wealth management, insurance and capital markets. As mentioned in my first newsletter, I originally purchased these shares for $22.375 in 1993. It has split 2:1 (where you get two shares for each one owned) two times, such that the current purchase cost is $5.60 per share. It has doubled its dividend over the past 10 years. While the stock price will fluctuate, BNS along with the other Canadian banks have been very consistent and I expect they will continue to be so. As such they deserve prominence in any portfolio.

Power Corporation: With $30 B in annual sales Power Corp is a very large and diversified Canadian insurance and wealth management company. It is still trading well below its pre-recession peak of $41.00. Its ownership interests include Power Financial, which includes Investors Group, Mackenzie Financial and Great West Life, which includes London Life and Canada Life. It has significant investments in Europe and Asia. As the saying goes, "Don't buy the mutual fund...buy the company managing the mutual funds." POW doubled its dividend between 2004 and 2008 and has held steady since the crisis. It could begin increasing the dividend again as was its habit before the crisis. I originally purchased POW in 1999 at $25.50 but it has split 2:1 once, making my cost $12.75 per current share.

Clarifications: As mentioned in the last newsletter, any of these companies would also be good choices for a TFSA. If you have both a TFSA and RRSP, then it's best to position US companies in the RRSP and Canadian (plus other non-withholding tax countries) in the TFSA. If, however, the TFSA is your only stock portfolio, then it makes sense to have 20-30% US exposure in it. I would also like to clarify that I am not totally against mutual funds and they may be the correct choice for many investors. I'm sure there are many well-managed ones. It's just that, for the time and effort, I have found it more productive trying to find well-managed companies.

Looking Back: I would like to clarify that our personal purchase price and time of purchase is mentioned in the company description, partly to illustrate how long holding periods actually tend to improve portfolio performance. The price and exchange rate in the chart is from the time I moved the company into the newsletter model portfolio. These are the numbers used to track the model portfolio over time. If I were to eliminate a stock personally that was in the model, I would also "sell" it in the model.

I have included market charts in Appendix #1 for reference of the market gyrations we experienced from June 2014 to February 2016.

Take the Pay from an Hour a Day to Put Away

Another month has passed and the September-October period lived up to its reputation as the most volatile and challenging two months of the year. While the US market has rapidly recovered its earlier losses, the resource sector remains seriously in the doldrums. Being heavily resource-oriented the Canadian market has lagged in its recovery. While not selling any positions in our model TFSA accounts which were resource heavy, the 2015 contribution next January will likely go to less cyclical sectors. Canadian investors with a home country bias (most investors have such a bias) will also be resource heavy, providing yet another reason to orient our RRSPs to at least 50% American companies.

In this issue we will add to our RRSP model portfolio, but would first like to discuss **WHY** a robust savings and investing program is important and some ideas on **HOW** to go about it. In previous issues, especially Issue #4, we went through how investments grow over time, but in some regards I may have put the cart before the horse. The first important question for all to answer for themselves is, "Why is it important to us?" The second and even more difficult question would be, "Our finances are strained enough with all our day-to-day needs...how can we possibly find the money to save and invest?"

WHY is it important?

Let me use a real life example from the past to illustrate. My first full-time job after university was with a large livestock feed company. After their extensive one-year training program I was assigned my own territory, taking over from a very nice gentleman who was about 50 to 55 years of age. He had been a successful lifelong territory manager with the company and had earned great commissions throughout his career. The feed industry was a growth industry through the 1960s and 1970s, and one of his dealers was a very large and rapidly growing integrated livestock enterprise. This dealer changed allegiance, leading to a sudden decline in sales. As is very common in our workplaces, this gentleman was deemed to have served his useful purpose with the company and was gracefully shown the door. There were newer, younger, more aggressive salesmen available!

Staying in touch with him and observing the sequence of events in his life afterwards was **very instructive** for me. To the best of my recollection here is how those events unfolded: 1) He had not saved much money even though he had earned great bonuses in his career 2) He had his house paid for 3) He always had an ambition to run a hardware store as he loved gadgets 4) Upon his early retirement he bought a very nice hardware store in a rural town 5) He remortgaged his house to buy the hardware store 6) Small-town retailing can be a very difficult business and in three or four years the hardware store went broke, taking with it the house he had previously owned mortgage free 7) The last I heard, he was once again a full-time salesman, selling products to farmers. This situation saddens me even to this day. He should have been enjoying a well-deserved retirement.

Whether a person is employed by a big company, a small company or self-employed, change is a constant and there will likely come a moment when you wish to **"take this job and shove it"** or, more likely, your boss will come to you and say, **"We took your job and shoved you."** No one is immune to this potential occurrence. **If a person has a robust savings and investment program, he/she could look upon that moment with a sense of relief and excitement rather than fear and trepidation.**

The story above illustrates one of my key reasons **WHY** to have a savings and investment program. Please list 3-4 of the reasons **WHY** this is important to you:

1)_____ 2)_____ 3)_____ 4)_____

HOW to save?

This is the more difficult of the two questions. Everyone has a myriad of financial obligations. Past issues, especially Issue #4, illustrated how small amounts can compound over time to become very significant amounts. It doesn't take a BIG start. A critical first step to saving is learning where the money is going. From a young age I put most expenses on a credit card and immediately paid the card off with each statement. **A credit card should never be used as a credit instrument...it should be strictly used as a convenience instrument.** When the monthly statement came in I would log the expenses in a personal accounting blue book, along with all other monthly expenses that were paid by cheque. This process is now more easily accomplished with an excel grid. The critical part of using a credit card is it outlines every expense. Have you ever taken money out of the bank, put it in your wallet and a few days later looked in your wallet and asked yourself "Where the (expletive deleted) did that money go?" Putting expenditures on a credit card eliminates this question as the statement lists everywhere it went. After a period of time we can figure out what we are spending money on and which expenses can be curtailed to create savings. Perhaps the morning visit to Tim's can go. Maybe packing a lunch will save money and be healthier too, and perhaps a new wardrobe every year isn't necessary. It's not about eliminating the fun parts of life but about striking a balance between today and tomorrow. We are all running our own personal "Me Inc." business.

As a suggestion, **Take the Pay from an Hour a Day to Put Away,** making it non-negotiable to yourself. $20/hr. x 250 working days per year = $5000 savings at year's end, almost enough to maximize a TFSA. To repeat and emphasize, little savings can add up and compound over time to become very significant. It's worth doing!

Please, once again, take a moment to think of 3-4 places where expenses can be reduced and savings created:

1)_____ 2)_____ 3)_____ 4)_____

At the beginning of this newsletter I referred to the September and October volatility. By way of terminology, a "pullback" is considered a drop by 5-10%. A "correction" is considered a drop of 10-20%, and a "bear market" is considered anything over a 20% drop, often lasting one to two years. During September/October, the Canadian market (TSX) dropped 12.8%, while the US market, as measured by the S&P 500, dropped 9.9%. However, the US small company index (Russell 2000) was down nearly 15%. Therefore by these definitions it is safe to suggest we experienced a full correction, albeit, a pretty mild one. Pullbacks occur quite frequently, whereas corrections usually occur on average about once every eighteen months but certainly cannot be timed. There was one in 2010, 2011 and 2012, but not in 2013. Oil is considered to be in a bear market as it has actually dropped about 27%. Gold and copper are in prolonged three-year bear markets with drops of 35-40% while grains are down in the range of 40-50%. As mentioned at the top, resources (commodities) are seriously in the doldrums, keeping the Canadian market well off its recent peak. The US S&P has however fully recovered.

The US market correction appears to be over but that is by no means a guarantee. I read a quote recently that is very appropriate. It went something like, "Guys who confidently know where the market is going are either retired or broke...and I can't think of any that are retired."

I made a couple of micro-adjustments to my personal RRSP during the correction. Noticing the portfolio was light on utilities I used some accumulated dividends to buy ATCO at $46.14. It is in our TFSA model so it will not go into the RRSP model to avoid overlap. I also sold a pharma company, Abbvie, near its current high at $60.52 and replaced it with another utility, Capital Power, and a software company, Constellation Software. These will go into the model this month, so let's now add to the RRSP model:

Company	Ticker	Date Added	# Shares	Price Added	Approx Exchange	Cost in CAD	Annual Dividend in CAD	Dividend Yield	Earnings Yield	Cash Flow Yield	Price Times Book
Model RRSP Portfolio											
US Companies											
Verizon	VZ	Sept 30/14	100	$ 49.99	1.12	$ 5,609	$ 246.40	4.4%	9.5%	19.6%	3.7
HCP Inc.	HCP	Sept 30/14	100	$ 39.71	1.12	$ 4,458	$ 244.16	5.4%	5.0%	7.1%	1.7
Hospitality Prop. Trust	HPT	Sept 30/14	150	$ 26.85	1.12	$ 4,521	$ 329.28	7.2%	3.1%	10.9%	1.3
United Technologies	**UTX**	**Oct 31/14**	**50**	**$ 107.00**	**1.12**	**$ 6,002**	**$ 132.16**	**2.2%**	**6.3%**	**8.8%**	**3.1**
Johnson & Johnson	**JNJ**	**Oct 31/14**	**50**	**$ 107.78**	**1.12**	**$ 6,045**	**$ 156.80**	**2.6%**	**5.7%**	**6.4%**	**3.9**
Canadian Companies											
Bank of Nova Scotia	BNS	Sept 30/14	100	$ 69.27		$ 6,937	$ 264.00	3.8%	8.4%	9.1%	1.9
Power Corp.	POW	Sept 30/14	200	$ 31.08		$ 6,226	$ 232.00	3.7%	7.2%	11.6%	1.3
Capital Power	**CPX**	**Oct 31/14**	**200**	**$ 25.58**		**$ 5,126**	**$ 272.00**	**5.3%**	**2.4%**	**12.8%**	**1.1**
Constellation Software	**CSU**	**Oct 31/14**	**10**	**$ 317.50**		**$ 3,185**	**$ 44.80**	**1.4%**	**1.7%**	**4.5%**	**14.4**
Total/Average						**$ 48,109**	**$ 1,921.60**	**4.0%**	**5.5%**	**10.1%**	**3.6**

United Technologies: With $65B in annual sales, UTX is a very large industrial conglomerate. It has two main areas of business: 1) Building and Industrial Systems, which includes OTIS elevators (look down when an elevator door closes, or at the logo on the button panel and most times you will see the OTIS name), Carrier heating, air conditioning and ventilation and Kidde fire safety technology. 2) Propulsion and Aerospace, which includes Sikorsky helicopters, Pratt and Whitney aircraft engines as well as a multitude of products used in the manufacture of civilian and military aircraft. Over the past four years profits have grown about 50%, and in the past 10 years it has increased its dividend by 168% from 22 to 59 cents per quarter. I purchased UTX in May of 2008 (before the crash) for $71.61 at par, adding to the position in May 2012 at $73.21 with a 1.04 conversion.

Johnson and Johnson is a name familiar to everyone as the maker of Band-Aids. JNJ is a large and highly diversified health care company with annual sales of $75B. About 40% of its revenue is derived from medical devices (joint replacements and instruments), another 40% from pharmaceuticals and 20% from consumer brands encompassing an array of over-the-counter medications, hair, skin, oral and vision care, including Tylenol, Listerine, Neutrogena, Aveeno and Visine. Over the past 10 years it has more than doubled its quarterly dividend from 28.5 to 70 cents and in the past four years increased profits by 25%. We owned JNJ in our RESP but sold it to raise the funds for this fall's tuition, then repurchased it in my RRSP at $104.32 and a 1.11 conversion.

Capital Power Corp is a smaller utility based in Alberta, with about $1.1B in sales. It has sold off somewhat due to a difficult year. In 2013 CPX had $2.08 in earnings and $4.24 of cash flow per share, but after nine months of 2014 it has a loss of $0.12 and cash flow of $2.57 per share. Its current losses seem to be related to a number of unique situations. It is trading at close to book value with a reasonable cash flow and dividend yield. CPX develops, acquires and operates generating facilities from a variety of energy sources including wind, coal and natural gas. Its facilities include the Halkirk, AB, Haldimand/Norfolk and Goderich, ON, wind farms, as well as coal and natural gas facilities in Alberta and BC and a couple of smaller facilities in the US. It is developing three new gas plants in Alberta and another wind project in Ontario. I paid $25.35 per share this past week.

Constellation Software Inc. is an exciting departure from my normal selection criteria and comes courtesy of my son who is in his final year of finance at the University of Calgary. He worked as an equity analyst for an asset management firm this past summer and is currently part of a small group of students selected to manage a trust fund on behalf of the university. I am learning new things from him while providing some experienced mentorship to him. He is convincing me to look at companies that represent greater growth potential. CSU has experienced dramatic growth since it was founded in 1995 and went public in 2006. With sales now over $1.5B, operating profit per share increased from $4.14 to $9.74 in 3 years from 2010 and 2013, and looks to be on pace to increase over 25% in 2014. CSU buys numerous smaller software companies that serve both public and private customers. After purchasing a company it allows that company to continue to operate independently. It has such a diverse customer base that its success is not tied to any single industry. The executive compensation plan is uniquely tied to shareholder interests as they DO NOT receive stock options. Their bonuses are paid in cash with 75% of it mandated to be invested in company stock. One of the big things to watch out for with rapidly growing companies with their higher valuations is that growth eventually slows. CSU maintains a database of 10,000 potential takeover candidates, providing plenty of

38

growth potential. While this is a departure from my normal comfort zone, it is not speculative in that CSU is making real money and paying a decent dividend for a rapidly growing company. I paid $296.95 this week and it is already up significantly on a very favourable third quarter report, with a dramatic 44% increase in earnings. Based on trailing earnings and cash flow it looks expensive, but relative to growth rate it appears reasonable. As a higher risk company the position in the model is smaller. One thing for sure...it will not be boring.

November 20, 2014 Update

I just wanted to pass along that today I purchased shares of Mullen Group (MTL) on the TSX for an RRSP account.

The money came from the sale of Contrans Group Inc., which was bought out by another trucking company. Contrans is a great example of the BUY VALUE...RARELY SELL strategy. I bought it in 2004 for $10.40. At the time it was an income trust (like Real Estate Investment Trusts) that paid an annualized dividend of 12%. In 2006 the government changed the rules on income trusts, causing an immediate and significant drop. During the 2008/09 big bear market Contrans fell further to a low of $3.50. After the rules changed, they reorganized themselves into a dividend paying company with a very nice but reduced dividend rate. They were bought out at $14.60 plus a special dividend of 40 cents for a total of $15.00. Doing some quick math, over the 10 year holding period they returned about 9% per year. Not great, but not bad considering the two major negative events that occurred over this time frame. By the way, it was the income trust rule change that led to the formation of the TFSA program. I owned a lot of income trusts at the time and thus took a significant immediate hit. However, in my opinion and with a longer-term view, the TFSA program is superior to the former income trust program.

I have owned Mullen Group Ltd. since 2007 in another account. It was an income trust, as well, but is now a dividend paying corporation. MTL is an Alberta-based trucking and oil & gas services company. It was selling at over $30.00 in the spring, but the current oil market (and all resource) sell-off has taken it down to a low of $21.00. My purchase price was $22.12. I will put it into the model RRSP portfolio at that cost. It pays a monthly dividend of .10 and thus yields 5.4%.

November 27, 2014 Update

I just wanted to update you on significant corporate news at Seadrill, which is part of our TFSA #2 model. Yesterday it eliminated its generous dividend. While a dividend cut was not surprising, the complete elimination took the market by surprise and with the market's normal "shoot first, ask questions later" orientation, Seadrill sold off by 22% to close at $15.99. I listened to their third quarter recorded conference call today to try to better understand what was happening. As you know oil has been in a bear market for four or five months and sold off another 4% today on OPEC's announcement they will not cut production. We will have to look tomorrow to see what further reaction there might be.

Summary of the conference call:

- Seadrill says it is going to use the money saved from the dividend for three purposes: to reduce debt, watch for potential acquisitions at depressed prices and/or buy back up to 10% of its own shares.

- Seadrill is currently trading for 74% of book value so if it buys its own shares below book value, it automatically increases the book value of the remaining shares. If it buys 10%, it also increases cash flow and earnings by 10% per share. If we take what it says at face value (not always the case but as small investors we can't talk to them over a beer to know what is really going on), then what they are doing makes good sense, thinking longer-term.

- Operations are solid with operating profit down slightly from the previous quarter and up as of the year-to-date.

- Cash flows are also up slightly year-to-date.

- It has a high percentage of rigs contracted through 2016.

- Thirty per cent of the ocean drilling industries fleet is over 30 years of age, so Seadrill thinks competitors will retire some older rigs during the downturn.

- It has the newest fleet with almost all rigs being less than 15 years old. Ensco has the second youngest fleet.

- Seadrill said it would reinstate a dividend "when we are comfortable the current cycle has turned."

What we do:

- As you could tell from my Contrans example I am not prone to panic selling at lows, but I feel bad for those of you newer to stock investing if you have recently purchased Seadrill. I would no longer purchase it for a TFSA as it no longer meets my dividend criteria but since we currently have it, we will not sell. I might actually consider purchasing in my non-registered accounts.

- Ensco sold off 7-8% in sympathy. This often happens as bad news affecting one industry player infects the entire industry. I would look at this as an opportune time to buy Ensco, if not already owned.

- It will take time for the company and the TFSA #2 model to recover. As always mentioned, this is a long-term process with lots of gyrations along the way. It is also a good example of the need for diversification.

I wish there were better news but the resource sell-off continues. The good news is opportunities occur during these sell-offs.

Looking Back: "Take the Pay from an Hour a Day to Put Away" is a GREAT message. Just don't invest it in Seadrill. Yikes. I should have panicked and sold. But for every Seadrill example there will be one or more Contrans examples and I will not change my overall approach due to this error. Mistakes happen and every investor will experience them.

UTX sold the Sikorsky business in 2015.

Sometimes the price we paid personally and the price in the model are different as the price in the model was as of publication date, whereas what we paid was when we purchased. I transitioned to immediately communicating new purchases that also went into the model. However, as our portfolios are larger than the models, I only communicate changes that affect the model.

ISSUE #7: DECEMBER 1, 2014

Investment, Expense or Speculation: Which Is It?

"A house is likely to be the biggest investment you will ever make." I'm sure we have all heard this saying. Then after purchasing a house we often invest in renovations to increase the value and of course we have to invest in furniture to make the house livable. We all need a vehicle to drive around in, so we invest in a new vehicle then some aftermarket upgrades like a roof rack or hitch. Safety is critical, so we must also invest in winter tires and of course for peace of mind we should invest in the extended warranty. Personal development is important so we invest in ourselves by completing a university degree or an evening continuing education course. Along the lines of personal development, to prevent burnout it's important to take a break from our hectic schedules so we invest in a vacation, and when I was young I invested a lot of time and money building friendships at pubs, bars and parties.....ya, right!!!

Problem is none of these are true investments. They are all expenses. The word "invest" is grossly overused in our consumption oriented society. It is often used by salespeople to make us feel like we are making wise purchase decisions. Which statement is more likely to trigger a purchase response? 1) Isn't that an investment you'll really enjoy? Or 2) Isn't that an expense you'll really enjoy? Clearly the word "investment" evokes a positive feeling while hearing the word "expense" makes us cringe.

To be a true investment the purchase must meet three criteria:

1. Interest paid to finance the purchase must be tax-deductible. Even if financing is not used, it would be tax-deductible if used.

2. The purchase has or has the potential to provide a steady stream of cash flow.

3. The purchase has the potential to appreciate in value.

Let's look at the items mentioned above to see if they pass these three requirements. Clearly money spent in bars, on vacations or in bars while on vacation, are enjoyable parts of life but don't qualify as investments. Neither does anything to do with automobiles as they create negative cash flow (i.e. cost money to operate) and depreciate in value. Education might be a little more controversial as it could be argued that your income will go up, thus providing cash flow. Interest may be tax-deductible on student loans but given that your education is not a saleable item (unless you are a slave and your owner could get more for you on the open market), it wouldn't pass the third criteria.

And now (drum roll, please) for the most controversial item mentioned above: a house. In Canada, interest on the purchase of an owner occupied primary residence is not tax-deductible. So much for criteria #1. The owner occupied residence is guaranteed to provide only negative cash flow. Like automobiles, houses require expensive upkeep. So much for criteria #2. A house purchase meets criteria #3, but unlike the Meatloaf song "Two Out Of Three Ain't Bad"...one out of three ain't good. I realize that what I am writing here flies in the face of conventional wisdom, but I do that at times. More often than not, "conventional wisdom" is an oxymoron. Therefore I consider a house serving as a personal residence as an asset that can go on your personal balance sheet like a car, but NOT an investment. Wait a minute, you say... in issue #5 I referred to my first house purchase as an "investment," didn't I? Correct. You caught me...that, however, was not an error. My first house purchase was an investment. It was a three bedroom raised bungalow with five student bedrooms in the basement which were rented out. On the top floor I used one of the bedrooms for myself, another as an office (required by my employment) and took in a roommate for the third bedroom. Thus I had a steady cash flow from rent and deducted 75 or 80% of the mortgage interest, making the purchase qualify as a true investment.

I'm not in any way suggesting that any of the above listed expenses are poor spending choices. Spending on what we like provides our daily enjoyment and enriches our lives. What I am trying to do is differentiate between what is a true **investment vs. an expense**. Training ourselves to distinguish between the two will help with the savings and investment program discussed in the last issue.

What about **speculations?** What are they? Let's look at a couple of items that could fall in the speculation category: lottery tickets and gambling. If one views these items as strictly entertainment they would be expenses. However, some may feel they have the potential to derive windfalls from these activities. Given that such a windfall is an extremely remote possibility, they would be speculations. I would define a speculation as a purchase with a very low probability of returning the initial purchase price to the purchaser. The reason we sometimes make such purchases is the remote possibility that when they do pay off, those payoffs can be very large. Speculative stocks (and there are many that are speculative) would be those without established businesses. A company with very little or no revenue and losing money would be regarded as speculative. Currently the hot speculative area is biotech stocks, just like Internet stocks were highly speculative in 1999. In my books most of the money made in these companies will be made by insiders and the venture capital funds, as they have the best chance of knowing which idea could make it to fruition. Outsiders and small investors like us are highly unlikely to succeed with these types of companies and are well advised to avoid such speculations. Promoters often show stock charts of the few speculative companies that make it big. They don't show the charts of the hundreds that go broke. Those charts are no longer available. With our RRSP model we would hope to avoid speculative companies and stick to established dividend paying organizations, albeit those that may currently be out of favour.

"Commodity Collapse"

This was the headline of the November 29th *Globe and Mail*, Report on Business section. The ensuing articles featured the imminent closing of two iron ore mines in Labrador and Quebec, and the expected slowdown of oil sands development in Alberta. As the old commodity saying goes, "the solution to high prices is high prices, and the solution to low prices is low prices." High prices motivate an increase in supply (shale oil) and a reduction in demand, thereby bringing about lower prices. Low prices cause a reduction in supply (mine closings) and an increase in demand (bigger vehicles), thereby causing the prices to eventually rise. A neighbour who manages a car dealership once told me that the consumer's reaction to a gasoline price changes was immediate. If prices at the pump drop while they are shopping for a new vehicle, they consider larger vehicles, and if the price rises they immediately consider smaller vehicles. From an investing standpoint I would much sooner invest after a "collapse" than before it.

We do not own many resource companies in our RRSPs, although it is important to have a few in a diversified portfolio. Given the current malaise, it appears to be an opportune time to add them to our model portfolio. However, it is impossible to know exactly when we have reached bottom and the commodity bear could continue for some time. Metals have been in a three-year downtrend, whereas oil had been more or less flat, fluctuating between yearly highs of about $110 and lows around $75.00 since the 2008-09 recession. Its current low of $65.99 is now the lowest since September of 2009.

Now for this month's additions:

Company	Ticker	Date Added	# Shares	Price Added	Approx Exchange	Cost in CAD	Annual Dividend in CAD	Dividend Yield	Earnings Yield	Cash Flow Yield	Price Times Book
Model RRSP Portfolio											
US Companies											
Verizon	VZ	Sept 30/14	100	$ 49.99	1.12	$ 5,609	$ 246.40	4.4%	9.5%	19.6%	3.7
HCP Inc.	HCP	Sept 30/14	100	$ 39.71	1.12	$ 4,458	$ 244.16	5.4%	5.0%	7.1%	1.7
Hospitality Prop. Trust	HPT	Sept 30/14	150	$ 26.85	1.12	$ 4,521	$ 329.28	7.2%	3.1%	10.9%	1.3
United Technologies	UTX	Oct 31/14	50	$ 107.00	1.12	$ 6,002	$ 132.16	2.2%	6.3%	8.8%	3.1
Johnson & Johnson	JNJ	Oct 31/14	50	$ 107.78	1.12	$ 6,045	$ 156.80	2.6%	5.7%	6.4%	3.9
Freeport-McMoRan	FCX	Nov 30/14	150	$ 26.85	1.14	$ 4,601	$ 213.75	4.7%	8.0%	25.0%	1.3
Chevron	CVX	Nov 30/14	50	$ 108.87	1.14	$ 6,216	$ 243.96	3.9%	10.0%	17.5%	1.4
Exelon	EXC	Nov 30/14	150	$ 36.17	1.14	$ 6,195	$ 212.04	3.4%	6.7%	19.2%	1.4
Canadian Companies											
Bank of Nova Scotia	BNS	Sept 30/14	100	$ 69.27		$ 6,937	$ 264.00	3.8%	8.4%	9.1%	1.9
Power Corp.	POW	Sept 30/14	200	$ 31.08		$ 6,226	$ 232.00	3.7%	7.2%	11.6%	1.3
Capital Power	CPX	Oct 31/14	200	$ 25.58		$ 5,126	$ 272.00	5.3%	2.4%	12.8%	1.1
Constellation Software	CSU	Oct 31/14	10	$ 317.50		$ 3,185	$ 44.80	1.4%	1.7%	4.5%	14.4
Mullen Group Ltd.	MTL	Nov 30/14	250	$ 22.12		$ 5,540	$ 300.00	5.4%	4.4%	8.5%	2.2
Total/Average						$ 70,661	$ 2,891.35	3.7%	5.7%	11.7%	2.8

Freeport McMoRan Inc: With over $20B in annual sales FCX is a leading international natural resources company. Its main products are copper, gold, molybdenum, cobalt, oil and gas. Copper represents over half its sales. Profits have been in decline since 2011, but compared to many other mining companies it remains solidly profitable. It is hard to predict when the current downturn will end but at some point it will. In the meantime FCX pays a very nice 4.7% dividend and with patience the resource sector will turn up. I originally purchased FCX in 2006 at $55.65 and an exchange rate of 1.13. It has since split two for one, such that my cost was $27.83 per current share. I added to the position in 2013 at $30.99 and a conversion rate of 1.04. It has traded as high as $60.00 in 2008 and again in 2010 and 2011. However, it dropped below $10.00 in the 2008/09 crash. Since recovering from that crash it has dropped just below $30.00 a few times but has always recovered and moved into the $40.00 range. While it missed making dividend payments for about a year during the recession, over the past 10 years it has increased its dividend from $0.06 to $0.31/quarter.

Chevron Corp: With over $200 B in annual revenues Chevron is one of the world's largest corporations. While there are three significant integrated oil and gas companies in Canada, Suncor, Husky and Imperial, I have Chevron in my RRSP as this US-based company provides a truly worldwide scope of business. Integrated energy companies are less impacted by commodity cycles than the Exploration and Production (E & P) companies that dominate the Canadian energy landscape. "Integrated" means they own all facets of the energy supply chain from exploration and production to refining and retail. Their operations include oil, natural gas and liquefied natural gas referred to as LNG. What drew me to purchase CVX way back in 2006, at a cost of $57.85 and exchange of 1.11, was its efforts in renewable energy. While still small, its work with bio-fuels, geothermal, solar and wind show the companies progressive nature. CVX's dividend has grown from 40 cents per quarter 10 years ago to its current $1.07. Its share price has recently declined from over $134 in July to $108 currently.

Exelon Corp: With about $25B in annual sales Exelon is a large integrated electrical power generating, distribution and marketing company across the US. Along with electricity it also distributes natural gas to residential and commercial customers. It has the largest fleet of nuclear generation facilities in the US. Its generating capacity is 55% from nuclear, 28% from natural gas, 3% from oil and just 4% from coal. Wind, solar, hydro and landfill gas make up the remaining 10%. With so little generation from coal it should benefit from new climate change regulations. US utilities had been relatively poor performers for a number of years but have come to life this past year. EXC has taken advantage of the situation by purchasing another large utility, Constellation Energy, in 2012 and is in the process of acquiring yet another, PEPCO Holdings. EXC traded for over $90/share in 2008. We originally purchased it in 2010 at $43.85 and a 1.06 exchange adding to the position in 2012 at $29.57 and a 1.01 exchange. EXC had a quarterly dividend of 40 cents 10 years ago, increased it to 52.5 cents but in 2013 cut it to the current 31 cents.

Mullen Group Ltd: While not super large like the above three US companies, MTL is a significant Alberta-based diversified trucking and oil & gas services company with about $1.5B in annual sales. It recently announced the intention of buying another Manitoba-based trucking firm, Gardewine Group, which will increase the trucking and logistics division to be the same size as its oil and gas services business. The current "commodity collapse" has driven its price from over $30.00 to $21.00. The recent purchase price for our RRSP was $22.12, although my original purchase price in another account was $18.70 in 2007. Their mission is "to acquire companies and improve their performance," although after acquiring they provide administrative services but essentially allow the independent businesses to operate on their own. The company CEO carries the Mullen name and the founding family still has significant ownership interest, which usually bodes well for smaller shareholders. I was impressed that throughout the 2008/09 recession they operated profitably, a sign of good management. Mullen was an income trust 10 years ago paying a monthly 13.5 cent dividend. It converted to a dividend-paying corporation after the income trust rules changed and now pays a still healthy 10 cent per month dividend for a yield of 5.4%. Did I mention that I liked dividends?

That summarizes this month additions...until next month. **Have fun investing.**

Please note the January 1st issue will be a few days late to allow time for year-end analysis, and to purchase our 2015 TFSA contribution stocks.

Looking Back: When a headline screams something like "Commodity Collapse" or "Sell Everything," it is often a pretty good signal that the malaise is in its final stages. Unfortunately, that was not the case this time as the commodity bear market lasted another full year and more, ending in February of 2016. Chevron as an integrated company actually performed reasonably well. Mullen Group declined significantly but has recovered most of these losses, but Freeport McMoRan has not done well. As it turned out I was clearly too early integrating these resource companies into the portfolio, but once again we shouldn't be too distracted by hindsight bias. A key learning is that market direction can last much longer than is rationally expected, both to the upside and to the downside. Catching a directional change is very difficult.

ISSUE #8: JANUARY 5, 2015

Is a 15% Gain Better Than a 22% Loss?

Happy New Year. Hope everyone had a wonderful holiday season and is ready for another year of fun and excitement in the investing world.

New Year's is a time of reflection. Relative to investments and to help the reflection process, we must first understand how to correctly calculate our own investment performance. How did we do this past year? How have we done over the past number of years? What, if any, tweaks should we make? As for that really dumb question in the title, we'll get to that as well. A recent article I came across had the following quote, which is paraphrased for brevity: "Most investors have no idea how they actually perform. Two professors asked investors how they thought they did and then looked at their brokerage statements. There was virtually NO correlation between what investors said and their actual performance based on their statements." Measuring performance correctly is a critical step to the reflection process and towards making progress whatever the pursuit, especially investing.

How do we calculate our actual performance? I try to follow a very simple, common sense portfolio approach, rather than looking at profits or losses on individual companies. Others may look at a number of completed transactions (purchase and subsequent sale) and if they are positive may surmise they had a good year. If, however, the entire portfolio is down, was it a good year? This difference in approach may be why investors referred to in the above quote didn't understand their own performance. What happens with individual companies is only important in how they contribute to the overall performance of the portfolio. In addition to calculating actual results, we should also look at the performance of the portfolio in relation to an appropriate benchmark, usually the S&P 500 in the US and TSX in Canada. There may be different ways to look at performance but keeping the process simple is my preference.

Example 1) The easiest situation is where there have neither been any additions nor subtractions from the investment account. If the account started 2014 with $10,000 and ended with $11,000, then the actual return was: $11,000 - $10,000 = $1000 gain divided by total invested capital at the start of $10,000 = 0.10 x 100 (to get to a per cent) = 10%.

Example 2) What if there was some money added during the year? Let's say an account started with $10,000, had an additional $2000 deposited on May 1st and ended up with $14,000 on December 31st. First, we need to calculate the average investment, then the gain and then the per cent gain over the average investment.

Average Invested: ($10,000 x 12 mos.) plus ($2,000 x 8 mos.) divided by 12 mos. = (120,000 + 16,000)/12 = $11,333.

Gain: $14,000 end value, minus $10,000 start value, minus $2,000 deposit = $2,000 gain.

Return: Gain divided by the average investment x 100 = ($2000/$11,333) x 100 = 17.6% return.

Example 3) What if there was some money withdrawn from the account during the year? Let's say an account started with $10,000, had $2000 withdrawn on May 1st and ended the year with $9,000?

Average invested: ($10,000 x 4 mos.) plus (($10,000-$2000) x 8 mos.) divided by 12 mos. = $8,667.

Gain: $9,000 end value minus total invested ($10,000 start - $2,000 withdrawn) of $8,000 = $1000 gain.

Return: $1000 gain/$8667 average invested = 11.5%.

These formulas are straightforward, but the process can get complicated if we are constantly moving money in and out of investment accounts. Normally with TFSAs or RRSPs there will only be one or two movements in or out (preferably in) during a year, which should make the calculations reasonably easy.

Project: Take your statements from December 31st, 2014, and December 31st, 2013, and calculate your actual return on whatever accounts you may have. Then go back as many years as possible and do the same. It is likely you can piece together three to four years of history without too much work unless you have really complicated investments, which is not a good sign. Understanding past performance will help the reflection process and enhance future performance. NOT KNOWING IS NOT THE ANSWER.

Personal real life results: Careful study of the following chart should be instructive in a number of areas I will discuss below. It might look a little complicated but highlights actual market and personal results over 22 years. The chart illustrates both the variability and the returns a well-structured stock portfolio can deliver. It should also paint a picture of what future expectations could be. I started the chart a long time ago. It goes back to when I started investing in stocks for my RRSP and then my wife's (Lillian's) a few years later. Although my chart is just handwritten (I am a low-tech guy), I have put it into Excel and added some shading for illustrative purposes.

Total Return by Year: Market				RRSPs		TFSAs	
	US S&P 500	Canadian TSX	US-CdnAvg.	Herman	Lillian	Herman	Lillian
CAGR	9.5%	10.0%	9.8%	11.7%	9.6%*	20.2%**	18.1%**
2014	13.7%	10.6%	12.2%	13.7%	22.9%	1.7%	-0.5%
2013	32.4%	11.5%	22.0%	26.9%	31.8%	23.0%	33.1%
2012	16.0%	8.2%	12.1%	10.2%	10.9%	22.2%	22.9%
2011	2.1%	-8.7%	-3.3%	-2.2%	2.9%	-4.2%	1.4%
2010	15.1%	17.6%	16.4%	12.9%	8.5%	20.2%	21.1%
2009	26.5%	35.9%	31.2%	15.4%	14.7%	71.4%	36.1%
2008	-37.0%	-33.0%	-35.0%	-27.7%	-17.2%		
2007	5.5%	9.2%	7.4%	-1.9%	-7.6%		
2006	15.8%	17.9%	16.9%	21.2%	18.0%		
2005	4.9%	25.6%	15.3%	26.1%	17.5%		
2004	10.9%	13.8%	12.4%	14.9%	12.2%		
2003	28.7%	27.1%	27.9%	22.6%	15.1%		
2002	-22.1%	-13.7%	-17.9%	-3.4%	-7.5%		
2001	-11.8%	-15.1%	-13.5%	4.2%	5.0%		
2000	-9.1%	9.3%	0.1%	18.1%	21.0%		
1999	21.0%	45.8%	33.4%	42.2%	10.3%		
1998	28.6%	1.2%	14.9%	-10.5%	-2.3%		
1997	33.3%	18.3%	25.8%	12.2%	13.7%		
1996	22.9%	29.9%	26.4%	27.0%	26.8%		
1995	37.5%	15.8%	26.7%	9.7%			
1994	1.3%	3.4%	2.4%	19.3%			
1993	10.0%	23.4%	16.7%	31.6%			

Notes:

CAGR is Compound Annual Growth Rate

*While the market and my RRSP results span 22 years, Lillian's span just 19 years. The correct Canada/US market benchmark average CAGR is 9.0% over those same 19 years vs. 9.8% for the 22 years. RRSPs are a combination of Canadian and US companies making the average of both markets an appropriate benchmark.

**The TFSAs are six years old. The Canadian market benchmark CAGR for this time frame is 11.7%. We didn't have many US companies, and as of now have no US companies, in these portfolios making the Canadian market the most appropriate benchmark.

First column — US S&P 500 Total Return Index: This was the total return on the US S&P 500 market. Many press articles, advisers etc., will refer to just the price return rather than total return. If the market started at 1000 and ended at 1100, they will say the market was up 10% but that only takes into account the stock price movement, not the dividends. Dividends are a significant part of the return so it is important to look at the total return, which includes the dividends paid by the stocks in the index. Total return is 2-3 percentage points higher than the price return. Using just price return benchmarks make individual result comparisons look better, which is maybe (being a little cynical here) why it is more commonly used. If meeting with a financial adviser who compares results to the market, be sure to ask if the market comparison is total return or price return.

Second column — Canadian TSX Total Return Index: This again includes dividends.

Third column — Average of the Canadian and US markets: Since our RRSPs contain a combination of Canadian and US companies, the best comparative benchmark is the average of both countries. There is also a little European and Asian content, but that is very small. Prior to 2005 the portfolios were largely Canadian stocks as there was a foreign content limit on RRSPs. When this restriction ended I moved aggressively into investing in US companies for the many reasons described in Issue #4. Both RRSP accounts are currently 60-65% US, which is highly unusual for a Canadian investor, as most investors exhibit a home country bias. I have started to tilt back slightly to Canadian companies, even though—and partly because—the Canadian side has been lagging.

Fourth and Fifth columns — Our actual annual RRSP performance.

Sixth and Seventh columns — Our actual annual TFSA performance.

OBSERVATIONS: While there are a lot of numbers on the chart, it is worth looking at closely as it brings to life real world situations that have happened and are likely to happen again. Understanding what has happened in the past is a critical element to preparing for likely outcomes in the future.

1. **Year-to-year performance can fluctuate dramatically:** I am after long-term results that are better than other investment options. The stock market presents this opportunity but we need to accept the fluctuations that go with it. Sticking with a disciplined strategy and not panicking in the face of adversity are keys to long-term success. The 37% drop of the S&P 500 in 2008 was actually its worst year since 1931, which had a 43.9% drop. 1937 was close at -35.3%. Many have shied away from stocks because of the financial crisis but this illustrates how rare an experience 2008 was.

2. **Larger, dividend-paying conservative companies do better during downturns:** Please note the performance of our portfolios during the 2000-2002 and 2008 bear markets. These were two of the four worst bear markets to have occurred in the past century, which has made the past fifteen years unusually challenging for investors. During these bears, our RRSPs dramatically outperformed the benchmark (Column 3, the average of the US and Canadian market), especially during the 2000-2002 bear.

3. **Canadian vs. US performance:** There is a widespread misperception that the Canadian and US markets are closely linked. As you can see they are not. There are significant differences between them from one year to another. I shaded in light grey which market outperformed the other. From 1993 to 2003 the leadership bounced around back and forth from year to year, but in 2004 something strange happened. The Canadian market took the lead and kept it for seven years. This was related to the great commodity bull market. In 2011 the lead switched to the US and has remained there for the past four years. It looked as if the lead was going to change in 2014. During the first half of the year Canada was up over 15% and the US just 8%, but that changed in dramatic fashion during the

second half of 2014 with the commodity collapse. I have no idea when this leadership will change again. Perhaps this year or perhaps in three or four years. It is very difficult to predict when, but it will change again. Right now the underlining sentiment in the market is that the best and safest place to invest is the US. European and especially emerging markets are very much out of favour. It is normal for investment sentiment to go to where the most recent outperformance has been, currently the US*. Four to five years ago, coming out of the Great Recession, Canada was widely praised as a model to the world while the US was supposedly a basket case. Thus the Canadian market was selling with an earnings yield premium of about 25% over the US market. Personally I never believed Canada was worth such a premium, which after the four recent years of US outperformance has nearly disappeared. The current exchange rate is also making it more expensive to invest in the US. For these two reasons (sentiment favouring US and exchange rate) I am tilting slightly back to Canada as well as Europe and emerging markets. Nothing dramatic, just a little over time.

*By comparison, the S&P 500 five-year total return CAGR was 15.5%, the EAFE index (Europe, Asia, Far East) total return was 5.3% and the Latin America price return (for some reason not quoted as total return) was -7.9%. To reiterate, it is very normal for investor sentiment to go to where the recent outperformance has been. This, however, does not tell us where the future returns will be the best.

4. **Our RRSP performance vs. the benchmark (column 3, average of US and Canada):** I shaded in darker grey the years our RRSPs outperformed the benchmark. Outperforming the benchmark every year is by no means a guarantee, but we strive to outperform over time. The CAGR of the US from 1993 to 2014 was 9.5%, whereas the Canadian TSX was 10.0% making an average of 9.8%. My own RRSP over this time frame yielded 11.7%, such that the market outperformance was a small but not insignificant 1.9%. Lillian's had a slightly shorter time frame and an outperformance of 0.6%. These outperformance percentages appear small, but over time compound to very significant differences (see Issue #4, "The Rule of 72"). The other interesting factor is that we achieved these results with significantly lower volatility than the market indexes. It is also important to compare against other investment options. Some real estate options, perhaps farmland, might have outperformed but there are very few options that can provide 9-12% annual returns.

A couple of other points of interest: It is widely accepted, especially in the academic community, that it is impossible to beat the market. This is referred to as the Efficient Market Hypothesis. Stats that show mutual funds, on average, underperform the market by 2-3% lend credence to the theory. Stats also show that investors, on average, underperform the market by an even wider margin. I agree that it is difficult to be equal or better than the market but not impossible. We are not practicing "rocket science," just trying to pick good companies at reasonable prices and "gut out" challenging periods.

5. **Our TFSA performance vs. the Canadian benchmark, 6 years:** The performance had been spectacular for five years and even after a flat 2014 is still well above the benchmark. The underperformance started coincidentally at the same time as I started the newsletter and as you will see below, our model TFSA portfolios are down almost 14% since mid-year. I feel bad for those who may have started their own portfolio with the first two or three issues and apologize for what has been a painful

start. Given my long-term investing history I can look back and view the successful outcomes, thus encouraging myself to "stay the course." If you are new to stock investing this will be more difficult to do. I hope you can look at the above results and see in them enough encouragement to stay on track. Neither the TFSA model nor the RRSP model (which is up nicely) have had anywhere close to enough time to work.

6. **The performance of the two RRSPs and the two TFSAs are pretty similar year to year:** There are only three or four stocks that overlap between the accounts. Most years the performance has been pretty similar, but a few years have shown big differences. The differences can easily happen based on a few individual companies that may have had a particularly great year (perhaps a buyout) or a bad year, like resources this past six months. Lillian's RRSP had no resources, explaining most of the 2014 difference.

7. **That dumb question in the title:** Clearly we are all likely happier if we end a year with a 15% gain rather than a 22% loss. However, which is the better result? Please look at our RRSP performance in 2008 and 2009. In 2008 the benchmark was down 35.0%, which was a disastrous result. Yet on average, our two RRSPs lost just 22% which was very significant market outperformance. In 2009 the benchmark was up 31.2% yet on average we were up just 15%, which was significant market underperformance. Which was a better result? This question could actually lead to quite a debate and is not as dumb as it first appears. Which outcome would you prefer?

My apologies for the lengthy explanations and overall length of this issue. I hope everyone found it worthwhile studying the longer-term results and remains motivated to either begin or continue their investment strategies. Let's review our different models' year-end performance.

TFSA MODEL # 1 — Began: June 1st, 2014

Company	Ticker	Date Added	# Shares	Price Added	Cost In CAD	Current Value in CAD	Share Price Change	Previous Quarter Total Dividends To Date	Oct 2014 Dividends	Nov 2014 Dividends	Dec 2014 Dividends	New Total Dividends To Date	Total Return
Ensco PLC	ESV	May 30/14	100	$ 52.66	$ 5,750	$ 3,474	$ (2,276)	$ 160.91			$ 85.99	$ 246.90	-35.3%
Glaxo Smithkline	GSK	May 30/14	100	$ 53.94	$ 5,890	$ 4,958	$ (932)	$ -	$ 71.85			$ 71.85	-14.6%
Ship Finance Int.	SFL	May 30/14	180	$ 18.52	$ 3,644	$ 2,948	$ (696)	$ 77.38	$ 81.25		$ 85.54	$ 244.17	-12.4%
TD Bank	TD	May 30/14	100	$ 53.76	$ 5,386	$ 5,551	$ 165	$ 47.00	$ 47.00			$ 94.00	4.8%
Innvest REIT	INN.UN	May 30/14	210	$ 5.16	$ 1,094	$ 1,256	$ 162	$ 20.97	$ 6.99	$ 6.99	$ 6.99	$ 41.94	18.6%
Rogers Communications	RCI.B	May 30/14	100	$ 43.82	$ 4,392	$ 4,517	$ 125	$ 45.75	$ 45.75			$ 91.50	4.9%
Teck Reources Ltd	TCK.B	May 30/14	200	$ 24.17	$ 4,844	$ 3,176	$ (1,668)	$ 90.00				$ 90.00	-32.6%
					$ 31,000	$ 25,880	$ (5,120)	$ 442.01	$ 252.84	$ 6.99	$ 178.52	$ 880.36	-13.7%
Cash						$ 880							
Total						$ 26,760							

TFSA MODEL # 2 — Began: July 26, 2014

Company	Ticker	Date Added	# Shares	Price Added	Cost In CAD	Current Value in CAD	Share Price Change	Previous Quarter Total Dividends To Date	Oct 2014 Dividends	Nov 2014 Dividends	Dec 2014 Dividends	New Total Dividends To Date	Total Return
Seadrill	SDRL	July 25/14	130	$ 37.49	$ 5,312	$ 1,801	$ (3,511)	$ 140.46				$ 140.46	-63.5%
HSBC Holdings PLC	HSBC	July 25/14	100	$ 52.82	$ 5,757	$ 5,479	$ (278)	$ -	$ 54.97		$ 56.82	$ 111.79	-2.9%
Vodaphone	VOD	July 25/14	150	$ 34.16	$ 5,585	$ 5,946	$ 361	$ -				$ -	6.5%
ATCO	ACO.X	July 25/14	100	$ 50.56	$ 5,066	$ 4,766	$ (300)	$ 21.50			$ 21.50	$ 43.00	-5.1%
Husky Energy	HSE	July 25/14	150	$ 33.72	$ 5,068	$ 4,125	$ (943)	$ -	$ 45.00			$ 45.00	-17.7%
Sunlife Financial	SLF	July 25/14	100	$ 41.40	$ 4,150	$ 4,192	$ 42	$ 36.00			$ 36.00	$ 72.00	2.7%
					$ 30,938	$ 26,309	$ (4,629)	$ 197.96	$ 99.97	$ -	$ 114.32	$ 412.25	-13.6%
Cash					$ 62	$ 474							
Total					$ 31,000	$ 26,783							

And now the RRSP model:

Company	Ticker	Date Added	# Shares	Price Added	Cost In CAD	Current Value in CAD	Share Price Change	Oct Dividend	Nov Dividend	Dec Dividend	Dividends Since Inception	Total Return
Model RRSP Portfolio												
US Companies												
Verizon	VZ	Sept 30/14	100	$ 49.99	$ 5,609	$ 5,426	$ (183)		$ 61.38		$ 61.38	-2.2%
HCP Inc	HCP	Sept 30/14	100	$ 39.71	$ 4,458	$ 5,107	$ 649		$ 60.85		$ 60.85	15.9%
Hospitality Prop. Trust	HPT	Sept 30/14	150	$ 26.85	$ 4,521	$ 5,394	$ 873		$ 82.58		$ 82.58	21.1%
United Technologies	UTX	Oct 31/14	50	$ 107.00	$ 6,002	$ 6,670	$ 668			$ 33.53	$ 33.53	11.7%
Johnson and Johnson	JNJ	Oct 31/14	50	$ 107.78	$ 6,045	$ 6,065	$ 20			$ 39.72	$ 39.72	1.0%
Freeport-McMoRan	FCX	Nov 30/14	150	$ 26.85	$ 4,601	$ 4,065	$ (536)				$ -	-11.6%
Chevron	CVX	Nov 30/14	50	$ 108.87	$ 6,216	$ 6,506	$ 290				$ -	4.7%
Exelon	EXC	Nov 30/14	150	$ 36.17	$ 6,195	$ 6,452	$ 257				$ -	4.1%
US Subtotal					$ 43,647	$45,685	$ 2,038				$ 278.06	5.3%
Canadian Companies												
Bank of Nova Scotia	BNS	Sept 30/14	100	$ 69.27	$ 6,937	$ 6,631	$ (306)	$ 66.00			$ 66.00	-3.5%
Power Corp	POW	Sept 30/14	200	$ 31.08	$ 6,226	$ 6,352	$ 126			$ 58.00	$ 58.00	3.0%
Capital Power	CPX	Oct 31/14	200	$ 25.58	$ 5,126	$ 5,200	$ 74				$ -	1.4%
Constellation Software	CSU	Oct 31/14	10	$ 317.50	$ 3,185	$ 3,454	$ 269				$ -	8.4%
Mullen Group Ltd.	MTL	Nov 20/14	250	$ 22.12	$ 5,540	$ 5,328	$ (212)			$ 25.00	$ 25.00	-3.4%
Cdn Subtotal					$ 27,014	$26,965	$ (49)				$ 149.00	0.4%
Total Cdn and US					$ 70,661	$72,650	$ 1,989				$ 427.06	3.4%
Cash						$ 427						
Portfolio Value						$73,077						

Prices are based on a December 31st closing and a 1.16 exchange rate. We are always trying to improve by tweaking a little here or there, but given the long-term results experienced will not make wholesale changes. Our TFSA model portfolio has experienced some real challenges with the commodity collapse. There is a very large difference in performance between the TFSA model and the RRSP model largely explained by the TFSA being Canada and resource focused, whereas the RRSP being US focused. Again, this different approach is driven by dividend withholding tax considerations. If the TFSA is your only stock account, it is advisable to have some US exposure.

One of the first projects each year is to decide where to invest new contributions to the TFSA. We always make our contribution early in the year to allow more time for the tax-free investments to work. We have made the following changes to our TFSAs as of January 2nd, 2015:

1. We made our $5500 contribution to each TFSA.

2. The discount brokerage I use recently introduced US dollar TFSA and RRSP accounts. This is great news and other banks will likely follow. Having US dollar-based accounts allows the splitting of the portfolios into companies that trade in US dollars separate from those that trade in Canadian dollars. In Canadian dollar accounts, if we sell a US or international company we would generate US dollars that would automatically be converted to Canadian and incur the exchange fee of 1-1.5%. A subsequent purchase of another US/international company would require re-conversion to US funds costing another 1-1.5%, such that the "round trip" would ding us a 2-3% fee as well as the trade commission of about 2 x $9.99. As well, all dividends are automatically converted to Canadian dollars and incur the exchange fee. With US dollar accounts there are no such fees. We only need to pay exchange when we originally convert to US and should we eventually wish to convert back. We had our TFSA accounts split into

Canadian and US. Even though we don't hold US companies in the TFSA, international companies trade in US dollars.

3. We sold the only two US companies, AT&T and Hospitality Property Trust, that we owned in our TFSAs. We purchased these before realizing the withholding tax consideration and with the desire to tilt away from the US thought it was an opportune time to sell these two. We still own both companies in other portfolios, so nothing against them. Neither was in the TFSA models.

4. **We purchased the following new companies for our TFSAs: Unilever, Diageo, BHP Billiton and Bank of Nova Scotia.**

Unilever PLC (UL): Based in London, England (no withholding tax), with about $60B in annual sales Unilever is very large consumer product's company. It has four product areas: 1) Personal Care, including well-known brands Dove, Vaseline, Axe, Lux and V05 2) Home Care, including Sunlight detergents, Cif cleaners and Comfort fabric softener 3) Foods, including Becel, Bertolli, Hellmann's and Knorr, and 4) Refreshments, including Lipton and Ben & Jerry's ice cream. It's a little on the expensive side but has traded sideways for two years. It has a dividend yield of 3.8%, earnings yield of 5.4%, cash flow yield of 7.0% and price times book of 6.6x. It has a very high ROE (Return on Equity) of 30-35% which is why it is a little expensive on the other metrics. I will discuss ROE in a future issue. It has major exposure to emerging markets and every day two billion people in the world use its products. Our price was $40.05 at a 1.18 (big Canadian $ drop on January 2nd) exchange rate.

Diageo PLC (DEO) is also based in London and also has significant exposure to emerging markets. With about $15B in annual sales DEO is a major player in the premium beverage industry. Some of its well-known spirits include Johnnie Walker, Crown Royal, J & B, Captain Morgan, Smirnoff and Baileys. It owns premium beers including Guinness, Harp, Kilkenny, Smithwick's and Red Stripe. It also has a smaller wine business including Piat d'Or and Dom Perignon. Like UL it has traded sideways for two years and is a little expensive but also has a very high ROE of 30-35%. It has a dividend yield of 3.0%, earnings yield of 5.1% and cash flow yield of 5.5%. It trades for 6.7 times book value. Our price was $112.73 at a 1.18 exchange rate. So after a tough day at work or on the markets, go ahead and reach for the Johnnie Walker...you deserve it. Part of the fun of investing is ownership in companies whose products we use ourselves and I expect DEO fits that bill. I hope both these companies will provide stability and modest growth to the portfolio. Both have share prices that have doubled over the past 10 years and have grown their dividends regularly. They both have highly recognized worldwide brands providing enduring value.

BHP Billiton Ltd. (BHP): The previous two consumer staples companies move us away from being too resource dependent in the TFSA, but I couldn't stay away from the bargain bin in resources. Based in Australia with $67B in annual sales, BHP is the largest mining company in the world. It is planning on spinning off its smaller operations to focus on copper, petroleum, coal and iron ore. This could result in ownership of few shares of a smaller company as well, which I don't particularly like, but its current valuation looks attractive. I bought a few shares in my non-registered account a while ago to make sure there were no withholding tax issues with BHP, listed in the UK and Australia. BHP sold at over $100 in 2011 but, like all miners, has ground down over four years to now trade at our cost of $47.27 with a 1.18 exchange rate. Unlike other miners it has remained very profitable with a dividend yield of 5.1%, earnings yield of 10.9%, cash flow yield of 19.6% and is currently trading at just below book value. BHP's income has been in decline since 2011 but ticked up a little in 2014. It is hard to predict when the commodity cycle might turn, but eventually it will and BHP should have the financial strength to survive the current situation and prosper when the turnaround arrives.

Bank of Nova Scotia (BNS): I described BNS when it was included in the RRSP model. It is currently selling at the best valuation of the big five Canadian banks. I believe this is because it is Canada's most international bank with lots of exposure to Latin America and the Caribbean, areas currently out of favour with the investment community. I will not be putting BNS in the model TFSA as it is in our RRSP model, but wanted to let you know that's how we rounded out our TFSAs for this year.

TFSA model change: Given that we now have Canadian and US dollar accounts, I will alter how the TFSA model is presented by merging all the positions into one portfolio and splitting between Canadian and international companies. If a family has two TFSAs, it doesn't really matter which TFSA owns which company. Thus, I propose presenting the chart the same way as the model RRSP portfolio, although instead of Canadian and US companies it will be Canadian and international. Adding the accumulated dividends received to date to the $11,000 (2 x $5500) eligible 2015 contribution converted at 1.18, allows the addition of 100 shares of UL, thirty shares of DEO and sixty-five shares of BHP to the model.

Again, my apologies for the length of the issue, but have a toast to your success getting through it. There was a lot to cover as we enter the new year. Until next time, **have fun investing.**

Looking Back: OK, this chapter had a lot of detail but reviewing it two years after it was written, it remains a pivotal chapter for stock investing success. A critical component of the journey is actually measuring bottom line results. This is an important reference chapter and periodic review will be beneficial. Enough said. Diageo products are a great way to celebrate.

ROE, ROE, ROE Your Boat...

...Gently down the stream. OK, the stock market is more like whitewater rafting than a gentle stream but I wanted to create a title related to the educational topic of the month, ROE or Return on Equity, which was introduced in the last issue. This issue will also include commentary on the new US exchange rate and add a couple more companies to our RRSP model.

Return on Equity is the bottom line profitability measure for a company. It is a simple **Profit/Equity** ratio. If a company makes $100 of profit and has $1000 of equity, then it has a 10% ROE. Back in Issue #2, I discussed the four main criteria used to evaluate a stock purchase: 1) Cash Flow Yield 2) Earnings Yield 3) Dividend Yield and 4) Price Times Book Value. I have tracked **Return on Equity** when doing the year-end analysis on all companies owned, but fully admit to not having placed enough emphasis on it. Two factors recently influenced my thoughts on the topic. First, the encouragement of my son to look at companies with higher ROE combined with higher growth potential, like Constellation Software, and second, reading a whole book on the topic (I know...I need a life). The investing world is filled with continual learning opportunities and while the above four criteria have served me well, we must continuously attempt to learn and improve.

To illustrate ROE we'll introduce two fictitious companies. They are both in the same industry and have ample growth opportunities. To keep the math simple and illustrate how ROE impacts longer-term valuation, we'll only look at the following: debt, equity, profit and number of shares. With this information we can calculate book value, profit per share, ROE and market value at a constant valuation factor of 8% earnings yield, which I arbitrarily picked. Both companies just reported their year-end which was very similar.

Company #1: $1000 of debt, $1000 of equity, $100 profit, 100 shares. For fun we will give this company the name **Mediocrity.**

Company #2: $1000 of debt, $1000 of equity, $200 profit, 200 shares. For fun we'll call this one **Excellence.** The names may not be very original, but they are descriptive.

Company #1, Mediocrity: Based on the information we can calculate that it earned $1.00 per share ($100 profit/100 shares) and has a book value of $10.00 per share ($1000 of equity/100 shares). It has an ROE of 10% ($100 profit/$1000 equity). It can be purchased for $12.50 per share based on 8% earnings yield ($12.50 x 8% = $1.00 per share earnings) and thus sells at 1.25 price times book ($12.50 price/$10.00 book value).

Company #2, Excellence: Based on the information it also has a profit of $1.00 per share ($200 profit/200 shares), but a book value of just $5.00 per share ($1000 equity/200 shares) and an ROE of 20% ($200 profit/$1000 equity). It can also be purchased for $12.50 per share based on the same earnings yield of 8% and thus sells for 2.5 price times book ($12.50 purchase price/$5.00 book value).

Which should we buy? Based on the original valuation criteria, both Mediocrity and Excellence have the same earnings yield of 8%, but Mediocrity represents better value from a price times book standpoint. Wouldn't we prefer to buy something that is the same on one valuation criteria but twice as good on another (1.25 vs. 2.5 price times book)? Stated another way, given that both companies have the same profit per share, wouldn't we prefer to pay only 1.25 times the equity in the firm, rather than 2.5 times the equity in the firm? Sometimes Mediocrity represents better **value** than Excellence.

But wait a minute. **How does the ROE factor into the longer-term performance?** The following grid illustrates this. Let's consider this Chapter One in the lives of these companies. To keep things simple both companies invest 100% of their profits back into the company. They also visit their friendly banker (that could be considered an oxymoron!) to ask for additional borrowings such that they maintain the same level of $1.00 of debt for every $1.00 of equity. This isn't important in Chapter One but will come into play in the future, as both companies evolve over time. Both companies also continue to trade with an earnings yield of 8%.

MEDIOCRITY	Start Line	Year 1	Year 2	Year 3	Year 4
Debt	$ 1,000.00	$1,100.00	$1,210.00	$1,331.00	$1,464.10
Equity	$ 1,000.00	$1,100.00	$1,210.00	$1,331.00	$1,464.10
Profit @ 10% ROE	$ 100.00	$ 110.00	$ 121.00	$ 133.10	$ 146.41
Profit/Share: 100 Shares	$ 1.00	$ 1.10	$ 1.21	$ 1.33	$ 1.46
Book Value/Share	$ 10.00	$ 11.00	$ 12.10	$ 13.31	$ 14.64
Market Value/Share @ 8% earnings yield	$ 12.50	$ 13.75	$ 15.12	$ 16.63	$ 18.25

EXCELLENCE					
Debt	$ 1,000.00	$1,200.00	$1,440.00	$1,728.00	$2,073.60
Equity	$ 1,000.00	$1,200.00	$1,440.00	$1,728.00	$2,073.60
Profit @ 20% ROE	$ 200.00	$ 240.00	$ 288.00	$ 345.60	$ 414.72
Profit/Share: 200 Shares	$ 1.00	$ 1.20	$ 1.44	$ 1.73	$ 2.07
Book Value/Share	$ 5.00	$ 6.00	$ 7.20	$ 8.86	$ 10.37
Market Value/Share @ 8% earnings yield	$ 12.50	$ 15.00	$ 18.00	$ 21.63	$ 25.88

Please observe that all the profits from the previous year are added to the equity for the following year. Profit is then calculated by the 10% or 20% ROE level. As mentioned these companies are in an industry with ample growth opportunities. Better management performance allows, but does not guarantee, Excellence to grow at a much faster pace of 20% per year vs. 10% per year. The Rule of 72 plays out in the example, as Excellence more than doubles its profit in four years (72/20 = 3.6 years). The importance of ROE seems blatantly obvious from the example, but real life is more complicated as higher ROE companies usually trade with lower earnings yield, making the decision more difficult. That said, ROE will become a more important valuation criteria in future purchase decisions. And there you have a whole book summarized in just two pages.

Exchange Rate: Speaking of whitewater rafting, both the Canadian and US markets have been rather choppy in January, but are essentially flat for the month. Commodities remain under pressure with copper taking a big hit, dropping from about $3.00 to $2.50 over two months. It was clearly too early adding FCX into the model on December 1st. Oil remains under pressure but seems to be stabilizing around $45.00. I am not a big believer in the current $20.00 predictions as extreme predictions often indicate a change in direction. The biggest loser, however, was the Canadian dollar. Already under pressure from the commodity sell-off, it dropped dramatically after the surprise announcement from the bank of Canada, cutting the overnight lending rate from 1% to 0.75%. The dollar now trades very close to 80 cents US, or said another way, it takes almost 1.25 loonies to buy a Yankee buck. I certainly didn't predict this kind of decline in oil, copper nor loonies. Did anyone? It illustrates the folly of predictions. Our energy is better spent learning to adapt as circumstances change. Below is an excerpt from the September 1st, 2014 Issue #4:

Exchange Rate: For about 40 of the past 50 years the Canadian dollar has been at a significant discount to the US dollar but for the past 10 years it has been close to parity, mostly between 90 cents and $1.05. I don't know where the exchange rate is going but figure that par is not the normal situation. Anytime our dollar is over 90 cents US is a good time to invest in US companies.

For the past 10 to 12 years I have been highly focused on US equities for many reasons listed in Issue #4 and now feel fortunate to have such a high percentage of stock investments in American companies. Over the years I have developed the following guidelines for new investments: Canadian dollar at 90 cents plus = mostly American investments. Canadian dollar at 80-90 cents = both American and Canadian investments. Canadian dollar below 80 cents = mostly Canadian investments. International companies are listed in the US and transact in US dollars but reflect the value of their home country currency. I certainly don't know where our dollar is headed next and think 80 cents is an appropriate level, but that doesn't mean it is going to stay there. Hopefully in three or four years subscribers' portfolios will also be organized in such a manner that currency and market swings represent new opportunities rather than concerns. We still have a few US companies in our personal RRSPs I would like to add to the model but will add just one at this time, plus a couple of Canadian companies.

Model RRSP Portfolio

Company	Ticker	Date Added	# Shares	Price Added	Approx Exchange	Cost in CAD	Annual Dividend in CAD	Dividend Yield	Earnings Yield	Cash Flow Yield	Price Times Book	ROE
US Companies												
Verizon	VZ	Sept 30/14	100	$ 49.99	1.12	$ 5,609	$ 246.40	4.4%	9.5%	19.6%	3.7	**37.6%**
HCP Inc.	HCP	Sept 30/14	100	$ 39.71	1.12	$ 4,458	$ 244.16	5.4%	5.0%	7.1%	1.7	**8.8%**
Hospitality Prop. Trust	HPT	Sept 30/14	150	$ 26.85	1.12	$ 4,521	$ 329.28	7.2%	3.1%	10.9%	1.3	**5.8%**
United Technologies	UTX	Oct 31/14	50	$ 107.00	1.12	$ 6,002	$ 132.16	2.2%	6.3%	8.8%	3.1	**19.7%**
Johnson & Johnson	JNJ	Oct 31/14	50	$ 107.78	1.12	$ 6,045	$ 156.80	2.6%	5.7%	6.4%	3.9	**23.7%**
Freeport-McMoRan	FCX	Nov 30/14	150	$ 26.85	1.14	$ 4,601	$ 213.75	4.7%	8.0%	25.0%	1.3	**10.7%**
Chevron	CVX	Nov 30/14	50	$ 108.87	1.14	$ 6,216	$ 243.96	3.9%	10.0%	17.5%	1.4	**13.8%**
Exelon	EXC	Nov 30/14	150	$ 36.17	1.14	$ 6,195	$ 212.04	3.4%	6.7%	19.2%	1.4	**9.2%**
General Electric	**GE**	**Jan 27/15**	**200**	**$ 24.38**	**1.24**	**$ 6,056**	**$ 228.16**	**3.8%**	**6.2%**	**7.4%**	**1.9**	**11.9%**
Canadian Companies												
Bank of Nova Scotia	BNS	Sept 30/14	100	$ 69.27		$ 6,937	$ 264.00	3.8%	8.4%	9.1%	1.9	**16.2%**
Power Corp.	POW	Sept 30/14	200	$ 31.08		$ 6,226	$ 232.00	3.7%	7.2%	11.6%	1.3	**11.9%**
Capital Power	CPX	Oct 31/14	200	$ 25.58		$ 5,126	$ 272.00	5.3%	2.4%	12.8%	1.1	**2.7%**
Constellation Software	CSU	Oct 31/14	10	$ 317.50		$ 3,185	$ 44.80	1.4%	1.7%	4.5%	14.4	**42.9%**
Mullen Group Ltd.	MTL	Nov 30/14	250	$ 22.12		$ 5,540	$ 300.00	5.4%	4.4%	8.5%	2.2	**10.3%**
Royal Bank	**RY**	**Jan 27/15**	**100**	**$ 75.12**		**$ 7,522**	**$ 300.00**	**4.0%**	**8.0%**	**9.1%**	**2.1**	**19.0%**
TransCanada Pipeline	**TRP**	**Jan 27/15**	**100**	**$ 55.99**		**$ 5,609**	**$ 192.00**	**3.5%**	**4.3%**	**8.7%**	**2.3**	**10.2%**
Total/Average						**$ 89,848**	**$ 3,611.51**	**4.0%**	**6.1%**	**11.6%**	**2.8**	**15.9%**

Notes: All valuation numbers are as of when the company was added to the model, except ROE which is current. VZ numbers are a little wonky because of their purchase of 100% of Verizon Wireless. Please keep in mind it is difficult to compare across industries. The chart now shows averages for all stocks in the portfolio with an average dividend yield of 4.0%, earnings yield of 6.1%, cash flow yield of 11.6% and ROE of 15.9%. I hope to update all numbers for the March 1st or April 1st issue when all year-ends are available.

Royal Bank needs no introduction as Canada's largest bank. The banking sector has sold off recently, with Royal down 10% from its recent high representing a decent time to buy. It has $22B in annual sales with two-thirds from Canada and the remainder split between US and international. It just announced a major US acquisition. Royal is my largest RRSP holding, having purchased some in December 2008 at $35.25, in 2004 at $30.51, and way back in 1999 at $16.01. One of the reasons Canadian banks have done so well in the past is they traditionally earn 15-20% ROE but still trade at very good earnings yields of 7-10%. High ROEs combined with high earnings yield (and cash flow yield) is a powerful combination. Royal has almost tripled its dividend the last 10 years.

TransCanada Pipeline is one of North America's largest energy infrastructure companies and again needs no introduction as the developer of the Keystone XL pipeline. TRP has a number of other big projects on the go, with Energy East gas to oil conversion and a couple of pipelines intended to take natural gas to the BC coast. Besides pipelines it has a growing portfolio of electricity generating facilities: 51% from natural gas, 23% nuclear (Bruce Nuclear), 15% coal, and 11% a combination of wind, solar and hydro. The share price is a little pricey but less expensive than most other pipeline companies. I believe the reason they all trade at high valuations is that the troika of supposed environmentalists, First Nations and Barrack Obama have made new pipelines very difficult to build, increasing the value of existing infrastructure. I first purchased TRP for $10.95 in 2000 and added to the position in 2011 at $37.17. Its dividend has increased by 60% in the past decade.

General Electric: While the previous two companies have been stars in our portfolios, GE has been a dog, but I remain optimistic it will once again become a high performance company. With $148B in sales it is a worldwide conglomerate encompassing aviation, health care, transportation, power generation, energy and water services. GE is downsizing its large financial services company to focus on the industrial products. Its share price was as high as $60.00 in 1999. It is a good example that "dropping in half" doesn't make it a bargain. I purchased GE in 2006 for $33.30 and added to the position in May 2008 at $30.92. It struggled during the recession and cut its dividend but has since increased it to where it is now a penny higher than 10 years ago.

I sincerely hope that sharing my purchase price and timing helps subscribers de-emphasize daily gyrations and focus on longer-term direction, like I have learned to do. These long-term gains increase the fun factor of investing in stocks.

Past Performance Is the BEST Indicator of Future Performance

Most ads and publications for mutual funds or other financial services have a disclaimer (as do I at the bottom of my newsletter) that will say something like "past performance does not guarantee future performance" or "past performance may not be the best indicator of future performance." If past performance isn't a good indicator of future performance, what is?

Through a thirty-five-year sales and sales management career I had the opportunity to participate in many training courses and seminars, usually one or two per year, which adds up to a lot of training. Maybe I was just a slow learner. Out of the plethora of programs only five or six were impactful enough to be memorable. One of the impactful programs was on conducting interviews to identify the best job candidates. The overall summary of the program (which could be useful to any subscriber hiring people) is that **how people behaved in the past will tell you how they will behave in the future.** In other words, a leopard doesn't change its spots.

How do you come to understand an individual's past behaviour? It's how the interview questions are structured. Theoretical questions such as "What do you think you can accomplish for our company?" are best avoided in favour of experiential questions like "During your time with Company X, what were your most memorable accomplishments?" The theoretical question invites speculation and the potential to blow the proverbial smoke. The answer to experiential questions gets at what the candidate actually did in the past. An individual with a history of significant achievements is likely to accomplish more of them in their future.

People can, of course, embellish their past, but a good interviewer in a 30-45 minute interview with good experiential questions and reference-checking, can usually catch those who embellish.

And there you have a two-day training program in two paragraphs.

The most critical element of building any team, whether a business team or a sports team, is the ability to identify, attract and evaluate the team members. Let's use the Edmonton Oilers as an example. It doesn't take much skill to draft, three times in a row, the first overall no-brainer draft pick. Oiler management, however, has been incapable of picking the other twenty players and coaches needed to make a valid team and thus has clearly displayed an inability to identify and hire the right people. Business teams operate similarly. Some organizations have a great ability to get the right people for long-term success; others don't. There are some teams where the TOP just has to go before the team will have any chance of performing. In other words, if the chess master makes a series of bad moves, there's not much sense blaming the pawns. However, in business as in sports, it is often the pawns that get the blame.

Why am I writing about hiring and team performance?

When picking a person or team to manage your funds, you are in fact "hiring" that person or team. If you are selecting a company to invest in, you are "hiring" the management team with the expectation of delivering a return for your investment. What is the best way to select those individuals or teams?

Question 1) Which money manager or company would you hire?

    a. One with a one-year performance of 10%.

    b. One with a one-year performance of 30%.

    c. One with a twenty year CAGR performance of 5%.

    d. One with a twenty year CAGR performance of 10%.

Question 2) Which money manager or company would you pick from this selection?

    a. One with a twenty-year CAGR performance of 5% but whose most recent year was 20%.

    b. One with a twenty-year CAGR performance of 10% but whose most recent year was zero.

The clear choice in question one is **d)**, although in real life many will choose **b)**. The October 1st, 2014 Issue #5, discussed luck vs. skill. One-year performance will have a much greater element of luck than twenty years. Question two is a little tougher, but my choice would be **b)**, as the most recent year (or any individual year) includes a greater element of luck. Answering a question like this on paper looks easy and logical, but in real life many would choose **a)** as they chase the "hot hand" in a phenomenon called "recency bias."

Whether hiring a money manager or a corporate management team, my preference is looking at long-term performance. This is one reason I tend to stay away from companies that are too young to evaluate. Unlike someone like Warren Buffett or a mutual fund manager, we, as small investors, do not get the opportunity to interview the management team, so how can we determine their past behaviour? The best way I know is studying a company's past financials. Generally, I like to view at least five years. There is lots of hype around new start-ups and the odd one does very well, but many don't. As with hiring people if a company (or financial manager) has achieved success in the past, it is likely to achieve more success in the future. This is by no means guaranteed because as the saying goes "the only guarantee in life is death and taxes." Corporate success rates can also change as will be illustrated with companies Mediocrity and Excellence in future issues. However, I would submit that **while past performance does not guarantee future performance, if of significant duration it is certainly the most reliable indicator.**

Ensco update (TFSA model): ESV reported fourth quarter and year-end results this past week. It reported a loss of $14.89 per share, which looks scary, but the loss was largely attributed to non-cash write-down of virtually all the goodwill on its balance sheet. Operating earnings for the year were actually $6.37 per share, and operating cash flows of $8.87 per share were very similar to 2013. To preserve capital in light of oil price weakness it cut its dividend by 80% to 15 cents per quarter, still representing 2.4% at the current share price. This all looks bad but I think it represents a great opportunity to buy at a discounted price. As a matter of fact I increased my exposure to ESV in my non-registered account through options.

Market update: The Canadian market was essentially flat in January but up about 4% in February. The US market was down about 3% in January, but up 5% in February to now have a modest gain so far this year. The Canadian dollar dropped about 6% in January and appears to be stabilizing around 80 cents (or $1.25/ USD). Similarly oil has bounced around but for now appears to have stabilized around $45.00-$52.00. My intention is to update all model portfolios quarterly in the next newsletter. It looks like they have done reasonably well over the past two months, with the decline in the Canadian dollar representing a boost to valuations in Canadian currency.

The exchange rate leads to the same conundrum as last month regarding new additions to the RRSP model. Interestingly I have read two recent articles extolling the virtues of being invested in the US, and one predicting a drop of our dollar to 69 cents. When ideas hit the popular press, it's often getting late to capitalize. Thus my main focus right now is Canada. That said I will keep the majority of our RRSPs in US companies for reasons previously explained. There are still a few US companies I would have liked to add to the model, but will add just two at this time (with some trepidation in regards to exchange) along with two Canadian companies, bringing the total to twenty companies. We have some accumulated dividends in our own RRSPs and intend to add two or three Canadian companies in the near future, which will be communicated and added to the model, bringing the total number of companies to 22-23, which is enough for a well-diversified portfolio with $50,000 to $1M of value. Smaller portfolios would work with 10 to 15 companies while larger ones might hold 30-40. My thought for subscribers: those lacking US exposure should still build some while those already heavily invested in the US could pull in the US reins. The Canadian dollar is below the midpoint of its fifty-year range, between about 63 cents and $1.10, and can go either way. It is closely correlated with the price of oil. And now for stock selections:

Company	Ticker	Date Added	# Shares	Price Added	Approx Exchange	Cost in CAD	Annual Dividend in CAD	Dividend Yield	Earnings Yield	Cash Flow Yield	Price Times Book	ROE
Model RRSP Portfolio												
US Companies												
Verizon	VZ	Sept 30/14	100	$ 49.99	1.12	$ 5,609	$ 246.40	4.4%	9.5%	19.6%	3.7	37.6%
HCP Inc.	HCP	Sept 30/14	100	$ 39.71	1.12	$ 4,458	$ 244.16	5.4%	5.0%	7.1%	1.7	8.8%
Hospitality Prop. Trust	HPT	Sept 30/14	150	$ 26.85	1.12	$ 4,521	$ 329.28	7.2%	3.1%	10.9%	1.3	5.8%
United Technologies	UTX	Oct 31/14	50	$ 107.00	1.12	$ 6,002	$ 132.16	2.2%	6.3%	8.8%	3.1	19.7%
Johnson & Johnson	JNJ	Oct 31/14	50	$ 107.78	1.12	$ 6,045	$ 156.80	2.6%	5.7%	6.4%	3.9	23.7%
Freeport-McMoRan	FCX	Nov 30/14	150	$ 26.85	1.14	$ 6,216	$ 213.75	4.7%	8.0%	25.0%	1.3	10.7%
Chevron	CVX	Nov 30/14	50	$ 108.87	1.14	$ 6,216	$ 243.96	3.9%	10.0%	17.5%	1.4	13.8%
Exelon	EXC	Nov 30/14	150	$ 36.17	1.14	$ 6,195	$ 212.04	3.4%	6.7%	19.2%	1.4	9.2%
General Electric	GE	Jan 27/15	200	$ 24.38	1.24	$ 6,056	$ 228.16	3.8%	6.2%	7.4%	1.9	11.9%
Praxair	**PX**	**Feb 28/15**	**25**	**$ 127.90**	**1.25**	**$ 4,007**	**$ 89.38**	**2.2%**	**4.5%**	**7.8%**	**8.8**	**27.7%**
Qualcomm	QCOM	Feb 28/15	50	$ 72.51	1.25	$ 4,542	$ 105.00	2.3%	6.6%	7.5%	3.1	21.3%
Canadian Companies												
Bank of Nova Scotia	BNS	Sept 30/14	100	$ 69.27		$ 6,937	$ 264.00	3.8%	8.4%	9.1%	1.9	16.2%
Power Corp.	POW	Sept 30/14	200	$ 31.08		$ 6,226	$ 232.00	3.7%	7.2%	11.6%	1.3	11.9%
Capital Power	CPX	Oct 31/14	200	$ 25.58		$ 5,126	$ 272.00	5.3%	2.4%	12.8%	1.1	2.7%
Constellation Software	CSU	Oct 31/14	10	$ 317.50		$ 3,185	$ 44.80	1.4%	1.7%	4.5%	14.4	42.9%
Mullen Group Ltd.	MTL	Nov 30/14	250	$ 22.12		$ 5,540	$ 300.00	5.4%	4.4%	8.5%	2.2	10.3%
Royal Bank	RY	Jan 27/15	100	$ 75.12		$ 7,522	$ 300.00	4.0%	8.0%	9.1%	2.1	19.0%
TransCanada Pipeline	TRP	Jan 27/15	100	$ 55.99		$ 5,609	$ 192.00	3.5%	4.3%	8.7%	2.3	10.2%
Bell Canada	**BCE**	**Feb 28/15**	**100**	**$ 54.71**		$ 5,481	$ 260.00	4.8%	5.4%	13.3%	4.3	21.0%
Brookfield Asset Mgmt	**BAM.A**	**Feb 28/15**	**100**	**$ 67.85**		$ 6,795	$ 85.00	1.2%	7.8%	9.5%	1.8	15.4%
Total/Average						$ 110,673	$ 4,150.89	3.8%	6.1%	11.2%	3.2	17.0%

Praxair: With over $12B in annual sales PX is North America's largest supplier of industrial gases, including oxygen, nitrogen, carbon dioxide, helium and hydrogen. Sales are almost evenly split between North America and the rest of the world. It serves a diverse set of industries such that overall sales are not dominated by any one industry and operates under long-term contracts. Its products are critical to customers, yet represent a small slice of their costs allowing PX to maintain pricing through difficult times. While earnings yield is lower than desired it has an excellent ROE, and even through the 2008/09 recession only experienced one year with declining profitability and by just 4%. It sports an excellent long-term record with 10-year earnings growth of 2.6x and dividend growth of over 3.5x. My original purchase was last December at $127.76, almost the same as today except for exchange.

Qualcomm has a "focus on a simple goal: invent mobile technology breakthroughs." With over $25B and rapidly growing annual sales, QCOM provides chips for many of the world's leading smart phones and other mobile devices like tablets and, increasingly, automobiles. I am not a tech expert, but it doesn't take one to know our use of mobile communications has grown rapidly. Over the past 10 years QCOM has grown sales by 5x, earnings per share by 3.5x and its dividend by 4.5x. Despite this growth rate it is selling for an above average 6.6% earnings yield. Earnings yields are usually lower with rapidly growing companies. The valuation is the result of uncertainty in China, possibly reducing growth for 2015. My original purchase last December was at a cost of $72.61, again almost the same as today except for exchange rate.

Bell Canada is a familiar name as one of Canada's leading communications companies. An interesting aspect to BCE is the ownership of Bell Media including the *Globe and Mail*, CTV, BNN, TSN, HBO Canada and the Discovery Channel. It also has significant ownership interest in the Montreal Canadiens, the Bell Centre and Maple Leaf Sports and Entertainment, including the Raptors, the Marlies and the Toronto Make Me Laughs

Issue #10: March 1, 2015

(oops sorry, Maple Leafs). With $20B in annual sales, BCE is large for a Canadian company but growing slowly. However, earnings per share and dividends have grown by 65 % over the past 10 years. My original purchase was at $34.69 in 2001 with additional shares purchased in 2013 at $42.62. The 4.8% stable yield is enticing.

Brookfield Asset Management is one of Canada's few truly international companies. It searches the world for undervalued, long life assets in three categories: real estate, infrastructure and renewable energy. Each segment is managed through a publicly traded subsidiary: Brookfield Property Partners, Brookfield Infrastructure Partners and Brookfield Renewable Energy Partners. It also invests and manages real assets on behalf of fee paying clients such as pension funds. It has over $200B of assets under management and is currently focusing on new investments in Brazil, Europe, Australia, and India. Brookfield share price has been on a tear, resulting from spectacular 2014 corporate performance and the devaluation of the Canadian currency, as many of its assets are outside Canada. It actually pays the dividend in US dollars. I don't particularly like buying at a peak but its valuation metrics still seem reasonable. I purchased in December 2014 at $57.19, hoping it would go down a little (didn't happen) before adding to the model. Over the last 10 years its earnings per share have grown by 5x, and dividend by 2.5x. While the share price is at a peak and could stagnate for a while, in 10 years today's value should look reasonable.

As mentioned above, I am looking at adding a couple more Canadian companies to the RRSP in the near future and will update you at that time.

Looking Back: I know the Oilers' owner was not reading my newsletter, but shortly after this issue was written they cleaned house at the TOP. Two years later the Oilers are a very respectable team. The house cleaning at the TOP of the Toronto Make Me Laughs started earlier but finished at the end of the 2015 season. They are the Make Me Laughs no more, and now need to be taken seriously. That's tough for a Habs' fan to write!

On a more serious note, oil had stabilized and actually rallied during this time frame only to resume its decline a few months later. The Canadian dollar did actually drop to 69 cents a year after this issue, boosting returns of US companies in Canadian dollar terms and illustrating the value of being diversified outside of Canada.

ISSUE #10 SUPPLEMENT: MARCH 3, 2015

This might be quicker than expected but I made my additional RRSP purchases today, adding three companies. They are smaller companies than my usual RRSP selections but all pay reasonable dividends and have good historical performance. Because they are smaller companies and are newer to me, I have kept the position size a little smaller. A twenty-three company portfolio works for RRSPs between about $50,000 of value and up to $500,000 or even $1M, although a larger portfolio could have a few more names. This portfolio yields 3.7%. By comparison the TSX average yield is 2.8% and the S&P 500 is 1.9%. The average earnings yield is 6.4%, above the TSX average of 5.1% and the US average of 5.6%. Based on purchase cost the portfolio is 48% US and 52% Canadian. While it is not as heavy on US companies as I would like due to the current exchange, the US share is much higher than most Canadians' portfolios. These will be the last additions to the model for the time being. After everyone receives their 2014 tax year Notice of Assessment, 2015 RRSP additions can be made.

Model RRSP Portfolio

Company	Ticker	Date Added	# Shares	Price Added	Approx Exchange	Cost in CAD	Annual Dividend in CAD	Dividend Yield	Earnings Yield	Cash Flow Yield	Price Times Book	ROE
US Companies												
Verizon	VZ	Sept 30/14	100	$ 49.99	1.12	$ 5,609	$ 246.40	4.4%	9.5%	19.6%	3.7	**37.6%**
HCP Inc.	HCP	Sept 30/14	100	$ 39.71	1.12	$ 4,458	$ 244.16	5.4%	5.0%	7.1%	1.7	**8.8%**
Hospitality Prop. Trust	HPT	Sept 30/14	150	$ 26.85	1.12	$ 4,521	$ 329.28	7.2%	3.1%	10.9%	1.3	**5.8%**
United Technologies	UTX	Oct 31/14	50	$ 107.00	1.12	$ 6,002	$ 132.16	2.2%	6.3%	8.8%	3.1	**19.7%**
Johnson & Johnson	JNJ	Oct 31/14	50	$ 107.78	1.12	$ 6,045	$ 156.80	2.6%	5.7%	6.4%	3.9	**23.7%**
Freeport-McMoRan	FCX	Nov 30/14	150	$ 26.85	1.14	$ 4,601	$ 213.75	4.7%	8.0%	25.0%	1.3	**10.7%**
Chevron	CVX	Nov 30/14	50	$ 108.87	1.14	$ 6,216	$ 243.96	3.9%	10.0%	17.5%	1.4	**13.8%**
Exelon	EXC	Nov 30/14	150	$ 36.17	1.14	$ 6,195	$ 212.04	3.4%	6.7%	19.2%	1.4	**9.2%**
General Electric	GE	Jan 27/15	200	$ 24.38	1.24	$ 6,056	$ 228.16	3.8%	6.2%	7.4%	1.9	11.9%
Praxair	PX	Feb 28/15	25	$ 127.90	1.25	$ 4,007	$ 89.38	2.2%	4.5%	7.8%	8.8	27.7%
Qualcomm	QCOM	Feb 28/15	50	$ 72.51	1.25	$ 4,542	$ 105.00	2.3%	6.6%	7.5%	3.1	21.3%
Canadian Companies												
Bank of Nova Scotia	BNS	Sept 30/14	100	$ 69.27		$ 6,937	$ 264.00	3.8%	8.4%	9.1%	1.9	**16.2%**
Power Corp.	POW	Sept 30/14	200	$ 31.08		$ 6,226	$ 232.00	3.7%	7.2%	11.6%	1.3	**11.9%**
Capital Power	CPX	Oct 31/14	200	$ 25.58		$ 5,126	$ 272.00	5.3%	2.4%	12.8%	1.1	**2.7%**
Constellation Software	CSU	Oct 31/14	10	$ 317.50		$ 3,185	$ 44.80	1.4%	1.7%	4.5%	14.4	**42.9%**
Mullen Group Ltd.	MTL	Nov 30/14	250	$ 22.12		$ 5,540	$ 300.00	5.4%	4.4%	8.5%	2.2	**10.3%**
Royal Bank	RY	Jan 27/15	100	$ 75.12		$ 7,522	$ 300.00	4.0%	8.0%	9.1%	2.1	19.0%
TransCanada Pipeline	TRP	Jan 27/15	100	$ 55.99		$ 5,609	$ 192.00	3.5%	4.3%	8.7%	2.3	10.2%
Bell Canada	BCE	Feb 28/15	100	$ 54.71		$ 5,481	$ 260.00	4.8%	5.4%	13.3%	4.3	21.0%
Brookfield Asset Mgmt	BAM.A	Feb 28/15	100	$ 67.85		$ 6,795	$ 85.00	1.2%	7.8%	9.5%	1.8	15.4%
Pason Systems	**PSI**	Mar 3/15	200	$ 18.48		$ 3,706	$ 136.00	3.7%	7.2%	13.7%	3.2	23.2%
Wajax Corp.	**WJX**	Mar 3/15	150	$ 24.31		$ 3,657	$ 150.00	4.1%	9.9%	12.8%	1.7	16.6%
Home Capital Group	**HCG**	Mar 3/15	100	$ 43.56		$ 4,366	$ 88.00	2.0%	10.0%	9.7%	2.2	23.8%
Total/Average						$ 122,402	$ 4,524.89	3.7%	6.4%	11.3%	3.0	17.5%

Pason Systems: With just $500M in annual sales, PSI is the smallest company in the portfolio. It is an oilfield services technology company. It provides instrumentation and data management systems for drilling rigs, optimizing performance and enhancing safety. The data is communicated to mobile devices and directly to corporate offices. It has about a 95% market share in Canada, grew to over 60% in the US and is small but growing internationally. Reasons for buying: 1) Hunting for value in the oil industry given the current state of affairs; PSI was $35.00 a few months ago 2) It has very little debt; it is highly unlikely a company with almost no debt will go broke, even in a tough environment. When a turnaround occurs, it should be able to capitalize 3) Through the last downturn in 2008/09 it lost money just one year and just 7 cents per share. 4) If its products are good enough to garner dominant market share in North America, it should be able to grow internationally. Its sales and profits will be down in 2015. Forward analyst earnings estimates are for a decline of about 50%. Most of that appears to be reflected in the current stock price.

Wajax Corp: I was waiting for Wajax to report year-end financials before making a final decision. With just over $1.4B in annual sales WJX is a distributor (rental and sales) of equipment (backhoes, forklifts, cranes, forestry equipment, mining trucks and shovels, etc.), power systems (diesel engines, transmissions, generators) and industrial components (bearings, hydraulics). It has over 150 years of history. During the last downturn in 2008/09, WJX still maintained profitability of $2.00 per share. WJX was trading over $50.00 per share in 2012. With resource exposure it has dropped significantly, but a diverse customer base mitigates some risk. WJX derives 18% of sales from construction, 18% oil and gas, 17% industrial, 12% transportation, 9% forestry, 7% mining as well as government, utilities and others. With this morning's earnings announcement WJX reduced its 9% dividend to 4.1% and is refocusing on growth. Very high dividends limit growth potential.

Home Capital Group is a holding company which owns Home Trust Company. It is effectively a small bank offering deposit, mortgage lending, retail credit and credit cards. It specializes in homeowners who often don't meet the big bank criteria for mortgages such as immigrants and small business owners, but protects itself with higher down payments and mortgage insurance, plus it charges higher interest rates. It has an incredible long-term record of success increasing revenue by 4x, earnings per share by 5x and dividends by 10x over the past 10 years. It didn't even skip a beat in the last recession, raising its dividend twice. HCG traded as high as $55.00 last fall. It's focused in Ontario but has offices in other major cities in Canada.

The April issue will contain updated grids with valuation numbers based on 2014 year-end financials. Until then keep having FUN, tough as it's been.

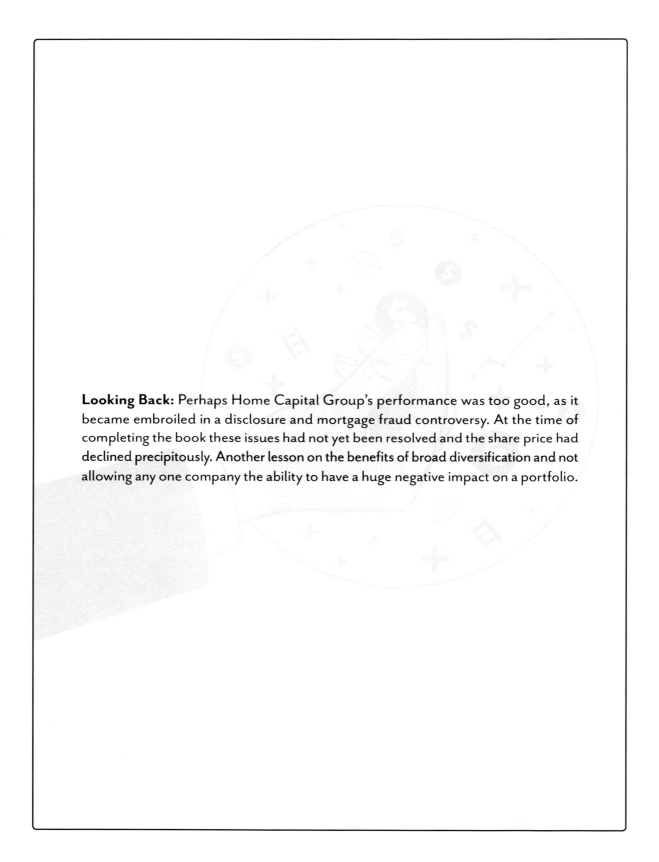

Looking Back: Perhaps Home Capital Group's performance was too good, as it became embroiled in a disclosure and mortgage fraud controversy. At the time of completing the book these issues had not yet been resolved and the share price had declined precipitously. Another lesson on the benefits of broad diversification and not allowing any one company the ability to have a huge negative impact on a portfolio.

ISSUE #11: APRIL 1, 2015

You Can't Always Be Right...But You Can Always Be Honest

Welcome to the April Fools' Day Issue. April Fools' Day provides an excuse to play pranks on friends and family having some fun with white lies that we would not ordinarily tell, all in the spirit of harmless fun. It makes a good backdrop for this month's title as the market regularly makes fools of us while simultaneously providing excellent profit opportunities. In this issue I will also discuss RESPs and provide updates on our RRSP and TFSA models.

The reason for the title was prompted by the behaviour of two newsletters that I subscribe to. The first is a newsletter that has a list of recommended companies, largely in the resource sector. With the commodity collapse of the past couple of years many of these positions were negative. Over the past six to eight months it has "sold" many of the previously recommended companies, most of which were down significantly. Going forward they will no longer be mentioned, leaving future subscribers the impression of a much higher winning record than the newsletter actually has. There is nothing inherently dishonest in what it has done. As a matter of fact that's how most newsletters work. The second example is more distasteful. In it the newsletter touted its "stock of the year." Shortly afterwards the company share price dropped by about 50%. Wow, that's embarrassing for a high profile newsletter, like Seadrill and Ensco are to me. I went on to the newsletter's website to check for commentary or an explanation. Many subscribers were similarly perplexed, questioning how a company described as "stock of the year" could drop in half almost overnight. The distasteful part was the newsletter defended itself by claiming the company had never been one of its "buy" recommendations.

Well, EXCUUUSE ME for thinking the "stock of the year" was a "buy." How could we, as subscribers, have been foolish enough to think that the "stock of the year" was actually a good company to invest in? So much for believing the reported long-term record of the newsletter. And it wasn't even April Fools' Day.

I get asked how my newsletter is different from the plethora of others available. I think the above illustrates how it is different. Because this newsletter integrates its recommendations into model portfolios, even if I sell a loser and remove it from the model, the result of that loss (or gain if a winner) will always show up in the bottom line results, just like it will show up in the bottom line results of any subscriber's portfolio.

Registered Education Savings Plans or RESPs: The RESP program is my least favourite of the three main tax-free investing programs due to its complexity. I will not get into the details of how the program works, as even though I am through the saving phase and now halfway through the withdrawal phase, I still don't understand its intricacies. This is a sign of either my lack of intelligence, the complexity of the program or both. Personally I would first maximize TFSA and RRSP contributions before moving to RESPs. That said, we have participated in the RESP program since 1998 and will readily admit that it is nice to have a separate pot of money to pay for most costs related to post-secondary education. We deposited the minimum amount to get the maximum government grant. When we started that was $2000/child to receive a $400 grant and has since moved to $2500 and $500. The grant isn't as exciting as it seems. If you are in a 30% marginal tax rate position and put $2500 into an RRSP you would get $750 back, which is more than $500! The grant must also be refunded if your children don't attend post-secondary education.

I made lots of mistakes (had many learning opportunities) managing the RESP. When we started, Internet investing was in its infancy, leaving the bank or brokerage as the two main choices. Buying small positions in individual stocks through a brokerage with high transaction fees didn't seem wise, so despite my reservations about mutual funds that's what we got. After six to eight years I moved to an ETF (exchange traded fund) and then individual stocks. ETFs were also in their infancy 15 years ago but have now become a staple investing option. An ETF is like a mutual fund but trades like individual stocks and is designed to track a specific index, like the TSX or S&P 500. They have very low fees compared to mutual funds and are thus, in my opinion, currently a better option for managing smaller accounts.

The premise of this newsletter is to build model portfolios around what we actually own ourselves. As our children are now in university and we are in the process of collapsing our RESP, that approach will not work. Thus, I will not build a model RESP portfolio but will provide the following suggestions:

1. The timeline for RESPs is dependent on the age of your children and time left until their post-secondary education. With this shorter-term nature, especially if less than 10 years, there is a case to be made for just going to the bank and buying GICs or bonds, accepting the low interest, taking the government grant and being assured of the amount of money you will have if and when your children attend college or university. This conservative approach works well in combination with a more aggressive approach in TFSAs and RRSPs.

2. If you would like better returns than today's low interest rates, and have a 10 to 17 year time frame (i.e. your children are still very young) then ETFs provide a valid option. They have broad diversification

without individual company risk, but with market risks and rewards. Here are five for consideration that all trade on the TSX and provide worldwide diversification: iShares S&P/TSX60 Index (ticker XIU), an index of the largest sixty companies in Canada; iShares Core S&P Capped Composite Index (XIC) which is broader, is composed of 250 companies and should closely mirror the TSX index; iShares Core MSCI EAFE Index (XEF) which provides exposure to the developed world markets of Europe, Asia, Japan and Australia; iShares Core MSCI Emerging Markets IMI Index (XEC), which provides exposure to the developing markets of Asia, Africa and Latin America; or for US exposure, Vanguard S&P 500 Index (VFV) tracks the broad US S&P 500 index. I do not own any of these but am confident they will closely track their respective indexes. They all pay a dividend and have fees ranging from 0.2% to 0.6%, which is significantly below mutual fund fees.

3. If you are more adventurous, my suggestion would be to pick stocks from the TFSA model portfolio. RESPs have the same withholding tax issue as TFSAs, such that it is better to invest in Canada and other jurisdictions without withholding taxes on dividends, such as the UK.

With the advent of low-cost Internet investing and low-fee ETFs, if I was starting today I would use the ETF strategy in 2) above. Be careful, however, if moving funds out of mutual funds to ETFs as many mutual funds have significant back-end fees when withdrawing before a specific time period has elapsed.

Market commentary: The first quarter of 2015 had an unusual number of days with daily movements of greater than 1%, both up and down, but in the end the US S&P 500 is flat and the TSX (mostly because it didn't drop yesterday like the US) is up 1.8%. In summary, there was a lot of volatility but very little real movement. Resources stayed firmly in the doldrums, although they appear to have stabilized. The American dollar was very strong worldwide as well as in relation to the Canadian dollar. Both our TFSA and RRSP models made progress in the quarter largely because of the exchange rate movement, illustrating the benefits of currency diversification. One somewhat rhetorical question I ask is, "Can anyone remember a time that Mid-East tensions were rising while oil prices were falling?" It does seem a little strange, doesn't it?

Model Updates

Model RRSP Portfolio

Company	Ticker	Date Added	# Shares	Price Added	Approx Exchange	Cost In CAD	Current Value in CAD	Annual Dividend in CAD	Dividend Yield	Earnings Yield	Cash Flow Yield	Price Times Book	ROE
US Companies													
Verizon	VZ	Sept 30/14	100	$ 49.99	1.12	$ 5,609	$ 6,127	$ 277.20	4.5%	5.1%	14.3%	16.4	37.7%
HCP Inc	HCP	Sept 30/14	100	$ 39.71	1.12	$ 4,458	$ 5,444	$ 284.76	5.2%	4.4%	6.7%	1.9	8.3%
Hospitality Prop. Trust	HPT	Sept 30/14	150	$ 26.85	1.12	$ 4,521	$ 6,235	$ 370.44	5.9%	3.5%	9.8%	1.8	6.4%
United Technologies	UTX	Oct 31/14	50	$ 107.00	1.12	$ 6,002	$ 7,384	$ 161.28	2.2%	5.7%	7.9%	3.5	19.7%
Johnson and Johnson	JNJ	Oct 31/14	50	$ 107.78	1.12	$ 6,045	$ 6,338	$ 176.40	2.8%	5.6%	7.1%	4.1	22.7%
Freeport-McMoRan	FCX	Nov 30/14	150	$ 26.85	1.14	$ 4,601	$ 3,582	$ 37.80	1.1%	-6.7%	15.4%	1.1	-6.7%
Chevron	CVX	Nov 30/14	50	$ 108.87	1.14	$ 6,216	$ 6,614	$ 269.64	4.1%	9.4%	17.9%	1.3	12.7%
Exelon	EXC	Nov 30/14	150	$ 36.17	1.14	$ 6,195	$ 6,352	$ 234.36	3.7%	5.6%	19.6%	1.3	7.2%
General Electric	GE	Jan 27/15	200	$ 24.38	1.24	$ 6,056	$ 6,252	$ 231.84	3.7%	6.0%	10.5%	2.0	11.9%
Praxair	PX	Feb 28/15	25	$ 127.90	1.25	$ 4,007	$ 3,803	$ 90.09	2.4%	4.7%	8.2%	6.3	27.7%
Qualcomm	QCOM	Feb 28/15	50	$ 72.51	1.25	$ 4,542	$ 4,368	$ 105.84	2.4%	6.8%	8.1%	2.9	21.3%
Canadian Companies													
Bank of Nova Scotia	BNS	Sept 30/14	100	$ 69.27		$ 6,937	$ 6,354	$ 272.00	4.3%	9.1%	10.2%	1.6	15.6%
Power Corp	POW	Sept 30/14	200	$ 31.08		$ 6,226	$ 6,704	$ 232.00	3.5%	8.3%	11.4%	1.4	12.2%
Capital Power	CPX	Oct 31/14	200	$ 25.58		$ 5,126	$ 4,902	$ 272.00	5.6%	1.1%	10.5%	1.0	1.0%
Constellation Software	CSU	Oct 31/14	10	$ 317.50		$ 3,185	$ 4,378	$ 40.00	1.2%	1.4%	3.9%	28.9	39.2%
Mullen Group Ltd.	MTL	Nov 20/14	250	$ 22.12		$ 5,540	$ 5,023	$ 300.00	6.0%	5.1%	9.7%	2.1	10.5%
Royal Bank	RY	Jan 27/15	100	$ 75.12		$ 7,522	$ 7,624	$ 308.00	4.0%	8.3%	9.6%	2.1	18.8%
TransCanada Pipelne	TRP	Jan 27/15	100	$ 55.99		$ 5,609	$ 5,416	$ 208.00	3.8%	4.5%	9.0%	2.3	10.4%
Bell Canada	BCE	Feb 28/15	100	$ 54.71		$ 5,481	$ 5,362	$ 260.00	4.9%	5.5%	13.3%	4.1	21.0%
Brookfield Asset Mgmt	BAM.A	Feb 28/15	100	$ 67.85		$ 6,795	$ 6,774	$ 85.68	1.3%	8.0%	16.9%	1.8	15.3%
Pason Systems	PSI	Mar 3/15	200	$ 18.48		$ 3,706	$ 3,992	$ 136.00	3.4%	6.7%	10.9%	3.4	26.4%
Wajax Corp	WJX	Mar 3/15	150	$ 24.31		$ 3,657	$ 3,629	$ 150.00	4.1%	10.1%	15.9%	1.6	16.6%
Home Capital Group	HCG	Mar 3/15	100	$ 43.56		$ 4,366	$ 4,256	$ 88.00	2.1%	10.3%	10.8%	2.1	23.9%
						$ 122,402	$ 126,913	$ 4,591.33	3.6%	5.6%	11.2%	4.1	16.5%

Model TFSA Portfolio

Company	Ticker	Date Added	# Shares	Price Added	Approx Exchange	Cost In CAD	Current Value in CAD	Annual Dividend in CAD	Dividend Yield	Earnings Yield	Cash Flow Yield	Price Times Book	ROE
International Companies													
Ensco PLC	ESV	May 30/14	100	$ 52.66	1.09	$ 5,750	$ 2,655	$ 75.60	2.9%	-59.9%	41.7%	0.6	-27.9%
Glaxo Smithkline	GSK	May 30/14	100	$ 53.94	1.09	$ 5,890	$ 5,815	$ 327.60	5.6%	3.6%	4.7%	18.2	49.0%
Ship Finance Int.	SFL	May 30/14	180	$ 18.52	1.09	$ 3,644	$ 3,357	$ 381.02	11.4%	8.5%	13.7%	1.2	9.8%
Seadrill	SDRL	Jul 25/14	130	$ 37.49	1.09	$ 5,312	$ 1,532	$ -	0.0%	86.2%	34.4%	0.5	46.0%
HSBC Holdings PLC	HSBC	Jul 25/14	100	$ 52.82	1.09	$ 5,757	$ 5,366	$ 315.00	5.9%	7.9%	4.6%	0.9	7.1%
Vodaphone	VOD	Jul 25/14	150	$ 34.16	1.09	$ 5,585	$ 6,177	$ 343.98	5.6%	1.6%	16.7%	0.8	1.3%
Unilever PLC	UL	Jan 2/15	100	$ 40.05	1.18	$ 4,736	$ 5,255	$ 185.22	3.5%	4.5%	5.8%	8.2	36.9%
Diagio PLC	DEO	Jan 2/15	30	$ 112.73	1.18	$ 4,001	$ 4,180	$ 127.01	3.0%	4.1%	5.2%	6.6	27.3%
BHP Billiton Ltd.	BHP	Jan 2/15	65	$ 47.27	1.18	$ 3,636	$ 3,806	$ 203.11	5.3%	7.9%	16.9%	0.9	12.8%
Canadian Companies													
TD Bank	TD	May 30/14	100	$ 53.76		$ 5,386	$ 5,421	$ 204.00	3.8%	7.8%	8.7%	1.7	14.2%
Innvest REIT	INN.UN	May 30/14	210	$ 5.16		$ 1,094	$ 1,212	$ 84.00	6.9%	-14.5%	9.7%	3.3	-8.6%
Rogers Communication	RCI.B	May 30/14	100	$ 43.82		$ 4,392	$ 4,240	$ 192.00	4.5%	6.0%	15.6%	4.1	26.4%
Teck Resources Ltd	TCK.B	May 30/14	200	$ 24.17		$ 4,844	$ 3,476	$ 180.00	5.2%	3.2%	15.3%	0.6	2.0%
ATCO	ACO.X	Jul 25/14	100	$ 50.56		$ 5,066	$ 4,512	$ 99.00	2.2%	7.9%	25.6%	1.7	13.9%
Husky Energy	HSE	Jul 25/14	150	$ 33.72		$ 5,068	$ 3,878	$ 180.00	4.6%	4.5%	20.4%	1.3	6.3%
Sunlife Financial	SLF	Jul 25/14	100	$ 41.40		$ 4,150	$ 3,903	$ 144.00	3.7%	7.3%	7.5%	1.4	11.2%
						$ 74,311	$ 64,785	$ 3,041.54	4.6%	5.4%	15.4%	3.3	14.2%

SDRL no longer suggested to buy but we are holding

These first two charts update the financial metric grids based on each company's year-end financials and will only be updated yearly. Most companies have a December 31st year-end with financial reporting in February/March, such that this update will be done for the April 1st issue. The chart shows year-end earnings and cash flow yields as well as price times book and ROE. The numbers are calculated using year-end financials and March 31st closing prices. ESV and SDRL have wonky earnings numbers but are both trading well below book value and still had strong cash flows in 2014. As a matter of fact, all the resource stocks had very good cash flows. FCX recently cut its dividend, which is now a trend amongst resource stocks and could happen with others. The current value in Canadian is based on $1.26 Canadian to buy a $1.00 US in all the grids. Let's have a look at the current value and dividend flow of both portfolios.

Model RRSP Portfolio

Company	Ticker	Date Added	# shares	Price Added	Cost In CAD	Current Value in CAD	Share Price Change	Previous Dividends Since Inception	Jan 2015 Dividend	Feb 2015 Dividend	Mar 2015 Dividends	Total Dividends to Date	Total Return
US Companies													
Verizon	VZ	Sept 30/14	100	$ 49.99	$ 5,609	$ 6,127	$ 518	$ 61.38		$ 69.36		$ 130.74	11.6%
HCP Inc	HCP	Sept 30/14	100	$ 39.71	$ 4,458	$ 5,444	$ 986	$ 60.85		$ 70.79		$ 131.64	25.1%
Hospitality Prop. Trust	HPT	Sept 30/14	150	$ 26.85	$ 4,521	$ 6,235	$ 1,714	$ 82.58		$ 92.09		$ 174.67	41.8%
United Technologies	UTX	Oct 31/14	50	$ 107.00	$ 6,002	$ 7,384	$ 1,382	$ 33.53			$ 40.32	$ 73.85	24.3%
Johnson and Johnson	JNJ	Oct 31/14	50	$ 107.78	$ 6,045	$ 6,338	$ 293	$ 39.72			$ 44.10	$ 83.82	6.2%
Freeport-McMoRan	FCX	Nov 30/14	150	$ 26.85	$ 4,601	$ 3,582	$ (1,019)	$ -		$ 59.11		$ 59.11	-20.9%
Chevron	CVX	Nov 30/14	50	$ 108.87	$ 6,216	$ 6,614	$ 398	$ -			$ 67.41	$ 67.41	7.5%
Exelon	EXC	Nov 30/14	150	$ 36.17	$ 6,195	$ 6,352	$ 157	$ -			$ 58.59	$ 58.59	3.5%
General Electric	GE	Jan 27/15	200	$ 24.38	$ 6,056	$ 6,252	$ 196					$ -	3.2%
Praxair	PX	Feb 28/15	25	$ 127.90	$ 4,007	$ 3,803	$ (204)				$ 22.52	$ 22.52	-4.5%
Qualcomm	QCOM	Feb 28/15	50	$ 72.51	$ 4,542	$ 4,368	$ (174)				$ 26.46	$ 26.46	-3.2%
US Subtotal					$ 58,252	$ 62,499	$ 4,247	$ 278.06				$ 828.81	8.7%
Canadian Companies													
Bank of Nova Scotia	BNS	Sept 30/14	100	$ 69.27	$ 6,937	$ 6,354	$ (583)	$ 66.00	$ 66.00			$ 132.00	-6.5%
Power Corp	POW	Sept 30/14	200	$ 31.08	$ 6,226	$ 6,704	$ 478	$ 58.00			$ 58.00	$ 116.00	9.5%
Capital Power	CPX	Oct 31/14	200	$ 25.58	$ 5,126	$ 4,902	$ (224)	$ -		$ 68.00		$ 68.00	-3.0%
Constellation Software	CSU	Oct 31/14	10	$ 317.50	$ 3,185	$ 4,378	$ 1,193	$ -	$ 10.00			$ 10.00	37.8%
Mullen Group Ltd.	MTL	Nov 20/14	250	$ 22.12	$ 5,540	$ 5,023	$ (517)	$ 25.00	$ 25.00	$ 25.00	$ 25.00	$ 100.00	-7.5%
Royal Bank	RY	Jan 27/15	100	$ 75.12	$ 7,522	$ 7,624	$ 102					$ -	1.4%
TransCanada Pipeline	TRP	Jan 27/15	100	$ 55.59	$ 5,609	$ 5,416	$ (193)					$ -	-3.4%
Bell Canada	BCE	Feb 28/15	100	$ 54.71	$ 5,481	$ 5,362	$ (119)					$ -	-2.2%
Brookfield Asset Mgmt	BAM.A	Feb 28/15	100	$ 67.85	$ 6,795	$ 6,774	$ (21)					$ -	-0.3%
Pason Systems	PSI	Mar 3/15	200	$ 18.48	$ 3,706	$ 3,992	$ 286					$ -	7.7%
Wajax Corp	WJX	Mar 3/15	150	$ 24.31	$ 3,657	$ 3,629	$ (28)				$ 34.00	$ 34.00	8.6%
Home Capital Group	HCG	Mar 3/15	100	$ 43.56	$ 4,366	$ 4,256	$ (110)					$ -	-0.8%
Cdn Subtotal					$ 64,150	$ 64,414	$ 264	$ 149.00				$ 460.00	-2.5%
Total Cdn and US					$ 122,402	$ 126,913	$ 4,511	$ 427.06				$ 1,288.81	1.1%
Cash						$ 887							
Portfolio Value						$ 127,800							4.8%

Cost in CAD total of $122,402 is derived from $122,000 invested plus $402 of reinvested dividends, leaving $887 of cash from unspent dividends.

TFSA Model Portfolio

Company	Ticker	Date Added	# Shares	Price Added	Cost In CAD	Current Value in CAD	Share Price Change	Previous Dividends Since Inception	Jan 2015 Dividends	Feb 2015 Dividends	Mar 2015 Dividends	New Total Divdends Since Inception	Total Return
International													
Ensco PLC	ESV	May 30/14	100	$ 52.66	$ 5,750	$ 2,655	$ (3,095)	$ 246.90			$ 18.90	$ 265.80	-49.2%
Glaxo Smithkline	GSK	May 30/14	100	$ 53.94	$ 5,890	$ 5,815	$ (75)	$ 71.85	$ 71.63			$ 143.48	1.2%
Ship Finance Int.	SFL	May 30/14	180	$ 18.52	$ 3,644	$ 3,357	$ (287)	$ 244.17			$ 95.26	$ 339.43	1.4%
Seadrill	SDRL	July 25/14	130	$ 37.49	$ 5,312	$ 1,532	$ (3,780)	$ 140.46				$ 140.46	-68.5%
HSBC Holdings PLC	HSBC	July 25/14	100	$ 52.82	$ 5,757	$ 5,366	$ (391)	$ 111.79				$ 111.79	-4.8%
Vodaphone	VOD	July 25/14	150	$ 34.16	$ 5,585	$ 6,177	$ 592	$ -		$ 97.30		$ 97.30	12.3%
Unilever PLC	UL	Jan 2/15	100	$ 40.05	$ 4,736	$ 5,255	$ 519				$ 40.99	$ 40.99	11.8%
Diagio PLC	DEO	Jan 2/15	30	$ 112.73	$ 4,001	$ 4,180	$ 179					$ -	4.5%
BHP Billiton Ltd	BHP	Jan 2/15	65	$ 47.27	$ 3,636	$ 3,806	$ 170					$ -	4.7%
Internatonal Subtotal					$ 44,311	$ 38,143	$ (6,168)	$ 815.17				$ 1,139.25	-11.3%
Canadian													
TD Bank	TD	May 30/14	100	$ 53.76	$ 5,386	$ 5,421	$ 35	$ 94.00		$ 47.00		$ 141.00	3.3%
Innvest REIT	INN.UN	May 30/14	210	$ 5.16	$ 1,094	$ 1,212	$ 118	$ 41.94	$ 6.99	$ 6.99	$ 6.99	$ 62.91	16.5%
Rogers Communications	RCI.B	May 30/14	100	$ 43.82	$ 4,392	$ 4,240	$ (152)	$ 91.50	$ 45.75			$ 137.25	-0.3%
Teck Reources Ltd	TCK.B	May 30/14	200	$ 24.17	$ 4,844	$ 3,476	$ (1,368)	$ 90.00	$ 90.00			$ 180.00	-24.5%
ATCO	ACO.X	July 25/14	100	$ 50.56	$ 5,066	$ 4,512	$ (554)	$ 43.00			$ 24.75	$ 67.75	-9.6%
Husky Energy	HSE	July 25/14	150	$ 33.72	$ 5,068	$ 3,878	$ (1,190)	$ 45.00	$ 45.00			$ 90.00	-21.7%
Sunlife Financial	SLF	July 25/14	100	$ 41.40	$ 4,150	$ 3,903	$ (247)	$ 72.00			$ 36.00	$ 108.00	-3.3%
Canadian Subtotal					$ 30,000	$ 26,642	$ (3,358)	$ 477.44				$ 786.91	-8.6%
Total Cdn and Int					$ 74,311	$ 64,785	$ (9,526)	$ 1,293				$ 1,926.16	
Cash						$ 615							
Total						$ 65,400							-10.4%

Cost in CAD total of $74,311 is derived from $73,000 investment plus $1311 of reinvested dividends, leaving $615 of cash from unspent dividends

Notes: All valuation numbers based on March 31st closing and $1.26 CAD to buy $1 USD. Dividends of US/INT companies are based on approximate exchange rate at the time dividend received. While FCX cut, HCP, UTX, PX, BNS, RY, TRP, BCE, BAM.A, SFL, TD, RCI.B, and ACO.X have all increased their dividends already in 2015. I am increasingly watching for regular dividend growth.

Issue #11: April 1, 2015

The RRSP model is off to a good start with a 4.8% gain to date, although adding FCX in December was a clear short-term mistake. I wish I would have started the newsletter with the RRSP rather than with the TFSA, as the US focus of the RRSP has been a big plus. However, investing isn't golf and there are no do-overs, just a need to adapt and adjust. The TFSA model has progressed in the first quarter and is down 10.4 per cent to date, rather than down 13.6 per cent at the beginning of the year. The resource orientation has not served it well. Even the non-resource stocks have been a little disappointing lately. That said, we have had some great long-term performance with these companies (see January 5, 2015 issue), so I am not thinking about any radical changes to the portfolio. That could be the orientation of many investors, but stickwithitness (Is that a word?) has served me well over the years. The three new additions, with our 2015 contributions, are nicely positive. No one knows how long the current commodity malaise will continue and indeed if it will get worse or better. I have seen the old adage of "it's always darkest before the dawn" play out many times in the past, so remain optimistic of renewal.

Even with the dividend cuts to FCX, ESV and SDRL, the overall dividend yield of the RRSP is 3.6% and of the TFSA is 4.6%, well above market averages. Earnings yields have dropped slightly and are now about market averages, but cash flows are strong and above market averages. As mentioned previously, I am big on cash flow and will even buy money loosing companies if they have good cash flow. It is rare to see companies trade below their book value, yet there are six such companies in the TFSA, which is an interesting phenomenon.

In the next issue I will discuss my real estate investing experiences before turning my attention to investing in a non-registered account with the June 1st anniversary issue. Real estate represents an important investment area and while not the purpose of this newsletter provides parallels and learnings.

April 14, 2015 Update

I did something a little unusual this morning in that I sold a company in our RRSP portfolio. To say Constellation Software was on a "bit of a tear" lately would be an understatement as it is up over 50% since we put in the model RRSP portfolio on October 31st, 2014, just over five months ago. While it appears to be very well run, the valuation now appears stretched. Thus I sold it in my RRSP this morning at $485.07/share.

I replaced it with AutoCanada (ticker ACQ) purchased at $34.15. ACQ is an auto dealership industry consolidator. Most auto dealerships are "mom and pop" operations. Consolidating these into larger multi-dealership companies is a trend across North America, similar to farm equipment dealerships being consolidated into Cervus and Rocky Mountain Dealerships. AutoCanada currently owns 48 dealerships across Canada, with concentration in Alberta and BC. It has sold off significantly due this resource exposure, having traded as high as $90.00 in mid-2014. It has dealerships representing most major car brands including Chrysler, GM, Hyundai, Nissan, Kia, Volkswagon, Audi, Subaru, and BMW. While there might be short-term concerns with new vehicle sales in western Canada, new vehicles represent 60% of revenue but just 28% of profit. Parts and service, which is less economic-dependent, represents 11% of revenue but 35% of profits. Used vehicles (22% of revenue, 8% of profit) and finance/insurance (6% revenue, 29% of profit) represent the remaining portions.

ACQ is growing rapidly as there are endless opportunities to amalgamate more dealerships. Currently there are 2000 dealer owners representing 3400 dealerships in Canada. ACQ is more in line with my normal RRSP criteria, with a dividend yield of 2.9%, earnings yield of 6.6%, cash flow yield of 8.5%, price times book of 2.2 and ROE of 18.6%. Using the proceeds from the sale of CSU ($4841) and some of the accumulated dividends, I could add 150 shares of ACQ to the model for a cost of $5133.

ISSUE #12: MAY 1, 2015

Is It Closer to the Bottom OR to the Top?

In a January 2013 phone conversation with a real estate broker, I made an observation that "it's closer to the bottom than to the top." The comment seemed to perplex him, so for clarification I said, "The way I see it the prices are down more than 50% and they ain't going to zero; therefore, mathematically, the price is closer to the bottom than the top."

We often overcomplicate things and a simple question as above can help crystallize our thoughts. It is relevant to real estate, stocks, exchange rate, oil and other commodities or just about anything we might wish to invest in. It is impossible to predict in advance where the bottom or the top will actually occur. This only becomes evident long afterwards. Yes, with the help of hindsight bias we might have thought we knew where it was going to occur and often regret NOT acting upon that "knowledge" when in reality we never knew. Has the following thought crossed through your brain?: "I knew oil was at the bottom when it hit 43 bucks...why didn't I load up then?" If so, you are victim of hindsight bias. By the way, we still don't know if $43.00 was the bottom, which now looks likely, or just a temporary bottom. The challenge with answering the question is stock and real estate tops often far exceed previous highs, whereas commodities and exchange rates often, though not always, trade within more defined ranges.

While this newsletter is based around stocks, I had a subscriber ask about thoughts on real estate. Given that real estate is an important investment medium and having significant experience with such investments, I thought it would be of value to write and reflect upon those experiences as they compare and relate to stock investing. In my real estate investing career, which isn't over, I have invested in almost all classes of real estate including farmland, multi-family residential, commercial, single-family residential (for rental as well as for living), student rentals and recreational. As with stocks I am the recipient of many lessons from the School of Hard Knocks and hope this summation will help those venturing into real estate achieve greater success with less nasty knocks. Please keep in mind that there are many classes of real estate and valuations are significantly influenced by local conditions. Thus my comments can only be broad-brush and are experiential. It is critical that prospective investors thoroughly understand local market conditions.

As for the conversation above, it was in relation to the purchase of hotel condos in Whistler. I enjoy skiing and have visited Whistler many times. Over the years I've periodically picked up a real estate magazine to dream about owing my own place in such a heavenly location. But the price...WOW. Turns out there was a cure for high prices which came via the Great Recession, a strong Canadian dollar and the Olympic hangover. Referring to my historic Whistler real estate magazines, I could compare current listing prices with 2011 and 2008. It's not an exact science (Is anything?) as listing magazines don't show final sale prices, but if listing prices are down by 50%, it stands to reason that selling prices are down similarly. I got a referral for a real estate agent and began to investigate an investment. It was an interesting process with many twists and turns, but I will do my best to explain with brevity. *(For clarification, many resort village hotel suites are individually owned but managed by a hotel company under a revenue sharing arrangement and are referred to as hotel condos.)*

The normal process would be to select an agent who would find listings to match the client's desires then travel to view those listings, pick the nicest one and try to negotiate a successful price. My primary desire was positive cash flow. Have I previously mentioned the importance of cash flow? Rather than take the traditional approach, I asked for year-end financial statements from a sample suite in each of the many hotels available to quickly weed out buildings that were not generating positive cash flows. What was disappointing and surprising was that numerous attractive buildings with great valuations on price per square foot basis did not have positive cash flow. There were just a few that did. What was equally surprising is that current owners are often reluctant to provide financial information and many buyers don't even ask for it. Most recreation property is purchased based on personal use desires and the hope of capital appreciation. However, in time, most property owners also tire of the regular maintenance and cash drain.

There was a good selection of suites available as is normal after prices have declined. Once the profitable buildings were identified we funnelled down to available suites. Using digital pictures and Google Earth, I could remotely identify the most desirable suites with the best views and eliminate less desirable ones. For instance, there was one suite in receivership with a very attractive price. However, googling down to Street View showed a bus stop outside its window. Stroke that one off the list.

Whistler is an international destination and, interestingly, I negotiated with owners from the US, Japan, Australia and Great Britain but not one Canadian. The first purchase was relatively modest, so I quickly started working on a second (despite the chilly atmosphere on the home front) and successfully completed a second purchase. To make a long story short, using today's information technology from the comfort of my home office I bought two hotel condos that I never saw through a real estate agent I never met, with all legal documents signed and scanned such that I also never stepped into my lawyer's office. Neat, eh? The following summer we went for a look and met the real estate agent, who, besides buying the beer, made a comment about buying at a good time as he felt Whistler was starting to turn around. "We'll only know that in 10 years," I replied. The chilly home atmosphere abated as both properties measured up to my better half's standards. During the two intervening years prices have moved up nicely. More important, cash flows have grown and are now a very acceptable 5-6%. It is difficult to find real estate opportunities that provide positive cash flow from the initial investment. While the short-term outcome has been good, 10 years have not yet passed.

What journey took me to this type of property? I hope my story, encapsulating over thirty years of experiences, will help illustrate some key truths and myths about real estate. Let's rewind the tape:

1983: I began my investing career shortly after graduating university. A KEY financial principle I have followed is a simple one: NEVER pay non tax-deductible interest. Prior to 2008/09, the 1980/82 recession was the worst since the depression. Interest rates reached 20% driving massive bankruptcies. Unemployment was in the 12-13 % range. As the calendar turned to 1983, interest rates were abating and the economy was in the early stages of recovery. I was single and had a fairly secure job paying about $20,000 and was paying $425/month rent such that rent was eating up 25% of my income. It was time to make my first big step into home ownership, but there was one problem: Interest on a house wasn't tax-deductible...or was it? Bungalows in my area ranged in value from $50-$75,000. Mortgage interest was about 14% such that if a house was purchased without income potential, monthly operating expenses of interest, utilities and taxes would be well over twice the rent costs. That wouldn't make much sense. House mortgage interest is not tax-deductible unless income is produced. Thus I looked for houses with a rentable suite. What I found was an opportunity that exceeded expectations, although involved extra work. It was a three bedroom bungalow in the shadow of two universities (Waterloo and Wilfred Laurier), with five student bedrooms in the basement. The purchase price was $70,000, about the same as a similar house without the income potential, and about the same as the previous owner paid a number of years earlier. Before the word "slumlord" enters your brain, I can assure you that after a fire inspection and some modest renovations these rooms were as good as campus residences and better than many other accommodations. The extra work came in renting room by room, semester by semester. There was no common area except a shared kitchenette, making it unconducive for student parties, attracting quieter students. Who would want to rent to a student like I had been? Living on the main floor with a friend/roommate and having a home office allowed the write-off of 75-80% of the interest and other expenses. The rental cash flow was tremendous. Four years later housing had recovered, and these student houses were now selling for a significant premium compared to standard bungalows. I certainly never anticipated the return generated but sold the property in 1987 for over two times the purchase price. That's what you call good luck rather than good skill. Capitalizing on good luck is, however, somewhat of a skill in itself.

1986: Supported by cash flow from the student rental house, I purchased my first farm on the edge of the city of Waterloo. The purchase price was $135,000 for 100 acres and once again, almost the same as the previous owner paid many years earlier. Land and house rental covered most costs, but not all. Securing financing was horrendously difficult as farmland was in the midst of a decade-long correction leading to value reductions in the range of 50%. Banks were exiting farm lending and Farm Credit Corp was only lending to full-time farmers.

1987: The main reason for selling the student house was my employer wanted me to move to their head office in Chatham. I refused (Ever been to Chatham? Sorry no offence intended) but agreed to go as far west as London. London housing had not appreciated nearly as much as Waterloo, such that I parlayed the capital gain from the student house into a mortgage-free similar sized house in London. Standard procedure for many others would be to buy a bigger house, resulting in once again becoming enslaved to non tax-deductible bank interest. Instead I mortgaged the house, only to provide down payment for another income-producing property purchased in 1989, thus making the mortgage interest tax-deductible. Personal residences are easy to finance even though they provide no income, whereas, paradoxically, income-producing real estate is more difficult to finance. (I don't understand how banks make so much money, but they do so I invest in them.) Another interesting historical event occurred in 1987. On October 19th the US stock market crashed by 22.6 % in a single day. The Canadian market only declined by a paltry 11%! That scared me as my modest stock portfolio dropped by five grand that day, erroneously convincing me of a real estate investing focus. Stocks went on a thirteen year upwards tear after that infamous day.

1989: By 1989 most real estate other than farmland was experiencing widespread speculation. I wasn't the only one scared off stocks in 1987, finding religion in real estate. (Sidebar question: Is today's real estate euphoria partly a result of fear of stocks after the 2008/09 stock collapse?) Despite elevated prices I ventured into my biggest investment yet, a 15,000-square-foot multi-family and commercial property with eight apartments and three commercial units, located in a small town close to London. I paid about two times what the previous owner paid, which was quite a departure from the previous value buys. It did have positive cash flow, however, and was below replacement cost. For the current market conditions it seemed like the best value available and I was keen to continue my education. **I got an education all right**. The building provided years of stress. It started off on the wrong foot, when in the first year, a glass door supposedly broke and fell on a tenant who sued. Then in 1991-92 things got really interesting.

The mortgage was held by Royal Trust. Another significant worldwide recession was in progress. US savings and loan (S&L) institutions, similar to credit unions, were dropping like flies precipitated by overvalued real estate on the decline. Does this sound familiar? 2008/09 wasn't a new invention. There was a famous Canadian family, the Reichmanns, who made their fortune in real estate development and were in the process of developing one of the largest ever commercial/office developments, Canary Warf in London, England. What does this all have to do with my building? Well, the mortgage came due for renewal at this time. Besides US Savings and Loans going broke, so did the aforementioned famous Canadian family, as well as Royal Trust. Normally renewing a mortgage is a pretty simple process if you have always made your payments. When the financial institution holding the mortgage goes broke, it's a different story. They demanded full payment of the entire mortgage. I didn't know they could do that! There was no negotiation, so I had to find another institution. As mentioned, banks are easy to deal with when borrowing for a personal residence, but not for financing income producing property, even with a good credit rating. If it's difficult at the best of times, try finding financing at a time of worldwide recession when the rich and famous are going broke. Next to impossible! I met with many bankers. The meetings were short. Fortuitously (big word for sh_t luck) I had joined the London Property Management Association which helped landlords stay abreast of regulations and provided education in landlord/tenant relations. I didn't attend many meetings but fortuitously (there it is again) attended one where a guest speaker from Guaranty Trust (subsequently purchased by Bank of Nova Scotia) made a presentation on how to secure financing during challenging times. What an opportunity to see if he would stand behind his words! So I approached him afterwards with my conundrum. He stood behind his words and I am forever grateful, as without his help I'm not sure how it would have turned out. You know that thing about dominoes!

The education didn't end there. I was fortunate to have a long-time superintendent who took care of most day-to-day issues while I took care of rent collection and re-leasing. While most tenants were very good, there were a few who stood out and not in a good way. A couple of the memorable ones were the alleged drug dealer and the hooker. The drug dealer had a lot of visitors for very short periods of time. After a couple of months my phone conversation with him went something like, "I know what you're doing. I also know a couple cops. If you move out cooperatively by month's end, I would appreciate it. If not, I'll have a cop car parked by the building every evening." He moved out. I also had a "lady" tenant who insisted on paying with cash, sometimes going to the bar where she waitressed to collect the rent. Not too big a deal until other tenants starting complaining about all the noise coming from her apartment late at night. 2 + 2 = hooker! She also moved out cooperatively. On a bright note, a tenant that stood out for the right reason was a developmentally handicapped young lady. Both the superintendent and I were concerned about what special needs she might have. Her case worker assuaged our concerns. She became the best tenant ever and was a real pleasure to deal with. She always paid on time and stayed for about seven or eight years. Tenant turnover is a big part of the risk, cost and workload with multi-family properties, making long-term tenants a real plus.

The commercial side also had challenges. When a residential tenant vacates, with some work a replacement can usually be found. When a commercial tenant vacates, replacements are more difficult to find, especially in economic downturns. Real estate is valued on what is referred to as Capitalization Rate (CAP rate), which is similar to earnings yield with stocks or interest rate. CAP rate is cash flow before financing cost, divided by value. A building with a CAP rate of 10% and annual cash flow before financing of $50,000 would be worth $500,000. If a tenant representing $10,000 of net rent vacates and a replacement can't be found, the value of the building drops to $400,000. If an expense, like taxes, goes up $8,000 in one year, as happened to me, it takes $80,000 off the value. A CAP rate of 7-10% was normal in the 1990s but is more likely 4-5% in today's interest rate environment. This has the effect of doubling the building valuation change with each dollar change in net rents. Great in boom times...not in bust.

To complete the saga, I sold the building after fifteen years of ownership for exactly the same amount as my purchase price. I got my education but lost my hair. The positive cash flow was hard-earned cash flow. I'm even exhausted reflecting and writing about it, but you can't win 'em all.

1990: Just a few months after buying the above-noted building, I sold the first farm on the edge of Waterloo. While farmland valuations remained depressed, this farm benefited from proximity to the city and urban price appreciation. It was largely a tax driven sale but also because I had moved. At the time there was a tax exemption on the first $100,000 of lifetime capital gains. Speculation was that the next budget would end this tax holiday. If I recall correctly, the exemption ended, later replaced by the current capital gains exemption for small businesses and farmers. I wish I still owned this one. Immediately after selling, I purchased another farm property closer to where I lived. Slightly further from an urban centre, it was valued on agricultural use. 1990 ended up being the very bottom of the farmland price cycle, although no one knew that at the time. The sellers could no longer meet their mortgage obligations. Rental of the house, hog barn and land covered expenses. It was difficult finding a land tenant at the time and it almost went unleased for a year. This is in stark contrast to today. The property was sold fifteen years later when I relocated to Calgary for about 2.5 times my purchase price. In the 10 years since, it has tripled in value such that it has appreciated by a factor of 7-8x since 1990. Is it closer to the bottom or to the top?

1992: I moved back into student rentals with a purchase of two side-by-side houses, close to University of Western Ontario in London. The kicker was an additional acre of undeveloped land. I purchased it for less than half of what the previous owner paid just a couple of years earlier. Remember the real estate speculation of the late '80s and the recession of the early '90s. I had building plans drawn for a new 8-10 unit student building but quickly learned (**BIG** hard knock) a project of that scope was clearly over my head. I sold the vacant land (one of those restaurant napkin deals) to an individual who owned a business specializing in developing student housing. Along the way I picked up a third neighbouring house, also on a large lot. Student housing is difficult to manage, and after struggles with a couple different management firms—one that quit without notice—I approached the aforementioned person who had purchased and developed the land. He had a very interesting business model. All his developments were 50/50 joint ventures with investors who provided the down payment money while he provided the expertise. The only way he would manage the properties was to set up a 50/50 JV. His offer for 50% was on the low side, but he promised I would make more money owning half with him managing than owning 100% on my own. He would also build another unit as part of the JV at the back of the third house. We knew and trusted each other from the land deal, so we concocted another napkin deal, which of course the lawyers formalized later. He was true to his word and my cash flow improved owning only half the property. That's the value of a good manager. We talked on the phone a couple times a year and he sent me the annual financial statement, which was all I needed to worry about afterwards. In the fall of 2007 I was getting a little nervous about the US housing shenanigans. So was he and he was already starting to see challenges with rentals. He called me one day and the conversation went like this: "How would you like to sell those houses?" "I was kinda thinking the same thing." "Good, what do you think for price?" "Well, you're the guy with the expertise. What do you think?" "How about $_____"? "That sounds reasonable," I said. "Good, I have a buyer. When can you sign the papers?" "We are going to Ontario in two weeks." "OK, we'll see you then." Here is another person, like the Guaranty Trust banker, who helped me in a tough spot and for whom I have nothing but respect. We made three separate deals, all of them quickly with little of the traditional haggling, but with fairness and mutual interest at heart. There was work and stress involved but after finding the right partner/manager, it was another good success.

1999: Our first recreational condo. Somewhere along the way, I found the right partner for life's journey. We had a couple of young boys and like many young couples desired a place to enjoy recreational time. We like to ski and had both kids on skis at a young age. The largest ski resort in Ontario is Blue Mountain on Georgian Bay. This area is a recreational hub full of activities. In 1999, Intrawest, the company that developed Whistler and numerous other ski resorts in North America, purchased a 50% interest in Blue Mountain. Having observed Whistler's development from its early years, and having skied Mount Tremblant before and after Intrawest purchased it, this looked like the right opportunity to move into recreational property. Our first condo was a short walk (long walk for a six-year-old in ski boots) from the base of the hill. It was not in the new Intrawest village but as close as you could get. We employed a management company to manage short-term rentals, which is common practice in resort areas. We really enjoyed our trips to the condo. The unfortunate part was that the best rental time was Christmas to the end of March and most ski tenants rented for that entire time frame, limiting our personal use during the ski season. The second drawback was that it seemed every time we went there was something that needed fixing. Not completely stress-free vacationing.

2002: We purchased our second recreational condo. This was an Intrawest-developed hotel condo in the new village at Blue, right at the base of the hill—not really a mountain! The price was too high and cash flow wasn't great to start, but we could book it when we wanted and management took care of all repairs as necessary. Two significant events impacted the property early on. 9/11 had a major impact on tourism, and just as occupancy was recovering the recession hit, representing another step backwards. The property value went from about $375,000 to $500,000 then dropped to $250,000 before recently recovering to close to the original purchase price. The best part of owning this property was it taught me the beauty of "no-work real estate" and familiarized me with hotel condos. They are true investments if entered into the rental pool. Even some travel expenses to see them are tax-deductible, as you have to check up on investments now and then, don't you? There are rules around this, and my accountant decides what qualifies. The property hit break-even before the recession then slipped back again but has recovered and is now earning a healthy cash flow.

2013: This brings us full circle to Whistler and my current interest in hotel condos. I like no-work real estate and current valuations remain well below peak. Tourism is rebounding and with proper research, positive-cash-flow properties can be found.

There is a lot more to the whole story, but I'm tired of writing and you're probably tired of reading. I hope the personal history illustrates both the profit potential and the trials and tribulations of real estate investing. The key reason I use the term "cash flow" rather than "profitability" is that one of the beauties of real estate is capital cost allowance (CCA) usually brings profitability to break-even for tax purposes. Recaptured CCA is, however, taxed upon the sale of the property.

In summation, following are a few myths and truths based on my experiences:

Myth #1 — Real estate always go up. What bunk! Reading this history illustrates that my most successful purchases were made after long periods of stagnation and/or decline, occasionally bought at 50% below previous peak value. I like 50% off sales! The big difference between real estate and stocks is you can't get minute by minute valuations on real estate, and it is much less liquid. While there may be good values in some local markets, many classes of real estate have been on a long bull run. Is it closer to the top or to the bottom? The one category which appears to be just in the early stages of recovery is recreational real estate.

Myth #2 — A house is likely to be your biggest investment. As discussed in Issue #7 and worth reiterating, a house used for living in, which derives no income and where interest payments are not tax-deductible, is an asset, like a car, but **not** an investment. Same goes for a recreational property strictly for personal use. I am not suggesting that such a purchase is unadvisable, just that it's important to understand the difference between personal property and a true investment. Real property, like an auto, is expensive to maintain.

Myth #3 — Owning is better than renting. From a month-to-month cost perspective, adding up interest, taxes, utilities, repair, etc., renting is usually cheaper. It is also less stressful and less work. There are times and locations where this may not be the case, so I stress the word "usually." However, most people will prefer to own for personal rather than financial reasons and ownership allows for participation in capital gains, as well as capital losses. Just because there haven't been capital losses for a period of time doesn't mean they won't occur in the future. Just ask our US neighbours. There are also greater relocation costs with ownership.

Truth #1 — Owning and managing property entails a lot of work. When considering real property for true investment purposes, it's important to think through the work and time commitment involved. Property managers are available but represent an additional expense. They may or may not do a better job managing than the owner. Finding a good one can reduce workload and stress immensely. After a quarter century I was delighted to retire from dealing directly with tenants and toilets.

Truth #2 — Cash flow is known, capital appreciation is not: Real estate investors may dream about the capital appreciation potential as that's what gets bragged about, but it's an unknown when purchasing just like it is with stocks. Cash flow might change in time, either up or down, but at least it's a known item at the time of purchase. Focusing on cash flow and cash flow growth is similar to dividend and dividend growth with stocks. Cash flow growth is also a significant contributor to capital appreciation. Experienced investors may purchase property for its capital appreciation potential but probably have good cash flowing properties supporting the purchase, or are already pretty well off. Focusing on cash flow will also reduce the chances of overpaying, and don't let anyone convince you that it's a "once in a lifetime opportunity."

Truth #3 — Interest rates impact real estate valuations. Are interest rates closer to the bottom or to the top?

Truth #4: Buying property sight unseen is probably a really dumb idea and wouldn't be advised.

I also have a theory for some thought provocation:

Theory #1 — The best time to buy is when it's almost impossible to find financing. Let's take farmland for example. I have seen banks enter and exit the farm lending business. They usually enter after a period of prosperity then exit after they have written off some loans, which happens after a period of financial stress and declining valuations in the industry. As such they are cycle followers. Getting the best valuations requires going against the trend or being somewhat contrarian. If a bank is eager to lend money on a purchase...think twice. If they don't want to talk to you, you might be on to something. When the banks (which seem to move together) are discriminating against a property class, it exacerbates the price decline as it removes most prospective purchasers from contention, like right now on recreational property. If buying a recreational property for personal use, financing is no problem. If it's income-producing, forget it. It makes no sense to me and, like I said, I have no idea how banks make so much money but they do (well, actually, I do have an idea... it's the fees). It will be interesting to observe but my guess is if hotel condos increase to their 2008 valuations, the banks will be back financing, bringing more potential purchasers into the market, fuelling further price increases. Then the cycle will repeat.

Are there other no-work real estate options?

1. **Real Estate Investment Trusts:** HCP, HPT and INN.UN from our model portfolios are REITs and amongst the plethora of REITs available. They trade like stocks and pay a high percentage of cash flow to owners through dividends.

2. **Private Equity:** There are many private equity firms that have real estate funds. Due diligence is required to make sure they are not scams that periodically make the news.

3. **Mutual Funds:** I have no personal experience with real estate mutual funds.

4. **Real Estate Company Stocks:** Most real estate public entities are organized as REITs but there are some organized as companies. Brookfield has many real estate investments, including part ownership in the aforementioned Canary Warf.

That concludes my long real estate journey and this long 12th issue. I wouldn't recommend what I did through the years to anyone. There are easier ways to achieve similar goals. That said, real estate has been profitable and many achieve financial success through it. I have written about these experiences to help prospective investors also understand the trials and tribulations. As I joked after returning from Africa many years ago, "It wasn't always pleasurable, but it was always interesting."

This also concludes the inaugural year of the newsletter. I would like to thank all subscribers for the encouragement and support of this new venture. I sincerely hope it has brought you value. There are many investing books, newsletters and guides. Many are written by enormously successful people but may have a scope beyond the reach of us ordinary folk. My aim is to stay within that scope.

May 19, 2015 Update

The federal budget has allowed an additional $4500 contribution to each TFSA and my Internet brokerage said it was OK to make additional contributions immediately.

This morning I made two additional purchases: Canadian Western Bank (CWB) at $28.99 and Jean Coutu Pharmacy (PJC.A) at $23.23. With the additional 2 x $4500 plus some accumulated dividends, I will add 170 CWB and 200 PJC.A to the model TFSA portfolio. More information in the June 1st issue, but wanted to pass along the purchase information as soon as I made them.

May 29, 2015 Update

I am busily working on the June 1st issue, but thought I would provide a quick update on a couple of changes this morning. Most people should have their tax Notice of Assessment back with the 2015 eligible RRSP contribution room. I made a contribution this morning and used accumulated dividends to purchase:

ATCO: ACO.X at $43.16

Home Capital Group: HCG at $42.21

Cogeco Inc.: CGO at 53.50

We have ACO.X personally in both our RRSPs and TFSAs, but trying to avoid duplicates in the model portfolios have not added it to the model RRSP. As it is in our TFSA model, I thought it should be mentioned.

Using a $6,500 contribution to the RRSP model and some accumulated dividends, I will add 50 HCG to our current position and 100 CGO, simulating what we have done personally. The market dropped shortly after making these purchases (isn't that the way), so they can be picked up marginally cheaper now.

More details to follow in the upcoming issue.

Looking Back: The hotel condo market continues to rebound but remains somewhat behind peak valuations of 2008. This is in stark contrast to most other property classes, which are well above previous highs. Are Toronto or Vancouver residential houses closer to the top or to the bottom? What I have observed in the past few years is the hotel condo market doesn't seem to be very highly correlated to single family residential. It seems to be more correlated to the American dollar. That makes some sense as a large per cent of buyers are foreign buyers, especially Americans. Cash flow is currently great with significant growth in tourism, again partly because of the strength of the American dollar and weakness of the Canadian dollar. I certainly don't miss those tenant and toilet days and continue to enjoy the no-work real estate.

My key question still is this: If I have made my best real estate investments after long periods of stagnation or after the price dropped in half, how come many believe that real estate never goes down?

Comment on oil: At the time of writing this newsletter, oil had rallied from $43 to almost $60 and it looked like the worst was over. It wasn't. Shortly afterwards oil started to decline again, dropping to $26 in early 2016.

Intrawest was a Canadian public company that developed numerous North American ski resorts. It was a company I admired and owned shares in. It was purchased by a US investment company in 2006, just prior to the recession and struggled financially through this time frame. Leveraged buyouts can go bad. You might remember the headlines about the possibility of Whistler Blackcomb going broke prior to the 2010 Vancouver Olympics. It still exists as a company but has sold off numerous assets, including Whistler Blackcomb.

ISSUE #13: JUNE 1, 2015

Value the Learning Experience

A long time ago in a land far, far away... Well, not exactly, but about twenty-five years ago, I had the privilege of participating in an excellent program put on by my then-employer. It was set up similar to an executive MBA program and designed specifically for our company by Purdue University. Those participating committed three separate weeks per year for three years. I was still quite young at the time and really enjoyed reliving many experiences from my university days, including all the fun evenings in a university town. Given the time that has elapsed I have very few specific recollections, but there is one that stands out. During one of the weekly sessions we had a consultant/guest lecturer for a whole day. We were doing a case study on a corporate venture or major investment that hadn't worked out so well with the overall question of "Was this a good or bad thing for the company?" For most of the day we were grumbling about wasting the day and not really understanding what we were supposed to be doing. We were struggling and frustrated with the assignment. However, at the end of the day we were left with one of the most enduring lessons, which is obvious as I am writing about it twenty-five years later. If the venture was a failure, was it good or bad for the company? Well, it depends. Did the failure prevent the company from making an even bigger mistake in the future? What did it learn from the mistake? Did the failure lead to some future success? To some failure is failure...end of story. But not to those people or companies that **"Value the Learning Experience."** To those, failure or setbacks are an important part of the growth process.

I thought this story would be fitting as we move into discussing non-registered accounts. Other than my 1980s experience, written about in a previous issue, our first non-registered account was set up in Lillian's name in the late 1990s. We had some spectacular success, even through the 2000-2002 bear market, by focusing on strong positive cash flow. Positive cash flow is the opposite of the burn rate that Internet stocks were being valued on. To me it made NO sense at all that the faster a company was burning money, the higher it was valued. I set out to find companies with the opposite of burn rate, having strong positive cash flow. Money-making companies were old school and totally out of favour at the time, thus easy to find. Through the bear market we achieved 43.0% return in 2000, 26.7% return in 2001, 14.0% return in 2002 and 51.2% in the recovery year of 2003, as these old school money-making companies came back into fashion while money-burning companies burnt up. These returns were enhanced by the use of leverage, which should have been a killer in a bear market. I will discuss leverage more in future issues.

My own non-registered account and first low-fee Internet account was started in the late winter/spring of 2008. Yes...GREAT TIMING, wasn't it? One of my fears setting up an Internet low-fee account was that I would overtrade, given that trading was very cheap compared regular broker commissions. That fear came true as the almost-free trades coincided with the second worst bear market in a hundred years. As well, contrasting with the 2000-02 bear, there were no safe havens in 2008/09. Everything got nailed and I did, too. Many investors gave up entirely. However, using logic rather than emotion (easier said than done), a fair bit of determination (too dumb to give up), some adjustment of strategy and the guidance of "**Value the Learning Experience,**" I persisted. Today this non-registered account is almost double the net invested capital. Not great, but not bad considering the bear market that greeted its first year. That said, I need to do better with this account. The current loss in our TFSA model is minor compared to my 2008/09 losses, which I hope provides encouragement to stay the course, frustrating as it currently might be.

I am more adventurous in my non-registered accounts, do more trial and error, don't focus as much on dividends and use options that will be discussed in future newsletters. I have way more stocks than I should (according to market mavens), often start with small positions and add when I get more comfortable with a company. I occasionally use the account as somewhat of a "farm team" for making selections to the more conservative registered accounts. I include smaller companies and more unique situations. I also integrate Exchange Traded Funds (ETFs) for specific industry and foreign market exposure. That said, I try to stay focused on the primary "**Buy Value...Rarely Sell**" strategy, although don't always succeed at this. I still consider it important to build a strong foundation of conservative companies in any portfolio. The larger conservative companies also have the most liquid options.

First, let's look at the tax consequences for non-registered accounts:

Highest tax rates: Interest income and dividends from foreign, including US corporations.

Middle tax rates: Dividends from Canadian corporations.

Lowest tax rates: Capital gains, either Canadian or foreign corporations. Capital losses can be deducted from capital gains in non-registered accounts, whereas they cannot be written off in registered accounts. This leads to more risk-taking, <u>which is not always productive</u>!

I firmly believe that making money, rather than tax consequences, should be the primary driver for investment decisions, but tax consequences are also relevant considerations. Taxes are based on individual circumstance, so please consider this brief summary as very generic in nature. Please consult with your tax professional about your own specific circumstances.

Current portfolio structure: Combining both Lillian's and my non-registered accounts we have about 64% US, 22% Canadian and 14% foreign holdings after recently converting a small amount back to Canadian. For the past three years our oldest son has been in charge of Lillian's portfolio, giving him some real world learning experience, which has been valuable. Prior to this she was trying to work with a broker, at my insistence, due to the potential "run over by a truck" risk with me doing it all, but that wasn't working out very well. She simply did not have the interest and the portfolio was not performing as well as desired. Our son displayed good judgement with his own TFSA funds and was in business school, so it looked like a good opportunity to augment his education and provide him with some valuable learning experiences. Our non-registered newsletter account will integrate some of his ideas as well.

Reason for heavy US exposure:

1. As mentioned in the preamble to the RRSP model (Issue #4, September 1st, 2014), the Canadian dollar was bouncing around parity with the US dollar for almost 10 years, with a brief precipitous drop during the 2008/09 recession and again recently. With all other assets, mainly real estate, invested in Canada, it only seemed natural to take advantage of the close to parity situation to invest in the US to diversify currency.

2. There are significantly more and much larger companies in the US, including some categories that hardly exist in Canada like health care, manufacturing and technology. With the exception of financials and resources, Canada is very much a branch plant economy.

3. I combine stock and simple option strategies. The option market is much more liquid in the US. Once I make a decision I don't like playing cat and mouse with bid/ask spreads. There are liquid options in Canada with large financials and resources, but otherwise it is a fairly illiquid options market.

The TFSA and RRSP models are simulations based on our own portfolios but are not exactly the same. They are different-sized accounts and, as mentioned, I had more US holdings to add to the RRSP model but hesitated as the exchange rate dropped into the 80 cent range. For the non-registered newsletter account, I have set up new Canadian and US dollar accounts at the Internet brokerage and intend to build, over time, an actual portfolio rather than a model. Subscribers will get updates as changes are made.

While the exchange rate remains a concern I think it is important to have US dollar exposure, so will build portfolios in both US and Canadian dollars. I will also integrate non-US foreign exposure into the US dollar account. I have not yet made any investments in these accounts as they are in the process of getting set up and I wanted to discuss some of the philosophy before making any actual investments.

TFSA and RRSP updates: There were a couple of updates in May. The new federal budget allowed an additional $4500 contribution to TFSA accounts, effective immediately. After a year's worth of newsletters I hope everyone shares my zeal for tax-free investing and thus contributed additional funds to these accounts. May is also the time that we normally get our Notice of Assessment confirming RRSP contribution limits. The quicker contributions are made, the more time tax-free compounding gets to work in our favour. Following are brief descriptions of the purchases:

RRSP Model

Home Capital Group (HCG): Added 50 more shares at $42.21/share. HCG rallied nicely after our original purchase in March then dropped again in May. This appears to be normal fluctuation and may be based on concern over the current status of the housing market. HCG loan to value ratio on non-insured mortgages is 55.7% such that it's unlikely to take a major financial hit even if house prices decline somewhat. It is maintaining conservative lending practices thereby slowing its growth rate, which also contributed to the recent decline. At over 10% earnings yield and 20% ROE it looks like pretty good value.

Cogeco Inc. (CGO): Purchased 100 shares at $53.50/share. CGO is an Eastern Canada-based holding company. It is majority owned by the founding family and has a complex ownership structure, which brings some positives and negatives. The positive is that companies with founding families at the helm often perform better than the market in general. The negative is the family effectively controls the voting rights and can run it for their own self-interest while ignoring the interests of the minority shareholders. Conglomerates and those with complex ownership structures tend to trade at a discount, which could disappear should the family decide to sell or streamline their business structure. Cogeco Inc. is the majority owner of Cogeco Cable (that trades under the symbol CCA) which provides cable services in Eastern Canada and Eastern US as well as IT business services, cloud services and data centres. It also owns a group of thirteen radio stations in Quebec and an advertising company. Over the past 10 years it has increased revenue and earnings by 3x, and dividends by almost 4x. It currently trades with a dividend yield of 2.0% earnings yield of 7.9%, operating cash flow yield of 16.2%, price times book value of 1.7, with an ROE of 13.1%.

TFSA Model

Canadian Western Bank (CWB): Purchased 170 shares at $28.99/share. As the name suggests, CWB is a regional bank focused in Alberta and BC, with a small presence in SK, MB and ON. It is focused on business banking rather than retail. The share price dropped from $43.00 to $25.00 with the oil price collapse. It has recovered a little. I have looked at CWB on and off a number of times. It normally traded at a premium to the big banks because of a faster growth rate but is now trading at a discount. It managed to grow nicely during the '90s despite low oil prices, which are now effecting its valuation. It trades with a dividend yield of 3.0%, earnings yield of 9.5%, price times book of 1.3 and ROE of 14.3%.

Le Groupe Jean Coutu Inc. (PJC.A): Purchased 200 shares at $23.23/share. PJC.A is a Quebec-based distribution and retail pharmacy operation. It has over 360 franchised outlets throughout New Brunswick, Ontario and Quebec, and is another company controlled by the founding family. The shares have come off from $28.00 to $23.00 recently over concerns regarding Quebec's budgetary difficulties and the potential of lower drug dispensing rates. These fears have been more than adequately priced into the stock, which is evident through the recent insider purchases from its founding owner and director Jean Coutu. He purchased nearly 15,000 shares on the market in late May around current prices. The company trades with a dividend yield of 1.9 %, earnings yield of 5.0%, cash flow yield of 5.7% and has an ROE of 22%. Interestingly, since Loblaws' recent purchase of Shoppers Drug Mart, PJC.A remains the only publicly traded pharmacy in Canada.

Other Notes:

Brookfield Asset Management recently split its stock 3:2, such that the 100 we owned in our RRSP model is now 150. Stock splits are very common after a company has done well and are intended to keep board lots of 100 shares priced low enough to attract retail investors. This is less important now in the computer age, but you sometimes still get a little better price when buying or selling a 100-share board lot.

BHP Billiton completed the spin-off of its smaller mining operations into a company called South32 (SOUHY). Every share of BHP owned received 0.4 shares of SOUHY, such that our model now owns 26 shares. They are trading at $8.27. This is a very small position but I intend to keep them to see how they perform. Spin-offs have historically been good for the share price of both companies, but I don't care for the tiny positions they have in the portfolio and tend to either add to or eliminate the spun-off company.

The July 1st issue will be a little late to allow compilation of the June 30 quarter-ending numbers and quarterly model updates. I will also begin building the non-registered portfolios. Until then, **have fun investing.**

"It Isn't the Bad Years That'll Break You IT'S THE GOOD ONES."

This bit of paradoxical financial wisdom recently came to me from a fellow seed seller, who is also a relatively young farmer. As he told it to me he said it was passed down by an "old timer" to him when he started farming a number of years ago. What brought up the saying? We were discussing the current state of the drought in western Canada. He mentioned that he could already sense the stress some of his customers were experiencing, particularly those with all new tractors and combines who were now looking at some pretty bleak crops. Crop farming has been pretty good over the last six to seven years and, as so often happens, good times leads to over exuberance, over investment, lax expense control, more debt and the inevitable financial struggle that follows when challenging times reassert themselves as they inevitably do. So often the "seeds" of success are consummated during tough times and the "seeds" of failure during good times.

This saying aptly applies to agriculture as well as any other field of business, including investing. The current malaise across the resource sector is a great example. When gold and other metals were at all-time highs a few years ago, mining companies were buying each other at peak prices. Oil had been strong for many years, with a brief but sharp interlude during the 2008/09 recession. Oil companies were investing heavily in new production. Now many are shedding non-strategic assets to "focus on their core holdings." Non-commodity companies are also subject to the same excitement, hubris, overinvestment and decline cycle. A perfect example is Blackberry. When the co-CEOs of Blackberry were shown the first iPhone, one of them dismissed it as "merely a toy." That toy went on to eat Blackberry's lunch.

Much has been written about the great investing prowess of Warren Buffett. I would submit that one of the keys to that prowess is his ability to stay humble. Ronald Reagan was one of the great world leaders of our generation. When he was in the hospital recovering from a gunshot wound (if you are old enough to remember), he accidently knocked over a glass of water. The nurse found him on his hands and knees cleaning up the mess, a clear sign of humility. Not only are companies subject to the above investment cycle, we as individuals are as well. Investing provides many opportunities to experience the cycle firsthand. Admittedly success requires a certain level of confidence, while always being mindful of the very fine line between confidence and cockiness.

Let's now have a look at how our model portfolios are doing at the end of the second quarter. I will then provide commentary on how I see the market today, especially in light of the current and ongoing Greek crisis. The numbers are based on a June 30th closing with a USD conversion rate of 80 cents or $1.25 Canadian per USD.

Company	Ticker	Date Added	# Shares	Price Added	Cost In CAD	Current Value in CAD	Share Price Change	Previous Total Dividends to Date	Apr 2015 Dividends	May 2015 Dividends	June 2015 Dividends	New Total Divdends to Date	Total Return
International													
Ensco PLC	ESV	May 30/14	100	$ 52.66	$ 5,750	$ 2,784	$ (2,966)	$ 265.80			$ 18.45	$ 284.25	-46.6%
Glaxo Smithkline	GSK	May 30/14	100	$ 53.94	$ 5,890	$ 5,206	$ (684)	$ 143.48	$ 86.90			$ 230.38	-7.7%
Ship Finance Int.	SFL	May 30/14	180	$ 18.52	$ 3,644	$ 3,672	$ 28	$ 339.43			$ 96.75	$ 436.18	12.7%
Seadrill	SDRL	July 25/14	130	$ 37.49	$ 5,312	$ 1,680	$ (3,632)	$ 140.46				$ 140.46	-65.7%
HSBC Holdings PLC	HSBC	July 25/14	100	$ 52.82	$ 5,757	$ 5,601	$ (156)	$ 111.79	$ 125.00			$ 236.79	1.4%
Vodaphone	VOD	July 25/14	150	$ 34.16	$ 5,585	$ 6,834	$ 1,249	$ 97.30				$ 97.30	24.1%
Unilever PLC	UL	Jan 2/15	100	$ 40.05	$ 4,736	$ 5,370	$ 634	$ 40.99			$ 31.40	$ 72.39	14.9%
Diagio PLC	DEO	Jan 2/15	30	$ 112.73	$ 4,001	$ 4,352	$ 351	$ -	$ 47.88			$ 47.88	10.0%
BHP Billiton Ltd	BHP	Jan 2/15	65	$ 47.27	$ 3,636	$ 3,308	$ (328)	$ -	$ 101.55		$ 266.71	$ 368.26	1.1%
South32 Ltd.	SOUHY	May30/15	26	$ 8.34	$ 267	$ 218	$ (49)	$ -				$ -	-18.3%
Internatonal Subtotal					$ 44,578	$ 39,025	$ (5,553)	$ 1,139.25				$ 1,913.89	-8.2%
Canadian													
TD Bank	TD	May 30/14	100	$ 53.76	$ 5,386	$ 5,304	$ (82)	$ 141.00	$ 51.00			$ 192.00	2.0%
Innvest REIT	INN.UN	May 30/14	210	$ 5.16	$ 1,094	$ 1,081	$ (13)	$ 62.91	$ 6.99	$ 6.99	$ 6.99	$ 83.88	6.5%
Rogers Communications	RCI.B	May 30/14	100	$ 43.82	$ 4,392	$ 4,430	$ 38	$ 137.25	$ 48.00			$ 185.25	5.1%
Teck Reources Ltd	TCK.B	May 30/14	200	$ 24.17	$ 4,844	$ 2,476	$ (2,368)	$ 180.00				$ 180.00	-45.2%
ATCO	ACO.X	July 25/14	100	$ 50.56	$ 5,066	$ 3,949	$ (1,117)	$ 67.75			$ 24.75	$ 92.50	-20.2%
Husky Energy	HSE	July 25/14	150	$ 33.72	$ 5,068	$ 3,584	$ (1,484)	$ 90.00	$ 45.00			$ 135.00	-26.6%
Sunlife Financial	SLF	July 25/14	100	$ 41.40	$ 4,150	$ 4,170	$ 20	$ 108.00			$ 38.00	$ 146.00	4.0%
Cdn. Western Bank	CWB	May 19/15	170	$ 28.99	$ 4,938	$ 4,891	$ (47)	$ -			$ 37.40	$ 37.40	-0.2%
Jean Coutu	PJC.A	May 19/15	200	$ 23.23	$ 4,656	$ 4,640	$ (16)	$ -				$ -	-0.3%
Canadian Subtotal					$ 39,594	$ 34,525	$ (5,069)	$ 786.91				$ 1,052.03	-10.1%
Total Cdn and Int					$ 84,172	$ 73,550	$ (10,622)	$ 1,926.16				$ 2,965.92	
Cash						$ 794							
Total						$ 74,344							-9.3%

TFSA Model Portfolio

Cost in CAD total of $84172 is derived from $82,000 investment plus $2172 of reinvested dividends, leaving $794 of cash from unspent dividends

RRSP Model Portfolio

Company	Ticker	Date Added	# Shares Added	Price Added	Cost In CAD	Current Value in CAD	Share Price Change	Previous Dividends to Date	April Dividends	May Dividends	June Dividends	New Dividends to Date	Total Return
US Companies													
Verizon	VZ	Sept 30/14	100	$ 49.99	$ 5,609	$ 5,826	$ 217	$ 130.74		$ 65.35		$ 196.09	6.2%
HCP Inc	HCP	Sept 30/14	100	$ 39.71	$ 4,458	$ 4,559	$ 101	$ 131.64		$ 68.91		$ 200.55	5.2%
Hospitality Prop. Trust	HPT	Sept 30/14	150	$ 26.85	$ 4,521	$ 5,403	$ 882	$ 174.67		$ 90.92		$ 265.59	23.4%
United Technologies	UTX	Oct 31/14	50	$ 107.00	$ 6,002	$ 6,933	$ 931	$ 73.85			$ 39.22	$ 113.07	16.7%
Johnson and Johnson	JNJ	Oct 31/14	50	$ 107.78	$ 6,045	$ 6,091	$ 46	$ 83.82			$ 46.30	$ 130.12	2.1%
Freeport-McMoRan	FCX	Nov 30/14	150	$ 26.85	$ 4,601	$ 3,491	$ (1,110)	$ 59.11		$ 8.91		$ 68.02	-22.8%
Chevron	CVX	Nov 30/14	50	$ 108.87	$ 6,216	$ 6,029	$ (187)	$ 67.41			$ 65.57	$ 132.98	-1.9%
Exelon	EXC	Nov 30/14	150	$ 36.17	$ 6,195	$ 5,891	$ (304)	$ 58.59			$ 56.99	$ 115.58	-4.0%
General Electric	GE	Jan 27/15	200	$ 24.38	$ 6,056	$ 6,643	$ 587	$ -	$ 55.35			$ 55.35	9.7%
Praxair	PX	Feb 28/15	25	$ 127.90	$ 4,007	$ 3,736	$ (271)	$ 22.52			$ 21.82	$ 44.34	-6.2%
Qualcomm	QCOM	Feb 28/15	50	$ 72.51	$ 4,542	$ 3,914	$ (628)	$ 26.46			$ 29.42	$ 55.88	-13.2%
US Subtotal					$ 58,252	$ 58,516	$ 264	$ 828.81				$ 1,377.57	2.8%
Canadian Companies													
Bank of Nova Scotia	BNS	Sept 30/14	100	$ 69.27	$ 6,937	$ 6,447	$ (490)	$ 132.00	$ 68.00			$ 200.00	-5.2%
Power Corp	POW	Sept 30/14	200	$ 31.08	$ 6,226	$ 6,388	$ 162	$ 116.00			$ 62.26	$ 178.26	4.5%
Capital Power	CPX	Oct 31/14	200	$ 25.58	$ 5,126	$ 4,308	$ (818)	$ 68.00	$ 68.00			$ 136.00	-14.6%
Mullen Group Ltd.	MTL	Nov 20/14	250	$ 22.12	$ 5,540	$ 5,102	$ (438)	$ 100.00	$ 25.00	$ 25.00	$ 25.00	$ 175.00	-6.1%
Royal Bank	RY	Jan 27/15	100	$ 75.12	$ 7,522	$ 7,638	$ 116	$ -		$ 77.00		$ 77.00	1.5%
TransCanada Pipeline	TRP	Jan 27/15	100	$ 55.59	$ 5,609	$ 5,076	$ (533)	$ -	$ 52.00			$ 52.00	-9.5%
Bell Canada	BCE	Feb 28/15	100	$ 54.71	$ 5,481	$ 5,306	$ (175)	$ -	$ 65.00			$ 65.00	-3.2%
Brookfield Asset Mgmt	BAM.A	Feb 28/15	150	$ 45.23	$ 6,795	$ 6,546	$ (249)	$ -			$ 22.32	$ 22.32	-3.7%
Pason Systems	PSI	Mar 3/15	200	$ 18.48	$ 3,706	$ 4,470	$ 764	$ 34.00			$ 34.00	$ 68.00	21.5%
Wajax Corp	WJX	Mar 3/15	150	$ 24.31	$ 3,657	$ 3,234	$ (423)	$ -	$ 12.50			$ 12.50	-11.6%
Home Capital Group	HCG	Mar3May29/15	150	$ 43.11	$ 6,475	$ 6,492	$ 17	$ -			$ 22.00	$ 22.00	0.3%
AutoCanada	ACQ	Apr 4/15	150	$ 34.15	$ 5,133	$ 6,195	$ 1,062	$ -			$ 37.50	$ 37.50	20.7%
Cogeco Inc.	CGO	May 29/15	100	$ 53.60	$ 5,370	$ 5,733	$ 363	$ -				$ -	6.8%
Cdn Subtotal					$ 73,577	$ 72,935	$ (642)	$ 450.00				$ 1,045.58	0.5%
Dividends from Sold Cos								$ 24.40				$ 24.40	
Total Cdn and US					$ 131,829	$ 131,451	$ (378)	$ 1,303.21				$ 2,447.55	
Cash						$ 775							
Portfolio Value						$ 132,226							2.9%

Cost in CAD total of $131829 is derived from $128,500 invested, $1656 capital gains, plus $1673 of reinvested dividends, leaving $775 of cash from unspent dividends.

Sales to Date	Ticker	Date Added	# Shares	Price	Exchange	Cost In CAD	Sold	Sold Price	Proceeds	Dividends	Profit	% Profit	
Constellation Software	CSU	Oct 31/14	10	$ 317.50		$ 3,185	Apr 14/15	$ 485.07	$ 4,841	$ 24.40	$ 1,679	52.7	

TFSA: Rather than two steps forward one step back, we are experiencing one step forward, one step back. I clearly slipped up on the oily stuff. The TFSA had always been heavier on resources and as such suffered with the commodity collapse. By comparison the TSX is down about 6.5 % from its peak last September. There was a really nice rally in March and April only to be undone in May and June, complicated by the Greek debt crisis. The 9.3% loss to date is dominated by losses in four resource companies: ESV, SDRL, TECK.B and HSE. SDRL reported a decent first quarter profit of 76 cents/share and is trading at an earnings yield of 28.5% while ESV reported a profit of $1.49 and is trading at an operating earnings yield (it wrote off significant assets not calculated in this number) of 30.3%. Clearly they are not being valued on current earnings but on expectations of much lower earnings and losses in the future. They are both valued at about half of their book value. HSE reported a quarterly loss of one cent but over the past twelve months has an earnings yield of 5.2% while TCK.B had a profit of 11 cents and has a current earnings yield of 6.0%. It is also trading about half of book value. While I would no longer recommend SDRL for this portfolio as it no longer pays a dividend, I am not contemplating selling any of these stocks at this time. BHP Billiton spun out new company South32 (SOUHY) as a stock dividend. Therefore you see the value of $266.71 under dividend and the same $267 under cost for SOUHY. I'm not a big fan of spin-offs as they leave investors with small positions, but they can be profitable. As such I will hold SOUHY and evaluate whether to add or sell at a later date. A surprising thing about oil stocks is they initially rallied when oil rallied back up to the $60.00 range, whereas more recently oil has held (until July 1-3) but stocks have sold back down close to their lows.

On a brighter note the two consumer stocks, UL and DEO, added in January are off to a good start. The other positive is that the portfolio illustrates how stock and currency diversification helps reduce the probability of big losses. Down 9.3% is not good, but many investors with a home country or local bias would have even greater oil exposure. The portfolio made very modest headway since the last update on April 1st when we were down 10.4%. The weighted average time of the investments is just 9.3 months. The early losses are disappointing, although it is still too young a portfolio to properly evaluate. The market has a way of providing humbling experiences.

RRSP: I was either dead wrong or way too early adding CVX and especially FCX on December 1st. Sometimes I am just too eager to jump on what looks like a bargain. Mining has been in a downtrend for four years and at some point will turn back up. Just don't know when. The other laggards are chip maker QCOM and utility CPX. Overall the portfolio is up a modest 2.9% with an average weighted time of investment of just over six months. The modest gain was driven by dividends, currency and the capital gain on CSU. CSU's replacement, ACQ is also off to a nice start. As with the TFSA it is once again too young a portfolio to truly evaluate.

Overall: Both the US and Canadian markets are essentially flat year-to-date. There is an advantage to the seesaw market that has gone nowhere. It allows ample time to establish positions. There has been a firming of longer-term US interest rates and widespread speculation on the timing of the first US interest rate increase in almost a decade, expected in September. As such, money-making dividend-paying companies, such as those I like to invest in, have been biased against in favour of sexier more speculative sectors, especially biotech and technology. This has also contributed to the modest showing in the above portfolios. I have no intention of trying to chase the current hot trends. It is a little déjà vu to 1998-1999 but still doesn't exhibit near the distortions of that era. As an example, one of the most blue-chip health care companies, JNJ, is down 5% in US dollars since January 1st but the Nasdaq biotech index is up 23%. Utilities and REITs have also been hurt by this current bias. There appear to be some good values emerging in the blue-chip arena.

Global growth: While there have been lots of headlines about China's slowing growth, there has been very little written about India's accelerating growth. Currently both countries are projecting growth around 7-8%. These two countries represent 35% of world population and are growing at a pretty good clip. Overall world growth is expected to grow from 2.6% in 2014 to 2.8 % in 2015 and 3.3% in 2016. In 2015, developed countries are expected to grow by 2.0% and developing countries by 4.4%. These may not be stellar numbers but growth is slowly improving, with even the EU and Japan beginning to show positive numbers.

Greek debt crisis: The investing world has been gyrating around Greek headlines, which contributed to 2% declines on Monday June 29th. In my opinion this crisis is way overblown. Greek finances have been like a Ponzi scheme for a long time. The area was booming around the time of the Greek 2004 Olympics, but even at that time was doing so on borrowed money (refer to headline). There is nothing like a financial crisis (2008-2009) to expose those emperors with no clothes and bring down Ponzi schemes (à la Madoff, Sorensen and Brost, and Greece). The only reason former Greek government officials aren't in jail is they were government officials, and part of both the European Union (EU) and the Euro currency. As I see it blue collar criminals often go to jail, white collar criminals sometimes go to jail and government criminals go to their summer homes!

While no one, including the Greek government or the EU, knows how this is going to play out, I am hopeful there will finally be a solution with some clarity. That solution could be default (which technically already occurred) or another injection of bailout cash. It could entail Greece leaving both the EU and the Euro currency, or reverting to its own currency while staying in the EU, or keeping both. By way of clarification, some countries like Great Britain are part of the EU but do not share the common currency and retain their own. I don't think it matters which way it goes as long as there is clarity. While I am hesitant to make any predictions, as long as the solution has good clarity I believe the markets will respond positively. The risk of Greece precipitating a contagion as in 2008/09 while not zero, is quite low. That said, until there is some clarity, markets could exhibit above-average volatility. This is one of the reasons I have been hesitant starting the non-registered account as discussed in the last newsletter, although I did start tentatively with one stock purchase.

This morning I purchased 100 shares of Bank of Montreal (ticker BMO) at $74.21. BMO traded as high as $85.00 last September and as low as $73.00 recently. It should benefit from its significant presence in the US, the growth leader of the developed world. It has a dividend yield of 4.4%, earnings yield of 8.3%, price times book of 1.4 and ROE of 12.8. I went ahead with the purchase despite the Greek vote risk. Canadian banks are a strong foundational building block in any portfolio.

July 6, 2015 Update

The Greek population overwhelmingly voted 61 to 39% to reject the latest bailout terms. While a yes vote may have sparked a rally, the NO vote did spark a sell-off but a pretty minor one. If we didn't know about the Greek situation, it would look like just an ordinary day with declines of between 0.5 and 3% depending on the market. Oil was the big loser, down $4.38.

To investors, a yes vote would have been preferred but at least the results were definitive. With these results, I would hope the EU and Greece will determine their status, in or out, in the near future. The markets don't like uncertainty, so getting a clear path forward, as mentioned in a recent newsletter, is a hopeful outcome.

Since the vote was completed and there was a small sell-off, I tried to take advantage with three positions in the new non-registered account on the US dollar side. In Issue #11, April 1st, I introduced Exchange Traded Funds (ETFs). They are like mutual funds except they track the respective index and have very low fees. This is my preferred route for investing outside the UK, US and Canada, and also for investing in specific sectors. Following are my purchases:

1) 100 shares of Vanguard FTSE Europe Index Fund (VGK) at $52.91 USD. This index was trading as high as $58.00 on May 1st. Europe had been recovering until this latest episode with Greece. From a longer-term perspective, this European index is still way off its all-time high of $80.00 in 2007. It fell as low as $30.00 in the 2008/09 bear market. It pays a 3.3% dividend.

2) 100 shares of iShares MSCI Emerging Markets ETF (EEM) at $38.63 USD. This index provides a "one stop shop" for the emerging (aka developing) markets of Asia, Africa and Latin America. It pays a dividend of 2.17%. This index, like Europe, is still significantly below its all-time high of $55.00 in 2007. It dropped just below $20.00 in 2008/09 and, since recovering, has bounced around between $35.00 and $50.00. With the US market having surpassed its 2007 highs by about 35%, it looks like other foreign markets represent a little better opportunity. They at least provide currency and country diversification.

3) 500 shares of First Trust ISE-Revere Natural Gas Index (FCG) at $8.57 USD. It tracks an index of North American natural gas companies. Nat gas has been in the doldrums for almost a decade, with its high being recorded at the time of Hurricane Katrina in 2005. The index traded at similar levels to today, life of the index lows, in 2008/09, and again briefly in 2010. Its all-time high was $32.00 in 2008. I am a little more optimistic about nat gas going forward as the US will start exporting Liquefied Nat Gas (LNG) later this year.

All three are very liquid, relatively large ETFs. They take away the individual security risk and provide exposure to their respective sectors.

I was fortunate to be able to transfer US dollars from my other non-registered account. If you have to convert from Canadian, the exchange rate would be 1.265 Canadian per USD.

When setting up non-registered accounts it is best to set up both US and Canadian dollar accounts to reduce the need for currency conversion.

Looking Back: The global growth forecast mentioned proved to be optimistic, with regular downgrades occurring afterwards. It looks like 2016 finally came in at about 3.1%. My initial picks for this portfolio haven't been great, with the exception of BMO. That all sounds pretty glum, doesn't it?

However, one of the wisest things I wrote over the entire two-and-a-half-year period was, "So often the 'seeds' of success are consummated during tough times and the 'seeds' of failure during good times." As you read through the remainder of 2015 and 2016 portion of the book, you will see how prescient this saying was. While the market had been tough, it was about to enter a phase of dramatic decline, with the TSX falling another 20% over the next seven months, until mid-February 2016. This provided the springboard for a dramatic recovery in the final 10 months of 2016, leading to exceptional performance results for the newsletter portfolios.

ISSUE #15: JULY 24, 2015

Many Bad Apples

Six months ago (January 28th issue) I introduced two fictitious companies for illustrative purposes. **Mediocrity** and **Excellence** are in the same industry but Excellence, as the name suggests, is operating much more efficiently with an ROE (Return on Equity) of 20% vs. 10% for Mediocrity. The example illustrated how a higher ROE drove much better share price appreciation, all else being equal. Now for the second chapter in the story.

The Board of Directors of Mediocrity had a "discussion" with their hired man, the CEO. "Mr. CEO, you have been in charge for four years and we are not pleased with your performance. Our nearest competitor has seen their share price double over four years, and we are up just 50%. This performance gap must change, or there will be another change...got it?"

After licking his wounds for a day or two, Mr. CEO comes up with a "brilliant" idea. He has been a company operations man and admits to himself that he is lacking some financial skills. Better hire those skills, so he brings in a young whippersnapper with an MBA (Masters of Business Administration or Many Bad Apples, whichever you prefer). As a matter of fact, this individual has two MBAs with different disciplines. Just what we need at Mediocrity, he thought. We'll catch up to those bozos at Excellence. They are no better than us!

Mr. MBA studies the books in the first few days and then goes to see his new boss, Mr. CEO. Always eager to impress the boss, he says, "This will be easy. All we need to do is use our profits to buy back some of our own shares...no problem." The boss asks, "Will we still be able to grow our business?" "Yep...just as fast as before.

We just need to borrow a little extra money, but with interest rates so low the cost of the extra borrowings is minimal." "When can we get started?" "Right now, so we make a big impact this year". "Get 'er done."

Mr. MBA applies his trade and immediately uses all the previous year's profits to buy back their own company shares. (This example may be extreme but easier math for illustration). They also visit their friendly banker to borrow the extra money as the boss insists on still growing the business, and it normally takes money to make money. To keep growing at the same pace without looking for ways to improve efficiency they must borrow twice as much as each previous year's profit, as they no longer have that profit to invest. It went into share buybacks. Let's have a look how this strategy plays out vs. Excellence over four years.

Excellence continues on its profitable way with 20% ROE, investing its annual profits plus additional borrowing, such that debt/equity stays 50:50.

Mediocrity uses Year 4 profits of $146.41 to buy back eight shares at its current price of $18.25. ($18.25 × 8 = $146 and to keep the calculations simple I rounded to the tenth of a share). To keep the rate of growth at 10%, they need to borrow an additional $292.82 or twice the previous year's profit. After one year (Year 5) you can see how the math works. The profit grew by 10% as usual, but with only 92 shares outstanding, profit per share growth was "juiced" to 20%. ROE also improved to 11% as now there was less equity as a per cent of total invested capital. Shareholders were happy and still paid 8% earnings yield, so the share price went up by 20% rather than the traditional 10%. A little bit of financial engineering and voila, big boost to share price. Pretty cool, eh? Or is it?

Mr. MBA gets a big raise, and the Board of Directors gives a big pat on the back to Mr. CEO, who keeps his job. Four years later, following the same process, the numbers look like this:

MEDIOCRITY	ROE, ROE, ROE Your Boat					Many Bad Apples			
	Start Line	Year 1	Year 2	Year 3	Year 4	Year 5	Year 6	Year 7	Year 8
Debt	$ 1,000.00	$1,100.00	$1,210.00	$1,331.00	$1,464.10	$1,756.92	$2,079.02	$2,433.34	$2,823.10
Equity	$ 1,000.00	$1,100.00	$1,210.00	$1,331.00	$1,464.10	$1,464.10	$1,464.10	$1,464.10	$1,464.10
Profit	$ 100.00	$ 110.00	$ 121.00	$ 133.10	$ 146.41	$ 161.05	$ 177.16	$ 194.88	$ 214.37
Share Number						92.0	84.6	77.8	71.7
ROE						11.0%	12.1%	13.3%	14.6%
Profit/Share	$ 1.00	$ 1.10	$ 1.21	$ 1.33	$ 1.46	$ 1.75	$ 2.09	$ 2.50	$ 2.99
Book Value/Share	$ 10.00	$ 11.00	$ 12.10	$ 13.31	$ 14.64	$ 15.91	$ 17.68	$ 18.82	$ 20.42
Market Value/Share @ 8% earnings yield	$ 12.50	$ 13.75	$ 15.12	$ 16.63	$ 18.25	$ 21.88	$ 26.13	$ 32.00	$ 37.38
EXCELLENCE									
Debt	$ 1,000.00	$1,200.00	$1,440.00	$1,728.00	$2,073.60	$2,488.32	$2,985.98	$3,583.18	$4,299.82
Equity	$ 1,000.00	$1,200.00	$1,440.00	$1,728.00	$2,073.60	$2,488.32	$2,985.98	$3,583.18	$4,299.82
Profit @ 20% ROE	$ 200.00	$ 240.00	$ 288.00	$ 345.60	$ 414.72	$ 497.66	$ 597.20	$ 716.64	$ 859.96
Profit/Share: 200 Shares	$ 1.00	$ 1.20	$ 1.44	$ 1.73	$ 2.07	$ 2.49	$ 2.99	$ 3.58	$ 4.30
Book Value/Share	$ 5.00	$ 6.00	$ 7.20	$ 8.86	$ 10.37	$ 12.44	$ 14.93	$ 17.91	$ 21.50
Market Value/Share @ 8% earnings yield	$ 12.50	$ 15.00	$ 18.00	$ 21.63	$ 25.88	$ 31.13	$ 37.38	$ 44.75	$ 53.75

After four years the CEO stands before the shareholders and the board at their annual meeting and declares they have effectively caught the performance of Excellence. ROE, the most critical efficiency measure is up almost 50% (14.6% vs 10%). Over the four years their profits per share have doubled, growing at the same pace as Excellence, and the share price has doubled, also just like Excellence (Compare Year 8 with Year 4). What a dramatic improvement over just four years. Mr. CEO announces his retirement with great fanfare and a big "golden parachute" for his efforts. The board announces that Mr. MBA is the unanimous selection of the board to take over as CEO, to continue his effort at actually overtaking Excellence. The shareholders give a resounding standing ovation to both.

We'll see how Mr. MBA makes out as Mr. CEO in Chapter 3, sometime in the future.

But what has changed? While the share profit has doubled, Mr. CEO and Mr. MBA have not enhanced the efficiency of the company. Return on Assets (ROA = Profit/(Debt + Equity)), ROE's first cousin is exactly the same in Year 8 as Year 4 at 5%. The biggest difference is debt capital has gone from 50% of capital employed to 66% of capital employed. It doesn't take a brain surgeon to see through this, does it? Yet investors almost always cheer share buyback programs by immediately bidding up share prices. In my books this is an easy exercise in financial engineering, but an exercise that has lately been taken to extremes. I have seen companies buy back so many shares they actually drive their book value to a negative number. That said, it is a more tax efficient way of returning capital to shareholders than dividends, as capital gains have lower tax rates than dividends, and share buybacks should, and usually do, increase share price. However, it is important for companies to avoid using buybacks to merely cover up mediocre performance. As with many things moderation is key.

I believe one of the reasons buybacks currently appear overused is the concurrent overuse of stock options as executive compensation. Stock option compensation provides incentive for short-term share price appreciation, at the peril of long-term appreciation, as executives can cash out options usually three years after they are awarded, profiting 100% of the share price appreciation between the date they are awarded and when they vest, at no cost to the executive. It's a "heads I win, tails I don't lose" practice. One of my big pet peeves is the outrageous level of executive compensation these days, with options being one of the key pieces of the outrageousness.

I will get off my soapbox now to discuss general market conditions and update the non-registered account.

Market update: It's a bit of a broken record but commodities and commodity stocks continue their downward spiral, which picked up steam recently. While currently very frustrating, this too will pass. We just don't know when or how low they will go. The key question is (Issue #12) "Is it closer to the bottom or to the top?" They certainly appear closer to the bottom. Adding to recent consternation, I read an article recently that TSX dividend stocks were down 7.8 % this year while the overall market is down just 1.8 %. It mentioned that dividend stocks have lagged the overall market for the past three years. This provides validation to what I mentioned last month in that it seems the type of companies I like to invest in have taken the back seat lately to sexier high-growth and tech stocks. The phenomenon appears to be the case in the US as well. As an example, Amazon just reported a surprise profit of 20 cents/share and investors responded with a 15% share price jump. It had a 12-cent loss in the first quarter, so the current 20 cent second quarter profit brings its total year-to-date profit to a whopping 8 cents. **It is trading at about $555.00/share!** Calculate the earnings yield on that! Did we learn anything through the year 2000 tech bubble? I'll stick to companies with more reasonable valuations as there are lots to choose from that have come down 10-20% or more.

Non-Registered Portfolio

This is an actual margin account with both US and Canadian sides. It began with the July 3rd issue and July 6th update. I transferred money from my other non-registered account to set this up and will continue to do so as we build the account. I transferred in $10,000 Canadian on July 3rd and another $10,000 on July 23rd. I transferred in $15,000 USD on July 6th (the exchange would have been 1.265) and a further $5000 July 24 (exchange of 1.30).

New Purchases

Crescent Point Energy (CPG): 200 shares at $20.33 made July 23rd. Last update I added FCG, which is a natural gas-based ETF, so this issue I am adding an oil-based company. CPG has a long history as a dividend-paying exploration and production (E & P) company. It started paying a 17 cent monthly dividend in 2003, increased it to 20 cents in 2005, and to 23 cents in 2008, which is where it is today. This represents a current yield of 13.5%, which the company says is sustainable but could get cut if low prices persist. In the last issue I mentioned the overinvestment cycle when prices are high and how mining companies were tripping over each other buying other companies. It's much better to make big investment purchases during tough times, which is what CPG has done recently with two purchases. Between 2010 and 2014 CPG bounced along between about $48 as a high and $35 as a low, before crashing to $21 last fall and then again in the last couple of days. It has a dividend yield of 13.5%, earnings yield of 4.8%, cash flow yield of 25.6% and price times book of 0.9. The reason it can make big investments now is it kept a fairly strong balance sheet with just 38% debt and thus 62% equity capital. Bottom fishing can be a perilous activity and it could go lower, but should be a long-term survivor.

CGI Group (GIB.A): 100 shares at $50.90 purchased July 23rd. With over $10B in annual sales GIB.A is the largest Canadian IT (Information Technology) and business consulting firm. It has a well-diversified customer and geographic base. Its customers include government, manufacturing, financial services, telecom and health. It operates in forty different countries with North America and Europe being the key markets. IT is a growing business and with the ever-increasing need for cyber security, GIB.A should be well positioned for future growth. It has grown earnings per share by 5x over the past decade. It has an earnings yield of 5.7%, cash flow yield of 9.4%, price times book of 2.9 and ROE of 18.2% but does not pay a dividend. It has seen a steady increase in stock price over the past decade from about $7.00 to its recent high of $57.00 before declining slightly to the current price.

And on the US side:

Parker Hannifin Corp (PH): 50 shares at $110.84 purchased this morning. I have looked at PH periodically but its recent sell-off from $130 to $110 had me looking more seriously. With $13B in annual sales PH is not large for a US company. It is a highly diversified worldwide manufacturer of precision products with a vision of "solving the world's greatest engineering challenges." It services many industries including food, water, energy, transportation, defence, environment, infrastructure, aerospace and life sciences with motion systems (hydraulics, etc.), pneumatics, electronic systems, climate control, fluid flow and filtration. It makes water filtration and desalination products. In the health field it builds an exoskeleton system that provides mobility to people often confined to wheelchairs, as well as medical and dental equipment. It has increased its dividend each year for over fifty years and has a current yield of 2.3%. It has earnings yield of 6.9%, cash flow yield of 9.4%, price times book of 3.0 and ROE of 19.5%. Over the last 10 years it has doubled earnings per share, which is decent considering all the challenges, although some of the earnings growth has come via share repurchases. PH looks like a very interesting company that has done well for a long time.

As an FYI, I also recently added more Home Capital Group to our own RRSP at $31.53 after it had a major price decline. We don't have enough accumulated dividends in the model to make any changes to it. The price decline was related to a reduction in new mortgage placements, which actually might be a good thing considering current real estate prices.

Hope you all have a chance for great summer vacation time, along with some **investing fun.**

Looking Back: No MBAs were injured during the writing of this issue and no disrespect is intended. Just trying to add a little humour while illustrating financial impacts of share buybacks.

I appear to have been wrong about Amazon. It actually started turning profits and building positive cash flow, although by traditional financial metrics it still appears very expensive.

ISSUE #16: AUGUST 31, 2015

Hair of the Dog That Bit You (Me)

Last week was full of ***fun and excitement*** to cap off a rather negative and volatile August. What happened? First of all, what happened was a fairly normal market correction that occurs every eighteen months or so. The correction was precipitated by rapidly declining Chinese stocks complementing and coinciding with what possibly appears to be a final capitulation in resource stocks. Lost in the headline hype was that the Chinese index, while down 40% since June, is still up over 40% in the past year. It surged from 2200 a year ago to almost 5200 in June, then sold off to 3000 early in the week before recovering to its current level of 3200. I would be a pretty happy investor with a one-year return of 40%. The problem is, most Chinese investors got in close to the top, creating the final big spike upwards.

What is a correction? It is defined as a 10-20% drop in a market. The S&P 500 peaked in July at 2128 and dropped to 1867 on Monday, representing a 12.3% drop. The more normally referenced US Dow Jones Industrial Average was off 14.4%. The TSX corrected from 15625 in August, 2014, to 13,869 in October, then from 15,111 to 13,705 (not quite 10% but close) in November/December and from 15,450 in April, 2015, to 13,052 on Monday. The current correction was thus 15.5% while the total decline since last August was 16.5%. Having three such corrections in a year is unusual. Making matters more difficult was that both US and Canadian markets were supported by high-flying biotech and technology, as mentioned previously. While gyrating significantly all these markets ended the week on the positive side.

Is the correction over? Maybe... Maybe not. In my books no one can predict these short-term gyrations with any level of accuracy or repeatability. September and October have the reputation of being the most volatile months with the lowest returns, so it is very possible we will see more interesting swings.

Will this lead to a full bear market? Possibly, but I don't think it will. The operative word here is "think" as I certainly don't "know" for sure. If we drop more than 20%, which is possible, I don't anticipate a major bear such as the 2008/09 bear for the following reasons:

1. Major bear markets usually coincide with major recessions. The US is growing nicely with second quarter GDP actually up 3.7% annualized. That's pretty good. US employment is growing. Canada is in an oil price driven recession. However, even with major layoffs in the oil and gas sector, Canadian employment has been steady indicating other sectors are picking up the slack.

2. China's growth on a percentage basis may be slowing, but on an absolute basis is holding up reasonably well. For example, if an economy has a GDP of 100 and grows 10%, its next year GDP is 110. If the following year it grows by 9.1%, it will have a GDP of 120. If the following year it grows by 8.2%, it will have a GDP of 130. You can see that the per cent growth is slowing but the absolute growth is 10/year. As an economy grows and becomes more advanced it is normal for the percentage growth to slow. There were many negative, scary headlines on the Chinese currency devaluation. The yuan is tied to the USD, so had been one of the strongest currencies in the world. A relatively small 2-3% decline was taken out of context and pales in comparison to many currencies, like the Canadian dollar decline over the past year.

3. Europe, Japan and especially India are improving. All four of these zones, including China, are large beneficiaries of decline in commodity prices, being major importers of them. Other fun facts: Greece's GDP grew by 0.9% in the second quarter, through its own debt negotiation brinkmanship and eventual capitulation. Former basket cases, Ireland and Spain, are now leading European GDP growth. Granted, Europe and Japan have major public debt issues, but these are easier addressed with growing economies.

4. Two of the worst bear markets of the past century occurred in the last fifteen years. Having a third of similar magnitude, while not impossible, would be highly unusual.

Why do I "think" this past week may represent the final capitulation in resource stocks? Final capitulation occurs after a long, agonizing downtrend rapidly accelerates, leading to a final epic collapse as investors give up all hope and do anything to get their money out. This pretty much describes resources, as mines were in a downtrend for four years and oil and gas for a year. Both sectors exhibited dramatic drops as illustrated by the 40% decline in CPG since we bought it last month. It has now recovered three bucks. I did mention that "bottom fishing can be perilous." Even though $40.00 oil is not sustainable long-term, these low prices may persist for some time until supply and demand come back to balance. From what I am reading that is likely to happen within a year. It looks like the bad news has now been factored in to share prices, which made nice recoveries towards the end of the week. One more anecdotal item: the resource newsletter I mentioned previously issued a "sell" on two-thirds of its recommended companies shortly before the Monday collapse. Most of the recommendations were in large loss positions. Those who sold would have crystallized those losses. When a newsletter dedicated to resources issues a "sell everything" alert after major declines, it sends me the opposite signal.

What did I do myself? Not much, other than watch with amusement. There were no changes to the model portfolios, or they would have been communicated. The prior week in our RRSPs, I sold half my positions in two cruise lines, which had moved up and looked expensive. I redeployed some of that cash by adding to an existing position in Enerplus (ERF), a Canadian energy E & P corporation that was selling at 30% of the price I originally paid. It was not in the RRSP model so I did not send an email alert. Besides, I was feeling a little squeamish after the CPG purchased declined so dramatically. ERF promptly declined another 15% but has since recovered and is up 7%, a swing of 22% in the week. That is the nature of capitulation. Also the previous week I did some portfolio house cleaning in my non-registered account, to raise the cash to move over to the newsletter account. It is usually best to SIT ON ONE'S HANDS during these type of sell-offs as emotions can cloud thought, resulting in errors. You are welcome to shoot me if I ever issue a "sell everything" alert. There are always tweaks and adjustments but never wholesale changes. *If I could predict the future I would make wholesale changes, but I can't, so I won't.*

The Canadian dollar: While I have converted some USD back to CAD between 75 and 80 cents, I don't intend to do more until after the federal election. Further declines are possible from uncertainty leading up to the election and the possibility of an NDP or a "Trudeau the 2nd" government being elected. For most of the past two decades we have been fortunate to have the federal finance department run by two exceptional finance ministers, Martin and Flaherty. Over that time we have taken our federal debt to GDP ratio down from about 67% to 31%. This picture is, however, complicated by profligate provincial governments, especially in Ontario and Quebec. I have absolutely no confidence that a federal NDP or "Trudeau the 2nd" government will ever balance the books, taking us back down the deficit path of "Trudeau the 1st" for those of us old enough to remember. This could have a negative impact on our currency. The price of oil and other resources will still be the largest driving force but government management impacts our currency status relative to others. That said, nothing goes up forever, and that includes the USD. As written about in previous issues, despite the current currency discount, I think it is wise to have significant investment in US stocks.

Bank Profits: The big Canadian banks reported their third quarter this past week with all of them meeting or exceeding expectations. Of those in our portfolios, BNS and RY increased dividends. This allays some fear about the oil collapse impact on bank profitability. Canadian banks are trading at good valuations compared to historical and bank profits are a pretty good indication of economic health.

What does dogs' hair have to do with investing? The saying "hair of the dog that bit you" comes from medieval times, when it was believed that rubbing the hair of the dog that bit you into the wound would aid healing and prevent rabies. The saying has been adapted to imply enjoying an alcoholic beverage for breakfast would also aid the healing process and recovery from the previous night's excessive activities. I'm not sure if it works but in my younger years it was often prescribed by friends, although never by doctors! The Enerplus example illustrates its application to investing.

Resources have bitten me hard. It is very difficult psychologically to add positions after "being taken behind the barn." The overwhelming tendency is to sell and try to forget, à la resource newsletter. However, companies we are already familiar with represent a good source of potential new or additional investments and buying when they are on sale makes sense to me. Precious metals have been some of my biggest losers, which is why with this issue we will be adding some precious metal exposure to the newsletter account. Not in all cases does it make sense to add to a losing position. The decision should be based on the circumstance at the time. Not all companies "on sale" recover, but many eventually do.

The place for precious metals in a portfolio: Opinions on precious metals, gold and silver, run the gamut from a "total waste of time" to an "absolute necessity." Those in the former camp can rightly argue that precious metals have short periods of dramatic gains followed by long periods of stagnation and decline. In the end they argue that our investment dollars are better rewarded with companies that can regularly grow earnings. Those in the latter camp argue that countries are forever defacing and devaluing their own currencies. They believe the only true currency that has withstood the test of time of many centuries is gold and silver, and as such they are an integral part of any portfolio as a hedge against government malfeasance. I tend to look at them in a more elementary fashion, as a commodity, and like other commodities they go up and down based on supply and demand. Certainly war, economic uncertainty and inflation tend to increase the demand. The price of gold rose through the recent market correction. Most central banks have gold reserves backing their currencies. Other uses include individual investors' holdings, jewellery and industrial uses, including some medical applications and in high-tech electrical devices such as cell phones. Silver is often referred to as poor man's gold and has a much larger industrial usage including electronics and in the growing solar industry, coins and medals, photography and jewellery. Precious metals tend to move in the opposite direction to the US dollar.

And now for this month's additions to our regular margin account (the first four are on the US side):

Market Vectors Gold Miners Index (GDX) is an ETF tracking the world's largest gold and a few silver miners. There is currently a lot of individual security risk with gold mining due to the four-year down market. Bankruptcies are possible. As well, many gold miners work in difficult political environments, where there is often government instability and potential rapid policy changes. To gain exposure to the gold industry yet mitigate individual security risk, I think it is prudent to purchase an ETF rather than individual companies. GDX peaked in 2011 at over $65.00. I think the miners as a group have put the past excesses behind them and are now focusing on driving profitability rather than just growth. You may wonder about going to the US for a gold index but the US offers the largest and most liquid index available. I purchased 200 shares at $13.71.

iShares Silver Trust (SLV): Most silver is mined as a byproduct of gold and copper. There are some specific silver miners but they tend to be smaller and quite volatile. The iShares index actually invests in physical silver held in vaults in New York and London and thus fluctuates directly with the price of silver. Over the past 10 years silver has traded as high as $48.00 and as low as $9.00. Its current price of $14.50 is pretty close to that bottom. Silver is also at the high end of the range of the gold/silver ratio. In 2011 it took about 40 ounces of silver to buy an ounce of gold. Today it takes 75, indicating that the price of silver is low in relation to the price of gold. I purchased 200 shares at $13.79.

Union Pacific Corp (UNP): The railroads have been consistent growth performers for many years. They just aren't building any more rail lines. UNP is the largest available with $24B in annual sales. While reliant on commodities, it is less reliant than Canadian railroads and trades with better valuation metrics. Revenues are derived from 18% agricultural, 11% autos, 18% chemicals including oil, 13% coal, 19% industrial products and 22% intermodal containers. It serves central and western USA. Profits were down this past quarter largely due to reduced coal shipments. Over the past 10 years revenues have almost doubled, profits are up by five times and dividends by six times. A combination of the recent profit decline and the overall market sell-off has taken the price from over $120 to the current price. It has a dividend yield of 2.5%, earnings yield of 6.7%, cash flow yield of 9.2%, price times book of 3.6 and ROE of 24.3%. I purchased 50 shares at $86.13.

Berkshire Hathaway Inc. (BRK.B): With $200B in annual sales BRK.B is managed by the famous Warren Buffett and his sidekick Charlie Munger. Insurance (Geico, General Re and others) is their base industry, but they are truly a conglomerate owning about sixty different companies outright and having significant ownership interest in many well-known public companies like Coca-Cola. Their success is unrivalled with the main concern being the age of Buffett and Munger, both in their 80s. They have successors in place to pave the way for a smooth transition. BRK.B has recently declined from over $150. It is valued with an earnings yield of 5.3%, cash flow yield of 8.3%, price times book of 1.4 and ROE 7.5%. BRK.B continues to deploy cash for prudent investments as illustrated by its recent $30B purchase of Precision Castparts, an aerospace parts manufacturer. Despite being a blue-chip company it doesn't pay a dividend, making it well suited for our non-registered account, because US dividends incur a higher tax rate than Canadian dividends. I purchased thirty shares at $134.31.

Suncor Energy Inc. (SU): Another resource "hair of the dog" stock. With $40B in annual sales SU is Canada's largest integrated oil company. Integrated companies are much more stable than E & P but still respond to the price of oil. The stability comes from making up some of the lost production profit through refining and retail. SU's retail brand is Petro-Canada. SU traded as high as $70.00 in 2008 but peaked last year at $45.00 before the recent oil price slide. SU was the oil sands pioneer. As a result it has great long-term reserves of 38 years, reducing the need and cost of finding new supplies. SU pays a 3.2% dividend and trades with an earnings yield of just 2.6%, but cash flow yield of 11.9%. It has a price times book of 1.3 and an ROE of 3.3%. Profitability is clearly down but it remains profitable. I purchased 100 shares at $35.78.

Telus Corp (T): Through all the volatility, it's nice to have something that provides better stability. The telecom sector provides that kind of stability and is an important foundation block for any portfolio. We have Rogers in our TFSA, Bell in our RRSP and now Telus in our non-registered, covering all three major Canadian telecoms. Telus is more of a pure telecom, whereas Rogers and Bell have numerous other complementary businesses as described previously. Over the past 10 years T has increased revenue by 50%, earnings/share by over 2x and has more than tripled its dividend, which is now 3.9%. It trades with an earnings yield of 5.4%, cash flow yield of 12.5%, price times book of 3.5 and ROE of 18.3%. I purchased 100 shares at $42.88.

All the above purchases were made the morning of August 31st. I transferred $5000 into the Canadian side and $13000 USD into the US side, which along with cash from previous transfers, provided the funds. As the USD was transferred from my other USD account there was no conversion, but for the record if conversion was necessary it would have been at 1.33.

The next issue will be a few days into October as I will once again provide our quarterly portfolio updates based on a September 30th close. Until then **have fun investing**.

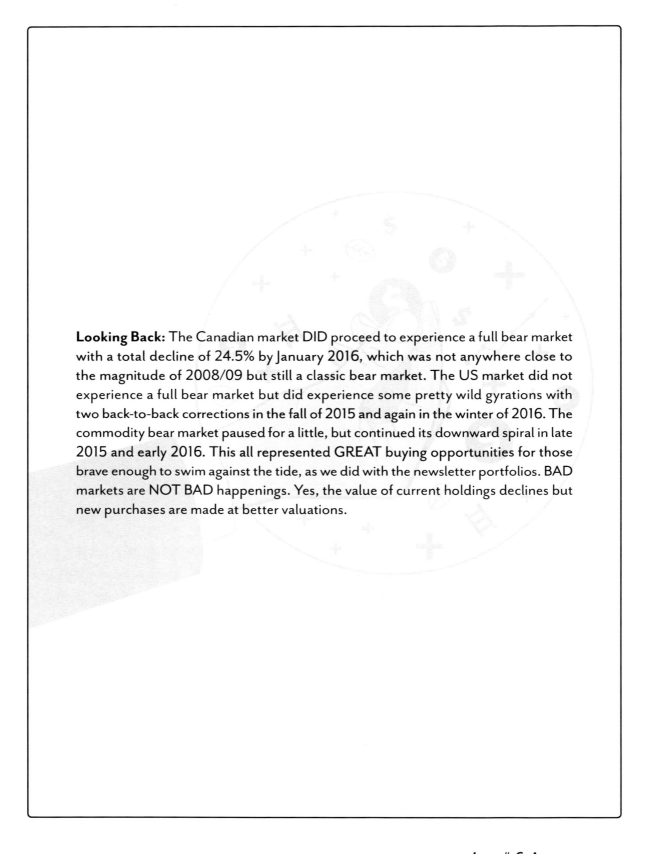

Looking Back: The Canadian market DID proceed to experience a full bear market with a total decline of 24.5% by January 2016, which was not anywhere close to the magnitude of 2008/09 but still a classic bear market. The US market did not experience a full bear market but did experience some pretty wild gyrations with two back-to-back corrections in the fall of 2015 and again in the winter of 2016. The commodity bear market paused for a little, but continued its downward spiral in late 2015 and early 2016. This all represented GREAT buying opportunities for those brave enough to swim against the tide, as we did with the newsletter portfolios. BAD markets are NOT BAD happenings. Yes, the value of current holdings declines but new purchases are made at better valuations.

If It Was EASY, It Would NOT Be as PROFITABLE

The investing world is full of paradoxes and contradictions, as you have gathered by now, so I start this newsletter with another paradox. The rationale for the title is the things that are easy to do attract crowds. These crowds then drive up prices in a desire to get in on the "easy" money, thus reducing the potential for future profitability. The fact that making money on stock investing is difficult makes it in fact more profitable. Easy money can be made going to the bank and investing in GICs, but that isn't particularly profitable. Similarly, if farming was easy it would attract lots of people who would bid up land prices and other inputs, overproduce and take the profitability out of the industry. The fact that farming is so difficult makes it profitable for the highly skilled long-term survivors in the industry. Housing has represented "easy" money for the past twenty years, especially in Toronto and Vancouver. All you had to do was buy a big house to become wealthy. House prices across Canada were up 8.3% in the past year alone making the stock market look like a mugs game. Through the years I have yet to find legal ways to make "easy" money. It all entails risk and work. In my books, buying a house in Vancouver right now would entail a lot of risk, even though it has been "easy" money for many years.

I can understand the sentiment, after reviewing the performance charts below, where you could say, "OK, I understand the difficult part, but where is the profitable part?" This is where we need to challenge ourselves to stay cool and stay the course. As previously mentioned, my own twenty-two year history in my RRSP has yielded almost 12% annual returns, through two very large bear markets where the S&P lost over 50% of its value. The objective of this newsletter remains to make it easier, but not easy for subscribers to profit from stock investing.

Market commentary: The third quarter was nasty with the S&P down about 7% and the TSX down about 9%. Year-to-date, as of October 2nd, the S&P is down 5.2% and the TSX is down 8.8%. Relative to other corrections and bear markets, this has actually been fairly mild so far but with a few wild days.

Is the correction over now? Same answer as last month: maybe, maybe not. October is historically a volatile month. However, if I was a gambler, I would bet on the fourth quarter being positive. That said 2015 could possibly be a negative year. The S&P has been negative 24 of the last 89 years or about one in four. The last negative year in Canada was 2011, and in the US was 2008, so in a way we are due a negative year. Why didn't we sell in January and stay in cash? Because predicting negative years in advance, like predicting any market direction in advance, is virtually impossible. My preference is to take advantage of the corrections when they occur to add to positions at better valuations. That's why I used some of the available cash in our personal RRSPs this past week to add TRP and BAM.A. This is one way we try to best the market by a couple of percentage points. The current US bull market has been referred to as the Rodney Dangerfield bull, as "it can't get no respect." Market sentiment has been very cautious all along. Perhaps it is a hangover effect from the 2008/09 bear that was extreme. Current market sentiment is almost as bad as it was in 2008/09. Market sentiment based on the bull/bear ratio is something I watch. More on that in a future issue.

The Canadian recession: Shortly after my last newsletter it was confirmed that Canada was in a recession the first two quarters of 2015. It is referred to as a technical recession because by definition a recession is two negative GDP quarters, so it met the technical definition. However, it was oil price-driven, thus localized and didn't have all the markings of a normal recession: 1) The feds ran a surplus, which doesn't happen during recessions, 2) Employment was steady to growing, again not normal recession behaviour and 3) Canadian house prices increased 8.3 % year over year. June actually recorded a 0.4% growth and July had 0.3 % growth. Annualized, these two most recent months (a couple months delay to get the data) would represent 4.2% annual growth, which is quite strong. As well, the US revised its second quarter growth upwards to 3.7%, which is the strongest growth since the Great Recession. Yesterday's weaker than expected US employment numbers with 142,000 jobs created vs 200,000 expected but unemployment holding steady at 5.1% was, however, a cautionary statistic.

How have our portfolios performed? In two words, NOT GREAT!

(Note: Prices in all charts taken from September 30th closing with conversion of 1USD = 1.33 CAD)

TFSA Model Portfolio

Company	Ticker	Date Added	# Shares	Price Added	Cost In CAD	Current Value in CAD	Share Price Change	Previous Total Dividends to Date	July 2015 Dividends	Aug 2015 Dividends	Sept 2015 Dividends	New Total Dividends to Date	Total Return
International													
Ensco PLC	ESV	May 30/14	100	$52.66	$5,750	$1,873	$(3,877)	$284.25			$19.95	$304.20	-62.1%
Glaxo Smithkline	GSK	May 30/14	100	$53.94	$5,890	$5,114	$(776)	$230.38	$75.55			$305.93	-8.0%
Ship Finance Int.	SFL	May 30/14	180	$18.52	$3,644	$3,890	$246	$436.18			$105.34	$541.52	21.6%
Seadrill	SDRL	July 25/14	130	$37.49	$5,312	$1,020	$(4,292)	$140.46				$140.46	-78.2%
HSBC Holdings PLC	HSBC	July 25/14	100	$52.82	$5,757	$5,038	$(719)	$236.79	$65.00			$301.79	-7.2%
Vodaphone	VOD	July 25/14	150	$34.16	$5,585	$6,332	$747	$97.30		$231.92		$329.22	19.3%
Unilever PLC	UL	Jan 2/15	100	$40.05	$4,736	$5,424	$688	$72.39			$42.99	$115.38	17.0%
Diagio PLC	DEO	Jan 2/15	30	$112.73	$4,001	$4,301	$300	$47.88				$47.88	8.7%
BHP Billiton Ltd	BHP	Jan 2/15	65	$47.27	$3,636	$2,734	$(902)	$368.26			$107.20	$475.46	-11.7%
South32 Ltd.	SOUHY	May30/15	26	$8.34	$267	$165	$(102)	$-				$-	-38.1%
Internatonal Subtotal					$44,578	$35,891	$(8,687)	$1,913.89				$2,561.84	-13.7%
Canadian													
TD Bank	TD	May 30/14	100	$53.76	$5,386	$5,260	$(126)	$192.00	$51.00			$243.00	2.2%
Innvest REIT	INN.UN	May 30/14	210	$5.16	$1,094	$1,046	$(48)	$83.88	$6.99	$6.99	$6.99	$104.85	5.2%
Rogers Communications	RCI.B	May 30/14	100	$43.82	$4,392	$4,598	$206	$185.25	$48.00			$233.25	10.0%
Teck Reources Ltd	TCK.B	May 30/14	200	$24.17	$4,844	$1,274	$(3,570)	$180.00	$30.00			$210.00	-69.4%
ATCO	ACO.X	July 25/14	100	$50.56	$5,066	$3,920	$(1,146)	$92.50			$24.75	$117.25	-20.3%
Husky Energy	HSE	July 25/14	150	$33.72	$5,068	$3,122	$(1,946)	$135.00	$45.00			$180.00	-34.8%
Sunlife Financial	SLF	July 25/14	100	$41.40	$4,150	$4,304	$154	$146.00			$38.00	$184.00	8.1%
Cdn. Western Bank	CWB	May 19/15	170	$28.99	$4,938	$3,993	$(945)	$37.40			$37.40	$74.80	-17.6%
Jean Coutu	PJC.A	May 19/15	200	$23.23	$4,656	$4,022	$(634)	$-		$22.00		$22.00	-13.1%
Canadian Subtotal					$39,594	$31,539	$(8,055)	$1,052.03				$1,369.15	
Total Cdn and Int					$84,172	$67,430	$(16,742)	$2,965.92				$3,930.99	-16.9%
Cash						$1,759							
Total						$69,189							-15.6%

Cost in CAD total of $84,172 is derived from $82,000 investment plus $2172 of reinvested dividends, leaving $1759 of cash from unspent dividends

The portfolio is down another 6.3% in the quarter to -15.6%. The good news is we are losing money more slowly than we would in Vegas. Please have faith. I have been here before and we will dig out of this hole! The market can change on a dime, as it did yesterday.

RRSP Model Portfolio

Company	Ticker	Date Added	# Shares	Price Added	Cost In CAD	Current Value in CAD	Share Price Change	Previous Dividends to Date	July Dividends	August Dividends	September Dividends	New Dividends to Date	Total Return
US Companies													
Verizon	VZ	Sept 30/14	100	$ 49.99	$ 5,609	$ 5,787	$ 178	$ 196.09		$ 71.12		$ 267.21	7.9%
HCP Inc	HCP	Sept 30/14	100	$ 39.71	$ 4,458	$ 4,954	$ 496	$ 200.55		$ 74.30		$ 274.85	17.3%
Hospitality Prop. Trust	HPT	Sept 30/14	150	$ 26.85	$ 4,521	$ 5,103	$ 582	$ 265.59		$ 97.39		$ 362.98	20.9%
United Technologies	UTX	Oct 31/14	50	$ 107.00	$ 6,002	$ 5,918	$ (84)	$ 113.07			$ 42.08	$ 155.15	1.2%
Johnson and Johnson	JNJ	Oct 31/14	50	$ 107.78	$ 6,045	$ 6,208	$ 163	$ 130.12			$ 49.25	$ 179.37	5.7%
Freeport-McMoRan	FCX	Nov 30/14	150	$ 26.85	$ 4,601	$ 1,933	$ (2,668)	$ 68.02		$ 31.13		$ 99.15	-55.8%
Chevron	CVX	Nov 30/14	50	$ 108.87	$ 6,216	$ 5,245	$ (971)	$ 132.98			$ 70.35	$ 203.33	-12.3%
Exelon	EXC	Nov 30/14	150	$ 36.17	$ 6,195	$ 5,925	$ (270)	$ 115.58			$ 61.15	$ 176.73	-1.5%
General Electric	GE	Jan 27/15	200	$ 24.38	$ 6,056	$ 6,709	$ 653	$ 55.35	$ 59.74			$ 115.09	12.7%
Praxair	PX	Feb 28/15	25	$ 127.90	$ 4,007	$ 3,387	$ (620)	$ 44.34			$ 23.54	$ 67.88	-13.8%
Qualcomm	QCOM	Feb 28/15	50	$ 72.51	$ 4,542	$ 3,573	$ (969)	$ 55.88			$ 31.62	$ 87.50	-19.4%
US Subtotal					$ 58,252	$ 54,742	$ (3,510)	$ 1,377.57				$ 1,989.24	-2.6%
Canadian Companies													
Bank of Nova Scotia	BNS	Sept 30/14	100	$ 69.27	$ 6,937	$ 5,883	$ (1,054)	$ 200.00	$ 68.00			$ 268.00	-11.3%
Power Corp	POW	Sept 30/14	200	$ 31.08	$ 6,226	$ 5,534	$ (692)	$ 178.26			$ 62.26	$ 240.52	-7.3%
Capital Power	CPX	Oct 31/14	200	$ 25.58	$ 5,126	$ 3,776	$ (1,350)	$ 136.00	$ 68.00			$ 204.00	-22.4%
Mullen Group Ltd.	MTL	Nov 20/14	250	$ 22.12	$ 5,540	$ 4,463	$ (1,077)	$ 175.00	$ 25.00	$ 25.00	$ 25.00	$ 250.00	-14.9%
Royal Bank	RY	Jan 27/15	100	$ 75.12	$ 7,522	$ 7,379	$ (143)	$ 77.00		$ 77.00		$ 154.00	0.1%
TransCanada Pipeline	TRP	Jan 27/15	100	$ 55.59	$ 5,609	$ 4,220	$ (1,389)	$ 52.00	$ 52.00			$ 104.00	-22.9%
Bell Canada	BCE	Feb 28/15	100	$ 54.71	$ 5,481	$ 5,462	$ (19)	$ 65.00	$ 65.00			$ 130.00	2.0%
Brookfield Asset Mgmt	BAM.A	Feb 28/15	150	$ 45.23	$ 6,795	$ 6,299	$ (496)	$ 22.32			$ 23.80	$ 46.12	-6.6%
Pason Systems	PSI	Mar 3/15	200	$ 18.48	$ 3,706	$ 3,752	$ 46	$ 68.00			$ 34.00	$ 102.00	4.0%
Wajax Corp	WJX	Mar 3/15	150	$ 24.31	$ 3,657	$ 3,314	$ (343)	$ 12.50	$ 37.50			$ 50.00	-8.0%
Home Capital Group	HCG	Mar3May29/15	150	$ 43.11	$ 6,475	$ 4,805	$ (1,670)	$ 22.00			$ 33.00	$ 55.00	-24.9%
AutoCanada	ACQ	Apr 4/15	150	$ 34.15	$ 5,133	$ 3,879	$ (1,254)	$ 37.50			$ 37.50	$ 75.00	-23.0%
Cogeco Inc.	CGO	May 29/15	100	$ 53.60	$ 5,370	$ 5,335	$ (35)	$ -		$ 25.50		$ 25.50	-0.2%
Cdn Subtotal					$ 73,577	$ 64,101	$ (9,476)	$ 1,045.58				$ 1,704.14	-10.6%
Dividends from Sold Cos								$ 24.40				$ 24.40	
Total Cdn and US					$ 131,829	$ 118,843	$ (12,986)	$ 2,447.55				$ 3,717.78	
Cash						$ 2,045							
Portfolio Value						$ 120,888							-5.9%

Cost in CAD total of $131,829 is derived from $128,500 invested, $1656 capital gains, plus $1673 of reinvested dividends, leaving $2045 of cash from unspent dividends.

Sales to Date	Ticker	Date Added	# Shares	Price	Exchange	Cost In CAD	Sold	Sold Price	Proceeds	Dividends	Profit	% Profit
Constellation Software	CSU	Oct 31/14	10	$ 317.50		$ 3,185	Apr 14/15	$ 485.07	$ 4,841	$ 24.40	$ 1,679	52.7

The RRSP portfolio fell from + 2.9% to -5.9 for an 8.8% loss in the quarter.

Non-Registered Margin Portfolio

Company	Ticker	Date Added	# Shares	Price Added	Cost In USD	Current Value in USD	Share Price Change	Previous Dividends to Date	July Dividends	August Dividends	September Dividends	New Dividends to Date	Total Return
US Dollar Purchases													
iShares MSCI Emerging	EEM	06-Jul-15	100	$ 38.62	$ 3,872	$ 3,278	$ (594)					$ -	-15.3%
Vanguard Europe ETF	VGK	06-Jul-15	100	$ 52.91	$ 5,301	$ 4,918	$ (383)					$ -	-7.2%
First Trust Nat GAS	FCG	06-Jul-15	500	$ 8.57	$ 4,297	$ 2,810	$ (1,487)				$ 14.92	$ 14.92	-34.3%
Parker Hannifin	PH	24-Jul-15	50	$ 110.84	$ 5,552	$ 4,865	$ (687)				$ 26.77	$ 26.77	-11.9%
iShares Silver Trust	SLV	31-Aug-15	200	$ 13.79	$ 2,767	$ 2,774	$ 7					$ -	0.3%
Market Vector Gold	GDX	31-Aug-15	200	$ 13.71	$ 2,751	$ 2,748	$ (3)					$ -	-0.1%
Berkshire Hathaway	BRK.B	31-Aug-15	30	$ 134.31	$ 4,039	$ 3,912	$ (127)					$ -	-3.1%
Union Pacific	UNP	31-Aug-15	50	$ 86.13	$ 4,316	$ 4,421	$ 105					$ -	2.4%
US Subtotal					$ 32,895	$ 29,726	$ (3,169)	$ -				$ 41.69	
Cash						$ 146							
Total USD						$ 29,872							-9.5%
Canadian Companies					CAD	CAD							
Bank of Montreal	BMO	03-Jul-15	100	$ 74.21	$ 7,431	$ 7,278	$ (153)			$ 82.00		$ 82.00	-1.0%
CGI Group	GIB.A	23-Jul-15	100	$ 50.90	$ 5,100	$ 4,835	$ (265)					$ -	-5.2%
Crescent Point Energy	CPG	23-Jul-15	200	$ 20.33	$ 4,076	$ 3,054	$ (1,022)			$ 46.00	$ 20.00	$ 66.00	-23.5%
Telus	T	31-Aug-15	100	$ 42.83	$ 4,293	$ 4,205	$ (88)					$ -	-2.0%
Suncor	SU	31-Aug-15	100	$ 35.78	$ 3,588	$ 3,569	$ (19)				$ 29.00	$ 29.00	0.3%
Stantec Inc	STN	29-Sep-15	200	$ 29.30	$ 5,870	$ 5,836	$ (34)					$ -	-0.6%
Cdn Subtotal					$ 30,358	$ 28,777	$ (1,581)	$ -				$ 177.00	
Cash						$ 319							
Total CAD						$ 29,096							-4.6%
Total Portfolio Value in CAD						$ 68,574							
Deposits in CAD Value						$ 73,265							-6.4%

Note: There is a slight format difference in this chart of the non-registered account. All institutions have non-registered USD and CAD currency accounts available, which is suggested. Therefore with the non-registered account, I am tracking in native currency and only converting to value in CAD at the bottom line. US dividends recorded are actual dividends minus the 15% US withholding tax. There is recognition for the withholding tax when paying Canadian income taxes.

And guess what? These, too, are down with resources once again the key culprits. Now please don't think I am crazy, but it is good to be down when you want to build positions. We can buy new companies or add to positions at better valuations.

New Additions

Stantec Inc. (STN): As per the email update on September 29th I added 200 shares of Stantec at $29.30. With over $2.5B in annual sales and growing, Stantec is an engineering and design consulting business with three operating units: Buildings, Energy and Resources, and Infrastructure. STN is geographically diversified with 53% of its business coming from Canada and 44% from the US with a small international presence in England, the Middle East and India. Most engineering firms are smaller "mom and pop" operations. Stantec's success has been in buying these smaller firms and consolidating them into a larger firm. Over the past 10 years STN has grown revenues by 5x and earnings per share by 3.5x. It pays a small dividend of 1.4%, preferring to invest its excess cash flow into new growth acquisitions. While its long-term growth chart is tremendous, it has recently declined from $38 to the current level of $29. It trades with an earnings yield of 6.1%, cash flow yield of 8.8%, price times book of 2.3x, and ROE of 15.5%.

Late yesterday afternoon I also added two companies not reflected in the September 30 chart:

Potash Corp. (POT): I keep drinking from the trough of decimated resource companies and POT is this month's "hair of the dog that bit me" company. Based in Saskatchewan, with $7B in annual sales, POT is the world's largest fertilizer company. It is the largest in potash with 20% world market share and also amongst the leaders in the other key nutrients of nitrogen and phosphorus. Like other commodities the world has gone from supposed shortages in 2008 to surpluses today. With its size, scope and strength of balance sheet, it should be able to survive the current malaise. The price of POT ranged from $4 to $8 for many years, but exploded to $80 from 2006 to 2008 before collapsing to $20 during the financial crisis. Since then it has gone as high as $60 and as low as its current price of $26. I purchased just 100 shares at $26.82. It has a dividend yield of 7.7%, earnings yield of 8.8%, cash flow yield of 13.0%, price times book of 1.9 and ROE of 16.8%. In the last 10 years sales have almost doubled while earnings are up by 3x, but have been trending down for the last four years. It will be a long time before it sees its previous high of $80 but today's price looks attractive.

ITC Holdings (ITC): This account did not yet have a utility so I added ITC on the US side. With just over $1B in annual sales it is quite small for an American Utility, but is unique in that it doesn't produce electricity. It just transports it, mostly in the US Midwest. Transmission is a highly regulated and fairly predictable business. Over the past 10 years, sales and earnings have grown five-fold, while dividends have doubled. It trades with a modest dividend yield of 2.3%. This is not a bad thing as we pay higher taxes on US dividends than Canadian dividends in non-registered accounts (see Issue #13) so growth and capital gains are a better focus for US companies. It has an earnings yield of 5.2%, cash flow yield of 7.9%, price times book of 2.8 and ROE of 15.6%. This is a fairly expensive valuation for a utility. Its lower risk and higher growth profile hopefully makes it worth the price. It traded as high as $44.00 early in the year. I purchased 100 shares at $32.10.

To make these purchases I transferred in another $8,000 CAD and $3,100 USD, which would have been at a conversion of 1.32 (the dollar gained a cent in the past two days) had I needed to convert.

A couple of other items:

World markets: While I generally refer to just the Canadian and US markets, it is important to note that almost all the key world markets are also down year-to-date. The few exceptions being Italy and France, which are up, and Japan and Korea being about breakeven.

USD vs. commodities: Besides current valuations and resources being completely out of favour, another reason I keep adding a little more resource exposure is that commodities tend to move in the opposite direction to the USD. It's like a teeter-totter. If the USD goes up, commodities tend to fall. If the USD falls, commodities go up. It's a chicken and egg scenario in that I'm not sure which causes what, just that they tend to move in opposite directions. The USD has risen dramatically in the past year. This benefited my personal accounts and to a lesser extent the model accounts, causing me to hesitate adding more US companies to the model after the dramatic rise. Adding commodities acts as a hedge against a decline in the USD. I am not hereby predicting the direction of the USD, just that it makes sense to me to have some counterbalance. Nothing goes up, or down, forever.

In the next issue I will begin the discussion on the exciting world of OPTIONS and how I use them in my non-registered portfolio to (hopefully) enhance returns. Options open up a whole new arena of fun and profit.

Looking Back: As a writer of a newsletter I never know what subscribers are actually doing with their portfolios, but I sure hope they were reading and following despite the tough markets to-date.

Options add some complexity, especially if you are new to stock investing. Most readers will only be interested in the simpler RRSP and TFSA portfolio strategies. I would encourage readers to read through the options information for the learning experience but only venture into them after significant stock investing experience and success. The book continues to build on the RRSP and TFSA portfolios in addition to general market knowledge. The option sections may be an area to revisit after gaining investing experience.

ISSUE #18: NOVEMBER 1, 2015

Leverage Is Not a Four-Letter Word

I am about to, once again, step on traditional financial management traditions and beliefs. One of the most controversial writings in the past is that an owner occupied house is NOT an investment but rather an asset, like a personal vehicle. Standard financial rhetoric is that one's house is *"likely to be one's largest ever investment."* True investments are those which provide steady cash flow (or at least the potential for such), allow for tax deductibility of interest and the potential for capital gains. An owner-occupied house does not meet two of these three principles, but other forms of real estate do. An accepted principle of real estate investing is that borrowing money, otherwise known as leverage, is widely accepted whereas with stock investing it is widely frowned upon. Why is there such a difference in perception of the use of leverage across these two asset classes? Both true investment real estate and dividend-paying stocks provide steady streams of cash flow. Both real estate investments and stock investments (in a regular account) allow tax deductibility of interest. Both real estate and stock values can fluctuate dramatically. The only real difference is you can't go to your computer and get second by second updates on real estate prices.

What is even more perplexing is that it is much easier to secure financing on owner-occupied residential property than to get financing on true investment real estate. Why is 80-90% debt widely accepted as "safe" with owner-occupied residential, whereas "unsafe" on true real estate investments or stock investments? This makes NO sense to me at all. A reason that high leverage might be considered safe with personal residential property is the ingrained but unwitting desire of the financial industry to keep people enslaved to perpetual mortgage payments, and that house prices go up forever! Do they?

I am NOT hereby suggesting that 80-90% leverage is safe with investments, just that it is no safer on owner-occupied residential than true investments. A realistic level of leverage could be 50%, although it depends on one's age and risk tolerance. I was much more comfortable with high leverage when I was younger. When 10 to 15 years ago I moved from being focused on real estate to stock investing, I chose to employ similar principals on leverage. Leverage is not allowed in registered TFSA, RESP or RRSP accounts, just non-registered. When a margin account is set up, the owner can buy more stocks than the deposited cash. The amount of overage is considered a loan and charged interest, which is tax-deductible. There is a limit on how much you can borrow, which ranges between 50% and 70% of the total value of the portfolio. The account details will show the amount of excess margin available.

Margin, like all debt, is a double-edged sword. It can enhance returns but will also exacerbate losses. It is important to keep in mind that this is a debt and it must be repaid, regardless of investment success. My original margin strategy was to make sure dividends covered the interest cost. This served me well for a number of years even during the 2000/02 bear market. However, during the 2008/09 financial crisis many companies cut or eliminated their dividends and there were no safe havens. Virtually every stock declined, causing a re-evaluation of the strategy. I also tired of the interest charges and looked for a better way. I had been introduced to options many years ago by a broker, but options tend to be smaller dollar transactions and brokerage fees chewed up most profits. Low fee Internet investing now makes option costs reasonable. Since about 2009 I have avoided interest payments while employing option strategies for leverage. **It is important to always be cognizant of the double-edged sword, which leverage provides.**

Part of my rationale for using options is the long-term record of the market being up much more than down. Over the past eighty-nine years the market has been down significantly, as defined by a 12.5% or more decline, in just seven years. It has been down some (0-12.5% decline) seventeen years and has been up sixty-five/eighty-nine years. The option strategies I use should theoretically only hurt in those really bad "down significantly" years, and should enhance returns in the sixty-five/eighty-nine up years. At least that's the theory, but security selection remains a critical component of realizing the theory.

What are options?

Options are the right to buy or sell a stock, at a specified price and up to a specified date in the future. One option contract usually represents 100 shares of the company. There are two types of options: **PUTS** and **CALLS.**

PUT: Is the right to **sell** the stock. The buyer of a PUT has a right to sell the stock, at a specified price and up to a specified date, to the seller of the PUT.

CALL: Is the right to **buy** the stock. The buyer of a CALL has the right to buy a stock, at a specified price and up to a specified date, from the seller of the CALL.

By far the most common and simple option strategy I use is the sale of PUTS. When I sell a PUT, the buyer pays me to buy the right to sell me the underlying stock at a specified price up to a specified date in the future. The option price is made up of the "intrinsic value" and the "time premium." The "intrinsic value" is the difference between the value of the stock and the option contract price and the "time premium" is the additional fee the seller collects (the buyer pays) for the risk the seller assumes for the duration of the contract. This may sound like mumbo jumbo if you are completely unfamiliar with options, but like I have done with TFSAs and RRSPs let me illustrate by doing and explaining along the way in this and future issues.

(Clarification: When I write "buyer," I mean anyone who bought the same contract, as we don't deal with a specific individual. For the real examples below I am excluding fees and commissions to better illustrate the math.)

On October 30th, in my non-registered account, I sold one PUT contract (representing 100 shares) of American Express, ticker AXP. The contract has a specified price of $75.00 and expires on January 20, 2017. The buyer of the contract paid me $7.73 per share or $773 for the 100 share contract. After fees and commissions, $761.74 USD was deposited in my account. The price of AXP at the time I sold the PUT was $73.60. The buyer can PUT (i.e. sell) me the stock for $75 any time up to and including January 20, 2017. Using this example, the intrinsic value is $1.40 ($75 minus $73.60) and the time premium is $6.33 ($7.73 contract price minus $1.40 intrinsic value)

Let's look at the various scenarios that could play out:

a. **The price of AXP goes up and is above $75.00 on expiration date:** I get to keep the premium of $7.73/share and the option expires worthless. This is the most desirable outcome for me. The buyer loses the $773 contract premium.

b. **The price ranges somewhere between $75.00 and $67.27 at expiration:** The $67.27 is derived from $75.00 minus the $7.73 option premium. If AXP is in this price range at expiration I have a couple of choices: 1) I can buy back the contract and could still make a profit but not the entire premium. As the option contract approaches expiry, the time premium diminishes and approaches zero. If the price of AXP drops to $70 on expiration date, I could buy the contract back at very close to $5.00, which would still net me a profit of almost $2.73/share or $273.00 on the contract. 2) Depending on the cash in the account, I could also choose to accept the shares. If I accept the shares, my effective cost is $67.27, which is the time premium of $6.33 below the cost of the shares at the time I sold the PUT options. Selling PUT options is designed to help buy shares below their current price.

c. **The price of AXP declines below $67.27 at expiration:** This is the least desirable outcome. There are the same two choices as above except buying out the contract will be at a loss. Let's say the price of AXP drops to $60.00, I will have to pay about $15.00 to buy back the contract, which would represent a loss of $15.00 minus $7.73 = $7.27 loss per share or $727.00 on the contract. This is, however, a smaller loss than if I bought the shares outright on October 30th for $73.60, which would represent a loss of $13.60, minus dividends collected. My decision on whether to accept the shares or buy out the contract depends on a number of factors including available cash in account, but mainly depends on whether I think the company still represents good value and is one I wish to own. I only sell PUTS on companies or ETFs I wish to own, but there are occasions when between the time of selling the PUT and the expiration date, I realize I'm doing something dumb and buy out the contract accepting the loss.

Over and above AXP I also did the following on October 30th:

Walmart (WMT): I sold one $60.00 PUT contract of Walmart with an expiry date January 20, 2017 at a price of $7.00 or $700 for the contract. After fees, $688.74 USD was deposited in my account. At the time I sold the PUT, WMT was $57.90, such that the intrinsic value was $2.10/share and the time premium was $4.90.

Emerson Electric (EMR): I sold one $50.00 PUT contract of Emerson Electric that also expires on January 20th, 2017, for a premium of $7.51/share or $751.00 for the contract, and $739.74 USD was deposited in my account. At the time EMR stock was $47.10, such that the intrinsic value was $2.90/share and the time premium was $4.61.

Berkshire Hathaway (BRK.B): Total proceeds from the three option sales were $2190.22 USD. I used this money to buy an additional fifteen shares of BRK.B for $137.55/share = $2063.25 plus $9.99 commission, thus using leverage (other people's money) to add to my account.

Where's the catch? This seems a little like money for nothing, but it's not. **It is leverage**. In doing the above I have obligated myself to buying 100 shares each of AXP, WMT and EMR. If things go as desired I get to keep all the premiums, but things don't always go as desired. I need to be prepared to accept the shares or buy out the contract if the price of any of the companies goes down. In total, I have obligated myself to $7500 of AXP, $6000 of WMT and $5000 of EMR should the prices decline for a total of $18,500. For this risk I was paid premiums of $2190.22. If things really go south I need to come up with the $18,500 or at least enough to buy out the contracts. Alternatively, I can use the bank margin loan available through the margin account but then need to start paying interest. **If options stretch your comfort zone, please watch for a period of time to see how they play out.**

Guidelines:

1. I only sell PUT contracts on companies or ETFs that I think represent good value and try to stay cognizant that I can make mistakes.

2. I try to keep my PUT sales in line with the size of positions of other securities in the portfolio. In other words, I could have sold three AXP contracts and raised a similar amount of cash but then my obligation for AXP purchases would be $22,500, which would be way out of line with the size of the other positions in the portfolio. Diversification is a key to success.

3. I have learned to sell PUTS on larger, more stable companies or ETFs. Unfortunately, the time premium is usually less on these types of companies as they tend to fluctuate less, but the last thing we want is for the company to drop dramatically or go broke. Larger companies also have much more liquid options. I don't like playing cat and mouse with bid/ask spreads. If the spread is too wide I usually don't bother. Liquidity is also important if there is a need to buy out the contract.

4. I tend to sell PUT options as far into the future as possible so that the time premium is higher. With the above option trades the furthest out month for WMT and EMR was January 2017. January 2018 contracts were available on AXP, but they are just recently available and still not very liquid. Option

contracts are available every month of the year, but not all months are available for all companies. January of each year is the most liquid, most available month. Options generally expire on the third Friday of each month, but some ETFs and companies have weekly options. January 2018 options will become much more prevalent and liquid over the next few months as January 2016 contracts expire.

5. I don't trade frequently. My intent is to sell the contract and wait for expiration time. I don't want options to become a daily task and, as with stocks, overtrading will lead to almost certain failure. I try to make a decision then stick with it.

6. Selling PUTS will use the available margin in the account but without interest charges. It is important to keep a reasonable margin cushion so that you are not forced to buy back contracts during short sharp market panics, such as those that recently occurred.

7. I also like to keep a little cash cushion in case I am PUT a stock unexpectedly. Generally the option will only get exercised close to or at expiration, but the buyer has the right to do it anytime. This will only occur if there is no longer a time premium, as the buyer would generally be better off to sell his contract than PUT the stock if there is any remaining time premium. There is no cash cushion in this account at this time because of its newness. It takes time to build.

8. I try to get about a 10% or better discount off the current stock price when I sell a PUT. This helps the sting during years that the market is down some but not when it is down significantly.

9. I started on the US side for a number of reasons: 1) The US has a much more liquid options market. 2) While I am not exchanging money myself to set up this portfolio, I am tracking it as if I was and am making an assumption that subscribers may need to convert CAD to USD. I don't like the exchange rate at this time for conversion to USD, so it makes sense to use the margin on the American side first. 3) There are far more large companies in the US to choose from.

Brief description of the three companies I sold PUTS on:

American Express (AXP): With $33B in sales AXP is a well-known US-based, global financial company. It is third to Visa and MasterCard in the credit card business, with its focus on prestige usage. It also provides travel and corporate services. AXP recently lost its Costco relationship, which represented a large but low margin account. It may take a year or two to recover from this loss, but AXP has been a highly successful company and credit cards remain a growth business. Like many financial companies AXP fell off a cliff in 2008/09 but recovered from a low of $10.00 to over $90.00 early in 2015. The recent sell-off has taken it to its current level in the lower $70s. It has a dividend yield of 1.6%, earnings yield of 7.6%, cash flow yield of 9.3%, price times book of 3.4x and spectacular ROE of 27.1%. As previously written, high earnings yield combined with high ROE makes a good combination. The risk with AXP is the length of time it takes to recover from the Costco loss.

Walmart (WMT): With almost half a trillion dollars in annual sales WMT is the largest company, by sales and employees, in the world. I am not a big fan of WMT and have rarely stepped inside one, but its success as a company is phenomenal. As a consumer staples retailer with the low price reputation, it tends to outperform during recessionary times. Like AXP it has sold down recently. It started paying its employees better and investing more heavily in Internet retail, leading to pressure on profits. It is currently valued with a dividend yield of 3.4%, earnings yield of 8.3%, cash flow yield of 13.7%, price times book of 2.3x and a very good ROE of 19.8%. It sold as high as $90.00 in early 2015, selling down to its recent price in the high $50s.

Emerson Electric (EMR): EMR may not be familiar name. With $24B in annual sales it is, however, a fairly large diversified US-based industrial company focused on industrial technology, automation, process improvement and engineering. It also provides climate control systems, heating, a/c, hvac and refrigeration systems to residential, commercial and industrial clients. The strong US dollar has hurt US industrial companies and Emerson is no exception. EMR peaked as high as $70.00 in late 2013 and has sold down to the mid $40s. However, it has a good record of long-term sales, profit and dividend growth. Profits and dividends have approximately doubled in the last 10 years. It has a dividend yield of 4.0%, earnings yield of 7.6%, cash flow yield of 10.6%, price times book of 3.6x and another spectacular ROE of 25.3%.

That concludes this **Intro to Options** issue. Until next month, **have fun with your investments.**

Risk Is a Four-Letter Word, but Not a Bad One

It is said that "beauty is in the eye of the beholder." I would suggest that "RISK is also in the eye of the beholder." Everything we do entails some element of risk. **To avoid risk is to avoid life itself.**

I googled riskiest sports and both skiing and cycling were amongst the very worst. Hey, those are my two favourites! Also high on the list were cheerleading, gymnastics and horseback riding. Who would have thought that cheerleading and gymnastics were riskier than football and hockey? How about risky activities we do every day? Driving, as we know, is amongst the worst along with BBQing and texting while walking. I can hardly walk and chew gum at the same time so have never tried texting and walking, but am confident it would be injurious. We all know the dangers of texting or talking while driving yet many continue to illegally do it on a regular basis, although like food intake I'm trying to cut back. For those who think staying at home is risk-free, think again. Falling down, especially down stairs, is a significant cause of death. There are also injuries related to brushing teeth, stapling paper and even reading, although the article didn't explain how.

Is stock investing risky? How about options? How do we look at risk? Summarizing the numerous articles I read on "riskiest investments," general consensus form least risky to most risky was: 1) Cash, CDs, GICs, Money Market Funds 2) Bonds 3) Stocks 4) Options and Futures. Following are a few abbreviated quotes that sum up the sentiment on options: "The prices of options can change quickly, and those who trade them can win or lose huge sums of money in very short periods of time. This type of trading is best left to professionals;" "The options arena is not to be treaded lightly and not by novices. A clear reason is the fact that roughly 90% of contracts expire worthless;" and a very succinct quote is "Basically they're gambling instruments."

However, in the context of "risk is in the eye of the beholder," a quote from Warren Buffett (rich guy who made his fortune investing) is "The investment you think is 'safe' is actually the riskiest in the world." Huh? Doesn't that fly in the face of all conventional wisdom? Yes, it does, and as mentioned before conventional wisdom is often an oxymoron. Buffett goes on to explain that the greatest investment risk is the loss of purchasing power, and cash has depreciated by 96% over the past century and by 85% over the past half century, whereas stocks have appreciated about 10% per year. He goes on to explain that virtually the entire investment community confuses "fluctuation" with "risk." While stocks fluctuate, referred to as "beta" in investing jargon, they are much safer than cash as they preserve purchasing power over multi-decade periods. Everyone has the right to choose who they believe and which strategies they wish to follow. I pick the rich guy.

Are options really as risky as purported? Yes, if used as a stand-alone strategy. Other than the leverage aspect when used in conjunction with a sound stock investment program, options can be employed without a disproportionate amount of additional risk. There are two main bullish strategies with options, selling PUTS and buying CALLS. As 90% of contracts expire worthless, my preference is selling but I will occasionally buy.

Once again, for the purposes of simplification, I have left commissions and dividends out of the example calculations and explanations. In reality, they need to be considered, but generally have limited impact on the overall result. As well, option owners do not collect dividends of the underlying stocks.

Selling PUTS: Let's build on the comments from last month's issue using this month's IBM example. I sold one $135.00 PUT contract of IBM, expiring on January 19, 2018, over two years from now. The stock was trading at $137.82 at the time and I received $18.70/share for the contract, or $1870 less commissions. If the price holds above $135, I get to keep the money. The worst case scenario is that IBM drops significantly and I get PUT the stock. My effective purchase price would then be $135 - $18.70 = $116.30, or 15.6% below its current price. Which is risker? Paying $137.82 today or $116.20 two years from now? Is this gambling?

Risk vs. reward: If we bought the stock outright, we would take all the downside risk and capture all upside potential. By selling the PUT we take less downside risk ($137.82 minus $116.30 = $21.52 less downside risk) but also cap our reward at $18.70, such that selling the PUT reduces both downside risk and potential upside returns. The biggest advantage is we receive the premium immediately and can deploy it immediately. To be fair while we take less downside risk than when buying the stock outright, we still take the risk that the company goes to zero and could lose $116.30, a much greater loss than our potential reward of $18.70. This is why I have learned to focus options on larger more stable companies that are highly unlikely to go to zero.

Buying CALLS: For purposes of illustration and just before writing this newsletter, the morning of November 27th I purchased two CALL option contracts of AT&T (ticker T) for $35.00 expiring on January 19, 2018. At the time AT&T was trading at $33.72. For the privilege of being able to buy AT&T anytime up to January 19th, 2018, for $35.00, I paid a price of $1.65, such that my total cost was 200 shares x $1.65 = $330 plus commissions. After the changes discussed below, there was $400 cash in the account, so I searched for a meaningful position that would cost less than the $400. A position of 200 shares of AT&T is in line with other holdings in the account. In two years, should I choose to CALL (i.e. purchase) the 200 AT&T my effective cost would be $35.00 plus $1.65 = $36.65, which is 8.7% over its current value. Why wouldn't I just buy the stock outright? In most cases I would but not wanting to convert any CAD to USD at today's exchange rate and not having any further funds available in the US account, this strategy locks in the price I need to pay in two years.

Let's look at how the various scenarios could play out and decide if this is truly gambling.

Most desired outcome: AT&T soars! First of all, AT&T is not likely to soar as a very stable high-dividend stock, which is why the premium was modest for a two-year-out contract. Many stocks would have a premium of 15-25%. But let's say the stock went to $40.00, I could sell the CALL for $5.00 and net a $5.00/$1.65 or 303% gain, or I could buy the stock for $35.00 with an effective purchase price of $36.65. Either way, all the upside potential above $36.65 is mine until January 19, 2018.

Second best outcome: AT&T tanks! It may surprise you that tanking is the second best outcome but if it drops to say $25.00, I lose my $1.65 but can then buy AT&T at a much more attractive price of $25.00. If I had purchased the shares, I would have lost $33.72 - $25.00 = $8.72, but instead have lost only $1.65.

Worst outcome: AT&T hangs around the $35 range. I lose my $1.65 and can't buy the shares any cheaper down the road. AT&T needs to decline to at least $32.07 (current price minus premium) for me to be happy that buying the CALL was better than buying the stock.

Risk vs. reward: Buying CALLS represents a way to lock in a future purchase price for a premium, in this case $1.65. The purchaser gains all the upside potential above the premium, with minimum and known downside risk of the premium. So you be the judge: Should I register for Gamblers Anonymous?

Portfolio Update

I have been active in adding to the non-registered portfolio with this issue for a couple of reasons:

1. December is usually a positive month. While it certainly doesn't happen all the time, there is often what is referred to as a Santa Claus rally. I don't know the cause, but it is partly believed to be that November and early December is when any tax loss selling occurs and when this is over the market rallies. It also may be that investors start looking optimistically towards the following year. I pay little attention to these calendar timing phenomenas and thus my main reason is:

2. The next issue will be dedicated to a year-end review and thus I may not change or add to the portfolio at that time.

3. It looks likely that we will exit 2015 with the US market up a little and the Canadian market down a little. If this is the case, it will be the fifth year in a row that the US has outperformed Canada, often by a wide margin. With each passing year the potential of a snapback, often referred to as "reversion to the mean," becomes more probable. Thus, I wanted to bolster the Canadian side before the new year.

US Companies

International Business Machines (IBM): As mentioned above, I sold one $135.00 put contract, expiring on January 19, 2018, for a price of $18.70/share. The actual share price at the time was $137.82. IBM is the granddaddy of the technology business. It is as much a business consulting firm as a technology company as it consults on almost all aspects of technology use in business and government. Those aspects include Analytics (big data), Cloud, Commerce, IT Infrastructure, Mobile, Security and Watson, their super computer. IBM has long been a very prolific patent producer. It is now aggressively moving into the health care data management arena. That said IBM is a definite turnaround situation. Revenues, while still north of $80B, have been in decline for four years. IBM was overly focused on share buybacks as a means to boost profits per share (please review Issue #15) but that strategy can hit a wall, which occurred to IBM in 2014. It now looks like it has recognized a need to grow top line revenue in order to grow profitability. Because of the aggressive share repurchase program, its financial metrics look a little wonky. It has a dividend yield of 3.8%, earnings yield of 10.5% (incredibly cheap if it can start to grow again) and cash flow yield of 13.7%. A very high 75% of this cash flow is "free cash flow" and is not required for reinvestment in capital projects. Operating cash flow minus capital expenditures equals free cash flow. Now for the wonky part: It has an ROE of 104.7% and a price times book of 10.1x, both extremely high as a result of the aggressive share buybacks. IBM traded as high as $215 in 2013 and has been in decline since. If misery loves company, we are in good company as Buffett's Berkshire Hathaway is a major shareholder, having recently increased its stake. IBM is new to me as an investment.

CVS Health Corp (CVS): I sold one $97.50 PUT contract, expiring on January 20, 2017, for a price of $11.00/share. The actual CVS share price at the time was $93.90 and my effective cost will be $86.50 if I get PUT. CVS is the second largest drug retailer and second largest pharmacy benefits manager in the US, with annual sales of $150B. In the US a pharmacy benefits manager is the intermediary and administrator between the drug manufacturers and the health insurer. They buy the drugs from manufactures, provide to patients and get paid by the insurance company or health plan. CVS is also the largest specialty pharmacy in the US and has over 1000 medical clinics located right in its retail pharmacies. It recently purchased a company that provides pharma services to long-term care facilities and is in the process of purchasing the in-store pharmacies at Target. Over the past 10 years CVS has grown sales by 4x, profits/share by 3x and dividends by 8x. Unlike IBM, this is definitely not a turnaround situation. CVS has a dividend yield of 1.5%, earnings yield of 4.7%, cash flow yield of 6.8%, ROE of 13.4% and price times book of 2.8x. CVS is not new to me, having purchased it for $29.11 in 2006. It did so well we sold 1/3 of our stake this past January for $103.34. I still liked the company, just thought it was getting too expensive. It is still expensive but has declined modestly. If it continues to drop and I get PUT it will be at an effective price of $86.50 or seventeen bucks less than where it was sold. If it goes back up, I get to keep the $1100.

I used the proceeds of these two transactions to buy twenty more BRK.B for $135.05 and the two AT&T CALLS.

AT&T (T): I purchased two $35.00 CALL contracts, expiring January 19, 2018, for a price of $1.65/share. The actual price of T at the time was $33.72. T is the largest US telecom with $140B in annual sales, although Verizon is very close in size. Key business segments are Business Solutions, Entertainment and Internet (which just expanded with the purchase of Direct TV) and Mobility, with increasing international presence, especially in Mexico and Latin America. T has a current dividend yield of 5.6%, and while this dividend is quite high, it has managed to increase this yield each year of the past decade. Its earnings yield of just 2.6% was impacted by unusual items in the fourth quarter last year. It is projected to have an earnings yield of 7.7%

in 2015. Its cash flow yield is 12.5%, ROE is 5.0% (again negatively impacted by fourth quarter last year) and price times book of 1.7x. T traded as high as $60.00 in 1999/2000 and as low as $20.00 in 2002/03 and again in 2008/09. It has been in the $30.00 to $40.00 range for the past four years. I have owned it in my RRSP since 2008, having purchased it at $29.25. It is rare to see a stock stay this stable for four years, so I'm hoping for a break to the upside.

Canadian Companies

Fortis Inc. (FTS): I purchased 100 shares at $36.67. Like with Telus, I am looking to build the portfolio with some key building blocks and utilities are one of those building blocks. Fortis looks like a "steady as she goes" company, having increased from $10/share in 2000 to its current level, all the while paying a reasonable dividend. Based out of Newfoundland, FTS provides natural gas and electricity to customers in many parts of Canada, in selected areas of the US, mainly New York and Arizona, and the Caribbean. Its annual sales are about $6B, making it one of the largest publicly traded utilities in Canada. While it has some electrical generation, mostly hydroelectric, its main business is transmission and delivery of both gas and electricity. It has increased its dividend 42 years in a row with a goal of increasing them by 6% per year, making it one of the most stable dividend growers on the market. It has a current dividend yield of 4.1%, earnings yield of 6.9%, cash flow yield of 15.3%, ROE of 11.1% and price times book of 1.3x. FTS is new to me as an investment.

Russell Metals (RUS): Also new to me as an investment I purchased 200 shares of RUS at $18.15. I have been thinking about RUS for a while but luckily held off as it has continued to decline along with other oil and gas services companies. With over $3B in annual sales, it is a significant North American metals distributor with 69% of revenue from Canada and 31% from the US. It has three operating segments: Metals Service Centres (48%), Energy Products (39%) and Steel Distribution (13%). The Metal Service Centre provides customized metal services to 38,000 customers, providing excellent diversification. While Energy Products is a key sector for success it is not wholly reliant on it, making it a slightly safer way to participate in a potential energy rebound. Profits are down but RUS remains solidly profitable. RUS grows through acquisitions buying about one other smaller "bolt-on" company per year. It has a dividend yield of 8.4% (which is too high and may get cut), an earnings yield of 6.9%, cash flow yield of 10.2%, ROE of 8.1% and price times book of 1.1x. Shares traded as high as $35.00 in mid-2014, before the big oil decline.

ShawCor Ltd. (SCL) is another energy services company but with a twist in that it services the pipeline industry. I purchased 200 shares at $28.94. With almost $2B in annual sales SCL is a world leader in anti-corrosion and insulated pipeline coatings with 25% market share. It also supplies the pipeline industry with numerous other products, including flexible composite pipe. While energy pipelines are SCLs main customer base, water and wastewater industries are also key customers. In addition, SCL provides inspection services for existing pipeline infrastructure and, somewhat unrelated, various cable products to the petrochemical, power generation and other industries. Once again, while energy is a key customer, SCL isn't solely reliant on the price of oil and gas to drive its business. With safety becoming increasingly important and aging existing pipeline infrastructure (50% of US pipelines were built over 45 years ago), SCL has the ability to grow regardless of oil and gas prices. Like RUS, SCL has a habit of picking up about one new company per year to help it grow. SCL has a dividend yield of 2.1%, earnings yield of 2.5% (although expectations are for

6.2% in 2015), cash flow yield of 6.7%, ROE of 4.6% and price times book of 1.7x. I originally purchased SCL for $39.85 in January 2014 and enjoyed a nice rally to $60.00 prior to its recent halving. This provided the opportunity to pick up these extra shares and add it into the newsletter account.

Hope you enjoyed reading the second issue on options. The January 1ˢᵗ issue will be sent about the 4ᵗʰ or 5ᵗʰ to allow time for compilation of year-end numbers. Until then, **have fun with your investments**.

December 9, 2015 Update

Hope all is well. If you have not yet made your RRSP contribution for the year, it might be a good time to do so.

This morning I purchased for our RRSP, Pembina Pipeline Corp. (ticker PPL) at $29.17. I personally used all accumulated dividends to make the purchase but for the purposes of our RRSP model portfolio will add $3000 to the model and use accumulated dividends to add 200 shares of PPL at $29.17.

While PPL has dropped from over $50 in mid-2014 to its current level, it is still not cheap from a valuation perspective. It has an earnings yield of just 3.3%, cash flow yield of 5.6%, price times book of 1.8x and ROE of just 3.2%. However, it has a dividend yield of 6.3%, and while on the smaller side with $4.7B in sales, it has been one of the more rapidly growing pipeline companies. It also has low debt relative to other pipe companies. It is the kind of company I like for an RRSP, that being one that provides steady and growing dividend income, having increased them by 75% over the past 10 years. All the pipeline companies have been hurt by the current oil and gas malaise, providing an opportunity to add a good company at much more reasonable valuation. PPL has minimal exposure to actual commodity prices, providing services largely on a fee basis. PPL's low debt level makes it highly unlikely to cut the dividend, and more likely to continue with the dividend growth focus. The company could also take advantage of the current environment to buy something themselves.

Other comment: For those watching the news in regards to the OPEC meeting last week, the announcement that OPEC will not be following any production quotas sent oil into another tailspin. While it is difficult to predict where this will end up, in my opinion we are "much closer to the bottom, than to the top," so picking away at some good companies that will likely survive, like PPL, makes sense to me. In reality none of the OPEC countries were following production quotas, so it seems a little like a non-announcement in that they are going to do what they have been doing over the past year anyway.

Looking Back: Geez, the Canadian market is in the grips of a grizzly BEAR, the US market isn't much better and I had a very busy month buying new positions and using leverage to boot. What's with that? THAT is how we enjoy market volatility and take advantage to build positions at reasonable valuations.

ISSUE #20: JANUARY 5, 2016

"Everybody" Is Often Wrong

Happy New Year. Hope everyone had a wonderful holiday season and is ready for another year of fun-filled investment excitement.

2015 was an interesting year with lots of ups and downs but in the end, the US market was relatively unchanged with the Canadian market down appreciably. Resources went from bad to worse as we proceeded from a "commodity collapse" to "commodity obliteration." The overall commodity complex is at 1999 levels. General market performance was worse than the indexes indicated as a very narrow group of companies performed very well, elevating overall market performance. Microsoft, Google (now Alphabet), Facebook and Amazon represented 4% towards the S&P returns. Without them it would have been down 4% rather than breakeven.

What does 2016 have in store for us?

In the October 3rd issue (Issue #17), I referred to market sentiment and mentioned elaborating in a future issue. As the holiday season coincides with prediction season, this seems like an appropriate issue to elaborate. The financial press is full of expert opinion on what will happen in 2016. A long time ago I coined the phrase "Everybody is often wrong" to succinctly express my thoughts on market sentiment and predictive powers.

Let's take a look at how last year's predictions worked out. The following numbers came from a recent *Globe Investor* article. A year ago Canadian bank economists' forecasts for the 2015 year-end value of the Canadian dollar ranged from .828 to .855. That was the range, meaning the closest prediction was off by 15% and the worst by 18%. Please note not just how wrong those predictions were, but also how tight together the forecasts were. Canadian GDP had a forecasted range from 2.2% to 2.7%, and the actual current estimate is 1.25%. The forecasts were out by 50%! The forecasted range for the TSX composite was 15,600 to 16,200, such that the best forecaster was out by 17%. This best forecaster predicted the market would go up by 6.6%, whereas it went down by 11.1% (price not total return). To be fair the average forecast was +8.7%, so the forecast was very accurate on the magnitude of the change, just completely wrong on the direction!

As mentioned before, most forecasts will actually predict a continuation of the recent trend. Interestingly the Canadian dollar ended 2014 at .848, such that the forecasts for 2015 were almost the same. The 2014 Canadian GDP growth was 2.4%, such that the 2015 predictions ranged close to this number and the TSX closed out 2014 at 14,632 and was up 7.4% in 2014. Was it a coincidence that the average of the forecasters predicted it to go up by a very similar 8.7% in 2015? This tendency to forecast the recent trend is underlined by a quote from another recent article in regards to 2016: "Next year is going to be challenging, too, because the same fundamental headwinds are in place."

Why do the forecasters cluster so closely together? My speculative guess is that, like mutual fund managers, nobody gets ridiculed or fired if they make a sane forecast similar to others, but they do get ridiculed and possibly fired if they go out on a limb and get it wrong. Yet, like growing crops, I can almost guarantee you that **next year will be different.** I just don't know exactly how and nobody really does. Interestingly, those same bank forecasters have 2016 GDP forecasted growth ranging from 1.6% to 2.2%, the dollar from .714 to .738 and the TSX from 13,750 to 15,300. Thus they have a slight recovery in GDP, the dollar exactly where it currently stands and a modest recovery for the TSX back to 2014 levels.

Market sentiment is the general orientation of market participants, economists, newsletter writers, fund managers, etc. An individual's prediction of where the market is going gives their market orientation, which falls into one of three categories: bullish, bearish or unsure. One financial magazine I subscribe to regularly reports the percentage of advisers in each category. Given that the market goes up more than it goes down, the bullish category is usually higher than bearish with a 2:1 bull to bear ratio being quite normal. It is, however, usually a very positive sign when there are more bears than bulls and usually a very negative sign when the per cent of bulls is 55-60% and the number of bears is around 20% (i.e. a bull to bear ratio of 3:1). Huh! Why is it a positive sign when the bears outnumber the bulls and negative when the bulls are 3:1 over the bears? Well, that's because **"Everybody is often wrong."** When everybody is doing something...it is generally best to run the other way. And as I hope you will see below, that's the only logical way the market can work.

What makes the market or a stock go up? Stocks are just like any other commodity and when there are more or more aggressive buyers than sellers, they will go up.

What makes the market or a stock go down? Simply more or more aggressive sellers than buyers. *(Note: The reason for writing "more or more aggressive" is that one could argue that for every trade there must be both a buyer and a seller; therefore, there can't be more of one than the other. However, at the end of the day there could be buyers or sellers who do not get filled. An aggressive seller would go "at the market," whereas the other party may simply bid at a price below the market and wait to see if the order gets filled).*

So you see it can't be any other way. When bulls outnumber bears by a big margin, there are more and more aggressive buyers than sellers pushing the market up but as soon as a few change their minds, the market starts going the opposite direction. This causes more people to change their mind, often resulting in a crescendo and precipitous drop creating a market low, at which point there will be more bears than bulls causing the process to reverse. This is only logical as someone predicting the market to rise would be recommending buying, and those predicting the market to fall would be recommending selling. It would be very unusual for someone to recommend the following to clients, "I think the market will rise, so we should sell." This is why, in the markets, "everybody" must often be wrong.

Market sentiment is not an exact science (Is anything?), so it is just a guideline. The one possibility is for the percentage of bulls or bears to stay high or low for extended periods of time. This can keep the market moving in the same direction for extended periods. In the 2008/09 bear, when the bears outnumbered bulls, I thought we were close to the bottom, but that unusual scenario lasted (as I recall) six to nine months, making the low period excruciatingly low and for a long time.

How does this ratio impact what I do? Given that I am not prone to making wholesale herky-jerky changes, and given the inexactness of the science, I just tend to be a little cautious buying when the bulls are 55-60% and try to get more enthused when bears outnumber bulls. Generally, I just keep plodding along trying to pick up decent companies at reasonable valuations. In any market there are usually some undervalued companies and some overvalued ones. When the market is really high, there are a lot more overvalued than undervalued and when it is low, there are more undervalued than overvalued, but there are always some of each. Given the difficulty (almost impossibility) of predicting when a market will change direction and given that the market is more up than down, I tend to stay fairly fully invested at all times.

Test question: Given 1) that the Canadian market had been in a downward direction for a year and a half, and the US market has been flat for a year and 2) my comment above that most of us humans will predict the same as the recent trend, what percentage of advisers do you think are currently bullish, bearish or unsure? *(Answer on next page.)*

Given the folly of predictions, why do so many try? Not sure but possibly one of our frailties is the delusion that we can. The other is that it helps newsletter writers and financial advisers, etc., sell their services if they can actually convince their audience of an ability to foresee future market direction. There is nothing too wrong with trying to predict, just with placing big bets on those predictions, thus, here is my New Year's rendition of fearless predictions:

Fearless Prediction #1: The vast majority of financial predictions you read at this time of year will be wrong. Confidence level of prediction: high.

Fearless Prediction #2: After being flat for over a year, in 2016 the US market will pick a direction. My best guess is the direction will be up with a magnitude of 20-25%. Confidence level of prediction: low. Please refer to Fearless Prediction #1, but see explanation below.

Fearless Prediction #3: In either 2016 or 2017, or at latest in 2018, the Canadian market will outperform the US market. Confidence level: fairly high, but once again please refer to Prediction #1.

I believe I have explained the rationale for Fearless Prediction #1, so here are explanations for #2 and #3.

US market direction: Looking at 90 years of S&P total return data, I was curious what happened in the past after a flat year, which I defined as plus or minus 5.0% or less. Here are the very interesting results:

Returns After a FLAT Year?

Year	% Total Return	Following Year	% Total Return
1925	0.0%	1926	11.0%
1934	-2.3%	1935	47.2%
1939	-0.9%	1940	-10.1%
1953	-1.1%	1954	52.4%
1960	0.5%	1961	26.8%
1970	3.9%	1971	14.3%
1981	-4.9%	1982	21.6%
1990	-3.1%	1991	30.5%
1994	1.3%	1995	37.6%
2005	4.9%	2006	15.8%
2011	2.1%	2012	16.0%
2015	1.4%	2016	???
Average			**23.9%**

There is only one case where a flat year led to a negative year, which was 1939/1940. I think we could all agree there was a very scary geopolitical situation going on at that time, with the big surprise being how little the market was down at the onset of WW2. Today's situation in Ukraine and with ISIS is concerning but not of the same magnitude. It's not just that the year following a flat year was up in all other cases, but the magnitude of the change was dramatic with an average of 23.9%, hence my 20-25% prediction. Current market sentiment, while not extreme in either direction, is a little on the bearish side with 36.7% bull, 29.6% bear and 33.7% unsure, which is a positive sign for the market. Congratulations if you were in the ballpark with your guess. These sentiment numbers make sense as a long period of ambivalent market direction combined with the preponderance of people to predict the recent past, leads to an ambivalent market forecast. Adding to my more optimistic than usual sentiment is the market normally goes up for a couple years after the initial US Federal Reserve rate hike in the economic cycle, which occurred in December. That said, please be careful with overenthusiasm as anything can happen.

Canadian vs. US market: The 2015 Canadian market has been described as "vomitous," which is a new word to me. There are only two markets in the developed world that did worse than Canada in 2015: Singapore and Greece. Yipee...we beat the Greeks! The updated table on page 148 illustrates the US and Canadian markets' total return, as well as our portfolios' performance. For now please look at the Canadian and US total return numbers year by year. The shading indicates which market was better for the year. You can see that prior to 2004, leadership alternated back and forth but for seven years, from 2004 to 2010, the Canadian market outperformed the US. This reversed and for the past five years the US market has been ahead each year. Interestingly for the seven year period from 2004 to 2010, the Canadian market was up from 8241 to 13530 or 64.2% (these numbers do not include dividends) and the US S&P 500 went from 1112 to 1257 or 13.0%, meaning over those seven years the Canadian market outperformed the US market by 51.2%. In the five years from 2011 through 2015, the US market has gone from 1257 to 2043, or 62.5% (Is it coincidence that it is so close to the Canadian performance the previous 7 years of 64.2%?) and the Canadian market has gone from 13,530 to 13,010, or a decline of 3.8%, such that in these five most recent years the US market has outperformed the Canadian market by 66.3%. Even though the time of US outperformance to date is two years less, the magnitude of the outperformance is already greater. I think it's time for another switcheroo. As it is impossible to predict when, I've suggested it will happen sometime in the next three years but feel it will be sooner than later.

On a more depressing note, the Canadian market is now at the same place as it was at some point in 2013, 2011, 2010, 2008, 2007, 2006 and just 15% above its peak in 2000. Dividends have been practically the only return. The US market has done better lately but is still just 32% above its 2000 peak or a tepid 2% per year price gain. Granted, both markets were significantly overvalued in 2000 at the end of a very long bull run. Is it any wonder that the general sentiment is that we investors must content ourselves with very modest market returns? Or is this merely once again a prediction based on the last fifteen years being tepid? In the fifteen years prior (1984 to 1999), the Canadian market was up 475% and the US by a whopping 900%. I would suggest that after long periods of strong performance come long periods of mediocre performance, and after long periods of mediocre performance come long periods of strong performance.

Canadian tilt: A year ago I mentioned tilting slightly back to Canada after then four years of US outperformance and with a declining Canadian dollar. It wasn't that the change in leadership was imminent, just that I wanted to prepare for its eventuality. If I could predict when I would make more dramatic changes, but I can't, so I won't. In our personal RRSPs through 2015, we sold some US and purchased just Canadian, but at the end of the year still have about 57% US, 38% CAD and 5% other foreign, down just 2% in the US and up just 2% in Canada. This is largely due to the declining dollar and the better US performance. The changes made were a short-term drag on our performance, but I will continue to tilt to Canadian in 2016. One thing to keep in mind is that for a long period of time while building heavy US positions, I was also sacrificing short-term performance due to the perpetually increasing value of the Canadian dollar. Those short-term sacrifices paid off nicely over the past three years with US outperformance and the decline of the Canadian dollar.

The following chart illustrates many of the characteristics of market performance. Please reference Issue #8, January 5th, 2015, for complete description. Dark grey shading represents years we outperformed the market.

Total Return by Year: Market			RRSPs		TFSAs		TFSA	RRSP
US S&P 500	Canadian TSX	US-CdnAvg.	Herman	Lillian	Herman	Lillian	Model	Model
CAGR								
9.1%	9.2%	9.2%	11.4%	*9.1%	**17.6%	**14.4%		
2015								
1.4%	-8.3%	-3.5%	3.3%	0.0%	2.9%	-6.1%	-5.3%	****-2.9%
2014								
13.7%	10.6%	12.2%	13.7%	22.9%	1.7%	-0.5%	***-13.6%	
2013								
32.4%	11.5%	22.0%	26.9%	31.8%	23.0%	33.1%		
2012								
16.0%	8.2%	12.1%	10.2%	10.9%	22.2%	22.9%		
2011								
2.1%	-8.7%	-3.3%	-2.2%	2.9%	-4.2%	1.4%		
2010								
15.1%	17.6%	16.4%	12.9%	8.5%	20.2%	21.1%		
2009								
26.5%	35.9%	31.2%	15.4%	14.7%	71.4%	36.1%		
2008								
-37.0%	-33.0%	-35.0%	-27.7%	-17.2%				
2007								
5.5%	9.2%	7.4%	-1.9%	-7.6%				
2006								
15.8%	17.9%	16.9%	21.2%	18.0%				
2005								
4.9%	25.6%	15.3%	26.1%	17.5%				
2004								
10.9%	13.8%	12.4%	14.9%	12.2%				
2003								
28.7%	27.1%	27.9%	22.6%	15.1%				
2002								
-22.1%	-13.7%	-17.9%	-3.4%	-7.5%				
2001								
-11.8%	-15.1%	-13.5%	4.2%	5.0%				
2000								
-9.1%	9.3%	0.1%	18.1%	21.0%				
1999								
21.0%	45.8%	33.4%	42.2%	10.3%				
1998								
28.6%	1.2%	14.9%	-10.5%	-2.3%				
1997								
33.3%	18.3%	25.8%	12.2%	13.7%				
1996								
22.9%	29.9%	26.4%	27.0%	26.8%				
1995								
37.5%	15.8%	26.7%	9.7%					
1994								
1.3%	3.4%	2.4%	19.3%					
1993								
10.0%	23.4%	16.7%	31.6%					

Notes:

*The market and my RRSP CAGR returns are twenty-three years, whereas Lillian's RRSP is just twenty years. The average US/Canadian market CAGR for the equivalent twenty years is 8.5%, for a 0.6% outperformance in Lillian's RRSP.

**The TFSAs are seven years old. As we do not have any US stocks in these portfolios, we are using just the Canadian market as a benchmark. The appropriate seven-year TSX CAGR is 8.6%, such that both our TFSAs are tracking well ahead of the benchmark, although by less of a margin than a year ago.

***I was surprised the model TFSA actually did better than the Canadian market in 2015 (-5.3 vs. -8.3). The real issue with this model was the last six months of 2014, where it was -13.6% vs. a market decline of -3.4% over the same time period. The average starting date for the model TFSA was July 1st, 2014.

****The average starting date for the RRSP model was very close to January 1st, 2015, so for simplicity I will consider it to have had a full year of performance. With a nice recovery in the fourth quarter, it was marginally ahead of the benchmark, down 2.9% vs. down 3.5%.

Now let's look at how each portfolio performed in detail:

TFSA Model Portfolio

Company	Ticker	Date Added	# Shares	Price Added	Cost In CAD	Current Value in CAD	Share Price Change	Previous Total Dividends to Date	Oct 2015 Dividends	Nov 2015 Dividends	Dec 2015 Dividends	New Total Divdends to Date	Total Return
International													
Ensco PLC	ESV	May 30/14	100	$52.66	$5,750	$2,124	$(3,626)	$304.20			$20.70	$324.90	-57.4%
Glaxo Smithkline	GSK	May 30/14	100	$53.94	$5,890	$5,568	$(322)	$305.93	$76.05			$381.98	1.0%
Ship Finance Int.	SFL	May 30/14	180	$18.52	$3,644	$4,116	$472	$541.52			$111.78	$653.30	30.9%
Seadrill	SDRL	July 25/14	130	$37.49	$5,312	$608	$(4,704)	$140.46				$140.46	-85.9%
HSBC Holdings PLC	HSBC	July 25/14	100	$52.82	$5,757	$5,447	$(310)	$301.79	$66.00		$69.00	$436.79	2.2%
Vodaphone	VOD	July 25/14	150	$34.16	$5,585	$6,678	$1,093	$329.22				$329.22	25.5%
Unilever PLC	UL	Jan 2/15	100	$40.05	$4,736	$5,951	$1,215	$115.38			$46.71	$162.09	29.1%
Diagio PLC	DEO	Jan 2/15	30	$112.73	$4,001	$4,515	$514	$47.88	$82.70			$130.58	16.1%
BHP Billiton Ltd	BHP	Jan 2/15	65	$47.27	$3,636	$2,311	$(1,325)	$475.46				$475.46	-23.4%
South32 Ltd.	SOUHY	May30/15	26	$8.34	$267	$137	$(130)	$ -				$ -	-48.6%
Internatonal Subtotal					$44,578	$37,455	$(7,123)	$2,561.84				$3,034.78	-9.2%
Canadian													
TD Bank	TD	May 30/14	100	$53.76	$5,386	$5,424	$38	$243.00	$51.00			$294.00	6.2%
Innvest REIT	INN.UN	May 30/14	210	$5.16	$1,094	$1,077	$(17)	$104.85	$6.99	$6.99	$6.99	$125.82	9.9%
Rogers Communications	RCI.B	May 30/14	100	$43.82	$4,392	$4,772	$380	$233.25	$48.00			$281.25	15.1%
Teck Reources Ltd	TCK.B	May 30/14	200	$24.17	$4,844	$1,068	$(3,776)	$210.00				$210.00	-73.4%
ATCO	ACO.X	July 25/14	100	$50.56	$5,066	$3,570	$(1,496)	$117.25			$10.00	$127.25	-26.7%
Husky Energy	HSE	July 25/14	150	$33.72	$5,068	$2,147	$(2,921)	$180.00	$45.00			$225.00	-53.2%
Sunlife Financial	SLF	July 25/14	100	$41.40	$4,150	$4,315	$165	$184.00			$24.75	$208.75	9.3%
Cdn. Western Bank	CWB	May 19/15	170	$28.99	$4,938	$3,975	$(963)	$74.80			$39.00	$113.80	-18.0%
Jean Coutu	PJC.A	May 19/15	200	$23.23	$4,656	$3,582	$(1,074)	$22.00			$22.00	$44.00	-22.1%
Canadian Subtotal					$39,594	$29,930	$(9,664)	$1,369.15				$1,629.87	-20.3%
Total Cdn and Int					$84,172	$67,385	$(16,787)	$3,930.99				$4,664.65	
Cash						$2,493							
Total						$69,878							-14.8%

Cost in CAD total of $84,172 is derived from $82,000 investment plus $2172 of reinvested dividends, leaving $2493 of cash from unspent dividends

Note: The current conversion used in the TFSA and RRSP charts was 1.38 CAD per USD.

The TFSA continues to suffer from heavy resource exposure, although now is not the time to abandon ship. Even some of the non-resource companies like GSK, HSBC and PJC.A have struggled. However, what goes around comes around. Most of these companies are Canadian or British, and the UK market was down 4.9% in 2015.

The RRSP model, on the next page, had a nice recovery in the fourth quarter and is down just 2.9%. It is certainly not without its blemishes. In the last update on October 1st, I commented on expecting a positive fourth quarter. In fact the S & P was up 6.4%, but the TSX was down 2.6% in the fourth quarter. Both US outperformance and dollar exchange helped the model RRSP portfolio. Neither market experienced a Santa Claus rally with both markets down in December. The RRSP model is not nearly as heavily US-based as our own, as we stopped integrating US companies when the dollar dropped below 80 cents. HPT spun off some of its ownership in RMR Group, thus the model has two shares of RMR. I'm not a big fan of these little spin-offs as it leaves small shareholders with stranded, very small positions. With all three portfolios the per cent total return is calculated by taking portfolio value gains and dividing into the time weighted total dollars invested in the portfolio, all converted to Canadian currency. Again, please see Issue #8 for a full explanation of calculating annual returns.

RRSP Model Portfolio

Company	Ticker	Date Added	# Shares	Price Added	Cost In CAD	Current Value in CAD	Share Price Change	Previous Dividends to Date	October Dividends	November Dividends	December Dividends	New Dividends to Date	Total Return
US Companies													
Verizon	VZ	Sept 30/14	100	$ 49.99	$ 5,609	$ 6,378	$ 769	$ 267.21		$ 73.42		$ 340.63	19.8%
HCP Inc	HCP	Sept 30/14	100	$ 39.71	$ 4,458	$ 5,277	$ 819	$ 274.85		$ 75.00		$ 349.85	26.2%
Hospitality Prop. Trust	HPT	Sept 30/14	150	$ 26.85	$ 4,521	$ 5,413	$ 892	$ 362.98		$ 99.23	$ 52.63	$ 514.84	31.1%
RMR Group	RMR	Dec 18/15	2	$ 16.95	$ 47	$ 40	$ (7)	$ -				$ -	-14.5%
United Technologies	UTX	Oct 31/14	50	$ 107.00	$ 6,002	$ 6,629	$ 627	$ 155.15			$ 43.26	$ 198.41	13.8%
Johnson and Johnson	JNJ	Oct 31/14	50	$ 107.78	$ 6,045	$ 7,088	$ 1,043	$ 179.37			$ 50.23	$ 229.60	21.1%
Freeport-McMoRan	FCX	Nov 30/14	150	$ 26.85	$ 4,601	$ 1,401	$ (3,200)	$ 99.15		$ 9.75		$ 108.90	-67.2%
Chevron	CVX	Nov 30/14	50	$ 108.87	$ 6,216	$ 6,207	$ (9)	$ 203.33			$ 72.33	$ 275.66	4.3%
Exelon	EXC	Nov 30/14	150	$ 36.17	$ 6,195	$ 5,748	$ (447)	$ 176.73			$ 62.87	$ 239.60	-3.3%
General Electric	GE	Jan 27/15	200	$ 24.38	$ 6,056	$ 8,597	$ 2,541	$ 115.09	$ 60.19			$ 175.28	44.9%
Praxair	PX	Feb 28/15	25	$ 127.90	$ 4,007	$ 3,533	$ (474)	$ 67.88			$ 24.45	$ 92.33	-9.5%
Qualcomm	QCOM	Feb 28/15	50	$ 72.51	$ 4,542	$ 3,449	$ (1,093)	$ 87.50			$ 33.33	$ 120.83	-21.4%
US Subtotal					$ 58,299	$ 59,760	$ 1,461	$ 1,989.24				$ 2,645.93	7.0%
Canadian Companies													
Bank of Nova Scotia	BNS	Sept 30/14	100	$ 69.27	$ 6,937	$ 5,597	$ (1,340)	$ 268.00	$ 70.00			$ 338.00	-14.4%
Power Corp	POW	Sept 30/14	200	$ 31.08	$ 6,226	$ 5,788	$ (438)	$ 240.52			$ 62.25	$ 302.77	-2.2%
Capital Power	CPX	Oct 31/14	200	$ 25.58	$ 5,126	$ 3,554	$ (1,572)	$ 204.00	$ 73.00			$ 277.00	-25.3%
Mullen Group Ltd.	MTL	Nov 20/14	250	$ 22.12	$ 5,540	$ 3,503	$ (2,037)	$ 250.00	$ 25.00	$ 25.00	$ 25.00	$ 325.00	-30.9%
Royal Bank	RY	Jan 27/15	100	$ 75.12	$ 7,522	$ 7,415	$ (107)	$ 154.00		$ 79.00		$ 233.00	1.7%
TransCanada Pipeline	TRP	Jan 27/15	100	$ 55.59	$ 5,609	$ 4,515	$ (1,094)	$ 104.00	$ 52.00			$ 156.00	-16.7%
Bell Canada	BCE	Feb 28/15	100	$ 54.71	$ 5,481	$ 5,346	$ (135)	$ 130.00	$ 65.00			$ 195.00	1.1%
Brookfield Asset Mgmt	BAM.A	Feb 28/15	150	$ 45.23	$ 6,795	$ 6,548	$ (247)	$ 46.12			$ 24.00	$ 70.12	-2.6%
Pason Systems	PSI	Mar 3/15	200	$ 18.48	$ 3,706	$ 3,878	$ 172	$ 102.00			$ 34.00	$ 136.00	8.3%
Wajax Corp	WJX	Mar 3/15	150	$ 24.31	$ 3,657	$ 2,519	$ (1,138)	$ 50.00	$ 37.50			$ 87.50	-28.7%
Home Capital Group	HCG	Mar3May29/15	150	$ 43.11	$ 6,475	$ 4,038	$ (2,437)	$ 55.00			$ 33.00	$ 88.00	-36.3%
AutoCanada	ACQ	Apr 4/15	150	$ 34.15	$ 5,133	$ 3,623	$ (1,510)	$ 75.00			$ 37.50	$ 112.50	-27.2%
Cogeco Inc.	CGO	May 29/15	100	$ 53.60	$ 5,370	$ 5,125	$ (245)	$ 25.50		$ 29.50		$ 55.00	-3.5%
Pembina Pipeline	PPL	Dec 9/15	200	$ 29.17	$ 5,844	$ 6,030	$ 186	$ -				$ -	3.2%
Cdn Subtotal					$ 79,421	$ 67,479	$ (11,942)	$ 1,704.14				$ 2,375.89	-12.0%
Dividends from Sold Cos								$ 24.40				$ 24.40	
Total Cdn and US					$ 137,720	$ 127,239	$ (10,481)	$ 3,717.78				$ 5,046.22	
Cash						$ 482							
Portfolio Value						$ 127,721							-2.9%

Cost in CAD total of $137,720 is derived from $131,500 invested, $1656 capital gains, plus $4564 of reinvested dividends, leaving $482 of cash from unspent dividends.

Sales to Date	Ticker	Date Added	# Shares	Price	Exchange	Cost In CAD	Sold	Sold Price	Proceeds	Dividends	Profit	% Profit
Constellation Software	CSU	Oct 31/14	10	$ 317.50		$ 3,185	Apr 14/15	$ 485.07	$ 4,841	$ 24.40	$ 1,679	52.7

The last portfolio below is our new non-registered account that I have set up and is a real portfolio rather than the TFSA and RRSP models that are based on our own portfolios. It makes it a little easier for tracking purposes. It also had a nice recovery in the fourth quarter and is now almost breakeven. As it is an actual account, the US portion is all shown in US dollars with the bottom line "Portfolio Value" being the value in CAD pulled from my Internet brokerage website.

Non-Registered Margin Portfolio

Company	Ticker	Date Added	# Shares	Price Added	Cost In USD	Current Value in USD	Share Price Change	Previous Dividends to Date	October Dividends	November Dividends	December Dividends	New Dividends to Date	Total Return
US Dollar Purchases													
iShares MSCI Emerging	EEM	06-Jul-15	100	$ 38.62	$ 3,872	$ 3,219	$ (653)	$ -			$ 42.57	$ 42.57	-15.8%
Vanguard Europe ETF	VGK	06-Jul-15	100	$ 52.91	$ 5,301	$ 4,988	$ (313)	$ -	$ 19.12		$ 17.17	$ 36.29	-5.2%
First Trust Nat GAS	FCG	06-Jul-15	500	$ 8.57	$ 4,297	$ 2,230	$ (2,067)	$ 14.92			$ 15.51	$ 30.43	-47.4%
Parker Hannifin	PH	24-Jul-15	50	$ 110.84	$ 5,552	$ 4,849	$ (703)	$ 26.77			$ 26.77	$ 53.54	-11.7%
iShares Silver Trust	SLV	31-Aug-15	200	$ 13.79	$ 2,767	$ 2,638	$ (129)	$ -				$ -	-4.7%
Market Vector Gold	GDX	31-Aug-15	200	$ 13.71	$ 2,751	$ 2,744	$ (7)	$ -			$ 19.72	$ 19.72	0.5%
Berkshire Hathaway	BRK.B	Aug-Nov/15	65	$ 135.28	$ 8,823	$ 8,583	$ (240)	$ -				$ -	-2.7%
Union Pacific	UNP	31-Aug-15	50	$ 86.13	$ 4,316	$ 3,910	$ (406)	$ -			$ 23.37	$ 23.37	-8.9%
ITC Holdings	ITC	02-Oct-15	100	$ 32.10	$ 3,220	$ 3,925	$ 705	$ -			$ 15.94	$ 15.94	22.4%
US Options													
American Express	AXP	30-Oct-15	1 Put	$ 73.60	$ (762)	$ (945)	$ (183)						-24.1%
Walmart	WMT	30-Oct-15	1 Put	$ 57.90	$ (689)	$ (445)	$ 244						35.4%
Emerson Electric	EMR	30-Oct-15	1 Put	$ 47.10	$ (740)	$ (640)	$ 100						13.5%
IBM	IBM	25-Nov-15	1 Put	$ 137.82	$ (1,859)	$ (1,790)	$ 69						3.7%
CVS Health Corp	CVS	25-Nov-15	1 Put	$ 93.90	$ (1,089)	$ (870)	$ 219						20.1%
A T & T	T	25-Nov-15	1 Call	$ 33.72	$ 342	$ 374	$ 32						9.4%
US Subtotal					$ 36,102	$ 32,770	$ (3,332)	$ 41.69				$ 221.86	
Cash						$ 217							
Total USD						$ 32,987							-8.6%
Canadian Companies					CAD	CAD							
Bank of Montreal	BMO	03-Jul-15	100	$ 74.21	$ 7,431	$ 7,808	$ 377	82			$ 82.00	$ 164.00	7.3%
CGI Group	GIB.A	23-Jul-15	100	$ 50.90	$ 5,100	$ 5,540	$ 440	$ -				$ -	8.6%
Crescent Point Energy	CPG	23-Jul-15	200	$ 20.33	$ 4,076	$ 3,224	$ (852)	$ 66.00	$ 20.00	$ 20.00	$ 20.00	$ 126.00	-17.8%
Telus	T	31-Aug-15	100	$ 42.83	$ 4,293	$ 3,826	$ (467)	$ -	$ 42.00			$ 42.00	-9.9%
Suncor	SU	31-Aug-15	100	$ 35.78	$ 3,588	$ 3,572	$ (16)	$ 29.00			$ 29.00	$ 58.00	1.2%
Stantec Inc.	STN	29-Sep-15	200	$ 29.30	$ 5,870	$ 6,864	$ 994	$ -				$ -	16.9%
Potash Corp	POT	02-Oct-15	100	$ 26.82	$ 2,692	$ 2,370	$ (322)	$ -		$ 49.12		$ 49.12	-10.1%
ShawCor	SCL	26-Nov-15	200	$ 28.94	$ 5,798	$ 5,614	$ (184)	$ -				$ -	-3.2%
Russel Metals	RUS	26-Nov-15	200	$ 18.15	$ 3,640	$ 3,214	$ (426)	$ -				$ -	-11.7%
Fortis Inc.	FTS	26-Nov-15	100	$ 36.67	$ 3,677	$ 3,741	$ 64	$ -				$ -	1.7%
Cdn Subtotal					$ 46,165	$ 45,773	$ (392)	$ 177.00				$ 439.12	
Cash						$ 318							
Total CAD						$ 46,091							
TotalPortfolio Value in CAD						$ 91,138							-0.2%
Deposits in CAD Value						$ 92,857							-1.9%

Closing Comments

The optimism I expressed early in the newsletter evaporated somewhat as I worked through the portfolios. This is not a bad thing as over exuberance can be fatal to one's financial health. There will always be challenges and unforeseen events. We should not, however, let these distract us from our long-term wealth-building strategies. 2015 was difficult and the most volatile year since 2008. That is exactly the kind of market that shakes people out, accepting permanent losses. One of the purposes of the newsletter is to help subscribers see through the short-term gyrations and focus on longer-term goals. While it will not happen every year, if we continue to meet or beat the market overall, in time the market will take care of us. The past year was particularly tough if just starting out, but also presented great learning opportunities. There will be both challenges and good times ahead. My best wishes for everyone's success, investing and otherwise, in 2016.

ISSUE #20 SUPPLEMENT: JANUARY 6, 2016

2016 TFSA Additions

I always like to start the new year with TFSA additions to reap the benefits of the tax-free aspect as long as possible. For 2016 we are each allowed to add $5500, such that I have added $11,000 to the model portfolio. Following are two new additions to the portfolio. I focused on stability with growth, while staying in Canada to eliminate the need for currency conversion.

CI Financial (CIX): I purchased 200 shares at $30.47. As the saying goes, "Buy the mutual fund company, not the mutual fund." CIX is both a mutual fund and a wealth management company, managing individual portfolios. It is one of the few independent, publicly traded wealth management companies in Canada with almost $2B in annual sales. I may have been a little hard on mutual funds in the past. They are appropriate for many smaller, less-educated investors who don't want to take responsibility themselves. CIX has a great record of fund performance, which has helped it continually grow assets under management and generates the fees collected. The wealth management side is focused on wealthier Canadians who want individual attention. Every two to three years it seems to pick up a bolt-on acquisition to help growth. CIX is also expanding into ETFs, which is a growing but lower-fee market. Over the past 10 years, which have not been great equity years, CIX has grown sales and earnings/share by 2x. It was structured as an investment trust, but since converting to a corporation in about 2009, it has grown its dividend from 5 cents monthly to 11 cents monthly, currently yielding 4.3%. It has an earnings yield of 6.7%, cash flow yield of 6.9%, price times book of 4.5x, but an enviable ROE of 30.1%. CIX traded as high as $36.00 in 2014 and 2015.

AltaGas (ALA): I purchased 200 shares at $30.96. ALA is a natural gas-focused utility and pipeline company. Many utilities have one main focus, pipelines or electrical generation or distribution, but ALA is diversified with about one-third of earnings from each of its three sectors, with the main theme being natural gas. The three sectors are: 1) Natural gas processing, storage and transportation (pipelines), generally referred to as midstream activities, therefore incurring minimal commodity risk; 2) Natural gas retail distribution to residential and commercial clients; and 3) Electric power generation with focus on clean energy from gas and renewables, although still with some coal. It is based in Alberta with operations across Canada and parts of the US, mainly California. Over the past 10 years it has grown sales by 50% with the biggest increase coming in the last three years, currently reaching $2B annually. Its debt level is modest for this type of company at 55%, whereas most others range from 70-80%. This strong balance sheet allows it to pursue growth as it is doing with plans to double its asset base. The earnings per share have not grown with focus on business growth, but operating cash flow, the best measure for infrastructure companies, has doubled in the past 10 years. It cut the dividends in the 2008 recession but has since increased them from 11 cents per month to 16.5 cents, such that its current yield is 6.4% with a 9% annual dividend growth target. It has earnings yield of just 1.8% but cash flow yield of 6.2% and price times book of 1.4x. ALA was trading at over $50.00 in late 2014. It would have been overvalued at that time, but today's price represents decent value.

Canadian Western Bank (CWB): I had enough cash left personally to add 80 shares of CWB at $23.16. The model account only had enough for 50 additional shares, so I will add those as well to use up the cash. As Yogi Berra quipped, "It's really hard to make predictions...especially about the future," but I think these additions will once again reduce the commodity risk in the portfolio and add reliable (at least as reliable as the market has to offer) dividend income. These additions will add about $700/year dividends to the TFSA.

RRSP: This week's, and especially this morning's, headlines put more scares into the market. China was once again in the news with currency devaluation issues and North Korea's reported but not verified successful hydrogen bomb test compounded matters. Oil and the Canadian dollar both tanked again. It can be difficult to brave the current negativity. However, I managed to this morning by also adding 100 shares of **Bank of Nova Scotia (BNS)** to my RRSP at $55.33. I had enough accumulated dividends for this addition but will need to add $5500 to the model RRSP to allow this addition. BNS is trading at valuations last seen in 2008/09 with a dividend yield of 5.1% and earnings yield of over 10%. It was trading at well over $70.00 in 2014, but has been in decline for a year and a half, which is a long period of decline for a Canadian bank. I also intended to add more ATCO (ACO.X) but was a few dollars short, so need a little extra dividend to land in the account before purchasing. I have ACO.X in the TFSA model, so this will not impact the RRSP model, but if you have extra cash I think it represents a good buy at its current price.

On the positive side there was a strong US employment report, but that headline seemed to get pushed aside. I certainly can't promise that the market won't go down further. There are clearly lots of concerns about worldwide growth. However, there also appear to be decent valuations emerging.

Looking Back: Still buying while "everybody" is heading for the hills. Must be crazy, eh?

$1 Lost = $1 Gained

As I write this month's newsletter the market is, at least temporarily, experiencing some relief after a very tumultuous January. Is it just another "relief" rally or the beginning of a true recovery? While it is impossible to know for sure, I will address this question in more detail below.

The gyrations of the recent past, and for that matter the past year and a half, make a good backdrop for the critical message in the title. Psychologists have measured our emotional response to losing money (or for that matter any property) and have found that we feel 2.5 times more pain in a loss than joy in a gain of equal magnitude. In other words, our emotions create an equation: $1.00 lost = $2.50 gained. Said another way, it takes a $2.50 gain to make up for the pain we feel losing a $1.00. Logically we all know that the value of a $1.00 loss is the same as the value of a $1.00 gain. This emotional vs. logical debate is one we will perpetually have in our minds as we pursue investing in stocks. The pain emotion being 2.5 times greater than what is logical is what causes us to "throw in the towel" at market bottoms. Falling markets are created when there are more or more aggressive sellers than buyers, making it fair to assume early January had numerous investors cashing out.

The key message is the more we can train ourselves that the value of a dollar lost is the very same as the value of a dollar gained, the more we will avoid the "throwing in the towel" emotion and the more successful we will be. New investors are more prone to giving up, as they have not yet experienced enough positive positions in their portfolio to offset the 2.5:1 emotions of negative positions. It is easier for a longer-term investor to feel "Well, I might be down 50% on this position, but I'm up 150% on this one, so no big deal." It is especially important for newer investors to fight the 2.5:1 loss emotion, to allow enough time for positive positions to manifest themselves in the portfolio. That said, it is not a bad thing to have a tough start as it can serve to keep one's hubris in check when things go well.

Is this the beginning of a true recovery or just another "relief" rally?

As mentioned many times in the past, it is virtually impossible to predict short-term market gyrations, so I will attempt to provide arguments for both sides:

Negative Side

1. **Recession timing**: Recessions seem to come along every six to 10 years. The last recession was in 2008/09, which is now seven to eight years ago, placing us smack in the middle of the timing where we would expect another one. Canada had a slight technical recession during the first and second quarters of 2015 and it is possible we are in a similar recession right now. Alberta is in a very serious recession but the rest of Canada appears to be growing, although at modest pace. Forty thousand jobs have reportedly been lost in the energy industry. Bear markets and recessions go hand in hand, although the bear market usually bottoms out about halfway through a recession.

2. **The US economy** is still performing well by most measures but not all. Transportation stocks like UNP are down as freight volume is in decline. Manufacturing is also in decline and has been for quite some time. Some of this decline is a result of the dramatic appreciation of the US dollar. Virtually every currency in the world has depreciated relative to the US dollar. This makes US exports more expensive and imports cheaper. Employment on the other hand has still been relatively strong, with the December jobs report well above expectations. The strong US dollar is also negatively impacting US corporate profits as those companies with international sales may have profit growth in local currency but a decline when translated back to USD. Should the US economy succumb to even a minor recession it could have a negative impact on the US stock market, which has been amongst the strongest in the world. New numbers have US fourth quarter GDP growth of just 0.7%, for full-year growth of 2.4%. Not bad, not great.

3. **Comparisons to 2008/09**: It's hard to pick up a newspaper (old school, I know) or read any Internet news site without reading about how today compares to what happened in 2008/09. These comparisons might include declarations like "The worst start to the year ever" or "As bad a start as 2009." The 2008/09 bear had numerous relief rallies along the way before it finally bottomed.

4. **China and resources:** Undoubtedly the slowdown in China has had an impact on resource pricing. While oil is the main headline resource, all have been impacted. The bigger issue, however, is the overinvestment cycle that created supply significantly larger than demand. Oil demand has been growing at a very steady pace but has been outstripped by supply growth. There are grave concerns being expressed should the Chinese economy slow even further. The resource slowdown has had a significant impact on economies like Canada's that rely on commodity exports, including Russia, Brazil, Australia and parts of Africa.

5. **Bankruptcies:** Worldwide corporate defaults almost doubled in 2015 to the highest level since 2008/09 (there is one of those comparisons) with almost half being resource-related. Glencore is the largest commodity trader in the world and its debt level is concerning. Their stock price has collapsed from $12.00 to $2.00. Given their size and reach, they represent potential systemic risk if they default. There is often a high-profile bankruptcy before the bear hibernates, like Dome Petroleum in the '80s, Reichmann's Olympia and York in the '90s, Nortel and Enron in the '00s, and Lehman Bros in 2008. Also troubling is the fiscal situation in Venezuela and especially the large Brazilian economy.

Positive Side

1. **Bear market stats:** The TSX is officially in a bear market as defined by a loss of over 20%. A number of other countries, especially resource-related, are in similar bear market territory. The TSX peaked on September 3rd, 2014, at 15,685 and fell to a low of 11,843 on January 20, 2016. Looking back at all Canadian bear markets since 1955, the average duration was 10.5 months. The current bear at seventeen months is longer than average. The TSX almost hit the September 2014 high again on April 26, 2015, when it reached 15,454. Even if we used this date to define the start of the bear, the duration would be nine months, still close to average. The total decline from September 2014 to January 20th, 2016, was 24.5%. The average decline of the previous nine bears was 31.7%, such that this decline (if it's over, which is not guaranteed) would be smaller than average. The bull markets between these bears lasted on average sixty-seven months with an average price appreciation of 173%. Even if we are not quite through the bear, it is worth hanging on as we should be close to the turning point and rewards on average have been very good after the turning point. Outside Canada the Emerging Market Index is the worst performing with a loss of 35%. The main US markets are in correction territory, defined as a loss of 10-20%, but not officially in a bear. The US small cap Russell 2000 index is, however, in a bear, down about 24%. *(Clarification: Market Capitalization is the size of a company as defined by its total market value: # shares x price/share. Small cap = smaller companies.)*

2. **Oil price:** While oil price and the Canadian market are closely related, the US market is not normally as closely linked to oil as recently. Reduction in the price of oil and other commodities should benefit importing regions such as Europe, India, China, and in the past, the US. The US is now producing more of its own oil so may not receive the same positive impact as before. Areas and sectors of the US economy not linked closely to oil should, however, benefit.

3. **More on oil:** Can someone explain how in 2006-2008 when we were using a mere 82M barrels/day the world was running out of oil, and currently when we are using 15% more or about 95M barrels per day we are swimming in it? The experts in 2006-2008 were clearly wrong and I suspect the experts today are similarly wrong, just in the opposite direction. I have read through a bunch of stats and commentary and believe the truth lies somewhere in the middle of these polar opposites. OPEC and the Saudis still hold the keys, even though they are choosing not to use them. They have recently indicated that if the rest of the world cuts production, they will also cooperate to bring back supply/demand balance. There have been about 40,000 layoffs in Canada's energy sector and probably similar cuts around many other parts of the oil world. There are two-thirds less land drill rigs working today in North America as two

years ago. Unless we believe those 40,000 people and two-thirds of drills were contributing nothing to supply, then eventually North American supply will drop.

4. **Lag time:** There is always a lag time between action and the reaction. There is a lag time between reduced drilling and reduced oil supply. There is a lag time between the US dollar rising relative to the Canadian dollar, and the building of a production plant in Canada to export to the US. There is a lag time between the lower oil price and its benefits showing up in importing nations. Eventually the lag ends and the benefits manifest.

5. **First US interest rate rise:** In December the US Federal Reserve raised interest rates for the first time this economic cycle. Since 1970, the average time from the first rate rise until the market peak has been 3.3 years, with a range of 1.5 to 6.1 years, and the average price appreciation has been 80.6% with a range from 21.3 to 225.1%. While these ranges display huge variations, they have one commonality in that the market went up after the first rate rise. Even if we consider the end of US quantitative easing in October, 2014, as the first rate rise we are still just 1.3 years into the tightening cycle.

6. **The US Dollar** has risen dramatically. Nothing goes up or down forever, and my gut feel is that the US dollar's rise will at least temporarily abate. The rapidity of the US dollar rise and oil's decline has been unnerving for the markets, which prefer slower, more gradual changes.

7. **Comparisons with 2008/09** could actually be positive and illustrate the very negative sentiment that permeates the market today. By the way, after the horrible start in 2009, the US market ended the year up 26.5%, and the TSX ended up 35.9%. Pretty decent considering they dropped 20% in January/February.

8. **Best time to buy in a long time:** And finally, to my simple way of thinking, while I can't predict the future, today represents a better time to buy Canadian stocks than any time in the past five years, and a better time to buy US stocks than any time in almost the past two years. While it is possible we may experience better buying opportunities in the future, given that it's already the best time in a long time, those opportunities are more likely to fade. Maybe "this time is different" and the market will not recover, but probably not. *("This time is different" is considered a dangerous phrase in the investing world.)*

What do we do? As mentioned last month I intend to keep plodding along, building the non-registered account, trying to find what looks like good value. Yes, it would be less stressful and more enjoyable if markets were rising, but that's not the reality of today. Let's try to take advantage of the situation.

Options: In the November 1ˢᵗ and December 1ˢᵗ issues, I covered selling PUTS and buying CALLS. This month I will provide an example of selling a COVERED CALL and have implemented an example. COVERED CALLS are often touted to enhance income from a portfolio. As with all strategies there are positives and negatives. It does provide income, lowers the cost base and provides some downside protection but also limits upside rewards. Selling a COVERED CALL means I own the underlying stock. It is not generally a good idea to sell naked CALLS when there is no ownership of underlying stock. If the stock rises, the seller of a naked CALL has to buy the stock at whatever the current price is if the stock gets CALLED. If, however, we sell a COVERED

CALL for the fee collected, we allow the buyer of the CALL to buy the stock from us at a predetermined price up to a predetermined time in the future. If the stock goes up, we lose on the option but win on the stock.

Crescent Point Energy (CPG): I purchased an additional 200 shares at a cost of $13.24/share. I simultaneously sold two covered CALL contracts that expire on January 20th, 2017, with a strike price of $16.00. I received $1.60 per share selling the CALLS and thus have an effective cost base on the 200 shares of $13.24 - $1.60 = $11.64, plus commissions and fees. If the price appreciates to over $16.00 by next January the purchaser of the CALL will CALL them from me, paying $16.00 at that time, netting me a profit of $16.00/$11.64 = 37.5%. Not bad for a year, if it goes up. In addition I will collect the dividend which is currently set at 12 cents per month or $1.20 for the year. This is an additional return of $1.20/ $11.64 = 10.3% for a total return of 47.8%. Of course CPG may not appreciate to $16.00, in which case I am left with the stock at whatever price it is, the dividend and the $1.60 for selling the CALL. Premiums for selling CALLS are rarely this good, but volatility increases option premiums and energy E & P companies are currently very volatile. The other reason this looks attractive is the high dividend. CPG already cut its dividend and has relatively low debt. It has 30% of its 2016 production hedged at about $80, so I think, but am definitely not sure the dividend is safe for a year.

Selling COVERED CALLS is similar to selling naked PUTS in that it limits upside potential, while reducing downside risk. I have not been a big user of the strategy but it can be a way to reduce losses during market downturns. That would have been a good thing this past year. I don't usually sell COVERED CALLS on my entire position as I don't like losing all the upside potential. In this case I would be very happy with the 47.8% return and still have my original 200 shares if CPG recovers quickly. If CPG goes down or goes broke, I lose $1.60 less than purchasing the shares outright without selling the CALL.

Other Portfolio Additions

I am employing similar strategies as in the past. I don't want to convert any CAD to USD and have actually slowly been converting from USD to CAD in other personal portfolios. For the newsletter portfolio I have added $10,000 CAD funds to the Canadian side and purchased more Canadian stocks. This enhances available margin, which is employed by selling PUTS on the American side, helping build this side as well. If in the future we get PUT some of these stocks, I am hopeful the Canadian currency will be stronger, allowing conversion.

Manulife Financial (MFC): I purchased 300 shares at $18.31. With over $25B in sales MFC is a leading Canada-based insurance and wealth management company. It operates principally in three geographies: Canada, US and Asia. It is the eighth largest life insurer in the world and third largest in North America. It actually derives about one-third of its income from each of the three main geographies serviced. It is targeting 10-12% earnings growth rate over the near future. MFC was severely wounded in the financial crisis but seems to be back on its feet. Insurance is one of the key building blocks of a sound portfolio and we now have three major Canadian insurers in our different portfolios. POW is in the RRSP, SLF in the TFSA and now MFC in the non-registered account. MFC was trading in the $40.00 range prior to the financial crisis and went as low as $10.00 during it. It recovered to the $23-24 range in mid-2015 but has since declined to its current price. It has a dividend yield of 3.7%, earnings yield of 6.9% and price times book of just 1.0x. Its current ROE is a modest 7.3% but it is expected to increase earnings substantially in 2016 to over $2.00/share. Should that occur, its earnings yield and ROE will increase markedly.

Potash Corp (POT): Like most commodities, fertilizer prices are dropping. POT reported earnings this week reflecting this reality but it was still profitable. It earned $1.52 USD (it reports in USD) and expects to earn between $0.90 and $1.20 in 2016. It also cut its dividend to $0.25 USD/quarter. It sold off on the news and was trading at the lowest price since 2006. I picked up another 100 shares at $20.86 adding to the existing position. While profits have come way down it is still a profitable commodity producer, which is a rarity these days. It has a good balance sheet and good cash flow. POT is very likely to survive the downturn and prosper if and when there is a commodity recovery. It is an example of how I often start small with a company but try to build the position over time.

US Side

iShares Russell 2000 ETF (IWM): As mentioned the Russell 2000 is a small cap index of 2000 companies in the US that rank in size from the 1000th to the 3000th. It is more volatile than the more common indices and is down about 24%, the most of any of the US indices. It could still go lower, but in a market rebound generally appreciates faster than the more familiar S&P 500 index. I sold one $100 PUT contract, expiring on January 19, 2018 and received $14.60/share. The price of IWM was about $99.50 when I sold the contract. By selling the contract my effective cost will be $85.40 if I get PUT. This would represent a price 35% below the peak of the index.

Berkshire Hathaway (BRK.B): I used most of the funds from the above PUT sale to purchase another 10 shares of BRK.B at $126.60. BRK.B is an excellent US holding for a non-registered account. It is very blue-chip but does not pay a dividend preferring to invest all cash flows into its own business. Buffett feels that he can make the best return for investors by managing the cash and investing it on their behalf and he has the track record to prove it. If we get a true US bear market there are few better places to be than in BRK.B. Buffett's best work comes during downturns. Berkshire made huge profits in the 2008/09 recession investing in numerous companies at the bottom.

You might also have noticed that there are pretty good dividend payers on the Canadian side but not on the US side of the non-registered account. This is because of tax treatment. We pay full taxes on US dividends similar to interest income but get a dividend tax credit on Canadian company dividends, reducing their tax load. The focus is more on capital gains on the US side. As I conclude the newsletter (three to four days after starting), the market is in true rally mode. What a RELIEF! But once again it is difficult to know whether this is just a relief rally or the beginning of a real move to the upside. Only in time will we know for sure. Stock investing is not unlike many other aspects of life. The past is a known but the future is a little foggy.

Looking Back: The Canadian market promptly went into another tailspin, but did not breach its mid-January low, then rallied again. The US market bottomed out in mid-February. While we do not know these things until well after the fact, the dance was finally on. Comments like "hang on," "close to turning point" and "best time to buy in a long time" hopefully provided motivation, as well as the fact that I kept putting my own money where my mouth was and kept buying up more stocks and selling more PUTS.

ISSUE #22: MARCH 1, 2016

TWO Primal Fears:
#1) The Fear of Losing What We Have
#2) The Fear of Not Getting What We Want

When planning a stock purchase, I experience the above two fears with regularity. While overall it is more pleasant to see the market go up than down, I always hope for a little downdraft when studying a stock to purchase and certainly hope it doesn't go up before being ready to purchase. Thus I experience the fear of not getting the desired price when buying. Concurrently there is the fear of the stock declining immediately after purchase, or worse that it goes down a lot over time, thus experiencing the fear of losing what we have. Those fears are now magnified as I am writing publicly about the process and experiencing the embarrassment of some major collapses on stock selections within the commodity sector. RATS! It will turn around; I just don't know when. There are many casualties on the downside of the commodity super cycle.

The rally at the end of January turned out to be just another relief rally, with another major leg down in early February. We are currently experiencing yet another market rally. Will this one last? Interestingly the Canadian dollar has rallied about 8% from January lows, while gold is up 15% and oil is up over 20%. Did you ever notice that the same value of a stock or commodity (i.e. oil at $33.00) looks a lot better when the direction is up, rather than when the direction is down? Did you pick up on the fact that through the turbulence when the market was down gold rallied, and when the market rallied gold dropped, thus illustrating its market hedge attributes? As mentioned previously, the US dollar and commodities go in opposite direction to each other. I'm not sure which is the chicken and which is the egg and it doesn't matter, just that they tend to go in opposite directions. However, the warm winter across North America has kicked the last bit of stuffing out of natural gas, which is trading at multi-decade lows. The first North American LNG export just occurred from the Gulf Coast. This new demand may start to revive natural gas but comes at a time of worldwide LNG surpluses.

Market sentiment remains very low. Commentary on Business News Network, BNN, indicated sentiment to be even worse than during the 2008/09 financial crisis. Another report had bears at 39.2%, outnumbering Bulls at 24.7%. This is a contrarian positive sign but, as mentioned in the January 1st issue, sentiment can remain poor for an extended period. The "when" question remains.

Inflation may not be as benign as everyone believes with all the deflation concerns. The Canadian January CPI registered 2.0%, which was not a surprise given the decline of the Canadian dollar driving up import prices. US CPI of 1.4% was surprising given the strength of the US dollar reducing their import prices and that gasoline is in the tank (pun intended). This was a pretty strong showing for US inflation. When oil and thus gasoline stops dropping in year over year comparisons, we may see stronger inflation than expected.

Investments for this month: Once again I deposited money into the Canadian side of the non-registered account and used options (leverage) to add to the US side. Over the past number of issues we have gone through selling PUTS, buying CALLS and selling COVERED CALLS. In this issue I will cover combining selling a COVERED CALL with selling a PUT on the same company. This is the most complex of the strategies I use. If you understood the other option strategies it should be within grasp. I normally prefer to sell options rather than buy as most options expire worthless, but the seller takes the most risk. This strategy reduces the risk a little and enhances the upside of both selling PUTS and selling COVERED CALLS. I will once again explain with an example just completed.

On Thursday, February 25th, I purchased 100 shares of Citigroup (ticker C) for $38.45/share. Concurrently I sold one COVERED CALL contract that expires January 20th, 2017 (in 11 months), at a strike price of $43.00 for $3.10, reducing my effective cost to $38.45-$3.10 = $35.35. My return would be $43.00/$35.35 = 21.6% plus dividends (0.5% with C) if CALLED using a standard COVERED CALL strategy. A decent return for eleven months. Thus my upside would be capped at 21.6%, but I accept all the downside risk.

To add to the potential return I also sold one PUT contract for the same date, at a strike price of $38.00 receiving another $4.80 and reducing my effective cost for the 100 shares of Citigroup to $38.45 - $3.10 (call) - $4.80 (put) = $30.55. Now if I get CALLED I would earn $43.00/$30.55 = 40.7% plus the 0.5% dividend, which is REALLY good for 11 months. If the 100 shares get CALLED, the PUT would naturally expire worthless, allowing me to subtract the $4.80 PUT from the price of $38.45, along with the CALL premium to get the effective price.

Where's the catch? The catch is that I now accept all the downside risk of the 100 shares purchased plus an additional 100 shares represented by the PUT. Why am I willing to accept this downside risk? I do this to potentially build a position at a cheaper price than today's price, just like when I sell PUTS outright, but now it's even cheaper. If the price of Citigroup goes down to below the PUT strike price of $38.00, then the CALL naturally expires and the effective purchase price of the extra 100 shares of C is $38.00 (put strike price) - $4.80 (put) - $3.10 (call) = $30.10 effective purchase price of second 100 shares, which is 21.7%

below the current price. If this occurs my average cost would be: $38.45 (cost of original purchase) plus $30.10 effective cost of second purchase /2 = $34.28 average cost of 200 shares. (*I am using the terminology of effective price because in fact each transaction is its own independent transaction and I am simply trying to illustrate how they work together. I am also excluding fees and commission from the calculations to keep the math simple.*)

In summary, if Citigroup goes over $43.00, the shares get CALLED to return 40.7%. If they go below $38.00, I get an extra 100 shares at an effective price of $30.10 and my average effective cost will then be $34.28. If the price stays between $38.00 and $43.00, both options expire worthless and I get to keep $4.80 plus $3.10 and can do the same thing again. The most desired outcome is for Citigroup to rise to $42.99 at expiration of the options, thus providing the 40.7 % return without having the stock CALLED. The least desired outcome is a big decline. As with all option strategies it is important to keep the value of the underlying stock in line with the value of other positions in the portfolio. I have only used this strategy a few times but plan on doing more in the future. We have witnessed some wild swings in a market that has really only gone sideways for a prolonged period. This strategy allows us to make some money during those sideways patterns.

Portfolio additions for this month: I have continued adding to the Canadian side with an $8500 transfer in, while employing margin to continue to build the US portfolio without converting to USD at today's exchange rate.

Canadian Additions

Enbridge Inc. (ENB): I purchased 100 shares at $44.26/share. With $33B in annual sales ENB is the big dog of the Canadian midstream pipeline companies. I have owned TRP (TransCanada Corp) for a very long time and while it has performed well, I was always a bit jealous that ENB did better. It seemed, however, to be always priced at a premium. The current energy malaise brought all the midstream companies back to earth from a valuation standpoint and thus my interest in ENB. It is still not cheap but reasonable given their consistent cash flows. ENB fell from $65.00 to as low as $40.00 erasing the premium valuation. While it officially lost 4 cents/share in 2015 due to a number of restructuring costs, its operating earnings were $2.20 for an earnings yield of 5.0%. Cash flow was $3.72 for a cash flow yield of 8.4% and it pays a dividend of 4.8% based on my purchase price. It has a goal of increasing the dividend by 10% per year until 2019. ENB also has a growing interest in renewable electrical power projects.

Transforce Inc. (TFI): I purchased 200 shares of TFI at $21.40/share. TFI is an Eastern Canadian-based trucking, courier (Canpar and Loomis) and logistics management enterprise with over $4B in annual sales. My portfolios do not have much transportation exposure, making an opportune investment in the industry logical. TFI derives 47% of revenue from Eastern Canada, 16% from Western Canada and 37% from the US, limiting the impact from the energy bust. It has a dividend yield of 3.1%, earnings yield of 6.7%, cash flow yield of 15.3%, ROE of 14.2% and price times book of 2.1. Its debt level was on the high side, but on February 1st it closed the sale of a smaller waste management division and can therefore reduce this debt substantially. It is using some of the proceeds to buy back shares and I wouldn't be surprised to see an acquisition in its core transportation business. TFI traded over $30.00 a year ago and fell to just under $20 recently.

US Additions

Citigroup Inc. (C): The trades were made as described above. C is a US-based large worldwide banking conglomerate. We didn't have any US banks in this portfolio yet so used the recent sell-off to make this purchase. C has $76B in annual sales with approximately half derived from North America and half from the other 100 countries served. C was a major casualty during the financial crisis, dropping from $500/share to $10/share. It had to undergo vary large reorganizations and downsizing to survive, but it has survived. Since 2009 its stock price recovered from $10.00 to $60.00 in July of 2015, only to be hit by the recent sell-off similar to almost all other financials. Should this panic abate C is trading a very cheap valuation of just 0.6 price times book with a strong 13.7% earnings yield. Its ROE is, however, on the low side at 8%. It pays a minimal dividend of 0.5%. New worldwide regulations have substantially reduced the leverage ratios of banks in an attempt to prevent another crisis like 2008. Never say never in this business, but I think the current sell-off was overdone and there is a low probability of a 2008 repeat.

Walt Disney Co (DIS): I had about $350 in cash in this account and the C trades cost about $3100, leaving me about $2750 short, which I covered selling a couple more PUTS. I sold one DIS PUT contract with a strike price of $100 and an expiration date of January 19, 2018, receiving $16.20/share for the sale. DIS was selling for $95.40 at the time. If I get PUT my effective price will be $100.00 - $16.40 = $83.60 or 12.4% below its current price. With over $50B in annual sales, DIS owns a number of the most iconic entertainment brands on the planet. Those brands include media networks ABC and ESPN, studio brands Pixar, Marvel, Touchstone and the recent addition Lucasfilm (Star Wars). It has Disney resorts in Hawaii, Florida, California, Shanghai, Tokyo, Paris and Hong Kong, and takes entertainment to the seas with Disney Cruise Lines. DIS has a dividend yield of 1.5%, earnings yield of 5.6%, cash flow yield of 7.6%, price times book of 3.7 and ROE of 20.6%. Perhaps still a little on the expensive side but it has an unbelievable track record of earnings growth, having more than tripled them in the past decade. It was trading at $120 in 2015 before falling to just below $90.00 recently. This is the third time I have sold PUTS on the company and I still don't own any shares!

iShares MSCI Emerging Markets ETF (EEM): I sold two PUT contracts with a strike price of $33.00, expiring on January 19th, 2018, and received $6.23/ share. EEM was trading at $30.30 at the time. My effective price if PUT will be $33.00 - $6.23 = $26.77 or almost 12% below its current price. Emerging markets are in tatters. Russia and Brazil are in deep commodity driven recessions while China has dominated the newswire, and not in a good way. Sounds like a good time to invest, eh? India is the star of the large emerging market countries. Other countries included in the index are South Korea, Taiwan, South Africa, Mexico, Malaysia, Indonesia and numerous smaller countries. EEM was over $50.00 in 2007/08, fell to $20.00 in 2008/09 then recovered to $50.00 again in 2011 but has been in decline since. What goes around comes around and emerging markets have trailed developed markets so much, there is a good chance they will start to play catch up. We own 100 shares in the account, making this PUT sale an attempt to add to the position at a better price. As with other PUT sales, I hope to fail in the attempt but am willing to accept the shares if PUT.

These additions make the US side of the account slightly over-margined, but because there is no margin on the Canadian side the overall margin is still reasonable, although approaching my comfort level. The margin will hurt if the markets stay in a downtrend but will help when things turnaround. Margin is a double-edged sword. Most company year-end reports are now available, and in March I will once again do my annual review of all portfolio companies and will provide a summary in the April issue. The April issue will also include the quarterly valuation updates and will arrive about the 4th or 5th to allow for compilation of those numbers.

ISSUE #23: APRIL 4, 2016

The GOOD, the Not BAD and the UGLY

The very interesting 2016 first quarter is now in the books. In this issue we will look at how our portfolios performed during the quarter as well as how all the companies in the portfolio performed during fiscal year 2015. Also a few thoughts on moving forward. I never saw the classic movie that inspired the title of this issue, but its name became famous for even those who didn't see it. While updating the portfolio information, it came to mind as an appropriate theme for this month with the slight not BAD twist, encapsulating how we performed in the first quarter and in general since beginning the newsletter. Let's start with the **GOOD**.

Non-Registered Margin Portfolio

Company	Ticker	Date Added	# Shares	Price Added	Cost In USD	Current Value in USD	Share Price Change	Previous Dividends to Date	January Dividends	February Dividends	March Dividends	New Dividends to Date	Total Return
US Dollar Purchases													
iShares MSCI Emerging	EEM	06-Jul-15	100	$ 38.62	$ 3,872	$ 3,423	$ (449)	$ 42.57				$ 42.57	-10.5%
Vanguard Europe ETF	VGK	06-Jul-15	100	$ 52.91	$ 5,301	$ 4,851	$ (450)	$ 36.29			$ 23.12	$ 59.41	-7.4%
First Trust Nat GAS	FCG	06-Jul-15	500	$ 8.57	$ 4,297	$ 2,060	$ (2,237)	$ 30.43			$ 9.48	$ 39.91	-51.1%
Parker Hannifin	PH	24-Jul-15	50	$ 110.84	$ 5,552	$ 5,554	$ 2	$ 53.54			$ 26.77	$ 80.31	1.5%
iShares Silver Trust	SLV	31-Aug-15	200	$ 13.79	$ 2,767	$ 2,934	$ 167	$ -				$ -	6.0%
Market Vector Gold	GDX	31-Aug-15	200	$ 13.71	$ 2,751	$ 3,992	$ 1,241	$ 19.72				$ 19.72	45.8%
Berkshire Hathaway	BRK.B	Aug15-Jan16	75	$ 134.12	$ 10,099	$ 10,636	$ 537	$ -				$ -	5.3%
Union Pacific	UNP	31-Aug-15	50	$ 86.13	$ 4,316	$ 3,976	$ (340)	$ 23.37			$ 23.37	$ 46.74	-6.8%
ITC Holdings	ITC	02-Oct-15	100	$ 32.10	$ 3,220	$ 4,354	$ 1,134	$ 15.94			$ 15.94	$ 31.88	36.2%
Citigroup Inc	C	25-Feb-16	100	$ 38.45	$ 3,855	$ 4,174	$ 319						8.3%
US Options													
American Express	AXP	30-Oct-15	1 Put	$ 73.60	$ (762)	$ (1,525)	$ (763)						-100.2%
Walmart	WMT	30-Oct-15	1 Put	$ 57.90	$ (689)	$ (187)	$ 502						72.9%
Emerson Electric	EMR	30-Oct-15	1 Put	$ 47.10	$ (740)	$ (320)	$ 420						56.8%
IBM	IBM	25-Nov-15	1 Put	$ 137.82	$ (1,859)	$ (1,325)	$ 534						28.7%
CVS Health Corp	CVS	25-Nov-15	1 Put	$ 93.90	$ (1,089)	$ (520)	$ 569						52.2%
A T & T	T	25-Nov-15	1 Call	$ 33.72	$ 342	$ 880	$ 538						157.3%
Russell 2000 ETF	IWM	28-Jan-16	1 Put	$ 99.50	$ (1,449)	$ (966)	$ 483						33.3%
Citigroup Inc	C	25-Feb-16	1 Put	$ 38.45	$ (469)	$ (269)	$ 200						42.6%
Citigroup Inc	C	25-Feb-16	1 CovCa	$ 38.45	$ (299)	$ (365)	$ (66)						-22.1%
Walt Disney	DIS	25-Feb-16	1 Put	$ 95.40	$ (1,609)	$ (1,305)	$ 304						18.9%
iShares MSCI Emerging	EEM	25-Feb-16	1 Put	$ 30.30	$ (1,233)	$ (840)	$ 393						31.9%
US Subtotal					$ 36,175	$ 39,212	$ 3,037	$ 221.86				$ 320.54	
Cash						$ 242							
Total USD						$ 39,454							9.1%
Canadian Companies					CAD	CAD							
Bank of Montreal	BMO	03-Jul-15	100	$ 74.21	$ 7,431	$ 7,880	$ 449	$ 164.00			$ 84.00	$ 248.00	9.4%
CGI Group	GIB.A	23-Jul-15	100	$ 50.90	$ 5,100	$ 6,203	$ 1,103	$ -				$ -	21.6%
Crescent Point Energy	CPG	Jul15/Jan16	400	$ 16.79	$ 6,734	$ 7,180	$ 446	$ 126.00	$ 20.00	$ 40.00	$ 40.00	$ 226.00	10.0%
Telus	T	31-Aug-15	100	$ 42.83	$ 4,293	$ 4,225	$ (68)	$ 42.00	$ 44.00			$ 86.00	0.4%
Suncor	SU	31-Aug-15	100	$ 35.78	$ 3,588	$ 3,612	$ 24	$ 58.00			$ 29.00	$ 87.00	3.1%
Stantec Inc.	STN	29-Sep-15	200	$ 29.30	$ 5,870	$ 6,598	$ 728	$ -	$ 21.00			$ 21.00	12.8%
Potash Corp	POT	Oct15/Jan16	200	$ 23.84	$ 4,788	$ 4,418	$ (370)	$ 49.12		$ 51.79		$ 100.91	-5.6%
ShawCor	SCL	26-Nov-15	200	$ 28.94	$ 5,798	$ 5,630	$ (168)	$ -			$ 30.00	$ 30.00	-2.4%
Russel Metals	RUS	26-Nov-15	200	$ 18.15	$ 3,640	$ 3,944	$ 304	$ -			$ 76.00	$ 76.00	10.4%
Fortis Inc.	FTS	26-Nov-15	100	$ 36.67	$ 3,677	$ 4,062	$ 385	$ -			$ 37.50	$ 37.50	11.5%
Manulife Financial	MFC	26-Jan-16	300	$ 18.31	$ 5,502	$ 5,505	$ 3				$ 55.50	$ 55.50	1.1%
Enbridge Inc	ENB	22-Feb-16	100	$ 44.26	$ 4,436	$ 5,051	$ 615					$ -	13.9%
Transforce Inc	TFI	22-Feb-16	200	$ 21.40	$ 4,290	$ 4,458	$ 168					$ -	3.9%
Cdn Options							$ -						
Crescent Point Energy	CPG	26-Jan-16	2 CovCa	$ 13.24	$ (308)	$ (710)	$ (402)						-130.5%
Cdn Subtotal					$ 64,839	$ 68,056	$ 3,217	$ 439.12				$ 967.91	
Cash						$ 673							
Total CAD						$ 68,729							6.0%
Total Portfolio Value in CAD						$ 119,863							
Deposits in CAD Value						$ 111,357							7.6%

The first quarter was very kind to this portfolio. We started the quarter with the US side down 8.6% USD and the Canadian side down 0.2%, with the overall portfolio being down 1.9% in Canadian dollar terms. We ended the quarter with the US side up 9.1% for a total change of 17.7%. The Canadian side ended the quarter up 6.0% for a gain of 6.2%. The overall portfolio in Canadian dollar terms ended the quarter up 7.6% for a gain of 9.5%. This is an actual portfolio set up for the newsletter purposes, making the tracking easier than the model portfolios. The above gains are very nice considering the significant downside market pressures, near panic, through mid-February. By March 31st, the Canadian and US markets had eked out modest year-to-date gains of 3.7% and 0.8% respectively.

Most of the positions are now positive with FCG being a real drag as a record warm winter hammered natural gas, over and above the general hammering energy has taken. Most of the option positions are also positive with the exception of the COVERED CALLS and AXP, which was hit even harder than the hard-hit financial sector through the mid-February panic. These early results illustrate the importance of keeping one's nerve during periods of market turbulence and the opportunities they create. The average invested time for the portfolio is 6.3 months. This is, as with the other portfolios, too little time to judge, but we are off to a good start.

Now for the not BAD:

RRSP Model Portfolio

Company	Ticker	Date Added	# Shares	Price Added	Cost In CAD	Current Value in CAD	Share Price Change	Previous Dividends to Date	January Dividends	February Dividends	March Dividends	New Dividends to Date	Total Return
US Companies													
Verizon	VZ	Sept 30/14	100	$49.99	$5,609	$7,030	$1,421	$340.63		$78.90		$419.53	32.8%
HCP Inc	HCP	Sept 30/14	100	$39.71	$4,458	$4,235	$(223)	$349.85		$58.61		$408.46	4.2%
Hospitality Prop. Trust	HPT	Sept 30/14	150	$26.85	$4,521	$5,179	$658	$514.84	$9.58	$101.93		$626.35	28.4%
RMR Group	RMR	Dec 18/15	2	$16.95	$47	$65	$18	$ -				$ -	38.9%
United Technologies	UTX	Oct 31/14	50	$107.00	$6,002	$6,507	$505	$198.41			$42.11	$240.52	12.4%
Johnson and Johnson	JNJ	Oct 31/14	50	$107.78	$6,045	$7,033	$988	$229.60			$49.52	$279.12	21.0%
Freeport-McMoRan	FCX	Nov 30/14	150	$26.85	$4,601	$2,016	$(2,585)	$108.90				$108.90	-53.8%
Chevron	CVX	Nov 30/14	50	$108.87	$6,216	$6,201	$(15)	$275.66			$70.41	$346.07	5.3%
Exelon	EXC	Nov 30/14	150	$36.17	$6,195	$6,993	$798	$239.60			$61.20	$300.80	17.7%
General Electric	GE	Jan 27/15	200	$24.38	$6,056	$8,265	$2,209	$175.28	$64.75			$240.03	40.4%
Praxair	PX	Feb 28/15	25	$127.90	$4,007	$3,720	$(287)	$92.33			$24.66	$116.99	-4.2%
Qualcomm	QCOM	Feb 28/15	50	$72.51	$4,542	$3,325	$(1,217)	$120.83			$31.19	$152.02	-23.4%
US Subtotal					$58,299	$60,569	$2,270	$2,645.93				$3,238.79	9.4%
Canadian Companies													
Bank of Nova Scotia	BNS	Sep14/Jan16	200	$62.30	$12,480	$12,694	$214	$338.00	$70.00			$408.00	5.0%
Power Corp	POW	Sept 30/14	200	$31.08	$6,226	$5,992	$(234)	$302.77			$62.25	$365.02	2.1%
Capital Power	CPX	Oct 31/14	200	$25.58	$5,126	$3,600	$(1,526)	$277.00	$73.00			$350.00	-22.9%
Mullen Group Ltd.	MTL	Nov 20/14	250	$22.12	$5,540	$3,598	$(1,942)	$325.00	$25.00	$20.00	$20.00	$390.00	-28.0%
Royal Bank	RY	Jan 27/15	100	$75.12	$7,522	$7,483	$(39)	$233.00		$79.00		$312.00	3.6%
TransCanada Pipeline	TRP	Jan 27/15	100	$55.59	$5,609	$5,106	$(503)	$156.00	$52.00			$208.00	-5.3%
Bell Canada	BCE	Feb 28/15	100	$54.71	$5,481	$5,919	$438	$195.00	$65.00			$260.00	12.7%
Brookfield Asset Mgmt	BAM.A	Feb 28/15	150	$45.23	$6,795	$6,775	$(20)	$70.12			$26.37	$96.49	1.1%
Pason Systems	PSI	Mar 3/15	200	$18.48	$3,706	$3,300	$(406)	$136.00			$34.00	$170.00	-6.4%
Wajax Corp	WJX	Mar 3/15	150	$24.31	$3,657	$2,621	$(1,036)	$87.50	$37.50			$125.00	-24.9%
Home Capital Group	HCG	Mar15/May15	150	$43.11	$6,475	$5,259	$(1,216)	$88.00			$36.00	$124.00	-16.9%
AutoCanada	ACQ	Apr 4/15	150	$34.15	$5,133	$2,733	$(2,400)	$112.50			$37.50	$150.00	-43.8%
Cogeco Inc.	CGO	May 29/15	100	$53.60	$5,370	$5,690	$320	$55.00			$29.50	$84.50	7.5%
Pembina Pipeline	PPL	Dec 9/15	200	$29.17	$5,844	$7,022	$1,178	$ -	$31.11	$30.81	$30.80	$92.72	21.7%
Cdn Subtotal					$84,964	$77,792	$(7,172)	$2,375.89				$3,043.01	-4.9%
Dividends from Sold Cos								$24.40				$24.40	
Total Cdn and US					$143,263	$138,361	$(4,902)	$5,046.22				$6,306.20	
Cash						$1,699							
Portfolio Value						$140,060							2.2%

Cost in CAD total of $143,263 is derived from $137,000 invested, $1656 capital gains, plus $4607 of reinvested dividends, leaving $1699 of cash from unspent dividends.

Sales to Date	Ticker	Date Added	# Shares	Price	Exchange	Cost In CAD	Sold	Sold Price	Proceeds	Dividends	Profit	% Profit
Constellation Software	CSU	Oct 31/14	10	$317.50		$3,185	Apr 14/15	$485.07	$4,841	$24.40	$1,679	52.7

This portfolio started the year in the red by 2.9% and ended the quarter in the green by 2.2% for a gain of 5.1%. Not BAD compared to the market movements discussed above.

The US side was up 2.4%, adjusted to Canadian dollars, even though our loonie appreciated markedly during the quarter. The conversion rate was 1.38 on the December 31st summary and 1.30 on this quarter's summary. The declining Canadian dollar helped American gains (or muted losses) in 2015, but the appreciating loonie is now muting the gains, illustrating how having a significant portion of an RRSP in USD provides a measure of stability. The current "unforeseen" loonie strengthening also validates the decision to avoid currency conversion once we fell below 80 cents USD (1.25), although I had to do a bit to get the regular account started. This was in contrast to many in the financial industry recommending investors "get out of Dodge" (i.e. Canada) in favour of the more lucrative, less commodity-reliant, safer American markets. The Canadian side of the portfolio, with the timely addition of 100 more shares of BNS, was up 7.1% and is now down a modest 4.9% overall. Not BAD considering the TSX is still down 10% from when we started the RRSP portfolio. The average time invested is now fifteen months. Over this fifteen month time frame you could have invested in very safe GICs and experienced similar results, but GICs don't provide near the entertainment value, do they?

Yes, GICs would have been every bit as good, but we have experienced a pretty tough market this past year and a half. If a year and a half ago I said, "In the next 18 months we are going to experience two major US market corrections and a full-on Canadian bear market and still be better than breakeven," that performance would be considered pretty darn good or at least not BAD.

And now the UGLY:

TFSA Model Portfolio

Company	Ticker	Date Added	# Shares	Price Added	Cost In CAD	Current Value in CAD	Share Price Change	Previous Total Dividends to Date	Jan 2016 Dividends	Feb 2016 Dividends	Mar 2016 Dividends	New Total Dividends to Date	Total Return
International													
Ensco PLC	ESV	May 30/14	100	$ 52.66	$ 5,750	$ 1,348	$ (4,402)	$ 324.90			$ 1.30	$ 326.20	-70.9%
Glaxo Smithkline	GSK	May 30/14	100	$ 53.94	$ 5,890	$ 5,271	$ (619)	$ 381.98	$ 77.96			$ 459.94	-2.7%
Ship Finance Int.	SFL	May 30/14	180	$ 18.52	$ 3,644	$ 2,665	$ (979)	$ 653.30			$ 105.74	$ 759.04	-6.0%
Seadrill	SDRL	July 25/14	130	$ 37.49	$ 5,312	$ 558	$ (4,754)	$ 140.46				$ 140.46	-86.9%
HSBC Holdings PLC	HSBC	July 25/14	100	$ 52.82	$ 5,757	$ 4,046	$ (1,711)	$ 436.79				$ 436.79	-22.1%
Vodaphone	VOD	July 25/14	150	$ 34.16	$ 5,585	$ 6,250	$ 665	$ 329.22		$ 104.83		$ 434.05	19.7%
Unilever PLC	UL	Jan 2/15	100	$ 40.05	$ 4,736	$ 5,873	$ 1,137	$ 162.09			$ 42.99	$ 205.08	28.3%
Diagio PLC	DEO	Jan 2/15	30	$ 112.73	$ 4,001	$ 4,207	$ 206	$ 130.58				$ 130.58	8.4%
BHP Billiton Ltd	BHP	Jan 2/15	65	$ 47.27	$ 3,636	$ 2,189	$ (1,447)	$ 475.46				$ 475.46	-26.7%
South32 Ltd.	SOUHY	May30/15	26	$ 8.34	$ 267	$ 185	$ (82)	$ -				$ -	-30.6%
Internatonal Subtotal					$ 44,578	$ 32,592	$ (11,986)	$ 3,034.78				$ 3,367.60	-19.3%
Canadian													
TD Bank	TD	May 30/14	100	$ 53.76	$ 5,386	$ 5,606	$ 220	$ 294.00	$ 51.00			$ 345.00	10.5%
Innvest REIT	INN.UN	May 30/14	210	$ 5.16	$ 1,094	$ 1,098	$ 4	$ 125.82	$ 6.99	$ 6.99	$ 6.99	$ 146.79	13.8%
Rogers Communications	RCI.B	May 30/14	100	$ 43.82	$ 4,392	$ 5,200	$ 808	$ 281.25	$ 48.00			$ 329.25	25.9%
Teck Reources Ltd	TCK.B	May 30/14	200	$ 24.17	$ 4,844	$ 1,970	$ (2,874)	$ 220.00				$ 220.00	-54.8%
ATCO	ACO.X	July 25/14	100	$ 50.56	$ 5,066	$ 3,928	$ (1,138)	$ 142.00			$ 28.50	$ 170.50	-19.1%
Husky Energy	HSE	July 25/14	153	$ 33.06	$ 5,068	$ 2,474	$ (2,594)	$ 225.00	$ 2.74			$ 227.74	-46.7%
Sunlife Financial	SLF	July 25/14	100	$ 41.40	$ 4,150	$ 4,190	$ 40	$ 223.00			$ 39.00	$ 262.00	7.3%
Cdn. Western Bank	CWB	May/15Jan/16	220	$ 27.67	$ 6,106	$ 5,313	$ (793)	$ 74.80	$ 39.10		$ 50.60	$ 164.50	-10.3%
Jean Coutu	PJC.A	May 19/15	200	$ 23.23	$ 4,656	$ 4,404	$ (252)	$ 44.00		$ 22.00		$ 66.00	-4.0%
AltaGas	ALA	Jan 4/16	200	$ 30.96	$ 6,202	$ 6,680	$ 478			$ 33.00	$ 33.00	$ 66.00	8.8%
CI Financial	CIX	Jan 6/16	200	$ 30.47	$ 6,104	$ 5,740	$ (364)			$ 22.00	$ 22.00	$ 44.00	-5.2%
Canadian Subtotal					$ 53,068	$ 46,603	$ (6,465)	$ 1,629.87				$ 1,931.78	-8.5%
Total Cdn and Int					$ 97,646	$ 79,195	$ (18,451)	$ 4,664.65				$ 5,299.38	
Cash						$ 653							
Total						$ 79,848							-14.1%

Cost in CAD total of $97,646 is derived from $93,000 investment plus $4646 of reinvested dividends, leaving $653 of cash from unspent dividends

During the quarter we moved from being down 14.8% to being down 14.1%, which, while similar to market performance, is still pretty UGLY. The international side was down 9.2% at year-end and declined another 10.1% to currently reside down 19.3% which is really UGLY. The causes were threefold: 1) The appreciating loonie; 2) The ocean drillers, SDRL and ESV, experienced another leg down and have only recovered modestly with the recent oil rally; and 3) HSBC and SFL took big beatings. HSBC, like other European and world-type banks fell on worldwide recession fears (I picked up Citigroup in the last issue because of this sell-off) and SFL is involved in all forms of ocean-going vessels, including dry bulk, container, tanker and drilling rigs, which are all under pressure. That said, if both these stocks are at this level in January 2017 when our next contribution is permitted, they would both rank high on my list for potential additions. On the bright side, the Canadian portion of the portfolio was -20.3% and gained 11.8% to currently reside down just -8.5%. Still down but recovering. While I do not intend to sell the beaten-up resource sector, except perhaps BHP's spin-off SOUHY, as it is too small to contribute, new deposits will be largely invested outside the resource sector. I have also implemented a new sector allocation process to help me avoid being accidentally overloaded in a certain sector, as occurred with resources in the TFSA. I will work out of this situation without making panicky changes.

How did the companies perform in 2015, and what are current valuations?

REG ACCT US Cos	Price	Dividend Yield	Earnings Yield	Adjusted Earnings Yield	Cash Flow Yield	Price Times Book	ROE
PH	$ 111.08	2.3%	5.4%	5.9%	7.2%	3.1	16.0
BRK.B	$ 141.88	0.0%	6.9%	6.9%	9.6%	1.4	9.7
UNP	$ 79.55	2.8%	6.9%	6.9%	10.6%	3.3	22.8
ITC	$ 43.57	1.7%	3.6%	4.8%	8.4%	4.0	14.4
C	$ 41.75	0.5%	12.9%	12.8%		0.6	8.0
Options		1.4%					
AXP	$ 61.40	1.9%	8.2%	9.1%		3.1	24.0
WMT	$ 68.49	2.9%	6.7%	6.7%	12.4%	3.8	20.8
EMR	$ 54.38	3.5%	7.3%	5.8%	6.9%	4.5	29.8
IBM	$ 151.45	3.4%	9.0%	9.9%	11.4%	10.3	91.4
CVS	$ 103.73	1.6%	4.5%	5.0%	7.2%	3.1	13.9
T	$ 39.17	4.9%	6.1%	6.9%	16.2%	1.9	12.8
DIS	$ 99.31	1.4%	4.9%	5.2%	6.8%	3.7	20.6
		6.9%	7.1%	9.7%		3.6	23.7
RRSP MODEL US Cos							
VZ	$ 54.08	4.2%	8.1%	7.4%	17.6%	13.5	109.0
HCP	$ 32.58	7.1%	-3.7%	0.5%	8.1%	1.5	-5.6
HPT	$ 26.56	7.5%	3.7%	4.6%	13.2%	1.5	5.6
RMR	$ 25.01	0.0%	0.6%	0.6%	17.5%	7.7	4.4
UTX	$ 100.10	2.6%	8.6%	4.5%	7.6%	3.1	26.0
JNJ	$ 108.20	2.8%	5.1%	5.7%	6.3%	4.2	21.9
FCX	$ 10.34	0.0%	-109.4%	-0.8%	26.4%	1.6	-93.7
CVX	$ 95.40	4.5%	2.6%	2.6%	10.9%	1.2	3.0
EXC	$ 35.86	3.5%	7.1%	7.2%	23.8%	1.3	9.4
GE	$ 31.79	2.9%	-1.9%	0.5%	6.2%	3.0	-5.4
PX	$ 114.45	2.6%	4.7%	5.1%	8.1%	6.9	30.9
QCOM	$ 51.14	3.8%	6.3%	9.1%	6.6%	2.4	16.7
		3.4%	-5.7%	3.9%	12.7%	4.0	10.2
TFSA MODEL Int. Cos							
ESV	$ 10.37	0.4%	-61.0%	37.3%	70.1%	0.4	-19.9
GSK	$ 40.55	5.9%	12.4%	5.4%	15.0%	13.4	179.6
SFL	$ 13.89	13.0%	14.0%	14.0%	18.0%	1.0	16.8
SDRL	$ 3.30	0.0%	-45.2%	33.0%	109.7%	0.2	-7.7
HSBC	$ 31.12	8.0%	10.3%	10.3%		0.7	7.2
VOD	$ 32.05	7.1%	-2.4%	-2.4%	16.7%	0.9	-2.1
UL	$ 45.18	3.7%	4.3%	4.3%	5.8%	7.3	33.8
DEO	$ 107.87	3.2%	5.2%	5.2%	6.6%	6.1	32.2
BHP	$ 25.90	2.5%	-8.9%	-8.9%	5.3%	0.6	-9.01
SOUHY	$ 5.48	0.0%	-24.5%	0.0%	17.7%	0.7	-9.2
		4.4%	-9.6%	9.8%	29.4%	3.1	22.2

REG ACCT Cdn Cos	Price	Dividend Yield	Earnings Yield	Adj Earnings Yield	Cash Flow Yield	Price Times Book	ROE
BMO	$ 78.87	4.3%	8.3%	8.9%		1.3	12.5
GIB.A	$ 62.07	0.0%	4.9%	5.0%	6.5%	3.2	17.7
CPG	$ 17.98	2.0%	-10.1%	3.9%	22.5%	0.9	-8.6
T	$ 42.28	4.2%	5.4%	5.4%	13.9%	3.4	18.3
SU	$ 36.17	3.2%	-3.8%	-3.8%	13.0%	1.8	-5.0
STN	$ 33.00	1.4%	5.0%	5.0%	6.6%	2.4	13.0
POT	$ 22.11	6.0%	9.1%	9.1%	16.8%	1.7	14.8
SCL	$ 28.23	2.1%	5.4%	5.4%	15.4%	1.6	8.8
RUS	$ 19.78	7.7%	-7.2%	5.0%	30.0%	1.4	-9.6
FTS	$ 40.71	3.7%	6.4%	5.2%	14.7%	1.4	9.1
MFC	$ 18.38	4.0%	5.7%	9.1%	0.0%	0.9	5.8
ENB	$ 50.56	4.2%	-0.1%	4.4%	10.5%	2.3	-0.2
TFI	$ 22.33	3.0%	7.2%	6.4%	16.0%	2.1	15.9
		3.5%	2.8%	5.3%	13.8%	1.9	7.1
RRSP MODEL Cdn Cos							
BNS	$ 63.47	4.5%	8.9%	9.0%		1.9	14.6
POW	$ 29.96	4.2%	12.9%	11.3%		1.5	14.7
CPX	$ 18.00	8.1%	3.9%	6.4%	25.3%	0.6	2.6
MTL	$ 14.39	6.7%	1.0%	5.6%	16.1%	1.6	1.6
RY	$ 74.83	4.3%	9.0%	9.0%	0.0%	1.7	18.4
TRP	$ 51.06	4.4%	-3.4%	4.9%	11.4%	2.2	-8.1
BCE	$ 59.19	4.6%	5.0%	5.7%	12.5%	3.9	21.1
BAM.A	$ 45.17	1.5%	6.4%	6.4%	7.1%	1.3	11.2
PSI	$ 16.50	4.1%	-1.0%	0.9%	6.8%	2.8	-3.0
WJX	$ 17.47	5.7%	-3.4%	8.6%	2.7%	1.2	-4.1
HCG	$ 35.06	2.7%	11.7%	11.7%	0.0%	1.5	18.7
ACQ	$ 18.22	5.5%	5.0%	8.9%	11.7%	1.0	5.4
CGO	$ 56.90	2.1%	9.3%	9.3%	23.9%	1.6	15.2
PPL	$ 35.11	5.5%	2.9%	2.9%	6.6%	1.8	5.1
		4.6%	4.9%	7.2%	10.3%	1.8	8.1
TFSA MODEL Cdn Cos							
TD	$ 56.06	3.9%	7.5%	8.2%		1.3	13.6
INN.UN	$ 5.23	7.6%	-1.9%	-1.9%	11.5%	2.9	-5.9
RCI.B	$ 52.00	3.7%	5.2%	5.6%	14.0%	4.7	24.0
TCK.B	$ 9.85	1.0%	-42.7%	3.4%	34.4%	0.3	-14.1
ACO.X	$ 39.28	2.9%	3.4%	6.5%	24.6%	1.4	4.7
HSE	$ 16.17	0.0%	-24.8%	1.1%	23.6%	1.0	-21.7
SLF	$ 41.90	3.7%	8.5%	9.0%		1.2	12.6
CWB	$ 24.15	3.8%	16.4%	10.7%		1.1	19.1
PJC.A	$ 22.02	2.0%	5.3%	5.3%	6.0%	4.0	20.5
ALA	$ 33.40	5.9%	0.2%	3.1%	10.2%	1.2	0.3
CIX	$ 28.70	4.6%	6.9%	7.0%	8.2%	4.2	29.2
		3.6%	-1.5%	5.3%	16.6%	2.1	7.5

(Notes: I used just the ticker symbol to save space and make the print larger. The very lightly shaded numbers at the bottom of each section are the averages for the portfolio. These may be a little misleading as will be discussed below. The average dividend on the US Reg Acct does not include the dividend rate on the optioned companies as we are not collecting dividends on them, but it is important to look at the other valuation metrics as we could end up owning the stock. I did not include cash flow yield on banks and insurance as it is not a good valuation metric for them but one of the best for other companies. The numbers are based on FY15 year-end except if the company had a year-end prior to September 2015, in which case I used the most recent results. I did my best to decipher the numbers and make the most accurate representation, but given the amount of work and the surprising grey areas of accounting, errors are possible. The list above does not include ETFs.)

One would think accounting was a black and white profession, but it is anything but black and white. I had more difficulty than usual getting these numbers put together. The three different websites I use often reported different numbers. There are various ways to calculate each of the metrics. One of the biggest challenges this year was differentiating between "earnings" and "adjusted earnings." In the past I have tended to look just at earnings but this year there were huge discrepancies, especially with resource companies. Therefore I included both metrics. Companies periodically undergo major reorganizations, buy or sell significant assets, or experience large changes in their outlook. All of these items can cause unusual profits (sale of an asset at significantly higher than book value) or losses (write-down of asset values, especially goodwill, because of the change in value of the underlying asset). When these situations occur, adjusted earnings better reflect the earnings of the ongoing business. In the past year most commodity companies made major write-down revisions to the value of their assets. When a company finally resolves to take write-downs, they often go overboard in what's referred to as the "kitchen sink quarter." The sentiment of the management is "If we are going to face investors with write-downs try to make sure we only do it once, so write down everything possible, including the kitchen sink".

The most extreme example is FCX, which had an earnings yield of -109.4%, meaning it lost more money than the current share price, but has an adjusted earnings yield of -0.8%, meaning the huge loss of 109.4% was largely the write-down of assets. While it lost money, it wasn't near as bad as the earnings yield would indicate. It has an operating cash flow yield of 26.4%, which is good. This means if it meets its target of cutting capital expenditures (capex) by 50% it has enough cash flow to survive, barring another leg lower for commodities. This is why, here in Calgary, many of the oil and gas companies are cutting capex by 50% or more with a couple announcing zero capex in 2016, meaning they will keep pumping what they are pumping, but as those wells run dry they are not replacing them by drilling or completing any others. Most resource companies have also dramatically cut or eliminated dividends to save cash.

The other extreme examples are the ocean drillers, ESV and SDRL. From an operating standpoint they still made good money, but the write-down of assets created big losses. SDRL had operating cash flow of 109.7% meaning its cash flow was greater than the current share price. These extremes make the averages somewhat misleading, but they are still a useful guideline when planning portfolio changes. The ROE is calculated using the earnings rather than adjusted earnings, creating numerous negative ROEs.

Portfolio structure: A portfolio should include a company from each of the key sectors, including bank, insurance or other non-bank financial (like CIX), electric utility, pipeline, telecom, manufacturing, consumer, technology, transportation, health care and resources. Each of the above portfolios has most of these bases covered. Overall, there are perhaps too many companies, but my preference is over diversification rather than under diversification. Watching many companies provides better insight across the market and helps me spot opportunities in companies that get hit, but which appear to have good long-term fundamentals. I also prefer to avoid letting any one individual company ruin the results of a portfolio. You never intend to buy a stock that goes down precipitously, but it happens. Even though the TFSA was overweight in resources, the current loss position of 14% is probably still mild compared to many Canadian investor portfolios over this time frame, despite the precipitous drop of SDRL, ESV, HSE and TECK.B. When companies go to almost zero, my attitude is that they will either go broke or recover, with most eventually recovering and only a few going broke. Given there is very little money left at risk and it is very difficult to predict which ones might actually go broke, I prefer to hold for recovery and accept the possibility of bankruptcy. If a recovery occurs it can often be very swift. TECK.B is already up over 250% since mid-February. Moving forward while I will add new companies and sell some existing ones, adding to current positions will now be a focus. There are, however, still a few holes to fill in individual sectors, like a US bank in the RRSP.

Government policy can have a significant impact on share price, especially in the short-term. Complicating the financial stress created by the resource sector decline on all Alberta-based industries was our government's decision to add additional carbon taxes to electric utilities and the complete elimination of coal by 2030. This had a sudden and direct impact on the share price of the two Alberta-based utilities, CPX and ACO.X. It would have been very difficult to predict the election of the NDP (No Darned Prosperity), but there are three election cycles left before 2030 and things could change again. The Quebec government also changed its drug pricing policy, negatively impacting PJC.A's share price. In both cases share prices have recovered most of the lost ground.

Corporate changes: Over the past year BHP spun off a separate company called South32 (SOUHY) and HPT spun off RMR Group. Both of these are very small positions and I will watch them with the intent of either buying more or selling. Husky replaced its cash dividend with a stock dividend for one quarter. This was a bizarre decision in an attempt to appear to be still making a dividend without using cash, increasing our share count to 153. Investors saw right through the charade and sold, prompting Husky to eliminate the stock dividend as well. In a somewhat unusual twist, FTS is buying ITC. I don't think I have ever experienced one of my portfolio companies buying another that's in the same account. ITC jumped when it put itself up for sale but both companies dropped upon the purchase announcement and have since recovered. ITC is still trading at about a 6% discount to the purchase offer of $22.57 USD cash plus 0.752 of a FTS share. If the discount narrows I intend to sell ITC. EXC just completed the purchase of another US utility it had been working on for two years. This was the impetus for its recent little rally. The sell-off in pipelines allowed me to add to my own position of TRP, as well as add ALA, PPL and ENB to our newsletter portfolios. TRP, ENB and PPL are also taking advantage by buying pipeline assets from others. The largest deal, worth about $13B, involves TRP buying US-based Columbia Pipeline Group. TRP is selling electricity assets to partially fund the purchase. It's a good sign when a company has the financial strength to make purchases during difficult periods. SU also recently completed the purchase of Canadian Oil Sands. Lastly, both HCG and TFI have mailed circulars for a Dutch auction buy-back of shares. I am not participating and plan to continue holding the companies. There has been lots of divestures, mergers and acquisitions as companies grapple with slower growth and stronger players pick up potential bargains. Darwin principles are at work in the business world.

Market commentary: While short-term market direction is very difficult to predict and anything can happen, I do believe we have now seen the worst of the commodity collapse and the market bear. The US economy continues to add jobs at a healthy pace and even the Canadian economy is showing signs of life. Exports were up recently and the January GDP number was very strong, indicating that the time lag between the decline of the loonie and the economic response (February 1st issue) has now closed. Market sentiment has improved but remains tepid, which is also a good sign. You can certainly accuse me of crying wolf and being too optimistic on a turnaround before, but I remain optimistic on overall long-term market direction. If you examine all the non-resource companies' dividends, earnings and cash flow yields, there are some pretty enticing numbers, especially when comparing to low bond and GIC yields.

The next issue will continue building the regular account. Until then, **have fun with your investments.**

Learnings from the Edge of a Bridge

A long time ago in a land far, far away, New Zealand to be exact, I had an opportunity to both skydive and bungee jump. I was young, single and enjoyed adventure and was on an adventurers' holiday. Both events were highly memorable. Upon my return, friends asked which I enjoyed the most. I gave a two-pronged answer. The skydive was far more enjoyable, but bungee jumping was more educational. Believe me, the nights before and after each event were rather sleepless; the night before because of anxiety, and the night after because of adrenalin still actively circulating throughout my body.

The skydive was done tandem, the only way for a tourist diver to experience a true free fall without going through extensive training. An experienced diver is tightly hooked to the back of the tourist diver and controls the entire process from jumping to orienting our bodies facing the ground, pulling the ripcord and landing. We dove from about 10,000 feet, free-falling at about 180 feet per second (about 120 miles per hour) for 30-35 seconds, at which time he pulled the ripcord and we floated down the remaining 4000 feet. The free fall was a pure adrenalin rush! Floating down with the parachute open was cool but not overly exciting by comparison. Afterwards I commented that I was actually disappointed when he had to pull the ripcord, upon which a fellow jumper remarked that I would have been much more disappointed if he hadn't pulled it. With the skydive, once our prepayment was made a few days earlier, the process was effectively out of our control unless we backed out prior to boarding the plane, forfeiting our not-insignificant stipend for participating. Not something a self-respecting Dutchman would do!

In contrast, bungee jumping was more in the jumper's control. Bungee jumping originated as a rite of passage for young men and a ritual to ensure a bountiful harvest, amongst natives in the South Pacific. The villagers built a tower from trees and branches and tied vines to the ankles of their young men, to jump from various heights. Injuries look like a distinct possibility! The newer version is a little more forgiving with huge elastic bands used, giving the participant a gentler ride down. I performed this ritual off a 220-foot bridge over a shallow river. The big difference between this and the skydive was the participant had to make the final decision to JUMP of their own free will while standing at the very edge of the bridge, 220 feet above the water. The guides offered encouragement to those who had second thoughts but would not push participants, not even those who asked to be pushed. Our own conscious decision was required to propel us from the safety of the bridge. We had to go through the mental process and trust that it would turn out all right. The descent was certainly less dramatic than skydiving as the free fall only seemed to last a second before I could feel the tug of the bungee cords slowing my descent. At many personal decision points, I still think of myself at the edge of that bridge deciding to jump...and trust!

While not on the same scale, each purchase and sale of a stock brings an element of anxiety and the perpetual question of, "Am I doing the right thing?" Each push of the buy or sell button creates some "jump and trust" anxiety. On the other hand investment decisions made with a high level of confidence, paradoxically, are often LESS likely to turn out well. *It is said that most great investments begin in discomfort.* Not all the decisions will work out but over time with experience most do if we trust the market to behave as it has in the past, which it always seems to. After a correction comes a recovery. After a bear market comes a bigger recovery. The analogy with bungee jumping certainly applies, not just to the "jump and trust" decision, but also to the trajectory of the price afterwards. The markets in April continued their recovering ways, especially the Canadian market, which is now up 20% from February lows, but still resides 10% below where it was two years ago. The US S&P 500 is up about 13% over the same period, and is within 3% of its all-time high recorded a year ago.

This month's "jump and trust" portfolio changes: After the dramatic recovery of the past two months I was a little more cautious adding funds to the regular portfolio. I still made some additions but less so than during the winter months. It is very possible for some giveback, but also the possibility for continued appreciation. As mentioned many times, short-term direction is difficult to predict. I added just $4200 CAD and $1000 USD. Yes, I added a small amount of USD as the exchange rate is back very close to 80 cents ($1.255 CAD buys $1 USD), where I would start to consider conversion to US again. The value of the regular account improved by 4% in the month and is now up 11% on an average investment time of seven months.

On Friday, April 29th, I added the following to the regular account:

Canadian Side

Badger Daylighting (BAD): I purchased 200 shares at $24.35 and managed to get them at almost the highest price they traded at during the day! They are lower now, representing a better value for you. While the short-term gyrations are frustrating, they will not meaningfully impact long-term growth of the portfolio. The process of daylighting is that of exposing underground facilities such as utilities and pipelines to daylight, much like excavating. Rather than traditional excavating, BAD uses high pressure water to liquefy the soil, then a powerful vacuum to suck up the liquefied soil. It is a much safer and faster process when working around underground utilities than traditional backhoe excavating. BAD is a Calgary-based company with utility and petroleum industries representing a significant part of its customer base. Needless to say, sales and earnings are lower. However, given that mobile trucks are its main asset, it has been able to redeploy these assets to areas with greater opportunity. The US now represents two-thirds of revenue compared to 50% just two years ago. The future seems bright as aging infrastructure requires attention. While it will benefit from any resurgence in the oil and gas sector, it is not wholly reliant on it. BAD traded as high as $40.00 in 2014 and just below $20.00 in late 2015. It is a smaller company but has a modest dividend of 1.5% paid monthly and trades with an earnings yield of 4.4%, cash flow yield of 9.4%, price times book of 3.2. It had an ROE of 15.6% in 2015, down from an average of 25% during the past decade. These metrics appear on the expensive side, but prior to the commodity collapse BAD was growing rapidly. This growth rate could return. I had about $700 of accumulated dividends and transferred in $4200 to make the purchase.

US Side

Market Vectors Gold Miners Index (GDX): In the August 31st issue, when adding GDX, I explained my rationale for adding precious metals exposure. In subsequent issues I explained the teeter-totter relationship between gold and other commodities and the US dollar. The past couple of months have illustrated this relationship perfectly as the American dollar declined while commodities rallied. GDX has almost doubled since purchasing it in August. It is quite possible for this dramatic rise to abate and as such I am following the same strategy with GDX as explained in the March 1st issue with Citigroup. I sold COVERED CALLS and PUTS on GDX. To employ this strategy we do not have to buy the stock and sell the CALLS and PUTS at the same time. In this case the price increase prompted the employment of options. As GDX is volatile there are decent option premiums to be had. The greater the volatility of the underlying stock, the bigger the option premium.

I sold two COVERED CALLS with a strike price of $30.00 that expire in nine months, on January 20, 2017, and at the same time sold two, $21.00 PUT contracts expiring on the same date. The price of GDX at the time was $25.50. I received $2.20/share for the CALLS and $1.75 for the PUTS. If GDX goes above $30 my 200 shares will get CALLED and I will receive $30.00 plus the $2.20 CALL premium plus the PUTS will expire for an additional $1.75 = $33.95, which represents a 33% potential gain for nine months. If the price drops to below $21.00 I will get PUT but my effective price will be $21.00 - $1.75 PUT premium and the CALLS will expire for and additional $2.20 off the purchase price. My effective price will be $17.05 or 33% below the current price. In other words I am happy to be a seller at $33.95 and a buyer at $17.05. If the price stays within the $21.00 to $30.00 range I get to keep both premiums. The ideal outcome is for the price to rise to $29.99, but that is unlikely to happen. After commissions these two option sales added $765 USD to my account. *(Please see March 1st 2016 issue for further explanation with the Citigroup example.)*

Monsanto (MON): I sold one PUT contract on MON with a strike price of $100.00 that expires January 19, 2018. I received $16.42 per share, such that my effective price if PUT will be $83.58 less commissions. MON was trading at $93.80 at the time, so my purchase price would be 11% below the current price. MON is a key competitor in my main business and while I may not like some of its business practices, there is no denying its technological prowess. It is the clear leader in GMO technology and neck and neck with DuPont in traditional genetics, making it the number one company overall. Genetics is a very high-tech business that serves the cyclical commodity agricultural business. There is no question its fortunes fluctuate with the commodity cycle and as such earnings were down in 2015 and likely to be down again in 2016. That said, the seed tech industry is very concentrated with just a few world-scale competitors and remains profitable even through the low parts of the cycle. MON doubled sales and tripled profits over the past 10 years. The industry is consolidating again with the Dow/DuPont Merger and with ChemChina buying Syngenta. These mergers may benefit MON short-term as both competitors deal with merger distractions. MON has a dividend yield of 2.3%, earnings yield of 3.3% (low but depressed due to current environment and reorganization costs), cash flow yield of 5.3% and ROE of 24.7%, although it has more debt than I like to see. MON traded for over $120 in both 2008 and again in 2014 and has been as low as about $85.00 recently.

With the money raised from these option sales and transferring in $1000 USD at an effective conversion rate of 1.255, I added five shares of Alphabet. The conversion rate is still expensive, but is approaching a level that I am comfortable moving some money back to US. Transferring $1000 allowed a small but meaningful purchase of Alphabet.

Alphabet (GOOGL): I purchased five shares at $706.77 per share. Alphabet is the new corporate name for a holding company which owns Google, a name synonymous with everything Internet. Almost everyone uses Google multiple times per day, which makes most of its money from advertising. I am hesitant buying tech companies because the environment can change very quickly. For instance a mere decade ago Nokia was the dominant cell phone provider, which quickly lost ground to Blackberry, which then quickly lost its place to Apple and Google Android phones. Google's growth has been phenomenal and it is hard to imagine any other company knocking off its search engine dominance. Alphabet also invests money in numerous other technology venture capital opportunities, including life sciences and drones, and has its own venture capital firm. Many of these new ventures will fail, but if one or two hit it will propel GOOGL even further. Over the past 10 years revenues have grown 7x, while profits have grown 5x. It made $22.84 per share in 2015 and is expected to earn $30.00 in 2016. It does not pay a dividend, making it a better choice for a regular account than an RRSP. It trades with an earnings yield of just 3.4%, cash flow yield of 4.6% and price times book of 4.0, making it expensive on my traditional value metrics. It has a very respectable ROE of 14.2%. If it makes $30/share this year, the earnings yield will increase to 4.2%, which is getting better. This is one company I hope drops in price after buying because I would like to build a bigger position. It has traded as high as $800 but has recently fallen to the current $700 range.

All three of these companies have more expensive valuation metrics (lower earnings and cash flow yield) than I often invest in, but they also have higher growth potential. Growth companies sell at premium prices and these three appear to be currently valued at less than their long-term potential.

Looking Back: Alphabet kept increasing in price so I have not added more. Monsanto became a takeover target itself, with Bayer trying to purchase. Regulatory hurdles still need to be completed. GDX rallied to $30.00 but then fell into the $21.00 range such that I made profit on both the PUTS and the CALLS.

Bear markets usually end with a sharp snap-back, bungee-jump-type reaction, just as this one did. One of the great market fallacies is the ability to time the market. Some may get it now or then, but nobody does it consistently. First, you have to sell at the right time and then you have to buy back in at the right time. From October to January, the TSX was down 18% and from January to June it was up 25%. Good luck trying to manage your emotions and time this when daily swings were often in the magnitude of 2%. The reason so many fail at stocks is the continual attempt to time the market despite the difficulty in doing so. As you have witnessed my approach is a "steady hand" approach. I might be a little more aggressive after big drops and a little more tentative after big increases, but overall just keep plugging away at trying to find decent companies at decent valuations.

ISSUE #25: JUNE 1, 2016

The Debt Trap

One of the enduring lessons of the commodity collapse and its effects on resource companies is the impact of debt levels. All companies have some cyclical elements but commodity companies are highly cyclical, whereas industries like health care and telecom have much more consistent cash flows and are referred to as non-cyclical. Other industries like manufacturing lie somewhere in the middle of these extremes. Those that are highly cyclical need to be much more vigilant managing debt levels, whereas those with steady cash flows can accept higher debt as a per cent of total capital employed. I will use our third instalment in the life cycle of our two fictitious companies, **Excellence** and **Mediocrity**, to illustrate the debt trap and its effect on company valuations when tough times occur, as they inevitably do.

Please review Issue #9, January 28, 2015 "ROE, ROE, ROE Your Boat," and Issue #15, July 24, 2015 "Many Bad Apples" for the first two instalments. During the "ROE Your Boat" years we illustrated how everything else being equal, companies with high ROEs would deliver better returns than those with lower ROEs. During the "MBA" years we illustrated how the financial engineering practice of "share buybacks" increases profit per share and ROE without having to increase overall corporate performance. This often elevates stock price at least in the short-term. The practice, however, also normally increases debt levels. When we finished the "MBA" years (year 8), the debt level of Mediocrity stood at 66% of total capital while equity was 34%. Excellence, however, maintained a debt level of 50% of total capital. Let's assume these companies are in a modestly cyclical industry and a RECESSION OCCURS. How does the recession impact their financials, and what are fairly normal investor reactions to these events? *(If you don't like details please skip to "The Bottom Line.")*

	ROE, ROE, ROE Your Boat				Many Bad Apples				The Debt Trap			
MEDIOCRITY	Start Line	Year 1	Year 2	Year 3	Year 4	Year 5	Year 6	Year 7	Year 8	Year 9	Year 10	Year 11	Year 12
Debt	$1,000.00	$1,100.00	$1,210.00	$1,331.00	$1,464.10	$1,756.92	$2,079.02	$2,433.34	$2,823.10	$3,251.84	$3,251.84	$3,251.84	$3,251.84
Equity	$1,000.00	$1,100.00	$1,210.00	$1,331.00	$1,464.10	$1,464.10	$1,464.10	$1,464.10	$1,464.10	$1,464.10	$1,082.00	$1,190.35	$1,653.19
Profit	$100.00	$110.00	$121.00	$133.10	$146.41	$161.05	$177.16	$194.88	$214.37	$117.90	$108.35	$88.84	$122.62
Share Number	100	100	100	100	100	92.0	84.6	77.8	71.7	66.0	66.0	66.0	100.0
ROE	10%	10%	10%	10%	10%	11.0%	12.1%	13.3%	14.6%	8.1%	10.0%	7.5%	7.4%
ROA	5%	5%	5%	5%	5%	5.0%	5.0%	5.0%	5.0%	2.5%	2.5%	2.0%	2.5%
Profit/Share	$1.00	$1.10	$1.21	$1.33	$1.46	$1.75	$2.09	$2.50	$2.99	$1.79	$1.64	$1.35	$1.23
Book Value/Share	$10.00	$11.00	$12.10	$13.31	$14.64	$15.91	$17.68	$18.82	$20.42	$22.18	$16.39	$18.04	$16.53
Market Value/Share @ 8% earnings yield	$12.50	$13.75	$15.12	$16.63	$18.25	$21.88	$26.13	$32.00	$37.38	$22.38	$16.39	$11.21	$12.30
EXCELLENCE													
Debt	$1,000.00	$1,200.00	$1,440.00	$1,728.00	$2,073.60	$2,488.32	$2,985.98	$3,583.18	$4,299.82	$5,159.78	$5,159.78	$5,159.78	$7,159.78
Equity	$1,000.00	$1,200.00	$1,440.00	$1,728.00	$2,073.60	$2,488.32	$2,985.98	$3,583.18	$4,299.82	$5,159.78	$5,175.76	$5,692.76	$6,235.38
Profit @ 20% ROE	$200.00	$240.00	$288.00	$345.60	$414.72	$497.66	$597.20	$716.64	$859.96	$515.98	$516.78	$542.62	$669.76
ROE	20%	20%	20%	20%	20%	20%	20%	20%	20%	10.0%	10.0%	9.5%	10.7%
ROA	10%	10%	10%	10%	10%	10%	10%	10%	10%	5.0%	5.0%	5.0%	5.0%
Profit/Share: 200 Shares	$1.00	$1.20	$1.44	$1.73	$2.07	$2.49	$2.99	$3.58	$4.30	$2.58	$2.58	$2.71	$3.35
Book Value/Share	$5.00	$6.00	$7.20	$8.86	$10.37	$12.44	$14.93	$17.91	$21.50	$25.80	$25.44	$28.46	$31.18
Market Value/Share @ 8% earnings yield	$12.50	$15.00	$18.00	$21.63	$25.88	$31.13	$37.38	$44.75	$53.75	$32.25	$32.30	$33.91	$41.86

Return on Assets (ROA): I will now introduce ROA because it is a more inclusive measure of profitability than ROE. It measures profits as a percentage of total assets employed, not just equity. Total Assets = All Liabilities + Equity.

Using ROA rather than ROE helps uncover companies that are merely using extra debt to cover up operational inefficiencies in an attempt to artificially elevate earnings. During the "MBA" years you can see that while Mediocrity increased its ROE through share buybacks, its ROA was static at 5%. The buyback strategy works until tough times hit at which point the Debt Trap rears its ugly head. *(Clarification: once again I am not totally against share buybacks, just their overuse and especially their use to mask other business issues while propelling short term share price appreciation for executive stock option benefits.)*

Year 9: A severe recession "surprises" the industry. Both companies experience a 50% decline in profits, calculated as a per cent of ROA. Investors continue to value both companies at 8% earnings yield, thus impacting the share price of both companies. At this point neither company borrows additional money keeping debt level flat going into Year 10.

Year 10: The recession continues. Both companies face the difficult decision of closing down one plant worth $500. The plant shutdown creates a write-off for both companies of $500. This illustrates the difference between "Adjusted Profit" and "Profit" as discussed in the April 4th issue. "Adjusted Profit" does not take into account the one-time asset write-down, whereas "Profit" does. I have used adjusted profit in the profit line of the chart and held it at the same ROA. I subtracted the $500 write-down from the equity. Thus Year 10 equity = Year 9 equity + Year 9 "adjusted profit" - $500. The write-down affected Mediocrity much more than Excellence, driving its liabilities as a per cent of total assets to new heights at 75%. Stock investors showed their concern by selling shares aggressively and were only placated when the earnings yield reached 10% rather than the traditional 8%, taking the share price down a greater per cent than the profit decline. Please note the chart says "Market Value/Share @ 8% earnings yield," but this is adjusted as described here for Years 10-12. Excellence on the other hand produced adjusted profits almost equal to the $500 write-down, thus keeping its debt level to about 50% of total assets. Investors were relatively pleased with management's response to the recession and kept the price of the shares trading at the traditional 8% earning yield.

Year 11: Because of its now excessive debt level, bankers and bondholders demanded significantly higher interest rates from Mediocrity. Higher interest rates result in higher expenses, driving Mediocrity's profits down further to 2% ROA. Stock investors continued their selling pressure due to continued declining profits and like the bankers and bondholders, demanded higher returns. They only stopped the selling pressure when the shares were trading at 12% earnings yield. Excellence maintained profits, albeit at the reduced levels, and investors maintained confidence in the company, holding shares prices with an 8% earnings yield.

Year 12: Mediocrity finally succumbed to both investor and banker pressure and went to the market with an equity offering to sell thirty-four shares at a price of $11.00, thus raising much needed equity capital and reducing its debt level but bringing its share total back to 100. The reduced debt level helped increase ROA back to 2.5%, increasing overall profits but reducing the profit per share as there were more shares. This effectively had the reverse effect on financials as during the "MBA" years, when it was buying up its own shares. Stock investors, however, breathed a sigh of relief and sensed a turnaround. They bid the shares back up marginally and once again accepted 10% earnings yield. Excellence, having maintained a strong balance sheet and sensing an end to the recession, bought out competitor #4 for $2000. It was an all debt acquisition adding $2000 to debt levels, but because it had maintained its balance sheet during the recession, it could do so and still maintain a debt level below 55% of total assets. It felt that within a year it could bring debt levels back to the normal 50:50 ratio with profits generated. Investors continue to pay an 8% earnings yield.

Twelve years after we began our story Mediocrity had a share price where we started, whereas Excellence had a share price more than triple where we started. The CEO, Mr. MBA, who four years earlier was promoted with such fanfare is now shown the exit door, unfortunately, taking with him a huge severance package, illustrating another reason executives often take gambling risks. Frankly, they are often in a no-lose situation. Gamble pays off; cash my big stock option grants. Gamble fails; cash my big severance check.

The bottom line: Leverage is a double-edged sword. Companies that overuse it to mask weak business practices will pay the piper when a recession arrives.

- When a company like Mediocrity faces weakening business prospects and has high debt levels, its risk level goes up. When risk levels go up, bondholders and bankers demand higher interest rates to offset that risk. Equity investors also generally demand higher potential returns by selling off until a higher earnings yield is created. This exacerbates the decline in the stock price, creating a larger whipsaw effect than from just the earnings reduction. When profits decline, it is not unusual to see share prices decline by an even greater percentage.

- Similarly when earnings accelerate, it is not unusual to see share prices climb by a greater per cent than the earnings increase.

- You might think the Mediocrity example is a bit far-fetched and it must be unusual to see a company buy back its own shares, only to have to sell them again at a much lower price at a later date to raise capital.

THIS IS NOT UNUSUAL AT ALL. Hundreds of companies did this through the 2008/09 recession. Company executives are as prone, and maybe even more prone due to stock option incentive structures, to buying high and selling low as any other typical investor.

- Companies with strong balance sheets can take advantage of business downturns to bulk up on assets at reduced prices. Right now numerous oil and gas companies are trying to sell what they position as "non-core assets." Who are they selling to? Other oil and gas companies with stronger balance sheets.

- *Companies with low cyclicality and steady cash flow are able to carry higher debt levels than companies with higher cyclicality.*

Portfolio Changes

May 12th Update, TFSA

I hope all is well with you. Two days ago a Hong Kong-backed Canadian private company, Bluesky Hotels, entered into an agreement to purchase Innvest REIT for $7.25 cash, representing about a 33% premium to its trading price. Innvest promptly rallied close to this purchase price. I owned Innvest in my TFSA, and a small 210-share position was in the model TFSA. When I put INN.UN in the model, I tried to have all companies personally owned represented in the model but set the model up based on the then maximum allowable contribution level. I generally had as many or more shares myself, having grown the TFSA substantially prior to starting the newsletter. I wrote the following about INN.UN at the time: "It is higher risk, thus a smaller part of the model portfolio".

I also owned INN.UN in my RRSP. Normally when something like this occurs with a company that I own in more than one account, I hedge my bets, so to speak. There are three things that can occur with a buyout:

1) The deal falls through and the price generally reverts to the trading price prior to the buyout offer. All deals are subject to regulatory review or the purchaser may get cold feet.

2) Another prospective purchaser bids more.

3) The deal goes through as planned.

Given that both parties have agreed to the price it is likely this deal will close, but that is not a certainty, which is why I hedged my bets and sold INN.UN in my TFSA but plan to continue holding for now in my RRSP. The buyout news provided a small boost to our TFSA portfolio.

Today I sold my shares in the TFSA for $7.09/share (2.4% below the buyout price) and purchased more HSBC at $30.99 and CI Financial (CIX) at $27.18 with the funds. As mentioned in the April 1st issue, if HSBC and SFL were at these prices next January, they would both rank high on my list for additional purchases. SFL has rallied but not HSBC, giving me the opportunity to buy more now. I also cleaned out the very small position of

SOUHY (a dividend spin-off from BHP) for $6.07 USD. In addition, I am very close to having enough cash for another 100 shares of AltaGas but need just a little more dividend to accumulate. I mention these purchases and intentions so you can see what I am doing myself, but the funds in the model are more restricted as we owned just 210 shares of INN. UN in the model. There were, however, enough funds in the model with the sale of SOUHY, INN.UN and accumulated dividends to buy 100 more CIX at $27.18. I also caught a slight error in my April 4th TFSA grid. Accumulated dividends were understated by $110.00.

The other goal through this process was to consolidate the number of positions, which is why instead of buying a new company I chose to add to existing positions, trying to pick the ones currently representing the best valuations. Until next time have fun with your investments. Buyouts usually represent a little FUN and PROFIT!

Regular Portfolio, Canadian Side

Canadian National Railroad (CNR): I purchased 100 shares for $78.20 per share. I transferred $7700 into the account to make the purchase. Overall my portfolios have been missing the Canadian rail segment. I owned CP a long time ago and did very well by it, but since selling have not replaced it. Both Canadian railroads have done very well over time and have a couple of unique attributes: 1) There are just two of them. Duopolies (two companies in an industry) and oligopolies (more than two but still just a few, like Canadian banks) tend to have better pricing power, as by definition they have less competition. They do, however, have to deal with more regulation because of the limited competition; and 2) They own critical, long-term infrastructure that cannot be duplicated. It is hard to imagine anyone trying to build a third trans-national railroad. CNR also owns significant US assets (where the railroads are an oligopoly) and connects the Atlantic, Pacific and Gulf of Mexico. CNR has been one of the best managed railroads in North America. It has been trading sideways for almost two years, coinciding with the biggest part of the commodity rout, but the fact it is maintaining profitability through this time period is a testament to its strength. There isn't much to split the difference between CP and CNR, with the exception of CNR's lower debt levels. CNR currently trades with a dividend yield of 1.9%, earnings yield of 5.8%, cash flow yield of 7.9 %, an unfortunately high price times book of 4.1, but an excellent ROE of 25.4% and ROA of 10.5%. In the past two years it has traded between $70.00 and $87.00, so we are not getting a bargain, but over the long haul (pun intended) it should serve us well.

US side: Since our last issue the USD has strengthened on signs of another US interest rate increase. Thus gold, silver and the Canadian dollar have declined. Uncharacteristically oil has continued to rally through the USD strengthening, which is a good sign. I am once again unwilling to convert any Canadian currency to USD. In order to continue to build the US side, I sold a couple more PUTS and bought shares of Williams-Sonoma Inc. While the markets have generally recovered since their February lows, some sectors have not participated in the rally. Retail and hotels are amongst the sectors still in the doldrums.

Hilton Worldwide Holdings Inc. (HLT): I sold four PUT contracts on HLT that expire on January 19, 2018, with a strike price of $23.00 and received $4.30/share for proceeds after commissions of $1705. The price of HLT was $20.60 at the time, so if I get PUT my effective price will be $18.70 or a 9% discount to the current price. I believe one of the concerns with hotels is the potential long-term impact of Airbnb and other such Internet sites, although they are likely more a threat to lower-end hotels than Hilton. While this is a concern, demographics are a positive. Baby boomers are now retiring in droves and will want to travel early in their retirement years. HLT is one of the largest hospitality companies in the world. One of its key competitors, Marriot, is in the process of buying another, Starwood (which includes Westin). On a much smaller scale Canadian Innvest REIT is also in the process of being bought out. HLT has three operating segments: 1) Hotel management and franchising 2) Hotel Ownership and 3) Timeshares. It owns just 150 hotels but manages or franchises a total of 4600 worldwide. Warning: HLT is in the process of splitting into three separate companies representing each of these segments, which it hopes to complete by the end of 2016. If this occurs and I get PUT, I will actually own shares of all three companies. I might try to buy the PUT out before this occurs, depending on share price movement. HLT has a dividend yield of 1.4%, earnings yield of 7.6% (inflated due to one-time gains with 2016 projected to be about 5%), cash flow yield of 11.0%, prices times book of 3.4, ROE of 28.7% and ROA of 6.1%. Over the past three years, since going public, it has traded as high as $30.00 and as low as $18.00.

iShares Silver Trust (SLV): The account already holds 200 shares. As mentioned above, gold and silver declined significantly recently. Thus I sold three PUT contracts in order to try to bulk up on the position at a lower price. The PUTS have a strike price of $17.00 and expire on January 19, 2018. I received $3.10/ share for total proceeds after commissions of $916. If I get PUT my effective price will be $13.90 or close to the original price on the first 200 shares. This represents a discount of 9% on the current price of SLV of $15.20.

Williams-Sonoma Inc. (WSM): I used the proceeds of the above PUT sales to buy 50 shares of WSM at a price of $54.09. I haven't been a big investor in the retail sector because of its faddish nature, but valuations are now enticing. One of the biggest concerns with retail is the growing trend of online retail, but WSM already derives half its revenues online. WSM is a home furnishings, home décor, small appliance, cookware, lighting and giftware retailer of higher end products. Besides Williams-Sonoma, its best-known brand is Pottery Barn. It is trading with a dividend yield of 2.7%, earnings yield of 6.5%, cash flow yield of 10.3%, price times book of 3.9 but a superb ROE of 25.6% and ROA of 13.1%. The US housing market continues to rebound from the 2008/09 implosion and WSM should benefit. US housing starts were reported to be up 6% year over year but still remain well below long-term averages. WSM traded as high $85.00 in 2015 and as low as $8.00 during the recession; however, it maintained some profitability even through those difficult years. With $5B in annual sales, WSM is a fairly large player in a fragmented industry with lots of consolidation potential.

In time I plan to add at least another 50 shares of WSM, as well as additional shares to many of the positions in the portfolio. As you have seen I tend to build breadth first, smaller positions in many companies and industries, then depth as I increase the number of shares at hopefully appropriate times.

Market commentary: May started tough but rallied strongly towards the end. Both sides of the border are up about 1% on the month. Shortly after last month's issue and PUT sale on Monsanto, it became a takeover target of Bayer, providing a fortuitous bounce to the shares. The July 1 issue will once again include portfolio summaries and will be sent to you about the 5th to allow time for compilation of the numbers. We are having a little more FUN these days.

ISSUE #26: JULY 4, 2016

The Brexit Blip and Other Such Market Calamities

In the next few pages we'll cover our portfolio review and this month's changes, but I wanted to start this edition with a sad and unfortunate story, but one that is entirely preventable. I was in a discussion with an acquaintance. During the discussion he related to me that he might be forced to leave the area. He had been unemployed for a little over a year and was close to losing his house. He had already given up one vehicle and was actively looking for work but not meeting much success in today's Calgary environment. He went on to explain that he had been a high-level employee with a very good annual income. I would guess his age to be approximately fifty. How does someone who has been a high-income earner throughout his career end up in such a predicament? This brings me back to the purpose of the newsletter. Having been an "amateur" but active investor throughout my career, I am trying to help and motivate other like-minded "amateurs" become conscious savers and investors, making wise investment decisions and building wealth through time. In sharing my experiences, strategies and portfolios I hope to help subscribers make their individual investment plans successful, without extraordinary effort.

Over the past month "Brexit" has dominated the regular and business news channels. The June 23rd vote in favour of the UK leaving the European Union took the market by surprise and precipitated a dramatic decline in stock markets around the world, especially those in Europe. It also precipitated a 10-12% decline in the value of the British pound and 3-4% of the euro. Why the market was taken by surprise is somewhat perplexing as the polls had the vote in a virtual dead heat. The underlying sentiment was the UK wouldn't and couldn't possibly vote to leave, could they? How could they possibly do this? Two days of dramatic selling took the US S&P 500 down 6% and the Canadian market down 4%. Key European markets dropped 6-10% over and above the currency devaluation. However, a funny thing then happened on the way to disaster. **It wasn't a disaster!** At least not at this time! And markets rallied back and have now regained most of those losses.

As mentioned many times in the past I cannot (nor do I believe can anyone else) predict the next market calamity, but I can assure you of the following:

1. There will be another market calamity, in fact many others.

2. Investing success entails sticking with the plan and not panicking.

3. Regular contributions to one's investments, especially the tax-advantaged plans (TFSA, RRSP, and RESP) will, over time, build wealth regardless of market gyrations, avoiding the fate of the above-mentioned individual.

4. A diversified portfolio of common shares of quality companies will provide excellent returns over the long-term.

5. While short-term market direction is very difficult to predict, one can enhance returns by making additional contributions after a market calamity and perhaps reducing after a big market run-up.

Now let's do our quarterly portfolio review: I endeavour to provide a completely accurate picture, but given the amount of information, slight errors are possible. The charts include this month's changes, which I will detail below. The per cent returns are all simple rates of return. At year-end, I will do the more complex total return and compounded return calculations. Values are as of June 30th closing, with 1.30 conversion rate.

Company	Ticker	Date Added	# Shares	Price Added	Cost In USD	Current Value in USD	Share Price Change	Previous Dividends to Date	April Dividends	May Dividends	June Dividends	New Dividends to Date	Total Return
US Dollar Purchases													
iShares MSCI Emerging	EEM	6-Jul-15	100	$ 38.62	$ 3,872	$ 3,436	$ (436)	$ 42.57			$ 22.61	$ 65.18	-9.6%
Vanguard Europe ETF	VGK	6-Jul-15	100	$ 52.91	$ 5,301	$ 4,666	$ (635)	$ 59.41			$ 78.54	$ 137.95	-9.4%
First Trust Nat GAS	FCG	6-Jul-15	100	$ 42.85	$ 4,297	$ 2,436	$ (1,861)	$ 39.91			$ 19.49	$ 59.40	-41.9%
Parker Hannifin	PH	24-Jul-15	50	$ 110.84	$ 5,552	$ 5,403	$ (149)	$ 80.31			$ 26.77	$ 107.08	-0.8%
iShares Silver Trust	SLV	31-Aug-15	200	$ 13.79	$ 2,767	$ 3,573	$ 806	$ -				$ -	29.1%
Market Vector Gold	GDX	31-Aug-15	200	$ 13.71	$ 2,751	$ 5,542	$ 2,791	$ 19.72				$ 19.72	102.2%
Berkshire Hathaway	BRK.B	Aug15-Jan16	75	$ 134.12	$ 10,099	$ 10,859	$ 760	$ -				$ -	7.5%
Union Pacific	UNP	31-Aug-15	50	$ 86.13	$ 4,316	$ 4,363	$ 47	$ 46.74			$ 23.37	$ 70.11	2.7%
Citigroup Inc	C	25-Feb-16	100	$ 38.45	$ 3,855	$ 4,239	$ 384		$ 4.25			$ 4.25	10.1%
Alphabet	GOOGL	29-Apr-16	5	$ 706.77	$ 3,544	$ 3,518	$ (26)					$ -	-0.7%
Williams Sonoma	WSM	May,Jun, 2016	100	$ 51.52	$ 5,172	$ 5,213	$ 41					$ -	0.8%
Capital One Financial	COF	30-Jun-16	65	$ 61.67	$ 4,019	$ 4,128	$ 109					$ -	2.7%
Dividends from Sold Cos								$ 31.88				$ 47.82	
US Options													
American Express	AXP	30-Oct-15	1 Put	$ 73.60	$ (762)	$ (1,365)	$ (603)						-79.2%
Walmart	WMT	30-Oct-15	1 Put	$ 57.90	$ (689)	$ (85)	$ 604						87.7%
Emerson Electric	EMR	30-Oct-15	1 Put	$ 47.10	$ (740)	$ (300)	$ 440						59.5%
IBM	IBM	25-Nov-15	1 Put	$ 137.82	$ (1,859)	$ (1,285)	$ 574						30.9%
CVS Health Corp	CVS	25-Nov-15	1 Put	$ 93.90	$ (1,089)	$ (850)	$ 239						21.9%
Russell 2000 ETF	IWM	28-Jan-16	1 Put	$ 99.50	$ (1,449)	$ (810)	$ 639						44.1%
Citigroup Inc	C	25-Feb-16	1 Put	$ 38.45	$ (469)	$ (214)	$ 255						54.3%
Citigroup Inc	C	25-Feb-16	1 CovCa	$ 38.45	$ (299)	$ (325)	$ (26)						-8.7%
Walt Disney	DIS	25-Feb-16	1 Put	$ 95.40	$ (1,609)	$ (1,432)	$ 177						11.0%
iShares MSCI Emerging	EEM	25-Feb-16	1 Put	$ 30.30	$ (1,233)	$ (790)	$ 443						35.9%
Market Vector Gold	GDX	29-Apr-16	2 CovCa	$ 25.50	$ (428)	$ (560)	$ (132)						-30.8%
Market Vector Gold	GDX	29-Apr-16	2 Put	$ 25.50	$ (337)	$ (204)	$ 133						39.5%
Monsanto	MON	29-Apr-16	1 Put	$ 93.80	$ (1,631)	$ (1,320)	$ 311						19.1%
Hilton	HLT	31-May-16	4 Put	$ 20.60	$ (1,705)	$ (1,588)	$ 117						6.9%
iShares Silver Trust	SLV	31-May-16	3 Put	$ 15.27	$ (916)	$ (579)	$ 337						36.8%
A T & T	T	30-Jun-16	2 Put	$ 42.60	$ (867)	$ (872)	$ (5)						-0.6%
Vanguard Europe ETF	VGK	30-Jun-16	2 Call	$ 46.00	$ 532	$ 560	$ 28						5.3%
US Subtotal					$ 39,996	$ 45,357	$ 5,361	$ 320.54				$ 511.51	
Cash						$ 123							
Total USD		Deposits		$ 37,100		$ 45,480							22.6%
Canadian Companies					CAD	CAD							
Bank of Montreal	BMO	3-Jul-15	100	$ 74.21	$ 7,431	$ 8,195	$ 764	$ 248.00		$ 84.00		$ 332.00	14.7%
CGI Group	GIB.A	23-Jul-15	100	$ 50.90	$ 5,100	$ 5,519	$ 419	$ -				$ -	8.2%
Crescent Point Energy	CPG	Jul15/Jan16	400	$ 16.79	$ 6,734	$ 8,164	$ 1,430	$ 226.00	$ 12.00	$ 12.00	$ 12.00	$ 262.00	25.1%
Telus	T	31-Aug-15	100	$ 42.83	$ 4,293	$ 4,160	$ (133)	$ 86.00	$ 44.00			$ 130.00	-0.1%
Suncor	SU	31-Aug-15	100	$ 35.78	$ 3,588	$ 3,584	$ (4)	$ 87.00			$ 29.00	$ 116.00	3.1%
Stantec Inc.	STN	29-Sep-15	200	$ 29.30	$ 5,870	$ 6,266	$ 396	$ 21.00	$ 22.50			$ 43.50	7.5%
Potash Corp	POT	Oct15/Jan16	200	$ 23.84	$ 4,788	$ 4,200	$ (588)	$ 100.91		$ 61.85		$ 162.76	-8.9%
ShawCor	SCL	26-Nov-15	200	$ 28.94	$ 5,798	$ 6,406	$ 608	$ 30.00		$ 30.00		$ 60.00	11.5%
Russel Metals	RUS	26-Nov-15	200	$ 18.15	$ 3,640	$ 4,576	$ 936	$ 76.00			$ 76.00	$ 152.00	29.9%
Fortis Inc.	FTS	26-Nov-15	100	$ 36.67	$ 3,677	$ 4,367	$ 690	$ 37.50			$ 37.50	$ 75.00	20.8%
Manulife Financial	MFC	Jan16/Jun16	500	$ 17.92	$ 8,978	$ 8,835	$ (143)	$ 55.50			$ 55.50	$ 111.00	-0.4%
Enbridge Inc	ENB	22-Feb-16	100	$ 44.26	$ 4,436	$ 5,473	$ 1,037	$ -			$ 53.00	$ 53.00	24.6%
Transforce Inc	TFI	22-Feb-16	200	$ 21.40	$ 4,290	$ 4,798	$ 508	$ -	$ 34.00			$ 34.00	12.6%
Badger Daylighting	BAD	29-Apr-16	200	$ 24.35	$ 4,880	$ 4,500	$ (380)				$ 6.60	$ 6.60	-7.7%
Cdn National Rail	CNR	30-May-16	100	$ 78.20	$ 7,830	$ 7,629	$ (201)				$ 37.50	$ 37.50	-2.1%
Cameco Corp	CCO	30-Jun-16	300	$ 13.98	$ 4,204	$ 4,257	$ 53					$ -	1.3%
Cdn Options							$ -						
Crescent Point Energy	CPG	26-Jan-16	2 CovCa	$ 13.24	$ (308)	$ (1,140)	$ (832)						-270.1%
Cdn Subtotal					$ 85,229	$ 89,789	$ 4,560	$ 967.91				$ 1,575.36	
Cash						$ 47							
Total CAD		Deposits		$ 83,700		$ 89,836							7.3%
Total Portfolio Value in CAD						$ 148,960							
Deposits in CAD Value						$ 131,812							13.0%

Sales to Date	Ticker	Date Added	#Shares	Price Added	Currency	Cost	Sold	Sold Price	Proceeds	Accum Div	Profit	% Profit	CapGainCdn
ITC Holdings	ITC	2-Oct-15	100	$ 32.10	USD	$ 3,220	27-Jun-16	$ 45.65	$ 4,554	$ 47.82	$ 1,382	43%	$ 1,715
A T & T Calls	T	27-Nov-16	2	$ 1.65	USD	$ 342	30-Jun-16	$ 7.65	$ 1,517	0	$ 1,175	344%	$ 1,517

WOW, that's pretty good. The average time invested is now eight months. The US side, which employs margin, is up 22.6% while the Canadian side without margin is up a very respectable 7.3%, for a combined weighted average growth in Canadian currency of 13.0%. This quarter's gain was 5.4%.

By way of comparison, the US market was up 2% and the Canadian market was up about 3% during the quarter. It is important to keep in mind that the Canadian market suffered a full bear market, while the US side had two large corrections during the time we have been building this portfolio. It is equally important to be aware that the portfolio employs margin and is still very young. I keep the margin at a relatively safe level by only employing it on the US side. While off to a strong start, please do not expect future returns to be as robust!

RRSP Model Portfolio

Company	Ticker	Date Added	# Shares	Price Added	Cost In CAD	Current Value in CAD	Share Price Change	Previous Dividends to Date	April Dividends	May Dividends	June Dividends	New Dividends to Date	Total Return
US Companies													
Verizon	VZ	Sept 30/14	100	$ 49.99	$ 5,609	$ 7,259	$ 1,650	$ 419.53		$ 70.26		$ 489.79	38.1%
HCP Inc	HCP	Sept 30/14	100	$ 39.71	$ 4,458	$ 4,599	$ 141	$ 408.46		$ 74.95		$ 483.41	14.0%
Hospitality Prop. Trust	HPT	Sept 30/14	150	$ 26.85	$ 4,521	$ 5,616	$ 1,095	$ 626.35		$ 98.91		$ 725.26	40.3%
RMR Group	RMR	Dec 18/15	2	$ 16.95	$ 47	$ 81	$ 34	$ -		$ 0.78		$ 0.78	74.8%
United Technologies	UTX	Oct 31/14	50	$ 107.00	$ 6,002	$ 6,666	$ 664	$ 240.52			$ 41.78	$ 282.30	15.8%
Johnson and Johnson	JNJ	Oct 31/14	50	$ 107.78	$ 6,045	$ 7,885	$ 1,840	$ 279.12			$ 50.90	$ 330.02	35.9%
Freeport-McMoRan	FCX	Nov 30/14	150	$ 26.85	$ 4,601	$ 2,172	$ (2,429)	$ 108.90				$ 108.90	-50.4%
Chevron	CVX	Nov 30/14	50	$ 108.87	$ 6,216	$ 6,814	$ 598	$ 346.07			$ 67.73	$ 413.80	16.3%
Exelon	EXC	Nov 30/14	150	$ 36.17	$ 6,195	$ 7,090	$ 895	$ 300.80			$ 60.39	$ 361.19	20.3%
General Electric	GE	Jan 27/15	200	$ 24.38	$ 6,056	$ 8,185	$ 2,129	$ 240.03	$ 58.03			$ 298.06	40.1%
Praxair	PX	Feb 28/15	25	$ 127.90	$ 4,007	$ 3,653	$ (354)	$ 116.99			$ 23.95	$ 140.94	-5.3%
Qualcomm	QCOM	Feb 28/15	50	$ 72.51	$ 4,542	$ 3,482	$ (1,060)	$ 152.02			$ 33.63	$ 185.65	-19.3%
US Subtotal					$ 58,299	$ 63,502	$ 5,203	$ 3,238.79				$ 3,820.10	15.5%
Canadian Companies													
Bank of Nova Scotia	BNS	Sep14/Jan16	200	$ 62.30	$ 12,480	$ 12,662	$ 182	$ 408.00	$ 144.00			$ 552.00	5.9%
Power Corp	POW	Sep/14/Jun16	300	$ 29.89	$ 8,986	$ 8,250	$ (736)	$ 365.02			$ 67.00	$ 432.02	-3.4%
Capital Power	CPX	Oct 31/14	200	$ 25.58	$ 5,126	$ 3,856	$ (1,270)	$ 350.00	$ 73.00			$ 423.00	-16.5%
Mullen Group Ltd.	MTL	Nov14/Jun16	500	$ 17.99	$ 9,013	$ 7,050	$ (1,963)	$ 390.00	$ 20.00	$ 16.00	$ 7.50	$ 433.50	-17.0%
Royal Bank	RY	Jan 27/15	100	$ 75.12	$ 7,522	$ 7,634	$ 112	$ 312.00		$ 81.00		$ 393.00	6.7%
TransCanada Pipeline	TRP	Jan 27/15	100	$ 55.59	$ 5,609	$ 5,846	$ 237	$ 208.00	$ 56.50			$ 264.50	8.9%
Bell Canada	BCE	Feb 28/15	100	$ 54.71	$ 5,481	$ 6,114	$ 633	$ 260.00	$ 68.25			$ 328.25	17.5%
Brookfield Asset Mgmt	BAM.A	Feb 28/15	150	$ 45.23	$ 6,795	$ 6,411	$ (384)	$ 96.49			$ 102.44	$ 198.93	-2.7%
Brookfield Business LP	BBU.UN	Jun 24,16	3	$ 25.67	$ 77	$ 74	$ (3)	$ -				$ -	-3.9%
Pason Systems	PSI	Mar 3/15	200	$ 18.48	$ 3,706	$ 3,572	$ (134)	$ 170.00			$ 34.00	$ 204.00	1.9%
Wajax Corp	WJX	Mar 3/15	150	$ 24.31	$ 3,657	$ 2,247	$ (1,410)	$ 125.00	$ 37.50			$ 162.50	-34.1%
Home Capital Group	HCG	Mar15/May15	150	$ 43.11	$ 6,475	$ 4,803	$ (1,672)	$ 124.00			$ 36.00	$ 160.00	-23.4%
AutoCanada	ACQ	Apr 4/15	150	$ 34.15	$ 5,133	$ 3,323	$ (1,810)	$ 150.00			$ 15.00	$ 165.00	-32.0%
Cogeco Inc.	CGO	May 29/15	100	$ 53.60	$ 5,370	$ 5,583	$ 213	$ 84.50		$ 29.50		$ 114.00	6.1%
Pembina Pipeline	PPL	Dec 9/15	200	$ 29.17	$ 5,844	$ 7,852	$ 2,008	$ 92.72	$ 30.81	$ 32.32	$ 32.32	$ 188.17	37.6%
Dividends from Sold Cos									$ 24.40			$ 24.40	
Cdn Subtotal					$ 91,274	$ 85,277	$ (5,997)	$ 3,160.13				$ 4,043.27	-2.1%
Total Cdn and US					$ 149,573	$ 148,779	$ (794)	$ 6,398.92				$ 7,863.37	
Cash						$ 446							
Portfolio Value						$ 149,225							6.2%

Cost in CAD total of $149,573 is derived from $140,500 invested, $1656 capital gains, plus $7417 of reinvested dividends, leaving $446 of cash from unspent dividends.

Sales to Date	Ticker	Date Added	# Shares	Price	Exchange	Cost In CAD	Sold	Sold Price	Proceeds	Dividends	Profit	% Profit
Constellation Software	CSU	Oct 31/14	10	$ 317.50		$ 3,185	Apr 14/15	$ 485.07	$ 4,841	$ 24.40	$ 1,679	52.7

The RRSP model was up 4.0% in the quarter and is now starting to show some nice gains for the eighteen months average time invested. Having started the year at -2.9% it is now up 9.1% so far this year, excellent in comparison to year-to-date gains of 8.1% in Canada and 2.5% in the US.

RRSP changes: As per the email on June 27, I added 250 Mullen Group (MTL) to the model portfolio at $13.85. Also after doing the calculation on dividends collected, I realized I had almost enough dividends for this purchase. As tax returns are now in hand and RRSP contribution room is known, this is an appropriate time to add to one's RRSP. Therefore I added $3500 to the model and increased Power Corp (POW) by 100 shares at its June 30th close of $27.50 for a new average cost base of $29.89. Financials took the biggest hit with the Brexit blip due to now anticipated "lower for longer" interest rates. To me POW looks like pretty good value and is one of the key foundation blocks of my RRSP. It looked like a good time to add to the model. It's a great habit to get into adding to one's RRSP when tax assessments are received rather than wait to the last minute. These are the habits that will help prevent the situation described in the first paragraph. It was a nice coincidence that a market sell-off occurred at this appropriate time for additions.

TFSA Model Portfolio

Company	Ticker	Date Added	# Shares	Price Added	Cost In CAD	Current Value in CAD	Share Price Change	Previous Total Dividends to Date	Apr 2016 Dividens	May 2016 Dividends	Jun 2016 Dividends	New Total Divdends to Date	Total Return
International													
Ensco PLC	ESV	May 30/14	100	$ 52.66	$ 5,750	$ 1,262	$ (4,488)	$ 326.20			$ 1.30	$ 327.50	-72.4%
Glaxo Smithkline	GSK	May 30/14	100	$ 53.94	$ 5,890	$ 5,634	$ (256)	$ 459.94	$ 156.95			$ 616.89	6.1%
Ship Finance Int.	SFL	May 30/14	180	$ 18.52	$ 3,644	$ 3,449	$ (195)	$ 759.04			$ 105.30	$ 864.34	18.4%
Seadrill	SDRL	July 25/14	130	$ 37.49	$ 5,312	$ 548	$ (4,764)	$ 140.46				$ 140.46	-87.0%
HSBC Holdings PLC	HSBC	July 25/14	100	$ 52.82	$ 5,757	$ 4,070	$ (1,687)	$ 436.79	$ 132.91			$ 569.70	-19.4%
Vodaphone	VOD	July 25/14	150	$ 34.16	$ 5,585	$ 6,024	$ 439	$ 434.05				$ 434.05	15.6%
Unilever PLC	UL	Jan 2/15	100	$ 40.05	$ 4,736	$ 6,228	$ 1,492	$ 205.08			$ 46.77	$ 251.85	36.8%
Diagio PLC	DEO	Jan 2/15	30	$ 112.73	$ 4,001	$ 4,402	$ 401	$ 130.58	$ 48.64			$ 179.22	14.5%
BHP Billiton Ltd	BHP	Jan 2/15	65	$ 47.27	$ 3,636	$ 2,413	$ (1,223)	$ 475.46	$ 27.05			$ 502.51	-19.8%
Internatonal Subtotal					$ 44,311	$ 34,030	$ (10,281)	$ 3,367.60				$ 3,886.52	-14.4%
Canadian													
TD Bank	TD	May 30/14	100	$ 53.76	$ 5,386	$ 5,548	$ 162	$ 345.00		$ 55.00		$ 400.00	10.4%
Rogers Communications	RCI.B	May 30/14	100	$ 43.82	$ 4,392	$ 5,230	$ 838	$ 329.25	$ 48.00			$ 377.25	27.7%
Teck Reources Ltd	TCK.B	May 30/14	200	$ 24.17	$ 4,844	$ 3,402	$ (1,442)	$ 220.00			$ 10.00	$ 230.00	-25.0%
ATCO	ACO.X	July 25/14	100	$ 50.56	$ 5,066	$ 4,532	$ (534)	$ 170.50			$ 28.50	$ 199.00	-6.6%
Husky Energy	HSE	July 25/14	153	$ 33.06	$ 5,068	$ 2,413	$ (2,655)	$ 227.74				$ 227.74	-47.9%
Sunlife Financial	SLF	July 25/14	100	$ 41.40	$ 4,150	$ 4,244	$ 94	$ 262.00			$ 40.50	$ 302.50	9.6%
Cdn. Western Bank	CWB	May/15Jan/16	220	$ 27.67	$ 6,106	$ 5,423	$ (683)	$ 164.50			$ 50.60	$ 215.10	-7.7%
Jean Coutu	PJC.A	May 19/15	200	$ 23.23	$ 4,656	$ 4,000	$ (656)	$ 66.00	$ 24.00			$ 90.00	-12.2%
AltaGas	ALA	Jan 4/16	200	$ 30.96	$ 6,202	$ 6,280	$ 78	$ 66.00	$ 33.00	$ 33.00	$ 33.33	$ 165.33	3.9%
CI Financial	CIX	Jan&May/16	300	$ 29.37	$ 8,832	$ 8,085	$ (747)	$ 44.00	$ 22.00	$ 22.00	$ 34.50	$ 122.50	-7.1%
Dividends from Sold Cos								$ 146.79				$ 167.96	
Canadian Subtotal					$ 54,702	$ 49,157	$ (5,545)	$ 2,041.78				$ 2,497.38	-5.6%
Total Cdn and Int					$ 99,013	$ 83,187	$ (15,826)	$ 5,409.38				$ 6,383.90	
Cash						$ 679							
Total						$ 83,866							-9.8%

Cost in CAD total of $99013 is derived from $93,000 investment plus $308 of capital gains plus $5705 of reinvested dividends, leaving $679 of cash from unspent dividends

Sales to Date	Ticker	Date Added	# Shares	Price	Exchange	Cost in CAD	Sold	Proceeds	Dividends	Profit	% Profit	
Innvest REIT	INN.UN	May30/14	210	$ 5.16		$ 1,094	May12/16	$ 1,479.00	$ 174.75	$ 559.75	51.2%	
South32	SOUHY	May30/15	26	$ 8.34	$ 1.23	$ 267	May12/16	$ 189.90	$ -	$ (77.10)	-28.9%	Rcvd via BHP Stock Div

Even the hard-luck TFSA model had a decent quarter growing by 4.3% but is still down 9.8% overall. I was very concerned prior to the Brexit vote given the number of UK-based corporations in the portfolio. However, I didn't make changes due to my long-term time horizon focus. The currency and market decline impacted these stocks but not nearly as much as the UK market overall. GSK, HSBC, VOD, UL, DEO are all UK-based large multinational corporations deriving income from many countries across the world. HSBC held particularly well compared to other European financials, many of which declined in the order of 25%. HSBC was down

15% but has since recovered half those losses. ESV, SDRL, HSE and BHP are slowly recovering from the commodity collapse while TECK.B has had a remarkable surge.

Lump sum investing: What occurred in the TFSA is a lesson in lump sum investing. One of my regrets with the newsletter was starting the TFSA model at the full allowable contribution room at the time. The stats show that lump sum investing provides the greatest probability of highest returns because the market is up more than it is down. This approach does not, however, allow for the psychological damage created if the market experiences a major calamity and performs an unceremonious face plant immediately afterwards. This calamity can cause an investor to retreat and potentially withdraw from the market entirely, giving up many future returns and may also be a key reason average investors underperform the market so dramatically, experiencing only 40% of total market returns (4% vs. 10%). Even with the smallish TFSA portfolios it would have been better to contribute over time. While not always providing the absolute best returns, it is a better approach taking into consideration both returns and the investor's emotional well-being. The TFSA lump sum approach was complicated by having too much resource exposure. Over time I am aiming to correct the issue without making panicky changes. It is also important to keep in mind the Canadian market benchmark remains down about 10% over the same time period, but is also now recovering nicely.

Regular non-registered margin account changes:

Sold ITC Holdings (ITC) and bought 50 more Williams-Sonoma (WSM): As communicated in the June 27th email update I sold 100 shares of ITC Holdings for $45.65 USD and purchased another 50 shares of WSM at $48.95. ITC is being purchased by Fortis and was trading at just a 3% discount to the purchase price, a combination of cash and shares of Fortis. To avoid holding a Canadian company in a US account, I wanted to sell the ITC before the deal closed. There is still some uncertainty related to the purchase, thus thought it would be wise to take advantage of the narrow discount and sell to take advantage of the Brexit blip to buy more WSM. The chart above includes a column "CapGainCdn." It is important to record the exchange rate at purchase and at sale of foreign companies in a taxable account in order to report capital gains in Canadian dollars for tax purposes.

On June 30th I also made the following changes on the US side:

Sold two AT&T $35.00 CALLS expiring on January 19, 2018: I had been pondering the sale of this CALL given the nice increase in AT&T share price and the large percentage gain in the CALL value. While not the original intention, after just seven months AT&T rallied from $33.72 to $42.60, driving the call price from $1.65 to $7.65. I decide to take the profit, which was relatively small on a dollar basis but very large on a percentage basis. With this example you can see how intoxicating option returns can be, but be careful as most CALLS expire worthless. The key to success is stock selection and using options in conjunction with stocks to enhance returns rather than using option only strategies (Please see Issue #19, December 1st, 2015, for purchasing rationale).

Sold two AT&T $42.00 PUTS expiring on January 19, 2018: I received $4.40/share or $880 for the contract, less commissions. This is a common strategy of mine. If a company I own and like experiences a nice surge and looks a little overvalued I often sell the shares and then also sell PUT options. This has the impact of stretching my upside a little (in this case $4.40/share) or at worst buying back the shares at a later date, at a lower price. In this case my effective lower price will be $42.00 - $4.40 = $37.60 or 12% below the then current price of $42.60. In this case I didn't own AT&T shares but rather CALL options, which is similar to owning the shares.

Vanguard Europe ETF (VGK): We already owned 100 shares of this European ETF. I had been thinking about adding more exposure to Europe as, contrary to the popular press, Europe's economy has been actually performing OK. I thought it would be best to wait for the Brexit vote before pursuing. After selling the AT&T CALLS, I thought I would derive this extra exposure through buying CALLS on VGK rather than the shares to keep at least one long CALL in the mix. What better to buy on than something which just dropped 10%, although it had already recovered half those losses? I purchased two $48.00 contracts which expire on January 19, 2018, and paid $2.60/share or $520 for the contract plus commissions. My effective price for the shares will be $48.00 + $2.60 = $50.60. VGK was trading at $46.00 at the time, such that I am paying a premium of 10%, but getting exposure to 200 shares for the small amount of $520. If VGK rallies to the same value as just before the Brexit vote, I will break even. VGK traded as high as $80.00 prior to the 2008 financial crisis providing great upside potential if the European economy defies the naysayers and continues to improve.

Capital One Financial (COF): I had enough cash left after these transactions on the US side to purchase 65 shares of COF for $61.67/share. COF has been a long time holding in another account. As mentioned, financials took the biggest hit during the Brexit blip, making it an opportune time to add. It is a large regional US banking and financial services company that grows organically and through acquisition, with emphasis on credit cards, consumer lending and commercial lending. It has active online banking presence with its purchase of ING Direct in the US. With $24B US in sales, it is one of the top 10 banking companies in the US. It is selling with a dividend yield of 2.5%, a very high earnings yield of 10.8%, price times book of just 0.69 but modest ROE of 8.0%. COF traded for $90.00 before the 2008 financial crisis, dropped to $10.00 bucks during it, recovered to $90.00 once again in 2015 but has since slid to $60.00 recently. Barring a significant US recession its valuation looks very good. COF has built a strong credit card brand with its "What's in Your Wallet?" slogan.

Canadian side: I added $7300 CAD to this side of the portfolio and made the following purchases on June 30th.

Manulife Financial fell during the Brexit blip, so I picked up an additional 200 shares at $17.33, such that I now own 500 with an average cost of $17.92. MFC trades with a dividend yield of 4.2%, earnings yield of 6.8% and price times book of just 0.82. It's not one of my favourites, but this looks like very good valuation.

Cameco Corp (CCO): I purchased 300 shares at $13.98. Over the past decade I have put a fair bit of effort into finding attractive alternative energy companies. Most of this effort has taken my down the path of speculative companies and cost me a fair bit of money. Alternative energy is, however, an important arena that is likely to grow over time. The experience has taken me back to relatively conservative companies with significant exposure to the alternative energy field. They still tend to be higher risk companies than many of the others invested in. CCO is the first such company I have added to this account. Based in Saskatchewan, CCO is a world leader in uranium production and refinement. There are 400 nuclear reactors in operation today, with another 86 under construction or expected to restart in the next five years and a further 172 in the planning stages. China is making an effort to clean up its air through both solar and nuclear, while India, Russia, South Korea and Japan represent other areas of demand growth. This growth should help uranium pricing, which declined during the financial crisis and again after Fukushima. Most of CCOs sales are on long-term contracts with utilities, providing a reasonable level of protection from swings in spot pricing. CCO, like most commodity producers has suffered over the past decade. Its price peaked in 2007 at over $55.00, declined to $16.00 in 2008, then rallied back up to $40.00 in 2011 and has been on a long, agonizing decline since then to its current price around $14.00. Compared to other commodity producers, however, while profits declined it has maintained profitability throughout the decade. It has a dividend yield of 2.8%, earnings yield of just 2.7%, cash flow yield of 7.9% and price times book of 1.0. One additional risk is a tax dispute with Revenue Canada. Winning the dispute could provide impetus for a rally. The current price looks like a good valuation.

Company Updates

First Trust Nat Gas ETF (FCG) performed a one for five reverse stock split, such that our share count dropped from 500 to 100 while the average cost per share is five times what it was. This has no impact on the valuation, which has been recovering slowly.

Brookfield Asset Management (BAM.A) spun out a new company, **Brookfield Business Partners LP (BBU. UN)**. We received one share for every 50 BAM.A owned for a total of three shares. It was a stock dividend and the value at the time of the spin-off was $25.67, which is now our cost base.

Looking Back: Do you notice a pattern here? Markets took a nosedive, and I was more active purchasing. Financials took the biggest hit of all, and that's where most purchases were made, with the addition of more POW and MFC as well as a new addition COF. This follows my "BUY VALUE...RARELY SELL" modus operandi (Issue #3, August 1st, 2014).

Financials went on to finish 2016 with very strong momentum. Six months after writing this issue, all three that were purchased at this time were up nicely. Europe has also done reasonably well, but the currency weakness in the British pound created another headwind for the TFSA with all its UK stocks.

ISSUE #27: AUGUST 1, 2016

Winning by NOT Losing

Welcome to a slimmed-down summer issue. In honour of Milos Raonic's runner-up success at Wimbledon and the final day of the Canadian Open, I thought a tennis analogy might be appropriate. Have you ever tried tennis? I have participated in many sports but found tennis the toughest to learn. Most of the exercise with tennis is running after errant balls. In my young adult years I did, however, play with friends. It was inexpensive to participate as tennis courts are a common recreational fixture and normally not too busy. While never gaining any level of proficiency, I found the best way to win was by NOT losing. Many of us amateurs will try our best to play like the pros, with ace serves and aggressive volleys. Unfortunately, these often go astray. Given the difficulty of the sport I found it best to just try to keep the ball in play and let my opponents attempt the testosterone-fuelled rocket shots. In other words I would try to win by NOT losing.

Winning at stock investing is similar to this strategy. Let others play the higher risk testosterone-fuelled moonshot companies. One in a hundred might turn out to be a 10-bagger (10x return), but most will fail. Many investors try to find the next Microsoft or the next Google but as you have seen I prefer the more established companies, like the current Microsoft or the current Google, that are much less likely to go broke. They will take much longer to become a 10-bagger, but it is still possible if held long enough, like my current holding of BNS purchased in the early 1990s.

Market comments: July started out with a nice rally taking both the TSX and the US S&P 500 up 3% by mid-July. They have effectively flatlined since then but July was still an excellent month for stocks. The TSX is now up 12.1% on the year and the S&P 500 is up 6.3%, breaking into new record territory. Whodathunkit with all the negativity in January and February? In the January issue I discussed market sentiment, which might be worth reviewing. The per cent bulls at the time was just 37%. That per cent dropped to 25% coincident with the markets bottoming in mid-February. The per cent bulls then started to rise along with the market and have now nudged over 50%. As mentioned in that issue, "That's the only logical way the market can work."

This month's changes: After the significant post-Brexit rally, I only made a couple of changes to the regular account.

Fortis (FTS): I added 100 shares at $43.12, such that I now hold 200 with an average cost of $39.89. When last month I sold ITC, which is being bought out by Fortis, it was my intention to add to Fortis and make it one of the key foundation blocks of the portfolio. I added $4200 to the Canadian side of the portfolio in order to make this purchase.

First Solar Inc. (FSLR): On the US side I sold two PUT contracts with a strike price of $52.50 and an expiry of January 19, 2018. I received $12.50 per share, or $2487.45 USD after commissions on the two contracts, such that my effective purchase price will be $40.00 if I get PUT. The price of FSLR shares was $46.80 at the time, so the effective purchase price is 14.5% lower than the current price. In January 2016 I sold 200 shares of FSLR in my other account for $63.76. If I get PUT I will get these shares back 37% below where I sold.

Capital One Financial (COF): I used the proceeds of the FSLR PUTS to purchase another 35 shares of COF at $67.47, such that I now have a board lot of 100 with an average purchase price of $63.67.

Alternative energy and First Solar: In the last issue I introduced the alternative energy field. Over the past decade I have spent a fair amount of time researching alternative energy investment ideas. This effort has largely been a waste of both time and money. While alternative energy is an exciting new area, most companies in the arena are smaller, higher-risk "moonshot" companies. I tried to win by winning and ended up losing! A number of alternative energy companies, including the largest at the time, Suntech, fell victim to over expansion, high debt and the financial crisis. The recent bankruptcy of SunEdison further highlights the risk in this area. I owned SunEdison but managed to escape at breakeven sometime before the bankruptcy. The entire solar industry has been referred to as a "solar coaster" to reflect its wild investment rides. All that might scare you off from investing in the area but the high volatility also provides larger option premiums, which is a benefit when using both stock and option strategies.

First Solar Inc: With $3.5B in sales FSLR is amongst the largest of the solar companies. Let's review some "solar coaster" numbers! FSLR has been a public company for about a decade. It traded at around $25.00 in 2007 then exploded to over $300 in 2008 when the world was running out of oil and other energy sources. Remember that era? The financial crisis bear market took it down to 100 bucks. It traded above this level from late 2008 until 2011. In late 2011 and 2012 the entire industry imploded from excessive over expansion combined with massive subsidy cuts in the European countries as part of their austerity programs. FSLR fell to below $15.00 in mid-2012. It then recovered and has traded between about $40.00 and $75.00 for the past three years. That's a real thrill ride, eh? Why would I invest in such a company?

At the current price, FSLR looks like a real bargain. It does not pay a dividend but has an earnings yield of 16.1%, cash flow yield of 20.8%, price times book of just 0.8, an ROE of 14.5% and ROA of 10.6%. Those look like great valuation numbers. The reason they are so good is FSLR earnings are expected to decline substantially in the near future as its pipeline of projects nears completion. However, one aspect that sets it apart from other solar companies is its excellent balance sheet. Its capitalization is 25% debt and 75% equity. This ratio can change quickly if losses occur and write-downs ensue, as we have seen with oil and gas. However, its low debt provides FSLR a better ability to survive tough times than many of its higher indebted competitors. While FSLR is higher risk than many of the other companies in the portfolio, it is "blue-chip" in the solar industry.

ISSUE #28: SEPTEMBER 1, 2016

Is It Risky, Volatile or Both?

Risk and volatility are usually considered synonymous, but are they? Many people are against investing in the stock market because it's so risky. But is it risky? Or is it just volatile? Are they the same, or am I just confused?

The following US stats might illustrate. One dollar invested 214 years ago in stocks would now be worth $704,997 after inflation. A "safer" investment in US bonds would be $1,178 and a "much safer" investment in US T-Bills would be $281. I don't plan on being alive in 214 years, but if I were to be so fortunate I would prefer the $704,997. What represents the greatest risk: a temporary 50% decline in the market (*all 50% declines in the market over the past 214 years have been temporary*) OR inflation outrunning current one to two per cent bond yields, thus eroding your wealth over time? While bonds and T-bills are considered safer, are they really, OR are they just less volatile?

Let's use a couple of examples to further illustrate my belief that risk and volatility are two separate entities. Please rate each of the following two items on a 1-10 scale for RISK, with a separate rating for VOLATILITY:

Bell Canada shares: Bell is a 135-year-old company. Over the past thirty years it has increased its quarterly dividend almost tenfold from 7 cents per share to 68.25 cents per share. During this time period it has not missed nor reduced its dividend. The 2008/09 bear market caused a share price decline of approximately 50%, from about $40.00 to about $20.00. How would you rate its risk? How about its volatility?

Private loan: A friend approaches you wishing to open a new restaurant. It is tough to borrow from a bank with an unproven business record, so he or she asks you for a $100,000 loan with a 12% interest rate. As a start-up business with constraints on initial cash flow, the loan is structured such that the interest accumulates and the entire loan plus all accumulated interest is to be paid off on the due date in five years. The rationale is that in five years the restaurant will be an ongoing business success, and the friend will be able to borrow from the bank to pay off the loan. This type of loan structure is sometimes used for a start-up business. How would you rate this debt instrument for risk? How about its volatility?

My ratings are as follows: I would rate Bell Canada shares as a 3/10 for risk (i.e. fairly low risk) but a higher 5/10 for volatility. There is certainly some business risk and it is possible for Bell to make a significant misstep, but the likelihood is pretty low. It is, however, higher on the volatility score due to the one occurrence in the recent past when its share price dropped in half, although it recovered within about three years.

How does the private loan rate? Let's first look at volatility. At any time during the five-year term the value of the debt instrument can be calculated. Simply add the accumulated interest to the original principal. There is effectively NO volatility and, thus, it rates a very low 1/10 for volatility. But that DOES NOT make it a safe investment. I would rate the private loan as a very high 9/10 on the risk scale. Most restaurants fail within their first five years. Will this friend beat the odds and succeed? In my books this would be a very risky investment.

September: Speaking of volatility, September is historically the most volatile and the only month of the year with a long-term negative return. Most think of October as the volatile month because the crash of 1929 and 1987 both occurred in October, but September is actually the worst month. On average over the past 88 years, the US market has had a negative average return of 0.5% in September and it has been a down month 55% of the years. However, a long-term investor can't plan around one month. December and January are the strongest months of the year, but last December and January sure didn't show strong results so I always take seasonality with some skepticism. The markets have effectively flatlined since mid-July so you would expect some volatility to return.

TINA is a new acronym circulating the business news media. It describes what I have been alluding to since starting the newsletter and stands for "There is No Alternative." Pundits were not saying such things back in January/February at the bottom of the Canadian bear market and the second major US correction in six months, but after the 20-25% rally since mid-February they are now coming to the conclusion that very low bond yields do not provide great investment returns, so what alternative is there to stocks? Wouldn't it have been better to be in the market for the rally, than to just now come to that conclusion? As discussed in the January issue, that's the way the market functions. The majority of market participants have to be negative when the market is falling and have to be positive when the market is rising. TINA, however, is a long way from a ringing endorsement for stocks. It's much more of an "Eeyore," reluctant-like endorsement.

The past two years, while somewhat painful, did provide lots of opportunities for market entry. That said, the sentiment has definitely shifted to the positive, which along with September's historical negative returns, creates a temporary cautionary note.

BUT because it is impossible to predict the short-term direction of the market I made the following additions to the regular portfolio on the US side.

Oceaneering International Inc. (OII): I purchased 100 shares of OII at $26.42. OII will not be a household name but it is a leader in underwater services to the oil and gas business. Its largest business segment is remote-operated vehicles which work underwater while being operated from a control centre on the drilling rig or vessel. It also manufactures complementary subsea products and provides a myriad of underwater installation, inspection, maintenance and repair services. Oil and gas is the main industry served, but it also provides similar services for the US Navy and NASA. As an oil and gas-service business it has naturally been hurt by the current state of affairs but has remained profitable to date. OII is one of my favourite long-time oil and gas-service company holdings. It peaked at over $80.00 in late 2013 and has been on a long steady decline since. At its current price OII has a dividend yield of 4.1% (which has not yet been cut), an earnings yield of 5.4%, cash flow yield of 14.5%, which is still very good, and price to book of 1.7x. Its current depressed profits still provide an ROE of 9.0% and ROA of 4.2%, which is much better than most other oil and gas service businesses. Approximately 30% of the world's oil and gas comes from offshore production and that isn't going away soon. A chart in one of their presentations shows that declining production from aging offshore fields is already outpacing new production. I also just read this morning that new conventional oil discoveries in 2015 represented a grand total of less than one month of current usage and so far in 2016 represent just nine days of consumption. The seeds of the next oil boom are being sown today with the virtual shutdown of new exploration and development. Another consideration is that with $2.5B in sales, OII is fairly small but big enough to make an interesting acquisition for a large service company should market challenges persist.

SPDR, S&P Biotech ETF (XBI): To pay for OII, I sold two PUT contracts on XBI with an exercise price of $60.00 that expire on January 19, 2018. I received $10.20 per share for a total of $2040 less fees. The price of XBI was exactly $60.00 at the time, so if I get PUT my effective price will be $49.80 or 17% below its current price. I have been looking to add to the health care part of the portfolio but health care has been a pretty hot investment theme making many companies look expensive. It is also difficult without extensive research to figure out which companies have good drug pipelines. Therefore I settled on this biotech ETF. XBI zoomed from $20.00 in 2011 to $90.00 in 2015 (about the time I commented on the speculation in biotech), then quickly dropped to below $50.00 before recovering to its current price of $60.00. The higher volatility level provides better option premiums but there is certainly a fair level of risk in biotech. However, I would sooner take that risk inside an ETF because while a few companies might go broke, the whole industry isn't going broke. This large ETF also provides good option liquidity. I was still just over $300 US greenbacks short, so I had to transfer in $305 at an exchange rate of 1.31. I did not make any additions to the Canadian side. As mentioned above, I am proceeding with a little more caution at this juncture but still proceeding!

I Hate Insurance...But It Is Often a Prudent Decision

Why do we buy insurance? It is something we buy at significant cost that provides no enjoyment, that we hope never to use, and we aren't really sure what we bought until something bad happens. But we still buy this nebulous product for various reasons. Auto liability insurance is mandatory, but for the most part we buy insurance to avoid a catastrophic loss and for peace of mind. Can we buy investment insurance? Is there a way to protect our portfolio from a catastrophic loss? Yes, there is, but just like all other insurance products there is a significant cost. I think the best way to buy portfolio insurance is to buy index ETF PUTS that are significantly below the current price (out of the money) to keep premiums lower. There are a number of ETFs that I have introduced to subscribers over the issues but a quick list of the bigger index ETFs would be **Canada:** XIU (Top 60) and XIC (whole index), **US:** SPY (S&P 500), IWM (Russell 2000), QQQ (Nasdaq) and **International:** VGK (Europe), EEM (Emerging Markets) and EFA (Europe, Asia and Far East). When buying this type of insurance, it is best to stick with the largest ETFs with the most liquid options. The US and international indexes listed above have significantly more liquid options than the Canadian ones. You can also buy PUTS on individual stocks. Selling COVERED CALLS also provides some insurance benefits. If the stock declines, we pocket the premium. I wished I had purchased portfolio insurance before the 2008/09 financial crisis and started to buy some afterwards but tired of the cost. Given that all bear markets and corrections are temporary, I have decided for the most part to gut out these market calamities without insurance. My September 29 email update did, however, illustrate how insurance works.

September 29 Update

The Bayer buyout of Monsanto (MON) is a little bizarre in that the market is almost completely discounting any possibility of the buyout occurring. The buyout price is $128 and MON is currently trading at about $102, just $10.00 above where it was when the discussion started. There is very little overlap between the two companies with the notable exception of canola. For the merger to occur it is likely the regulators will insist on the sale of the Monsanto canola program. Two likely interested parties could be Syngenta or Agrium. Given the lack of other overlap it looks to me like the probability of completing the deal is better than how the market is currently pricing MON, which based on its own fundamentals is probably worth $80-100 without a buyout offer.

This represents a unique opportunity. Over the past two days, I sold one PUT contract on MON with a strike price of $125, just below the buyout offer, that expires on January 18, 2019, which is well after the buyout is likely to close, if it closes. The targeted date for closure is late 2017. I received $26.00 per share or $2600 less fees for this option. Because I had sold one PUT contract on MON previously, I thought this was a little too much exposure to one company relative to the size of the portfolio and keeping in mind that I try to transact options contracts representing a similar position size, as with outright stock purchases. Therefore, I decided to buy (and thus illustrate) some insurance on the transaction. I concurrently purchased one PUT contract with a strike price of $80.00 and the same expiry date. This cost me $5.62 per share or $562 plus fees for the contract netting me $2038 less fees on both transactions. Like any insurance I do not expect nor wish to collect on the policy. I would far sooner see MON increase to the buyout price. I purchased it strictly as insurance if something goes completely awry, the deal falls through and MON drops dramatically. The insurance kicks in if MON falls below $80.00. I will explain this more thoroughly in the upcoming issue but wanted to let you know what I did as I did it.

Monsanto was trading at $102.50 at the time I made these option transactions. This PUT sale was much further "in the money" (i.e. above the current MON price) than I would normally transact, but in this case it makes sense to do so just below the prospective purchase price, to maximize the upside. I received $26/share on the transaction. If I get PUT my effective price is $125-$26 = $99 or just $3.50 below the current price. This illustrates that if we sell PUTS deep "in the money" we get more cash up front and more upside potential, but if the stock goes down the effective purchase price is closer to the actual price at the time of the option sale. I chose to go for the 2019 options as they recently became available and provided a little more time premium of about $2/share. While the target closing is late 2017 it could easily slide well past this date. The 2019 date also provides extra time for MON to recover if the deal fails. I purchased an insurance PUT contract because this is the second MON PUT sale I made. The previous one was at $100, expiring January 19, 2018, so that my total commitment to MON is now $10,000 (first contract) + $12,500 (second contract) = $22,500 which is large in relation to the rest of the portfolio. The insurance PUT was at a strike price of $80.00 and cost me $5.62 per share. If the deal doesn't conclude and MON falls below $80.00, I will be able to sell this PUT to partially offset the cost of getting PUT the 100 shares at $125. If the stock drops to $50.00, I will need to come up with the $125/share, but part of coming up with this money will be the sale of the insurance PUT contract which will be worth $80 - $50 = $30. This is clearly not the desired outcome but provides a little peace of mind. Given the entire portfolio has some leverage it also makes sense to have a few insurance items in it, like the covered calls and now the purchased PUT.

One other point of interest is that if the regulators stop the deal, Bayer is required to pay Monsanto a $2B breakup fee. This is not an insignificant sum and shows Bayer's commitment to completing the purchase. $2B represents an entire year of profit for Monsanto of about $4.50/share and should cushion any sell-off if the deal falls apart. There is always risk in any transaction but this looks reasonably safe to me.

And now for our quarterly review: September brought a little more excitement after a couple of pretty boring summer months, but in the end provided very little in the way of real movement. The US S&P was down a little on the month, and the TSX was up a little. While both markets had some days with greater than 1% moves, neither moved more than 1% over the entire month. The third quarter, however, was very productive, especially with our newsletter portfolios. The TSX was up a very nice 4.7% (price rather than total return) in the third quarter with a year to date gain of 13.2%. The S&P 500 was up a respectable 3.3% for the quarter contributing nicely with its more modest 6.1% year-to-date gain. These are much better outcomes than pundits were predicting early in the year. That said, anything can happen and full-year returns are still not guaranteed.

The fourth quarter is historically the best quarter of the year but that is certainly not guaranteed. We experienced weak fourth quarters the last two years. The US election is providing lots of entertainment value on its own but will surely contribute to some entertaining market gyrations as well. While I am quite optimistic, market sentiment has fallen again contributing somewhat to my optimism. The average US market forecast is for the S&P to finish the year at its current level.

How did our portfolios do in the third quarter?

TFSA: The hard-luck TFSA continued its recovery gaining a respectable 4.5 % in the quarter, but remains 5.3% in the red. TECK.B has made a remarkable recovery but our three oil companies, ESV, SDRL and HSE continue to drag. While many oil stocks are recovering, the ocean drillers remain in a deep funk. As mentioned before, we will continue to work out of this whole and continue to diversify the portfolio away from resources, which will be the main topic in next month's newsletter. I am determined to use this portfolio as an example of not giving up, a key trait to succeeding long-term. (Please note that Teck Resources changed its ticker from TCK.B to TECK.B. This is why you may see both throughout the book.)

RRSP: Had another very solid quarter gaining 3.2% with a 12.3% gain year to date. Total return since inception is 9.4% over the twenty-one month average weighted time frame. Given the market conditions over this period and returns on competing fixed-income investments, this is a very acceptable result, but I expect better in the future.

TFSA Model Portfolio

Company	Ticker	Date Added	# Shares	Price Added	Cost In CAD	Current Value in CAD	Share Price Change	Previous Total Dividends to Date	Jul 2016 Dividens	Aug 2016 Dividends	Sep 2016 Dividends	New Total Divdends to Date	Total Return
International													
Ensco PLC	ESV	May 30/14	100	$ 52.66	$ 5,750	$ 1,114	$ (4,636)	$ 327.50			$ 1.32	$ 328.82	-74.9%
Glaxo Smithkline	GSK	May 30/14	100	$ 53.94	$ 5,890	$ 5,650	$ (240)	$ 616.89	$ 63.85			$ 680.74	7.5%
Ship Finance Int.	SFL	May 30/14	180	$ 18.52	$ 3,644	$ 3,473	$ (171)	$ 864.34			$ 106.33	$ 970.67	21.9%
Seadrill	SDRL	July 25/14	130	$ 37.49	$ 5,312	$ 404	$ (4,908)	$ 140.46				$ 140.46	-89.8%
HSBC Holdings PLC	HSBC	July 25/14	100	$ 52.82	$ 5,757	$ 4,927	$ (830)	$ 569.70	$ 64.80		$ 65.42	$ 699.92	-2.3%
Vodaphone	VOD	July 25/14	150	$ 34.16	$ 5,585	$ 5,728	$ 143	$ 434.05		$ 196.83		$ 630.88	13.9%
Unilever PLC	UL	Jan 2/15	100	$ 40.05	$ 4,736	$ 6,209	$ 1,473	$ 251.85			$ 44.87	$ 296.72	37.4%
Diagio PLC	DEO	Jan 2/15	30	$ 112.73	$ 4,001	$ 4,560	$ 559	$ 179.22				$ 179.22	18.5%
BHP Billiton Ltd	BHP	Jan 2/15	65	$ 47.27	$ 3,636	$ 2,950	$ (686)	$ 502.51			$ 24.01	$ 526.52	-4.4%
Internatonal Subtotal					$ 44,311	$ 35,015	$ (9,296)	$ 3,886.52				$ 4,453.95	-10.9%
Canadian													
TD Bank	TD	May 30/14	100	$ 53.76	$ 5,386	$ 5,824	$ 438	$ 400.00		$ 55.00		$ 455.00	16.6%
Rogers Communications	RCI.B	May 30/14	100	$ 43.82	$ 4,392	$ 5,566	$ 1,174	$ 377.25	$ 48.00			$ 425.25	36.4%
Teck Reources Ltd	TCK.B	May 30/14	200	$ 24.17	$ 4,844	$ 4,730	$ (114)	$ 230.00				$ 230.00	2.4%
ATCO	ACO.X	July 25/14	100	$ 50.56	$ 5,066	$ 4,662	$ (404)	$ 199.00			$ 28.50	$ 227.50	-3.5%
Husky Energy	HSE	July 25/14	153	$ 33.06	$ 5,068	$ 2,459	$ (2,609)	$ 227.74				$ 227.74	-47.0%
Sunlife Financial	SLF	July 25/14	100	$ 41.40	$ 4,150	$ 4,269	$ 119	$ 302.50			$ 40.50	$ 343.00	11.1%
Cdn. Western Bank	CWB	May/15Jan/16	220	$ 27.67	$ 6,106	$ 5,555	$ (551)	$ 215.10			$ 50.60	$ 265.70	-4.7%
Jean Coutu	PJC.A	May 19/15	200	$ 23.23	$ 4,656	$ 4,026	$ (630)	$ 90.00		$ 24.00		$ 114.00	-11.1%
AltaGas	ALA	Jan 4/16	200	$ 30.96	$ 6,202	$ 6,748	$ 546	$ 165.33	$ 33.33	$ 33.33	$ 35.35	$ 267.34	13.1%
CI Financial	CIX	Jan&May/16	300	$ 29.37	$ 8,832	$ 7,551	$ (1,281)	$ 122.50	$ 34.50	$ 34.50	$ 34.50	$ 226.00	-11.9%
Dividends from Sold Cos								$ 167.96				$ 167.96	
Canadian Subtotal					$ 54,702	$ 51,390	$ (3,312)	$ 2,497.38				$ 2,949.49	-0.7%
Total Cdn and Int					$ 99,013	$ 86,405	$ (12,608)	$ 6,383.90				$ 7,403.44	
Cash						$ 1,698							
Total						$ 88,103							-5.3%

Cost in CAD total of $99013 is derived from $93,000 investment plus $308 of capital gains plus $5705 of reinvested dividends, leaving $1698 of cash from unspent dividends

Sales to Date	Ticker	Date Added	# Shares	Price	Exchange	Cost in CAD	Sold	Proceeds	Dividends	Profit	% Profit	
Innvest REIT	INN.UN	May30/14	210	$ 5.16		$ 1,094	May12/16	$ 1,479.00	$ 174.75	$ 559.75	51.2%	
South32	SOUHY	May30/15	26	$ 8.34	$ 1.23	$ 267	May12/16	$ 189.90	$ -	$ (77.10)	-28.9%	Rcvd via BHP Stock Div

RRSP Model Portfolio

Company	Ticker	Date Added	# Shares	Price Added	Cost In CAD	Current Value in CAD	Share Price Change	Previous Dividends to Date	July Dividends	August Dividends	September Dividends	New Dividends to Date	Total Return
US Companies													
Verizon	VZ	Sept 30/14	100	$ 49.99	$ 5,609	$ 6,813	$ 1,204	$ 489.79					31.5%
HCP Inc	HCP	Sept 30/14	100	$ 39.71	$ 4,458	$ 4,974	$ 516	$ 483.41		$ 73.05		$ 562.84	24.1%
Hospitality Prop. Trust	HPT	Sept 30/14	150	$ 26.85	$ 4,521	$ 5,844	$ 1,323	$ 725.26		$ 73.72		$ 557.13	47.5%
RMR Group	RMR	Dec 18/15	2	$ 16.95	$ 47	$ 99	$ 52	$ 0.78		$ 97.85		$ 823.11	114.6%
United Technologies	UTX	Oct 31/14	50	$ 107.00	$ 6,002	$ 6,660	$ 658	$ 282.30		$ 0.64		$ 1.42	16.4%
Johnson and Johnson	JNJ	Oct 31/14	50	$ 107.78	$ 6,045	$ 7,743	$ 1,698	$ 330.02			$ 42.75	$ 325.05	34.4%
Freeport-McMoRan	FCX	Nov 30/14	150	$ 26.85	$ 4,601	$ 2,138	$ (2,463)	$ 108.90			$ 51.74	$ 381.76	-51.2%
Chevron	CVX	Nov 30/14	50	$ 108.87	$ 6,216	$ 6,746	$ 530	$ 413.80				$ 108.90	16.3%
Exelon	EXC	Nov 30/14	150	$ 36.17	$ 6,195	$ 6,546	$ 351	$ 361.19			$ 69.15	$ 482.95	12.5%
General Electric	GE	Jan 27/15	200	$ 24.38	$ 6,056	$ 7,769	$ 1,713	$ 298.06	$ 60.21		$ 61.01	$ 422.20	34.2%
Praxair	PX	Feb 28/15	25	$ 127.90	$ 4,007	$ 3,959	$ (48)	$ 140.94				$ 358.27	2.9%
Qualcomm	QCOM	Feb 28/15	50	$ 72.51	$ 4,542	$ 4,490	$ (52)	$ 185.65			$ 24.54	$ 165.48	3.7%
US Subtotal					$ 58,299	$ 63,781	$ 5,482	$ 3,820.10			$ 34.81	$ 220.46	17.0%
												$ 4,409.57	
Canadian Companies													
Bank of Nova Scotia	BNS	Sep14/Jan16	200	$ 62.30	$ 12,480	$ 13,904	$ 1,424	$ 552.00	$ 144.00			$ 696.00	17.0%
Power Corp	POW	Sep14/Jun16	300	$ 29.89	$ 8,986	$ 8,337	$ (649)	$ 432.02			$ 100.50	$ 532.52	-1.3%
Capital Power	CPX	Oct 31/14	200	$ 25.58	$ 5,126	$ 4,124	$ (1,002)	$ 423.00	$ 73.00			$ 496.00	-9.9%
Mullen Group Ltd.	MTL	Nov14/Jun16	500	$ 17.99	$ 9,013	$ 8,230	$ (783)	$ 433.50	$ 15.00	$ 15.00	$ 15.00	$ 478.50	-3.4%
Royal Bank	RY	Jan 27/15	100	$ 75.12	$ 7,522	$ 8,126	$ 604	$ 393.00		$ 81.00		$ 474.00	14.3%
TransCanada Pipeline	TRP	Jan 27/15	100	$ 55.59	$ 5,609	$ 6,231	$ 622	$ 264.50	$ 56.50			$ 321.00	16.8%
Bell Canada	BCE	Feb 28/15	100	$ 54.71	$ 5,481	$ 6,059	$ 578	$ 328.25	$ 68.25			$ 396.50	17.8%
Brookfield Asset Mgmt	BAM.A	Feb 28/15	150	$ 45.23	$ 6,795	$ 6,920	$ 125	$ 198.93			$ 25.76	$ 224.69	5.1%
Brookfield BusinessLP	BBU.UN	Jun 24,16	3	$ 25.67	$ 77	$ 104	$ 27	$ -			$ 0.27	$ 0.27	35.4%
Pason Systems	PSI	Mar 3/15	200	$ 18.48	$ 3,706	$ 3,358	$ (348)	$ 204.00			$ 34.00	$ 238.00	-3.0%
Wajax Corp	WJX	Mar 3/15	150	$ 24.31	$ 3,657	$ 2,171	$ (1,486)	$ 162.50	$ 37.50			$ 200.00	-35.2%
Home Capital Group	HCG	Mar15/May15	150	$ 43.11	$ 6,475	$ 4,050	$ (2,425)	$ 160.00			$ 36.00	$ 196.00	-34.4%
AutoCanada	ACQ	Apr 4/15	150	$ 34.15	$ 5,133	$ 3,323	$ (1,810)	$ 165.00			$ 15.00	$ 180.00	-31.8%
Cogeco Inc.	CGO	May 29/15	100	$ 53.60	$ 5,370	$ 5,142	$ (228)	$ 114.00		$ 29.50		$ 143.50	-1.6%
Pembina Pipeline	PPL	Dec 9/15	200	$ 29.17	$ 5,844	$ 7,996	$ 2,152	$ 188.17	$ 32.32	$ 32.32	$ 32.32	$ 285.13	41.7%
Dividends from Sold Cos												$ 24.40	
Cdn Subtotal					$ 91,274	$ 88,075	$ (3,199)	$ 4,043.27				$ 4,886.51	1.8%
Total Cdn and US					$ 149,573	$ 151,856	$ 2,283	$ 7,863.37				$ 9,296.08	
Cash						$ 1,879							
Portfolio Value						$ 153,735							9.4%

Cost in CAD total of $149,573 is derived from $140,500 invested, $1656 capital gains, plus $7417 of reinvested dividends, leaving $1879 of cash from unspent dividends.

Sales to Date	Ticker	Date Added	# Shares	Price	Exchange	Cost In CAD	Sold	Sold Price	Proceeds	Dividends	Profit	% Profit
Constellation Software	CSU	Oct 31/14	10	$ 317.50		$ 3,185	Apr 14/15	$ 485.07	$ 4,841	$ 24.40	$ 1,679	52.7

And now for something spectacular:

Non-Registered Margin Portfolio

Company	Ticker	Date Added	# Shares	Price Added	Cost In USD	Current Value in USD	Share Price Change	Previous Dividends to Date	July Dividends	August Dividends	September Dividends	New Dividends to Date	Total Return
US Dollar Purchases													
iShares MSCI Emerging	EEM	6-Jul-15	100	$ 38.62	$ 3,872	$ 3,745	$ (127)	$ 65.18				$ 65.18	-1.6%
Vanguard Europe ETF	VGK	6-Jul-15	100	$ 52.91	$ 5,301	$ 4,873	$ (428)	$ 137.95			$ 22.52	$ 160.47	-5.0%
First Trust Nat GAS	FCG	6-Jul-15	100	$ 42.85	$ 4,297	$ 2,642	$ (1,655)	$ 59.40			$ 1.80	$ 61.20	-37.1%
Parker Hannifin	PH	24-Jul-15	50	$ 110.84	$ 5,552	$ 6,277	$ 725	$ 107.08			$ 26.77	$ 133.85	15.5%
iShares Silver Trust	SLV	31-Aug-15	200	$ 13.79	$ 2,767	$ 3,640	$ 873	$ -				$ -	31.6%
Market Vector Gold	GDX	31-Aug-15	200	$ 13.71	$ 2,751	$ 5,286	$ 2,535	$ 19.72				$ 19.72	92.9%
Berkshire Hathaway	BRK.B	Aug15-Jan16	75	$ 134.12	$ 10,099	$ 10,835	$ 736	$ -				$ -	7.3%
Union Pacific	UNP	31-Aug-15	50	$ 86.13	$ 4,316	$ 4,877	$ 561	$ 70.11			$ 23.37	$ 93.48	15.2%
Citigroup Inc	C	25-Feb-16	100	$ 38.45	$ 3,855	$ 4,723	$ 868	$ 4.25		$ 13.60		$ 17.85	23.0%
Alphabet	GOOGL	29-Apr-16	5	$ 706.77	$ 3,544	$ 4,020	$ 476	$ -				$ -	13.4%
Williams Sonoma	WSM	May/Jun2016	100	$ 51.52	$ 5,172	$ 5,108	$ (64)	$ -		$ 31.45		$ 31.45	-0.6%
Capital One Financial	COF	Jun/Jul2016	100	$ 63.67	$ 6,387	$ 7,183	$ 796	$ -		$ 34.00		$ -	12.5%
Oceaneering Intl Inc	OII	31-Aug-16	100	$ 26.42	$ 2,652	$ 2,751	$ 99	$ -				$ -	3.7%
Dividends from Sold Cos								$ 47.82				$ 47.82	
US Options													
American Express	AXP	30-Oct-15	1 Put	$ 73.60	$ (762)	$ (1,110)	$ (348)						-45.7%
Walmart	WMT	30-Oct-15	1 Put	$ 57.90	$ (689)	$ (43)	$ 646						93.8%
Emerson Electric	EMR	30-Oct-15	1 Put	$ 47.10	$ (740)	$ (115)	$ 625						84.5%
IBM	IBM	25-Nov-15	1 Put	$ 137.82	$ (1,859)	$ (865)	$ 994						53.5%
CVS Health Corp	CVS	25-Nov-15	1 Put	$ 93.90	$ (1,089)	$ (925)	$ 164						15.1%
Russell 2000 ETF	IWM	28-Jan-16	1 Put	$ 99.50	$ (1,449)	$ (457)	$ 992						68.5%
Citigroup Inc	C	25-Feb-16	1 Put	$ 38.45	$ (469)	$ (49)	$ 420						89.5%
Citigroup Inc	C	25-Feb-16	1 CovCa	$ 38.45	$ (299)	$ (560)	$ (261)						-87.3%
Walt Disney	DIS	25-Feb-16	1 Put	$ 95.40	$ (1,609)	$ (1,345)	$ 264						16.4%
iShares MSCI Emerging	EEM	25-Feb-16	1 Put	$ 30.30	$ (1,233)	$ (584)	$ 649						52.6%
Market Vector Gold	GDX	29-Apr-16	2 CovCa	$ 25.50	$ (428)	$ (218)	$ 210						49.1%
Market Vector Gold	GDX	29-Apr-16	2 Put	$ 25.50	$ (337)	$ (112)	$ 225						66.8%
Monsanto	MON	29-Apr-16	1 Put	$ 93.80	$ (1,631)	$ (1,050)	$ 581						35.6%
Hilton	HLT	31-May-16	4 Put	$ 20.60	$ (1,705)	$ (1,040)	$ 665						39.0%
iShares Silver Trust	SLV	31-May-16	3 Put	$ 15.27	$ (916)	$ (441)	$ 475						51.9%
A T & T	T	30-Jun-16	2 Put	$ 42.60	$ (867)	$ (1,022)	$ (155)						-17.9%
Vanguard Europe ETF	VGK	30-Jun-16	2 Call	$ 46.00	$ 532	$ 820	$ 288						54.1%
First Solar	FSLR	29-Jul-16	2 Put	$ 46.80	$ (2,487)	$ (3,862)	$ (1,375)						-55.3%
SPDR Series Biotech	XBI	31-Aug-16	2 Put	$ 60.00	$ (2,028)	$ (1,540)	$ 488						24.1%
Monsanto	MON	28-Sep-16	1 Put	$ 102.50	$ (2,589)	$ (2,600)	$ (11)						-0.4%
Monsanto	MON	28-Sep-16	1 Put-L	$ 102.50	$ 573	$ 600	$ 27						4.7%
US Subtotal					$ 38,485	$ 49,442	$ 10,957	$ 511.51				$ 631.02	
Cash						$ 2,092							
Total USD		Deposits		$ 37,405		$ 51,534							37.8%
Canadian Companies						CAD							
Bank of Montreal	BMO	3-Jul-15	100	$ 74.21	$ 7,431	$ 8,597	$ 1,166	$ 332.00		$ 86.00		$ 418.00	21.3%
CGI Group	GIB.A	23-Jul-15	100	$ 50.90	$ 5,100	$ 6,249	$ 1,149	$ -				$ -	22.5%
Crescent Point Energy	CPG	Jul15/Jan16	400	$ 16.79	$ 6,734	$ 6,920	$ 186	$ 262.00	$ 12.00	$ 12.00	$ 12.00	$ 298.00	7.2%
Telus	T	31-Aug-15	100	$ 42.83	$ 4,293	$ 4,329	$ 36	$ 130.00	$ 46.00			$ 176.00	4.9%
Suncor	SU	31-Aug-15	100	$ 35.78	$ 3,588	$ 3,642	$ 54	$ 116.00			$ 29.00	$ 145.00	5.5%
Stantec Inc.	STN	29-Sep-15	200	$ 29.30	$ 5,870	$ 6,166	$ 296	$ 43.50	$ 22.50			$ 66.00	6.2%
Potash Corp	POT	Oct15/Jan16	200	$ 23.84	$ 4,788	$ 4,270	$ (518)	$ 162.76		$ 64.63		$ 227.39	-6.1%
ShawCor	SCL	26-Nov-15	200	$ 28.94	$ 5,798	$ 6,474	$ 676	$ 60.00		$ 30.00		$ 90.00	13.2%
Russel Metals	RUS	26-Nov-15	200	$ 18.15	$ 3,640	$ 4,190	$ 550	$ 152.00			$ 76.00	$ 228.00	21.4%
Fortis Inc.	FTS	Nov15/Jul16	200	$ 39.89	$ 7,998	$ 8,438	$ 440	$ 75.00			$ 75.00	$ 150.00	7.4%
Manulife Financial	MFC	Jan16/Jun16	500	$ 17.92	$ 8,978	$ 9,255	$ 277	$ 111.00			$ 92.50	$ 203.50	5.4%
Enbridge Inc	ENB	22-Feb-16	100	$ 44.26	$ 4,436	$ 5,766	$ 1,330	$ 53.00			$ 53.00	$ 106.00	32.4%
Transforce Inc	TFI	22-Feb-16	200	$ 21.40	$ 4,290	$ 5,434	$ 1,144	$ 34.00	$ 34.00			$ 68.00	28.3%
Badger Daylighting	BAD	29-Apr-16	200	$ 24.35	$ 4,880	$ 5,670	$ 790	$ 6.60	$ 6.60	$ 6.60	$ 6.60	$ 26.40	16.7%
Cdn National Rail	CNR	30-May-16	100	$ 78.20	$ 7,830	$ 8,576	$ 746	$ 37.50			$ 37.50	$ 75.00	10.5%
Cameco Corp	CCO	Jun/Sep 16	600	$ 12.64	$ 7,604	$ 6,726	$ (878)	$ -				$ -	-11.5%
Cdn Options							$ -						
Crescent Point Energy	CPG	26-Jan-16	2 CovCa	$ 13.24	$ (308)	$ (440)	$ (132.00)						-42.9%
Cdn Subtotal					$ 92,950	$ 100,262	$ 7,312	$ 1,575.36				$ 2,277.29	
Cash						$ (2,769)							
Total CAD		Deposits		$ 87,900		$ 97,493							10.9%
TotalPortfolio Value in CAD						$ 165,003							
Deposits in CAD Value						$ 136,411							21.0%

Sales to Date	Ticker	Date Added	#Shares	Price Added	Currency	Cost	Sold	Sold Price	Proceeds	Accum Div	Profit	% Profit	CapGainCdn
ITC Holdings	ITC	2-Oct-15	100	$ 32.10	USD	$ 3,220	27-Jun-16	$ 45.65	$ 4,554	$ 47.82	$ 1,382	43%	$ 1,715
A T & T Calls	T	27-Nov-16	2	$ 1.65	USD	$ 342	30-Jun-16	$ 7.65	$ 1,517	0	$ 1,175	344%	$ 1,517

Note: The numbers in all the charts are as of closing on September 30th, with a conversion rate of 1.31. Changes made on October 3rd, discussed below, have not been reflected in the charts.

There are very few negative signs on any of the positions in the regular account. Considering the gnashing of teeth which occurred in the latter half of 2015 and especially in early 2016, this is a remarkable result if I don't say so myself! The US side is up an amazing 37.8% aided by the leverage employed (but keep in mind leverage cuts both ways) and the Canadian side is up 10.9% for a total portfolio increase of 21.0% in Canadian dollar terms over a 10.7 month weighted average time frame. The performance is the result of exceptional skill, unadulterated s--t luck or some combination thereof. I would suggest it is the combination thereof, but with the short time frame mostly luck. Nobody is that good and these results are unlikely to be sustainable over the long-term! **That said, it illustrates the benefits of building positions during periods of market weakness.**

Other portfolio changes, Regular Account:

Cameco (CCO): On September 30th I doubled my position with an additional 300 shares at a cost of $11.29/share. My new average cost is $12.64. We are bottom-fishing with Cameco. It is highly unlikely to go bankrupt with its modest debt levels. Eventually uranium prices will turn around with the restart of Japanese reactors and new builds in China and India. We will have to be patient as the current oversupply will persist for some time, but after declining for most of a decade we are "closer to the bottom than to the top."

The North West Company Inc. (NWC): On October 3rd I started a new position in NWC of 150 shares at $25.79. NWC is a food and dry goods retailer focused on rural and remote communities mostly in northern and western Canada and Alaska but also in the Caribbean and South Pacific. It has some urban presence focusing on underserved indigenous and lower income sectors. Food represents 80% of revenue but offerings include clothing, housewares, appliances, gasoline, pharmacy, quick serve food and financial services, as it is a "one stop shop" in many of the small communities served. Its main brands are Giant Tiger and Northern. With $1.8B in sales NWC is not large, but it is a critical and often sole supplier in these remote communities. As such it is less subject to the rigorous competitive pressures of the larger urban centres and also less susceptible to getting Amazoned with challenging logistics into these areas. NWC should benefit from the perpetually increasing funding for indigenous communities and any resurgence in resources, as they are often extracted in remote areas. NWC trades with a dividend yield of 4.8%, earnings yield of 5.6%, cash flow yield of 9.3%, price to book of 3.7x, a very strong ROE of 20.6% and ROA of 9.1%. Its debt level is reasonable at 57% vs. 43% equity and has been stable. NWC's growth has been modest but generally steady.

The cash balance in the chart is negative as the CCO trade was made on September 30 and I had not yet transferred funds into the account. With the NWC trade I have now transferred $6700 to cover both. On the other hand, you will see a positive cash position on the US side as I have not yet deployed the cash generated from the MON option trades. I plan on holding to see if short-term opportunities occur during the US election period. As well, the January 20, 2017, option expiry date is approaching and I usually try to build a little cash cushion in case I get PUT any of the stocks. AXP and CVS are currently trading below the strike price. You usually don't get PUT until close to or on the expiry date when the time premium has virtually disappeared, but the owner of the PUT has the right to exercise any time up to expiry.

RRSP: On October 3ʳᵈ I sold the very small positions in RMR at $37.94 USD, netting $88.57 CAD for the model account and BBU.UN for $34.21, netting $92.63 CAD for the model account after taking off the $10.00 transaction fees. These were small spin-offs from their parent companies, and while they have done well, they cannot contribute significantly to the overall portfolio. As mentioned before I still work with a full-service brokerage on the RRSP, and they periodically have commission-free days to allow customers to sell these very minor positions. I took advantage of this opportunity to clean up the positions.

Looking Back: I don't want to steal my own thunder from the January 4th, 2017 issue, but the experts were forecasting the S&P 500 to end the year at the same level it was at the end of the third quarter. This was way off base as the market surged after the US election.

Also please note how the dividends collected are contributing to portfolio growth.

ISSUE #30: NOVEMBER 1, 2016

Build It with Straw, Sticks, or Bricks?

What should we use to build a strong portfolio? Straw, sticks or bricks? We all know the classic fairy tale and its enduring lesson to build our house with only the strongest material, BRICKS, so it can withstand the huffing and puffing of the Big Bad Wolf. With all due respect to our three friendly piglets, is this the correct answer? Should we make the roof out of bricks? Perhaps the roof would be better made of sticks covered with straw thatch. Like any well-constructed edifice a portfolio should also be constructed with various materials (stocks), each with its own purpose and complementary to each other for maximum overall strength to power upwards during favourable markets and better withstand the huffing and puffing of the Big Bad Bear when it rears its ugly head.

There has been much written about the benefits of diversification, but there are also proponents for portfolio concentration. One of the strongest proponents of concentration is actually Warren Buffett. This is one of the few areas where I personally disagree with his investing philosophy. Concentration may work for larger investors who can regularly meet with company executives but would be difficult for smaller investors. Company CEOs are unlikely to return our calls but would surely respond to Warren's if he were to call. Thus, large investors have the opportunity to better understand what is really going on inside a company. A contrary opinion, however, comes via Peter Lynch, now retired but one of the most successful mutual fund managers of all-time. He managed his funds with a very high level of diversification and advocated starting with small positions to learn about a company before building larger positions.

Below is a chart showing how our portfolio companies fit into each of the seventeen market segments I use to build portfolio diversification:

Group	Sector	TFSA		RRSP		Non-Registered			
		CDN	INTL	CDN	US	CDN	US	INTL	US-Options
1	Bank	TD,CWB	HSBC	BNS,RY		BMO	COF,C		C
	Non-Bank Financial	SLF,CIX	SFL	POW,HCG		MFC	BRK.B		AXP
	Telecom	RCI.B	VOD	BCE,CGO	VZ	T			T
	Pipeline	ALA		TRP,PPL		SCL,ENB			
	Electric Utility	ACO.X		CPX	EXC	FTS			
2	Consumer	NWC	UL,DEO	ACQ		NWC,CJR.B	WSM		WMT
	Health	PJC.A	GSK		HCP,JNJ				XBI,CVS
	Industrial/Manufacturing			WJX	UTX,GE,PX	RUS	PH		EMR
	Technology				QCOM	GIB.A	GOOGL		MON,IBM
	Transportation			MTL		TFI,CNR	UNP		
	Infrastructure/Building			BAM.A		STN,BAD			
	Real Estate/Hotel/Leisure				HPT				DIS,HLT
	Index ETF'S							VGK,EEM	IWM,VGK,EEM
3	Oil and Gas	HSE	ESV,SDRL	PSI	CVX	CPG,SU	OII,FCG		
	Metals/Materials	TCK.B	BHP		FCX	POT			
	Gold and Silver						SLV,GDX		SLV,GDX
	Alt Energy/Environment					CCO			FSLR

There are a couple of considerations for Canadian investors which provide impetus to enhance diversification: 1) Tax-advantaged government programs create a need to build portfolios separately for each program, and 2) There is a need to significantly diversify outside Canada for large world-class companies. Many investors do not avail themselves of these opportunities and maintain a strong home country bias. I feel this is a mistake and diversify heavily outside Canada for the many reason previously written about.

I have divided each of the seventeen sectors into three groups. The first group tends to be the most stable companies with lower cyclicality and higher dividends but slower growth, although US banks have proven to be more cyclical than Canadian banks. The second group has more cyclicality, but also somewhat higher growth potential and the third group are very cyclical and thus exhibit greatest volatility as we have seen over the past two to three years. Issue #3, way back on August 1st, 2014, was titled "Buy Value...Rarely Sell." I still stick to this main philosophy but fully admit, especially with the third group of companies, the need to be readier to sell at opportune times. Some companies bridge two or more sectors. Examples: MTL is 50% oil and gas and 50% transportation. I have put in the transportation segment as this is my main reason for purchasing. CCO could easily be put in the materials sector but because the material it mines is used to power nuclear plants I have categorized it as alternative energy. BAM.A could easily be considered a non-bank financial but because many of the investments it makes and manages are long-life infrastructure investments, I have categorized it that way. Below are a few comments on each portfolio:

Non-registered account: Is focused on Canadian and US equities, with a little international exposure through ETFs. Each of the 17 sectors is now covered, with the sale of PUT options providing coverage in some areas. Index ETFs aren't really a segment as they include all industries, but I wanted to represent this through a separate line.

RRSP: Again, the focus is Canada and the US. Most of the sectors are covered with the exception of a couple of Group 3 segments. Given the more conservative approach taken with this fund, this is appropriate.

TFSA: The reason for 2014 and 2015 underachievement should be obvious. Avoiding US withholding tax has led to being under-diversified. Another contributing factor is the limits put on annual contributions leading to modest-sized accounts, which are inherently more difficult to diversify. Financials and resources make up 70% of the Canadian market, making it difficult to fully diversify with just Canadian stocks. International stocks, largely based out of the UK without dividend withholding taxes, help the diversification effort. The chart is as it is today, with the exception of leaving TECK.B in for visual effects, even though it was recently sold. If we go back 2.5 years at the beginning of the commodity collapse, there were only two Group 2 companies: INN.UN recently sold because of a buyout and GSK. The other companies that now appear have been added more recently to provide diversification. Prior to these additions the portfolio was even more skewed than today. Over the next two to three years, contributions will be focused towards filling the other segments. One of the fun aspects of stock investing is the endless opportunities for learning and improving.

The GOOD news: If you followed the newsletter recommendations over the past 2.5 years you will have done significantly better than many Canadian investors. Most investors exhibit home country bias and have over two-thirds Canadian exposure, with minimal US and international diversification. The RRSP has especially benefited from heavy US equity exposure. The non-registered portfolio has been built largely during the period of weak Canadian currency and has not had the same benefit while the TFSA has not benefited because the British pound has been equally as weak as the Canadian dollar partly thanks to Brexit.

Conclusion: While what I have added in the newsletter accounts may have appeared a little helter skelter, there was some method to the madness. I try to cover each segment with both a Canadian and US (or in the case of TFSA, Canadian and UK) equity. Some segments will have two to four representative companies, especially the first group as they are my preferred sectors. I always try to buy companies that represent reasonable value and can be held long-term, but in this business it is impossible to be perfect. I once read that if two-thirds of a portfolio's positions are positive, it is a successful portfolio. My goal is to be better than this and aim for 80% positive. Like building a strong house and contrary to the fable of the three little pigs, many ingredients are necessary for a strong portfolio. These ingredients are all connected and work together. When the US dollar strengthens, benefiting US exposure, commodities tend to decline hurting those sectors. When the US is believed to be on the verge of increasing interest rates, financials rally as they benefit from higher interest rates, but what are considered interest sensitive sectors (utilities, pipelines, telecom and REITs) tend to decline. When economic growth is strong Group 2 and Group 3 stocks tend to benefit, but in a recession Group 1 companies hold their value better. This is clearly an oversimplification but all these factors weigh in for overall portfolio performance. If one could predict with any level of accuracy which factors would occur over the next 12 months then one could pick the companies benefiting from those conditions. But we can't so do our best bet is to have full diversification and buy during market or sector weakness.

And now for this month's portfolio changes:

Issue #30: November 1, 2016

TFSA: On October 18, I forwarded the following TFSA update to further diversify the portfolio away from resources.

October 18 Update

Hope all is well. I wanted to bring you up to date on some changes I made this morning in my TFSA accounts.

Teck Resources has made a remarkable comeback and has proven to be a very well-managed mining company. However, I wanted to take advantage of the rebound to reduce exposure to the volatile resource sector in the TFSA, add to the dividends collected and take advantage of the recent surge in TECK.B. I still own a fair bit of TECK.B in a personal non-registered account, which is a more appropriate place for it given its current minimal dividend.

Thus, this morning in my TFSA, I sold 200 TECK.B at $26.69 and used the proceeds plus some accumulated dividends to buy 200 North West Company (NWC) at $25.91 plus add 100 more Jean Coutu Group (PJC.A) at $19.62. I will make the same changes to the model TFSA account. The new average purchase price for PJC.A is $22.03.

The NWC purchase is a duplication of last issue's non-registered account addition. I have tried to avoid duplicates in the newsletter accounts but when making this addition to the non-registered account I was thinking that NWC would also be appropriate for a TFSA or RRSP.

In the end we made a 15% return, including dividends, on TECK.B over the two and a half years it was in the model TFSA account. This is what I refer to as a successful failure and an example of "winning by not losing." Not a bad return by any means but a somewhat harrowing journey. We still hold BHP, the world's largest mining company, in the TFSA.

Regular Account

Corus Entertainment Inc. (CJR.B): Late Friday I transferred $4200 to the Canadian side of the regular account and added 400 shares of CJR.B at $10.92 per share. Corus is not without its risks but those risks seem to be factored into its stock price. It is a media and entertainment company with 45 specialty channels and 15 conventional TV stations. Its many recognized brands including Global, Teletoon and Treehouse children's programming. Its Canadian broadcast rights include HGTV, OWN, National Geographic Channel, History Channel, Disney Channel, The Food Network and numerous others. It owns 39 Canadian radio stations including Country 105 in Calgary and Q107 in both Calgary and Toronto. CJR.B produces children-focused content including *Babar*, *Franklin* and a library of children's books. It also provides animation software to other studios including Disney and Fox. The higher risk level is because it recently purchased many of these assets from Shaw Communications, in effect doubling the overall size of the company and taking on significant new debt. The process of integrating new assets doesn't always go smoothly. Over the past year the company has traded between $9.00 and $14.00 but in 2012-2014 it was in the $20.00 to $28.00 range. It pays an oversized monthly dividend of 9.5 cents equating to a dividend yield of 10.5% at today's price. CJR.B has an

August 31st year-end and for fiscal 2016 it had earnings yield of 7.1%, cash flow yield of 26.3%, price to book ratio of just 0.9, ROE of 7.2% and ROA of 3.3%, although all of this could change significantly in 2017 due to the Shaw asset purchase. It needs to improve profitability (ROE and ROA) but is cheap from a cash flow perspective. If successful with integration, profitability should improve to help sustain the dividend while chipping away at debt.

S&P 500 ETF (SPY): I am a little nervous about the endless US election circus. Both candidates for president could face criminal charges, one for sexual assault and the other for sending classified emails through a personal server. I'm not sure how this is criminal but it was certainly a lapse of judgement. The other very concerning aspect is both candidates, especially Trump, are spouting significant trade protectionist sentiment. As a reminder, the Great Depression started with the 1929 market crash but got into high gear when trade wars erupted. I am in no way suggesting we are entering such an era but the trade war rhetoric is concerning the markets. Since early July the S&P 500 has effectively flatlined, trading within a very narrow band of 2120 to 2185. I think the election could provide the impetus to break this low-volatility four-month cycle. Problem is, it is impossible to predict which way. Thus I purchased a little PUT insurance for downside protection until the election is over. I purchased four PUT contracts on SPY with a strike price of $208, which expires on November 11th, three days after the election. They cost me $1.55/share or $155 plus fees per contract. The SPY ETF was trading at $212.50 at the time of the purchase. Should we have a negative reaction prior to or immediately after the election (like Brexit) and SPY falls below $208, I will sell the PUT contracts to collect on the insurance policy. SPY really needs to fall to $206.45 ($208.00-$1.55 cost) or 2.9% to provide a positive return, but keep in mind this is insurance and the preference is not collecting.

On the other hand, markets hate uncertainty and this election in particular is providing plenty of uncertainty. Thus it is very possible for the end of the election to spark a relief rally of significance. November and December are also historically amongst the best months of the year for returns. Therefore I concurrently purchased two CALL contracts on SPY that expire on December 16, 2016, with a strike price of $216. My cost was $2.58 per share plus fees. If SPY rallies over $216 I will sell the CALL. If it goes over $218.58 ($216.00 plus $2.58 cost) I will profit. This is an increase of 2.8% over the value at the time of the CALL purchase. The reason I went further into the future with the CALL is, as we have seen, market shocks can cause rapid and precipitous declines, whereas rallies tend to take longer. The cost of option contracts is always greater for longer time frames.

I have written many times that we cannot predict short-term market gyrations. Combining both the purchase of a PUT and a CALL concurrently, I am not making such a prediction. My only thought is that after four months of flat markets and with an unpredictable election approaching, I think there could easily be a return to volatility and am thus trying to protect the downside while hoping to capitalize if there is a significant relief rally. If the markets continue to stagnate, I will lose both premiums. This is a risk I am willing to take given the circumstances.

Looking Back: TECK.B continued to rally afterwards then fell back in early 2017. Its replacement in the TFSA, NWC, has done nicely and has brought better stability. This was one of my goals in making the change.

ISSUE #31: DECEMBER 1, 2016

The Certainty of Uncertainty

The US election provided plenty of uncertainty with unexpected results and unexpected market reaction to the results. Conventional wisdom (remember this is often an oxymoron) was that if Trump won the market would immediately decline by 5-10%, potentially precipitating a bear market. This was a very unconventional election in many ways, including that stock market participants were cheering for a Democratic win, whereas normally a Republican win is favoured as Republicans are perceived* to be more business-friendly. To demonstrate that the market was cheering for Hillary, on the Monday before the election and after the US Department of Justice cleared her once again over the email scandal, the S&P 500 was up 2.2% in confidence of a Hillary win. Like with Brexit, the polls were close but pundits were widely predicting a Hillary win. However, as John Diefenbaker, the Canadian prime minister from 1957-1963, famously quipped, "Dogs know best what to do with polls," and American voters did the same to Hillary. *(*Even though Republicans are perceived to be more business-friendly, long-term statistics show that the markets tend to do better under Democratic rule.)*

How did the market react to this unexpected Trump win? Initially, as the results became evident late in the evening of the 8th, US stock futures, which trade overnight, declined 5% but by morning this reaction had abated. On the morning of the 9th, US indices opened down slightly but then quickly moved into positive territory and the S&P closed the day up 1.1%. The rally continued almost uninterrupted to this date. How can this be so different than the widely expected market reaction if Trump unexpectedly won? It simply goes back to the title of my January 5th, 2016 issue, "Everybody Is Often Wrong." If something is widely expected to occur, it gets priced into the market ahead of time. While the market was expecting Hillary to win it had been very cautious. The market was very flat for an extended three-month period prior to the election. Then, as mentioned in the last issue, the great election uncertainty passed and a relief rally ensued. While there was widespread fear of a Trump win, he has conducted himself more professionally since winning (you could argue that point) and the market is now focusing on the positive side of his promises, like infrastructure spending and big corporate tax cuts, which will be positive for markets.

The insurance PUT contracts I purchased prior to the election have expired worthless but I don't feel bad about this at all. They provided some sense of comfort the evening of the election. The CALL contracts I purchased concurrently, for the possibility of a relief rally, are now in the money and I will sell. I certainly didn't predict the election outcome or the market reaction, only that after three months of flatlining the market would begin to move one way or the other. I always maintain an upwards bias because the market is up a lot more than it is down.

With election uncertainty removed are we now in an era of certainty? Absolutely NOT. One great constant is the "Certainty of Uncertainty." When uncertainty is greatest, opportunities are also greatest. Times of widespread consensus or certainty are actually times we must be most cautious, as that certainty will then be priced into the market and uncertainty will return with negative consequences. That should make sense even though it is somewhat counterintuitive, and is consistent with "Everybody Is Often Wrong."

It was fortuitous that last month I wrote about portfolio diversification across sectors, as the aftermath of the election illustrated its importance. Some sectors like utilities, consumer staples and real estate were down significantly, while financials, health care and industrials were up significantly.

Interest Rates: While the US has yet to increase short-term interest rates, long-term rates are driven by the market and have increased fairly dramatically since the election. This is again contrary to popular opinion prior to the election of what would transpire if Trump won. 10 year US bond rates experienced about a 0.5% interest rate increase from approximately 1.85% to 2.35%. That may not seem like a lot but is a 27% movement. As bond prices move in opposite direction to interest rates, ten-year US bonds have declined in value by 5-7%. Will we finally see an end to ridiculously low interest rates? How will this affect stock markets? While I'm not sure what will happen this time, long-term stats show that stock markets do well during early stages of the interest-rate tightening part of the cycle.

How will this all play out, and what do we as investors do? I am not big on making predictions but would predict that Trump's bark will prove to be exponentially larger than his bite. His pledge to "RIP UP NAFTA" reminds me of Chretien's promise to "RIP UP the GST." While Chretien won an election on the promise, in the end he increased the rate, tried to get provinces to coordinate with their PST and renamed it HST. That doesn't quite hit my definition of "RIP IT UP." In regards to NAFTA, my cynical view* is that all three countries will agree to renegotiate, and there is really nothing wrong with adjusting a 25-year-old agreement. Trump could win a few concessions, perhaps the agreement will get renamed and Trump will "trumpet" it as a huge win for American workers. In politics it is more important to be seen as doing something than actually doing anything substantive. Unfortunately, this also holds true in the world of corporate politics. While it is impossible to predict how it will all play out, I do think the Trump presidency will be very interesting. *(*I have a saying that cynicism and age are directly correlated.)*

My approach to investing will remain unchanged. We will continue to work through all the short-term uncertainty, look for companies that represent reasonable value and capitalize on long-term market fundamentals, which demonstrate about 10% total returns per year, even though current "conventional wisdom" is that those historic returns are no longer achievable.

Managing options: We are now approaching the January 17th, 2017, option expiry date and need to start managing the options that expire on or before this date. I do not expect to see the Canadian dollar rise past the 80 cent level and will continue to be hesitant adding USD to the account. Thus, we must manage within this fiscal constraint. I have built a theoretical decision tree grid to help understand the potentialities:

	Situation	Decision	Further Decision
Covered CALLS	Out of the Money	Allow to expire	Sell another covered CALL or just hold stock
		Profitably buy out to assure no CALL	Sell another covered CALL or just hold stock
	At the Money	Allow to expire if so happens	Sell another covered CALL or just hold stock
		Profitable buy out to assure no CALL	Sell another covered CALL or just hold stock
		Allow Call if so happens	Sell PUT to maintain interest in company
	In the Money	Allow Call	Sell PUT to maintain interest in company
		Buy out at loss to prevent CALL	Sell another covered CALL or just hold stock
Sold PUTS	Out of the Money	Allow to expire	Sell another PUT if still good valuation
		Profitable buy out to assure no PUT	Sell another PUT if still good valuation
	At the Money	Allow to expire if so happens	Sell another PUT if still good valuation
		Profitable buy out to assure no PUT	Sell another PUT if still good valuation
		Allow PUT if so happens	Hold stock, potentially sell covered CALL
	In the Money	Buy out at loss	Roll the position by selling another PUT
		Allow PUT	Hold the stock, potentially sell covered call

Most **options** in the account are COVERED CALLS or sold PUTS as we have mostly sold rather than bought options, gaining the time premiums and adding money to help purchase stocks. Definitions: For covered calls, "Out of the Money" means the current stock price is below the option price and the stock is unlikely to get CALLED unless there is a big rebound in the stock price between now and expiry. "In the Money" means the stock price is above the option price and the stock is likely to get CALLED unless there is a big drop in the stock price between now and expiry. "At the Money" means the stock price and option price are close at this time.

For the sold PUTS, "Out of the Money" means the stock price is above the option price and the stock is unlikely to get PUT unless there is a big drop in the stock price between now and option expiry. "In the Money" means the stock price is below the option price and I will likely get PUT at the option price, sometime between now and expiry date. "At the Money" means the stock price and option price are close and it could go either way. This all may be hard to follow theoretically but will become more evident as I go through the options which expire between now and January 17th, 2017, and what my intentions are for each one.

Option	Expiry	Strike Price	Cur. Stock Pr.	Status	Intention	Further Decision Intention
Naked Call						
SPY	16-Dec-16	$ 216.00	$ 220.38	In the Money	Sell	
Covered Calls						
CPG (Cdn)	20-Jan-17	$ 16.00	$ 17.10	At the Money	Undecided	Undecided
GDX	20-Jan-17	$ 30.00	$ 20.83	Out of the Money	Allow to expire	Sell another CALL if big rally up
C	20-Jan-17	$ 43.00	$ 56.39	In the Money	Allow CALL to raise cash	Sell PUT if significant decline
Sold Puts						
GDX	20-Jan-17	$ 21.00	$ 20.83	At the Money	Allow to expire or buy out profitably	Probably sell another PUT
C	20-Jan-17	$ 38.00	$ 56.78	Out of the Money	Allow to expire	Sell PUT if significant decline
EMR	20-Jan-17	$ 50.00	$ 56.44	Out of the Money	Allow to expire	Sell another PUT
WMT	20-Jan-17	$ 60.00	$ 70.43	Out of the Money	Allow to expire	Sell PUT if significant decline
AXP	20-Jan-17	$ 75.00	$ 72.04	At the Money	Buy out profitably	Sell another PUT
CVS	20-Jan-17	$ 97.50	$ 76.89	In the Money	Allow getting PUT	Possibly sell another PUT

Regular Account Changes

US side:

In order to accept getting PUT the CVS shares on January 20th I need to accumulate $9750 of cash and hope to do this without adding money to the account. Citigroup is likely to get CALLED, which will raise $4300 but also illustrates why I don't sell too many covered calls. They reduce risk but also reduce upside potential as I now need to sell at the option price rather than the market price. The following changes were made November 30th. *(All the calculations below are before fees to make the math simpler to understand.)*

SPDR S&P 500 (SPY) CALL: I sold the two CALL contracts that I purchased coincidental with the insurance PUTS purchased last month. I received $5.83/share for a profit of $3.25/share or 126% gain over the purchase price of $2.58. Pretty good return for a month. I would have liked to hold until expiry but given the need to raise cash I figured "one in the hand was worth two in the bush." Given the recent run, it wouldn't be a surprise to see a market pause or give back, and these CALLS could easily still expire worthless with a small 2.3% S&P decline. Another way to look at it is the profit from this trade paid for the cost of the insurance PUTS, which expired. Not bad given the rest of the portfolio has gained significantly through this relief rally. I rarely trade short-term but thought it was a good idea given the extra dose of uncertainty around the election.

American Express (AXP): I purchased back the AXP $75.00 PUT sold for $7.73 just over a year ago. AXP had a tumultuous ride over this time period but in the end rallied back such that I could buy the PUT out profitably. I paid $4.30 per share and profited by $3.43 per share. I concurrently sold another PUT contract, with the same $75.00 strike price that expires January 18th, 2019, or just over two years from now. I received $11.50 per share for this contract such that if I get PUT my effective cost will be $75.00 - $11.50 = $63.50 or 12% below the current price of $71.95. These trades demonstrate two features of PUTS and the strategy I follow: 1) AXP was trading at $73.60 when I sold the original PUT. It was trading at $71.95 when I purchased the PUT back. I got to use the $773 (one contract is 100 shares) during this time frame for other investments. Even though AXP lost $1.65 itself, the PUTS gained $3.43 as the time premium portion eroded. The stock went down but I still made money! Pretty cool, eh? 2) With today's trades I effectively traded with someone else, the right to sell me AXP for $75.00 up to January 20, 2017, for the right to sell me the same stock at the same price up to January 18, 2019. I received $11.50 - $4.30 = $7.20/share for the extra time I gave him/her to sell me the stock.

This is referred to as "rolling the position." My preference is for the stock price to go up and the option to expire but rolling the position profitably is still a pretty good outcome. Options don't usually get exercised until close to the expiry date, but it can happen and the seller accepts that risk for the premium received.

Hilton (HLT): HLT options are not noted in the above chart as these options expire in 2018. However, HLT is undergoing a corporate reorganization where it is splitting into three companies. Options often get illiquid after such reorganizations as the option will then represent all three companies. We made almost 60% of the potential profit, so I chose to buy back the HLT PUTS, which were sold May 31st, 2016, for $4.30/share. I paid $1.85/share to buy them back, profiting by $2.45/share. The four contracts made a $980 profit. I still think HLT will do well and will relook at their options after the reorganization.

iShares MSCI Mexico ETF (EWW): Given that I wrote Trump's "bark will prove to be exponentially larger than his bite," I thought I should "put my money where my mouth is" (Ha ha—Get it?). I sold two PUT contracts on EWW with a strike price of $45.00 that expire January 18, 2019. I received $6.85/share or $1370 for the two contracts, more than making up for the $740 cash spent buying back the HLT PUTS. EWW was trading at $44.17 at the time of the PUT sale. If I get PUT my effective price will be $38.15 or about 14% below the current price. EWW is now trading at its lowest level since recovering from the 2008/09 financial crisis and has been as high as $70.00 in 2013/14. Most of the decline is Mexican peso-related rather than stock market related. In the three days after the election EWW fell from about $52.00 to $42.00. Ripping up NAFTA will likely prove "easier said than done" (How do you like the use of all these clichés?), with all three countries' manufacturing economies being closely integrated. If the US economy improves it will likely help both Canada and Mexico.

Cash position: With the above adjustments, the US side of the account now has $3461 in cash. When Citigroup gets CALLED, which looks very likely, it will add another $4300 to bring the cash to $7761 within $2000 of the cash needed if CVS gets PUT. I will likely raise that money by...you guessed it...selling more PUTS and perhaps a covered CALL. The market is always fluid and some of the PUTS, which currently look like they will expire, could still be exercised if the underlying stock declines below the strike price. Monitoring the situation is necessary as we approach expiry date. Overall margin level in the account is pretty strong and when the current PUTS expire, their margin requirement is released allowing the sale of more PUTS.

Canadian side:

Linamar (LNR): In my November 14th update I discussed the purchase of 100 shares of Linamar at $48.10. LNR is a Canadian auto parts manufacturer trading at what appears to be great valuation. It has a small dividend yield of just 0.8% but an earnings yield of 15.9%, cash flow yield of 26.3%, ROE of 21.5%, ROA of 10.8% and price times book of 1.2. This company traded at over $80.00 in 2015. The reason it is trading this cheaply is there is widespread concern that the cyclical auto sector is at the peak of the cycle and auto sales volume could decline from here. This may or may not be true but even if it is, it appears to be already priced into the stock. There may also be some "RIP UP NAFTA" concerns. With almost $6B in annual sales LNR is a mid-sized auto parts supplier. It is the second largest in Canada, 33rd in North America and 65th in the world. While automotive represents over 80% of sales and 75% of profits, LNR also has a growing industrial business serving energy, marine, off-road and agricultural markets. The Skyjack powerlift segment is a key piece of this industrial business. LNR appears to be a well-managed company. I moved $5,000 CAD into the account to pay for the purchase.

"If I Claim to Be a Wise Man... It Surely Means That I Don't Know"

Happy New Year. Wishing everyone a healthy and prosperous 2017. I sincerely hope 2017 matches the prosperous, "surprising" investment environment of 2016!

Physical fitness, like financial fitness, requires discipline, effort, determination and commitment. While my favourite fitness activity is riding a road bike through the Calgary area foothills, I am only a fair-weather rider, which confines the activity to six or seven months of the year. The remainder of the year I attempt to maintain a reasonable level of fitness at the local gym. I find most gym activities a complete bore requiring additional entertainment. I derive this from my iPod loaded with '70s style classic rock, complemented with newer rock and even some heavy metal. Motivation for exercise requires high-energy music. While I enjoy other genres, they just don't cut it at the gym. Song lyrics often go in one ear and out the other, but the mindless activity of the gym combined with frequent repetition allows one to comprehend some of the meaning woven through the poetry of good rock music. While I mindlessly "row a boat" to nowhere, an occasional epiphany strikes. The title of this issue comes thanks to the classic philosophical rock band **Kansas** and their '70s hit, "Carry on Wayward Son." It eloquently encapsulates a warning vis-à-vis those who might claim to be "wise men" or so called experts. JFK was blunter with his wording after the Bay of Pigs fiasco when he famously quipped about "NEVER relying solely on experts."

A year ago, in the January 5th, 2016 issue I made my three non-expert predictions for 2016 compared to what the experts were calling for. How did it all turn out?

1. Fearless Prediction #1 was that most predictions would be wrong. This prediction was fairly accurate, but hey, it's an easy one to make. Most predictions were for very modest market returns. As markets spiralled downwards early in the year many analysts were also revising their projections further downwards. But let's give the experts some credit as their predictions were better than in 2015.

2. Fearless Prediction #2 was that after a flat 2015, the US market would find a direction, and my guess was that the direction would be upwards with an aggressive magnitude of 20-25%. I got this about half right. The direction was upwards and the magnitude was 12.0%. While this was only half-right, it was much more correct than the very tepid expert opinions. One could have easily missed the market gains by thinking, "If the market is only going to be up a little it's not worth the risk, so might as well stay in cash or bonds and play it safe." Many took that approach with the average investor gaining much less than the overall market.

3. Fearless Prediction #3 was that the Canadian market would outperform the US market in 2016, 2017 or 2018, but I also felt that it would be sooner than later. This was bang-on with the Canadian market returning 20.2%, right in the 20-25% range. Again, this was out of sync with the experts, as the year began with the continuing commodity rout and the Canadian market in the grips of a grizzly bear. Overall, my predictions look fairly prescient, especially compared to or contrasted with the "wise men."

What will 2017 bring? Fresh off the success of the 2016 predictions and my demonstrated skill as a market prognosticator, I must be able to see clearly into the future to provide clear guidance of how to invest for maximum returns. NOT. But for fun I will once again attempt a few predictions:

Fearless Prediction #1: Same as last year. Most predictions you read at this time of year will be wrong. The world will continue to unfold in an unpredictable fashion. Most important, accurate predictions are NOT a prerequisite for market success. By the way, most of the experts are once again calling for very tepid 0-5% returns. While most analysts are positive and market sentiment has now swung positive (a negative sign), the apprehensive nature of the positivity is surprising given the strength of 2016 returns and is a positive sign for future returns.

Fearless Prediction #2: I am once again going to stick my neck out and call for market returns of 15-20%, much bolder than the general consensus.

Returns After a FLAT Year?					
Year	% Total Return	Following Year	% Total Return	2nd year after	% Total Return
1925	0.0%	1926	11.0%	1927	37.1%
1934	-2.3%	1935	47.2%	1936	32.8%
1939	-0.9%	1940	-10.1%	1941	-11.8%
1953	-1.1%	1954	52.4%	1955	31.4%
1960	0.5%	1961	26.8%	1962	-8.8%
1970	3.9%	1971	14.3%	1972	19.0%
1981	-4.9%	1982	21.6%	1983	22.6%
1990	-3.1%	1991	30.5%	1992	7.6%
1994	1.3%	1995	37.6%	1996	23.0%
2005	4.9%	2006	15.8%	2007	5.5%
2011	2.1%	2012	16.0%	2013	32.4%
2015	1.4%	2016	12.0%	2017	???
Average			22.9%		17.3%

Last year I provided the first part of this chart demonstrating what happened historically to S&P 500 returns after a flat year like 2015. I recently wondered if there would be any further trend for the second year after a flat year, and to my surprise there appears to be. While on average the market is down 1/4 of the years, it was down just 2/11 of the years, two years after a flat year. There may be too few reps of data to suggest a firm trend, but the average return two years after a flat year still shows significant market outperformance of 17.3% vs. long-term performance of just below 10%. Hence, my 15-20% prediction for 2017. Caveat and warning: Prediction #1

Fearless Prediction #3: Now that the Canadian market has outperformed the US for a year I have no idea whether it will do so again. I do think, however, that Canadian vs. US performance will seesaw back and forth as occurred historically prior to 2004, the great commodity bull and great commodity bust.

Fearless Prediction #4: This one is longer-term. Current overwhelming market commentary is that 10% average historical market returns are no longer possible. That we must accept and expect much smaller 4-6% average returns at best. My question is this: Is this because for 17 years since 2000 inclusive, average returns have been below average and thus (discussed in last year's January issue), as most predictions "predict" what has occurred in the recent past, the conservative longer-term forecasts are merely the result of recent (17-year) below-average market performance? Since 2000 the US S&P 500 CAGR (compound annual growth rate) has been just 4.5% and TSX CAGR has been 6.0%. My prediction is that over the next 17 years market performance will revert back to more historical long-term 10% average returns. That said, negative years occur a quarter of the time so we must always be wary of the potential of a negative return year and not panic when it occurs. Caveat and warning: Prediction #1.

Fun predictions aside, it is important that we not think we are now "wise men." As humans we have many frailties. One of them is a desire to latch on to and believe precise predictions from experts, as it seems the precision of the prediction creates a sense of expertise. We tend to believe these precise predictions even though they are regularly proven wrong. Why do we prefer these to imprecise generalities, which are more likely to provide better guidance? I don't know the psychological reason, but it is a frailty we must conquer to be successful at many things including successful investing.

How did we do in 2016?

Total Return by Year: Market				RRSPs			REG	TFSAs		
	US S&P 500	Canadian TSX	US-CdnAvg.	Herman	Lillian	Model	SFP Acct.	Herman	Lillian	Model
Correct Time, Benchmark CAGR for Each Portfolio:				9.4%	8.9%	5.8%	16.1%	10.0%	10.0%	2.5%
CAGR	9.2%	9.6%	9.4%	11.7%	9.6%	8.9%	30.6%	18.0%	13.8%	-0.4%
2016	12.0%	20.2%	16.1%	20.9%	19.0%	22.2%	30.6%	21.3%	9.9%	13.9%
2015	1.4%	-8.3%	-3.5%	3.3%	0.0%	-2.9%		2.9%	-6.1%	-5.3%
2014	13.7%	10.6%	12.2%	13.7%	22.9%			1.7%	-0.5%	*-13.6%
2013	32.4%	11.5%	22.0%	26.9%	31.8%			23.0%	33.1%	
2012	16.0%	8.2%	12.1%	10.2%	10.9%			22.2%	22.9%	
2011	2.1%	-8.7%	-3.3%	-2.2%	2.9%			-4.2%	1.4%	
2010	15.1%	17.6%	16.4%	12.9%	8.5%			20.2%	21.1%	
2009	26.5%	35.9%	31.2%	15.4%	14.7%			71.4%	36.1%	
2008	-37.0%	-33.0%	-35.0%	-27.7%	-17.2%					
2007	5.5%	9.2%	7.4%	-1.9%	-7.6%					
2006	15.8%	17.9%	16.9%	21.2%	18.0%					
2005	4.9%	25.6%	15.3%	26.1%	17.5%					
2004	10.9%	13.8%	12.4%	14.9%	12.2%					
2003	28.7%	27.1%	27.9%	22.6%	15.1%					
2002	-22.1%	-13.7%	-17.9%	-3.4%	-7.5%					
2001	-11.8%	-15.1%	-13.5%	4.2%	5.0%					
2000	-9.1%	9.3%	0.1%	18.1%	21.0%					
1999	21.0%	45.8%	33.4%	42.2%	10.3%					
1998	28.6%	1.2%	14.9%	-10.5%	-2.3%					
1997	33.3%	18.3%	25.8%	12.2%	13.7%					
1996	22.9%	29.9%	26.4%	27.0%	26.8%					
1995	37.5%	15.8%	26.7%	9.7%						
1994	1.3%	3.4%	2.4%	19.3%						
1993	10.0%	23.4%	16.7%	31.6%						

*Half-year results compared with half-year Canadian market results of -3.4%.

This is a critical chart to understanding long-term performance. For complete description see Issue #8, January 5, 2015. Light grey shade: Canadian or US outperformance. Third column: US/CDN average performance, which is our benchmark for RRSPs and the regular account as both are invested in both Canada and the US. We only use the Canadian market for our TFSA benchmark as we don't invest in US companies due to withholding tax on dividends. I added a new line titled "Correct Time, Benchmark CAGR for Each Portfolio" at the top. This shows the benchmark CAGR for the same time period as the actual portfolio so correct comparisons can be made. My objective is to beat the market performance by 1-2 % on average, a feat that is considered impossible by many academics. The dark grey shading shows years where the portfolio beat the benchmark.

With the exception of the newsletter TFSA model portfolio, each other portfolio has managed to beat the benchmark CAGR over the equivalent time frame. For example, the "Herman RRSP" has a 24-year CAGR of 11.7%, or 2.3% greater than the 24-year US/CDN average CAGR of 9.4%. The "Lillian TFSA" portfolio has an eight-year CAGR of 13.8% or 3.8% greater than the eight-year Canadian market benchmark CAGR of 10.0%.

I continue to share our own portfolios' performance because investing is a long game. I hope they illustrate the potential outcomes one can achieve with stocks that are vastly superior to bonds or GICs if one is prepared to accept the volatility of stocks. Please review Issue #28, "Is It Risky, Volatile or Both?" where I try to distinguish between RISK and VOLATILITY. They are different even though most consider them synonymous. Achieving these results didn't require the employment of any "rocket science," with the possible exception of options in the regular account. Just try to pick companies that look like good value at the time and stick with it through difficult times like the period from mid-2014 to early 2016. *(Caveat: all the charts contain an enormous amount of data, such that perfect accuracy is not guaranteed. I am trying to calculate and present in a simple and understandable format.)*

2016 newsletter portfolio review:

TFSA Model Portfolio

Company	Ticker	Date Added	# Shares	Price Added	Cost In CAD	Current Value in CAD	Share Price Change	Previous Total Dividends to Date	October Dividends	November Dividends	December Dividends	New Total Divdends to Date	Total Return
International													
Ensco PLC	ESV	May 30/14	100	$ 52.66	$ 5,750	$ 1,302	$ (4,448)	$ 328.82			$ 1.33	$ 330.15	-71.6%
Glaxo Smithkline	GSK	May 30/14	100	$ 53.94	$ 5,890	$ 5,160	$ (730)	$ 680.74	$ 61.28			$ 742.02	0.2%
Ship Finance Int.	SFL	May 30/14	180	$ 18.52	$ 3,644	$ 3,582	$ (62)	$ 970.67			$ 109.42	$ 1,080.09	27.9%
Seadrill	SDRL	July 25/14	130	$ 37.49	$ 5,312	$ 594	$ (4,718)	$ 140.46				$ 140.46	-86.2%
HSBC Holdings PLC	HSBC	July 25/14	100	$ 52.82	$ 5,757	$ 5,384	$ (373)	$ 699.92			$ 66.41	$ 766.33	6.8%
Vodaphone	VOD	July 25/14	150	$ 34.16	$ 5,585	$ 4,908	$ (677)	$ 630.88				$ 630.88	-0.8%
Unilever PLC	UL	Jan 2/15	100	$ 40.05	$ 4,736	$ 5,455	$ 719	$ 296.72			$ 46.28	$ 343.00	22.4%
Diagio PLC	DEO	Jan 2/15	30	$ 112.73	$ 4,001	$ 4,178	$ 177	$ 179.22	$ 73.55			$ 252.77	10.7%
BHP Billiton Ltd	BHP	Jan 2/15	65	$ 47.27	$ 3,636	$ 3,116	$ (520)	$ 526.52				$ 526.52	0.2%
Internatonal Subtotal					$ 44,311	$ 33,679	$ (10,632)	$ 4,453.95				$ 4,812.22	-13.1%
Canadian													
TD Bank	TD	May 30/14	100	$ 53.76	$ 5,386	$ 6,621	$ 1,235	$ 455.00	$ 55.00			$ 510.00	32.4%
Rogers Communications	RCI.B	May 30/14	100	$ 43.82	$ 4,392	$ 5,178	$ 786	$ 425.25	$ 48.00			$ 473.25	28.7%
ATCO	ACO.X	July 25/14	100	$ 50.56	$ 5,066	$ 4,449	$ (617)	$ 227.50			$ 28.50	$ 256.00	-7.1%
Husky Energy	HSE	July 25/14	153	$ 33.06	$ 5,068	$ 2,490	$ (2,578)	$ 227.74				$ 227.74	-46.4%
Sunlife Financial	SLF	July 25/14	100	$ 41.40	$ 4,150	$ 5,154	$ 1,004	$ 343.00			$ 42.00	$ 385.00	33.5%
Cdn. Western Bank	CWB	May/15Jan/16	220	$ 27.67	$ 6,106	$ 6,670	$ 564	$ 265.70				$ 265.70	13.6%
Jean Coutu	PJC.A	May/15Oct/16	300	$ 22.03	$ 6,628	$ 6,276	$ (352)	$ 114.00		$ 36.00		$ 150.00	-3.0%
AltaGas	ALA	Jan 4/16	200	$ 30.96	$ 6,202	$ 6,780	$ 578	$ 267.34	$ 35.35	$ 35.35	$ 35.35	$ 373.39	15.3%
CI Financial	CIX	Jan&May/16	300	$ 29.37	$ 8,832	$ 8,658	$ (174)	$ 226.00	$ 34.50	$ 34.50	$ 34.50	$ 329.50	1.8%
North West Company Inc	NWC	Oct 18/16	200	$ 25.91	$ 5,192	$ 5,492	$ 300	$ -				$ -	5.8%
Dividends from Sold Cos								$ 404.75				$ 404.75	
Canadian Subtotal					$ 57,022	$ 57,768	$ 746	$ 2,956.28				$ 3,375.33	7.2%
Total Cdn and Int					$ 101,333	$ 91,447	$ (9,886)	$ 7,410.23				$ 8,187.55	
Cash						$ 636							
Total						$ 92,083							-1.0%

Cost in CAD total of $101,333 is derived from $93,000 investment plus $781 of capital gains plus $7552 of reinvested dividends, leaving $636 of cash from unspent dividends

Sales to Date	Ticker	Date Added	# Shares	Price	Exchange	Cost in CAD	Sold	Proceeds	Dividends	Profit	% Profit	
Innvest REIT	INN.UN	May30/14	210	$ 5.16		$ 1,094	May12/16	$ 1,479.00	$ 174.75	$ 559.75	51.2%	
South32	SOUHY	May30/15	26	$ 8.34	$ 1.23	$ 267	May12/16	$ 189.90	$ -	$ (77.10)	-28.9%	Rcvd via BHP Stock Div
Teck Resources Ltd	TCK.B	May 30/15	200	$ 24.17		$ 4,855	Oct18/16	$ 5,328.00	$ 230.00	$ 703.00	14.5%	

This is the portfolio that just couldn't seem to get no lovin'. However, we stuck with it and unlike many who would have given up at the depth of the Canadian bear, we are now very close to breakeven. I hope the challenges with this portfolio illustrate the importance of sticking with it through tough times. During 2016 the TFSA model was up a very respectable 13.9%. As it is based on a combo of both Lillian's and my own TFSAs its performance fell between the two. The main reason my TFSA did better was the buyout of INN. UN, which represented a large holding in my portfolio. If you work with stocks long enough these periodic buyouts provide positive boosts to performance. There have been two main issues with my unsatisfactory performance on the portfolio since the beginning of the newsletter:

1. Too much exposure to resources, especially oil. I wasn't watching portfolio diversification closely enough. Part of the decent 2016 performance was the dramatic recovery of TECK.B, subsequently sold for a small profit for diversification purposes.

2. Brexit: While the above issue was clearly my fault, the Brexit election in June 2016 was out of my control. I still feel it is wise to avoid US dividend withholding tax in the TFSA and focus on US stocks in the RRSP, where there is no withholding. To get larger international companies and those outside the financial and resource sectors, which dominate the Canadian market, into our TFSA requires buying companies in jurisdictions without withholding taxes, mostly the UK. The UK market did fine, being up 16.3% total return on a local currency, British pound, basis. The currency, however, declined significantly, such that the return in USD terms was -3.6%. It was slightly worse in Canadian dollar terms as the Canadian dollar appreciated slightly to the USD. I used a 1.38 CAD: USD conversion a year ago and a 1.34 CAD: USD this year. I am not concerned long-term with the pound value, as what goes around comes around, and plan to take advantage of this as a buying opportunity for my 2017 TFSA additions.

RRSP Model Portfolio

Company	Ticker	Date Added	# Shares	Price Added	Cost In CAD	Current Value in CAD	Share Price Change	Previous Dividends to Date	October Dividends	November Dividends	December Dividends	New Dividends to Date	Total Return
US Companies													
Verizon	VZ	Sept 30/14	100	$ 49.99	$ 5,609	$ 7,153	$ 1,544	$ 562.84		$ 76.84		$ 639.68	38.9%
HCP Inc	HCP	Sept 30/14	100	$ 39.71	$ 4,458	$ 3,982	$ (476)	$ 557.13		$ 409.40		$ 966.53	11.0%
Hospitality Prop. Trust	HPT	Sept 30/14	150	$ 26.85	$ 4,521	$ 6,380	$ 1,859	$ 823.11		$ 101.97		$ 925.08	61.6%
United Technologies	UTX	Oct 31/14	50	$ 107.00	$ 6,002	$ 7,345	$ 1,343	$ 325.05			$ 43.21	$ 368.26	28.5%
Johnson and Johnson	JNJ	Oct 31/14	50	$ 107.78	$ 6,045	$ 7,719	$ 1,674	$ 381.76			$ 52.64	$ 434.40	28.5%
Freeport-McMoRan	FCX	Nov 30/14	150	$ 26.85	$ 4,601	$ 2,651	$ (1,950)	$ 108.90				$ 108.90	-40.0%
Chevron	CVX	Nov 30/14	50	$ 108.87	$ 6,216	$ 7,886	$ 1,670	$ 482.95			$ 70.71	$ 553.66	35.8%
Exelon	EXC	Nov 30/14	150	$ 36.17	$ 6,195	$ 7,133	$ 938	$ 422.20			$ 62.56	$ 484.76	23.0%
General Electric	GE	Jan 27/15	200	$ 24.38	$ 6,056	$ 8,469	$ 2,413	$ 358.27	$ 60.97			$ 419.24	46.8%
Praxair	PX	Feb 28/15	25	$ 127.90	$ 4,007	$ 3,926	$ (81)	$ 165.48			$ 24.67	$ 190.15	2.7%
Qualcomm	QCOM	Feb 28/15	50	$ 72.51	$ 4,542	$ 4,368	$ (174)	$ 220.46			$ 35.25	$ 255.71	1.8%
Quality Care Properties	QCP	Nov 1/16	20	$ 13.43	$ 360	$ 415	$ 55	$ -					15.3%
US Subtotal					$ 58,612	$ 67,427	$ 8,815	$ 4,408.15				$ 5,346.37	24.2%
Canadian Companies													
Bank of Nova Scotia	BNS	Sep14/Jan16	200	$ 62.30	$ 12,480	$ 14,952	$ 2,472	$ 696.00	$ 148.00			$ 844.00	26.6%
Power Corp	POW	Sep14/Jun16	300	$ 29.89	$ 8,986	$ 9,015	$ 29	$ 532.52			$ 100.50	$ 633.02	7.4%
Capital Power	CPX	Oct 31/14	200	$ 25.58	$ 5,126	$ 4,646	$ (480)	$ 496.00	$ 78.00			$ 574.00	1.8%
Mullen Group Ltd.	MTL	Nov14/Jun16	500	$ 17.99	$ 9,013	$ 9,915	$ 902	$ 478.50	$ 15.00	$ 15.00	$ 15.00	$ 523.50	15.8%
Royal Bank	RY	Jan 27/15	100	$ 75.12	$ 7,522	$ 9,087	$ 1,565	$ 474.00		$ 83.00		$ 557.00	28.2%
TransCanada Pipeline	TRP	Jan 27/15	100	$ 55.59	$ 5,609	$ 6,054	$ 445	$ 321.00	$ 56.50			$ 377.50	14.7%
Bell Canada	BCE	Feb 28/15	100	$ 54.71	$ 5,481	$ 5,803	$ 322	$ 396.50	$ 68.25			$ 464.75	14.4%
Brookfield Asset Mgmt	BAM.A	Feb 28/15	150	$ 45.23	$ 6,795	$ 6,645	$ (150)	$ 224.69			$ 26.20	$ 250.89	1.5%
Pason Systems	PSI	Mar 3/15	200	$ 18.48	$ 3,706	$ 3,928	$ 222	$ 238.00			$ 34.00	$ 272.00	13.3%
Wajax Corp	WJX	Mar 3/15	150	$ 24.31	$ 3,657	$ 3,459	$ (198)	$ 200.00	$ 37.50			$ 237.50	1.1%
Home Capital Group	HCG	Mar15/May15	150	$ 43.11	$ 6,475	$ 4,701	$ (1,774)	$ 196.00			$ 39.00	$ 235.00	-23.8%
AutoCanada	ACQ	Apr 4/15	150	$ 34.15	$ 5,133	$ 3,468	$ (1,665)	$ 180.00			$ 15.00	$ 195.00	-28.6%
Cogeco Inc.	CGO	May 29/15	100	$ 53.60	$ 5,370	$ 5,672	$ 302	$ 143.50			$ 34.00	$ 177.50	8.9%
Pembina Pipeline	PPL	Dec 9/15	200	$ 29.17	$ 5,844	$ 8,392	$ 2,548	$ 285.13	$ 32.32	$ 32.32	$ 32.32	$ 382.09	50.1%
Dividends from Sold Cos								$ 26.09				$ 26.09	
Cdn Subtotal					$ 91,197	$ 95,737	$ 4,540	$ 4,887.93				$ 5,749.84	11.3%
Total Cdn and US					$ 149,809	$ 163,164	$ 13,355	$ 9,296.08				$ 11,096.21	
Cash						$ 3,501							
Portfolio Value						$ 166,665							18.6%

Cost in CAD total of $149,809 is derived from $140,500 invested, $1714 capital gains, plus $7595 of reinvested dividends, leaving $3501 of cash from unspent dividends.

Sales to Date	Ticker	Date Added	# Shares	Price	Exchange	Cost In CAD	Sold	Sold Price	Proceeds	Dividends	Profit	% Profit	
Constellation Software	CSU	Oct 31/14	10	$ 317.50		$ 3,185	Apr 14/15	$ 485.07	$ 4,841	$ 24.40	$ 1,679	52.7	
RMR Group	RMR	Dec 18/15	2	$ 16.95		$ 47	Oct 3/16	$ 37.94	$ 89	$ 1.42	$ 43	91.5	HPT Div
Brookfield Business LP	BBU.UN	Jun 24/16	3	$ 25.67		$ 77	Oct 3/16	$ 34.21	$ 93	$ 0.27	$ 16	20.8	BAM.A Div

(Note: QCP came via a small spin-off from HCP in November.)

The RRSP model had a great year with a 22.2% gain, exceeding both Lillian's and my portfolios. It beat the US/CDN benchmark average by 6.1%. The portfolio is now up, in simple terms, 18.6% over the approximate two-year time frame which is a strong performance in light of the environment. There are only three out of 26 companies showing a negative return at this time and 23/26 or 88% are positive. The 2016 performance came about even with a slight headwind from stronger Canadian currency. Last year we made extra returns due to the declining currency, so a little give and take on the issue. With -2.9% in 2015 and 22.2% in 2016, the two-year CAGR calculated to 8.9%. For a review on how I calculate the annual returns, please see Issue #8.

And now, drumroll please, the STAR of the portfolios:

Non-Registered Margin Portfolio

Company	Ticker	Date Added	# Shares	Price Added	Cost In USD	Current Value in USD	Share Price Change	Previous Dividends to Date	October Dividends	November Dividends	December Dividends	New Dividends to Date	Total Return
US Dollar Purchases									US dividends collected minus 15% witholding tax				
iShares MSCI Emerging	EEM	6-Jul-15	100	$ 38.62	$ 3,872	$ 3,501	$ (371)	$ 65.18			$ 33.68	$ 98.86	-7.0%
Vanguard Europe ETF	VGK	6-Jul-15	100	$ 52.91	$ 5,301	$ 4,792	$ (509)	$ 160.47			$ 19.21	$ 179.68	-6.2%
First Trust Nat GAS	FCG	6-Jul-15	100	$ 42.85	$ 4,297	$ 2,615	$ (1,682)	$ 61.20			$ 7.04	$ 68.24	-37.6%
Parker Hannifin	PH	24-Jul-15	50	$ 110.84	$ 5,552	$ 7,000	$ 1,448	$ 133.85			$ 26.77	$ 160.62	29.0%
iShares Silver Trust	SLV	31-Aug-15	200	$ 13.79	$ 2,767	$ 3,020	$ 253	$ -				$ -	9.1%
Market Vector Gold	GDX	31-Aug-15	200	$ 13.71	$ 2,751	$ 4,174	$ 1,423	$ 19.72			$ 9.35	$ 29.07	52.8%
Berkshire Hathaway	BRK.B	Aug15-Jan16	75	$ 134.12	$ 10,099	$ 12,227	$ 2,128	$ -				$ -	21.1%
Union Pacific	UNP	31-Aug-15	50	$ 86.13	$ 4,316	$ 5,187	$ 871	$ 93.48			$ 25.71	$ 119.19	22.9%
Citigroup Inc	C	25-Feb-16	100	$ 38.45	$ 3,855	$ 5,943	$ 2,088	$ 17.85	$ 13.60			$ 31.45	55.0%
Alphabet	GOOGL	29-Apr-16	5	$ 706.77	$ 3,544	$ 3,963	$ 419	$ -				$ -	11.8%
Williams Sonoma	WSM	May/Jun2016	100	$ 51.52	$ 5,172	$ 4,838	$ (334)	$ 31.45	$ 31.45			$ 62.90	-5.2%
Capital One Financial	COF	Jun/Jul2016	100	$ 63.67	$ 6,387	$ 8,724	$ 2,337	$ -	$ 34.00			$ -	36.6%
Oceaneering Intl Inc	OII	31-Aug-16	100	$ 26.42	$ 2,652	$ 2,821	$ 169	$ -				$ 12.75	6.9%
Dividends from Sold Cos								$ 47.82				$ 47.82	
US Options													
American Express	AXP	30-Nov-16	1 Put	$ 71.95	$ (1,139)	$ (1,215)	$ (76)						-6.7%
Walmart	WMT	30-Oct-15	1 Put	$ 57.90	$ (689)	$ (8)	$ 681						98.8%
Emerson Electric	EMR	30-Oct-15	1 Put	$ 47.10	$ (740)	$ (25)	$ 715						96.6%
IBM	IBM	25-Nov-15	1 Put	$ 137.82	$ (1,859)	$ (590)	$ 1,269						68.3%
CVS Health Corp	CVS	25-Nov-15	1 Put	$ 93.90	$ (1,089)	$ (1,910)	$ (821)						-75.4%
Russell 2000 ETF	IWM	28-Jan-16	1 Put	$ 99.50	$ (1,449)	$ (287)	$ 1,162						80.2%
Citigroup Inc	C	25-Feb-16	1 Put	$ 38.45	$ (469)	$ (3)	$ 466						99.4%
Citigroup Inc	C	25-Feb-16	1 CovCa	$ 38.45	$ (299)	$ (1,660)	$ (1,361)						-455.2%
Walt Disney	DIS	25-Feb-16	1 Put	$ 95.40	$ (1,609)	$ (715)	$ 894						55.6%
iShares MSCI Emerging	EEM	25-Feb-16	2 Put	$ 30.30	$ (1,233)	$ (546)	$ 687						55.7%
Market Vector Gold	GDX	29-Apr-16	2 CovCa	$ 25.50	$ (428)	$ (2)	$ 426						99.5%
Market Vector Gold	GDX	29-Apr-16	2 Put	$ 25.50	$ (337)	$ (196)	$ 141						41.8%
Monsanto	MON	29-Apr-16	1 Put	$ 93.80	$ (1,631)	$ (1,050)	$ 581						35.6%
iShares Silver Trust	SLV	31-May-16	3 Put	$ 15.27	$ (916)	$ (843)	$ 73						8.0%
A T & T	T	30-Jun-16	2 Put	$ 42.60	$ (867)	$ (780)	$ 87						10.0%
Vanguard Europe ETF	VGK	30-Jun-16	2 Call	$ 46.00	$ 532	$ 440	$ (92)						-17.3%
First Solar	FSLR	29-Jul-16	2 Put	$ 46.80	$ (2,487)	$ (4,450)	$ (1,963)						-78.9%
SPDR Series Biotech	XBI	31-Aug-16	2 Put	$ 60.00	$ (2,028)	$ (2,010)	$ 18						0.9%
Monsanto	MON	28-Sep-16	1 Put	$ 102.50	$ (2,589)	$ (2,600)	$ (11)						-0.4%
Monsanto	MON	28-Sep-16	1 Put-L	$ 102.50	$ 573	$ 300	$ (273)						-47.6%
ishares Mexico	EWW	30-Nov-16	2 Put	$ 44.17	$ (1,357)	$ (1,450)	$ (93)						
US Subtotal					**$ 38,455**	**$ 49,205**	**$ 10,750**	**$ 631.02**				**$ 810.58**	
Cash						**$ 3,596**							
Total USD		Deposits			**$ 37,405**	**$ 52,801**							**41.2%**
Canadian Companies						CAD	CAD						
Bank of Montreal	BMO	3-Jul-15	100	$ 74.21	$ 7,431	$ 9,656	$ 2,225	$ 418.00		$ 86.00		$ 504.00	36.7%
CGI Group	GIB.A	23-Jul-15	100	$ 50.90	$ 5,100	$ 6,433	$ 1,333	$ -				$ -	26.1%
Crescent Point Energy	CPG	Jul15/Jan16	400	$ 16.79	$ 6,734	$ 7,300	$ 566	$ 298.00	$ 12.00	$ 12.00	$ 12.00	$ 334.00	13.4%
Telus	T	31-Aug-15	100	$ 42.83	$ 4,293	$ 4,266	$ (27)	$ 176.00	$ 46.00			$ 222.00	4.5%
Suncor	SU	31-Aug-15	100	$ 35.78	$ 3,588	$ 4,390	$ 802	$ 145.00			$ 29.00	$ 174.00	27.2%
Stantec Inc.	STN	29-Sep-15	200	$ 29.30	$ 5,870	$ 6,776	$ 906	$ 66.00	$ 22.50			$ 88.50	16.9%
Potash Corp	POT	Oct15/Jan16	200	$ 23.84	$ 4,788	$ 4,858	$ 70	$ 227.39		$ 26.47		$ 253.86	6.8%
ShawCor	SCL	26-Nov-15	200	$ 28.94	$ 5,798	$ 7,168	$ 1,370	$ 90.00		$ 30.00		$ 120.00	25.7%
Russel Metals	RUS	26-Nov-15	200	$ 18.15	$ 3,640	$ 5,104	$ 1,464	$ 228.00			$ 76.00	$ 304.00	48.6%
Fortis Inc.	FTS	Nov15/Jul16	200	$ 39.89	$ 7,998	$ 8,292	$ 294	$ 150.00			$ 80.00	$ 230.00	6.6%
Manulife Financial	MFC	Jan16/Jun16	500	$ 17.92	$ 8,978	$ 11,950	$ 2,972	$ 203.50			$ 92.50	$ 296.00	36.4%
Enbridge Inc	ENB	22-Feb-16	100	$ 44.26	$ 4,436	$ 5,649	$ 1,213	$ 106.00			$ 53.00	$ 159.00	30.9%
Transforce Inc	TFI	22-Feb-16	200	$ 21.40	$ 4,290	$ 6,992	$ 2,702	$ 68.00	$ 34.00			$ 102.00	65.4%
Badger Daylighting	BAD	29-Apr-16	200	$ 24.35	$ 4,880	$ 6,404	$ 1,524	$ 26.40	$ 6.60	$ 6.60	$ 6.60	$ 46.20	32.2%
Cdn National Rail	CNR	30-May-16	100	$ 78.20	$ 7,830	$ 9,026	$ 1,196	$ 75.00			$ 37.50	$ 112.50	16.7%
Cameco Corp	CCO	Jun/Sep 16	600	$ 12.64	$ 7,604	$ 8,418	$ 814	$ -	$ 30.00			$ 30.00	11.1%
The North West Co.	NWC	3-Oct-16	150	$ 25.79	$ 3,878	$ 4,119	$ 241					$ -	6.2%
Corus Entertainment	CJR.B	28-Oct-16	400	$ 10.92	$ 4,378	$ 5,036	$ 658			$ 38.00	$ 38.00	$ 76.00	16.8%
Linamar	LNR	14-Nov-16	100	$ 48.10	$ 4,820	$ 5,760	$ 940				$ 10.00	$ 10.00	19.7%
Cdn Options							$ -						
Crescent Point Energy	CPG	26-Jan-16	2 CovCa	$ 13.24	$ (308)	$ (472)	$ (164.00)						-53.2%
Cdn Subtotal					**$ 106,026**	**$ 127,125**	**$ 21,099**	**$ 2,277.29**				**$ 3,062.06**	
Cash						**$ 840**							
Total CAD		Deposits			**$ 103,800**	**$ 127,965**							**23.3%**
TotalPortfolio Value in CAD						**$ 198,860**							
Deposits in CAD Value						**$ 152,312**							**30.6%**

Sales to Date	Ticker	Date Added	#Shares	Price Added	Currency	Cost	Sold	Sold Price	Proceeds	Accum Div	Profit	% Profit	CapGainCdn
ITC Holdings	ITC	2-Oct-15	100	$ 32.10	USD	$ 3,220	27-Jun-16	$ 45.65	$ 4,554	$ 47.82	$ 1,382	43%	$ 1,715
A T & T Calls	T	27-Nov-16	2	$ 1.65	USD	$ 342	30-Jun-16	$ 7.65	$ 1,517	$ -	$ 1,175	344%	$ 1,517
S&P 500 PUTS	SPY	28-Oct-16	4	$ 1.55	USD	$ 635	Expired	$ -	$ -	$ -	$ (635)	-100%	$ (851)
S & P 500 CALLS	SPY	28-Oct-16	2	$ 2.58	USD	$ 528	30-Nov-16	$ 5.83	$ 1,153	0	$ 625	118%	$ 837
Hilton PUTS	HLT	30-Nov-16	4	$ 1.85	USD	$ 755	31-May-16	$ 4.30	$ 1,705	0	$ 950	126%	$ 1,222
American Express PUT	AXP	30-Nov-16	1	$ 4.30	USD	$ 441	30-Oct-15	$ 7.73	$ 762	0	$ 321	73%	$ 998
													$ 5,438.11

2016 returns on the regular account were pretty fantastic at 30.6% comprised of 41.2% on the US side with the use of leverage, and a very strong 23.3% on the Canadian side. Try doing that with bonds! The weighted average time invested is now 11.6 months, and while not quite technically correct, for simplicity we will use this as our first full year of returns. The 30.6% is almost double our benchmark of 16.1%. There are 8/53, or just 15% of positions with a negative sign and two of those are covered calls, where we accepted a maximum return when we purchased the stock and simultaneously sold the call. This is an actual portfolio set up for newsletter purposes, making tracking much easier. The exceptional performance is the result of good luck, good stock selection and a generally rising market for the last 10 months. In Issue #5, "Luck vs. Skill," I outlined that luck contributes more to shorter-term performance, whereas skill contributes more towards longer-term performance. Unfortunately, many investors never get out of the luck phase as they turn over positions much too quickly or give up entirely after experiencing negative unlucky returns early in their investing careers. Despite emphasizing the influence of luck on results to date, it is equally important to recognize the importance of staying the course through challenging times. In some ways we make our own luck. Good luck partially comes from good design when preparation, knowledge, courage and action intersect with opportunity.

Please keep in mind that I am trying to build a robust US and international portfolio without using many US dollars due to the current depressed value of the Canadian dollar. Thus I am employing leverage through options. For those of you not comfortable with options, or who would sooner not use these slightly more complex strategies but wish to employ cash purchasing stocks outright, the companies I sell PUTS on are companies that I think represent good value. Selling a PUT is similar to buying the stock but without the immediate outlay of cash. The tradeoff is the strategy limits upside potential equal to the value of the PUT but doesn't limit downside. I do not sell PUTS unless I am prepared to get PUT and thus buy the stock, so I only sell PUTS where I think the stock is good value. As an example, when I sold a PUT on MON, which was trading for $102.50, I thought this was a pretty good value for purchasing the stock.

Portfolio Updates, Regular Account

It looks like the PUTS sold on C, WMT and EMR will expire. It also looks like COVERED CALLS sold on GDX will expire, but those sold on C and CPG will get CALLED or "exercised," as this is referred to. I decided to let the C covered CALLS be exercised but to buy back the CPG covered CALLS on the Canadian side. On January 3rd I purchased back the two CPG CALL contracts at a price of $2.59/share, accepting a small loss of $0.99/share. The shares themselves have appreciated by about $5.25 in the 11 months since purchased, so I gave up a portion of this gain. The reason for buying the CALLS back is that CPG looks like decent value with the oil recovery, and as the portfolio has grown it is best to build larger individual positions. If I allowed the 200 shares to be CALLED the remaining position of just 200 shares of CPG would be pretty small.

I also decided to allow CVS to get PUT to me, which will require $9750 USD cash. This will be covered by $3596 current cash and the $4300 from C being CALLED but I am still $1854 short. The GDX PUT was "at the money," so I have chosen to roll that position and make it larger. On January 3rd I purchased back the two GDX PUT contracts for $0.76/share, making a small profit, coincidentally the same as the CPG loss of $0.99/share. I concurrently sold four GDX PUT contracts at a strike price of $24.00 which expire on January 19, 2018. I received $5.20/share, such that my effective price if I get PUT will be $24.00 - $5.20 = $18.80 or about 11% lower than its current price of $21.20. Selling this PUT provided just enough extra cash to cover me when CVS gets PUT. I went a little further "into the money" than usual so that I could generate enough cash to cover CVS and because at today's price I am more optimistic than pessimistic on the price of gold.

TFSA: I added $5500 to each of our TFSA accounts, thus adding $11000 to the TFSA model. Currently the TFSA has about 35% international and 65% Canadian positions so adding all this to the international side would bring that up to a more acceptable 45%. The British pound is even weaker than the Canadian dollar, so it also makes sense to try to take advantage of this situation. Remember that while we transact UK purchases in USD on a US exchange, we are really buying UK companies with pound valuations. The exchange rate was 1.359 as the bank makes a big fee on exchange. We had enough money with the deposits and accumulated dividends for the following additions:

National Grid PLC (NGG): I purchased 75 shares at $57.74 in the model account. With over $15B in sales NGG is a large UK-based utility with 30% of its operations in the northeast US, providing a small backdoor way for some US exposure in the TFSA. It has three main businesses in the UK. It is a midstream operator owning transmission lines and pipelines transporting electricity and natural gas from producers to market. It is also one of the largest natural gas distributors in the UK, taking the gas from the midstream operation and distributing to end use customers. It is, however, in the process of selling 61% of this distribution business and will distribute part of the proceeds to shareholders through a special one-time dividend, probably in March. Its US business is also focused on electricity and natural gas but is more diversified than UK operations. It produces, transmits and distributes electricity plus transmits and distributes gas. This company is a "Group 1" company and covers the international portfolio gap in both the electric utility and pipeline sectors. (See November 1st, 2016 issue). Its regular dividend yield is 5.1% and it has an earnings yield of 5.7%, cash flow yield of 10.5%, price to book of 2.8x, ROE of 16.5% and ROA of 3.5%. Its ROE is amongst the highest in this industry. NGG has been on my radar for a TFSA investment for some time but I felt it was too expensive. The share price has recently become more reasonable after declining from $73.00 to its current level.

Pentair PLC (PNR) has also been on my TFSA radar for a while. I also purchased 75 shares at a price of $57.69. With about $6B in annual sales it is a reasonably large diversified industrial company based out of the UK. It has four segments, each representing about 25% of the business: 1) valves and controls 2) flow and filtration 3) water quality and 4) technical solutions for protection of sensitive equipment. The valves and controls segment, which services mostly energy-related customers, is in the process of being sold to Emerson Electric. The second and third business segments are focused on water and other fluid management for both residential and commercial customers, including agriculture, food and beverage, water infrastructure and desalination. Water is an interesting investment theme with ever increasing needs. After selling the valves and controls segment, PNR will be one of the most focused water-related industrial companies. It pays a 2.5% dividend but has more than doubled the payout with steady increases each year for the past 10 years. It has an earnings yield of 6.7% based on operating earnings but technically has not recorded net income due to write-downs in the valves and controls business. Its cash flow yield is about 8.8% and price times book is 2.3x. As with all companies involved with large write-downs its financials look wonky at this time, but these issues have brought the share price down from $80.00 three years ago to their current level. Given the company's long-term track record and very interesting business mix, I think it will turn itself around and get back on track. One aspect of trying to find good value is finding companies that have been recently wounded with the expectation they can heal their wounds. PNR fills a gap in the Group 2, industrial sector of the portfolio.

(Note: Personally we managed to buy 90 NGG and 85 PNR at these prices, but the model had less accumulated dividends.)

That concludes this month's lengthy issue. I hope you endured it all. 2016 started tough but turned into a super **fun and profitable year.**

Disclosure: As of the time of writing this issue, we owned all the stocks mentioned in our RRSPs, TFSAs or non-registered accounts. In addition, we have bought and sold the PUTS and CALLS as described above plus have sold PUTS on 100 shares each of AXP and EMR, 200 shares each of COF, SLF, 300 shares of HSE, and 600 shares of EEM that expire on Jan 20th, 2017. We have also sold PUT options representing 100 shares of CVS, 200 shares each of BHP, COF, BNS, TRP, SU, 300 shares of GE and 500 shares each of GDX and SLV that expire on Jan 19, 2018 and 100 shares of UNP that expire Jan 18, 2019.We also have CALL options representing 200 shares of SDRL that expire in Jan 20th, 2017, and all the options listed in the non-registered portfolio above. Options are not suggested until an investor has significant stock investing experience and is very comfortable with their stock investing success.

STOCKS FOR FUN AND PROFIT

Concluding Chapter: Next Steps in Your Journey

What you have just read is truly unique. I have read in the range of 40 investment books and have not seen any that chronicles actual investments in actual portfolios over time. As I read and reread the monthly newsletters for editing purposes, I found very few embarrassing moments in the over two and a half years of chronicling my investments, despite the challenging climate over this period of time. That is a pretty good accomplishment considering the stock market is often referred to as "the great humiliator." On the contrary, I found lots to be proud of and hope the effort bears fruit for readers. The investing world is full of advice and analysis, much more than can be readily used, so it is up to us to figure out who is providing valuable, concise and non-sensational guidance.

I recently read another sad story about a person's investment experience with their retirement account, in which they had invested more than $100,000. Over a 10 year period the account had grown by a measly $1,500. And here's the kicker: it had accumulated $25,000 of fees over the same period of time. Whose fault is this? While most would pin the blame on an irresponsible adviser, does the client not share part of the blame? What did this person do to oversee the adviser's efforts? If this person had read Issue #8, January 5, 2015, "Is a 15% Gain Better Than a 22% Loss?" would they have been better prepared to evaluate their own portfolio performance and been more educated in discussing the performance of the account with their adviser? Whether working with an adviser or investing on your own, the issue outlining how to calculate annual returns is one of the most critical.

While writing this newsletter, I tried to integrate many other useful educational components in addition to providing stock selections organized into portfolios. Those portfolios were developed quicker than they would likely be developed in real life, especially if you are just starting out. They do, however, illustrate how to build a stable and resilient portfolio over time. I hope to have adequately illustrated that better performance comes from minimal change, rather than perpetual tinkering. It is important to think like an investor, not a trader. This investing rather than trading mentality will reduce workload managing investments but is contingent on making good stock selection decisions to begin with. While the amount of material in the book may have seemed overwhelming, please keep in mind that only a few changes were made each month and the book covered two and a half years worth of material. It is my aim with the newsletter to have subscribers spend just a couple hours per month on their investments.

The stock market may be considered risky but I don't look at it that way. It may be volatile and there might be risky, speculative stocks, but overall every bear market has given way to recovery and growth. **The real risk resides in oneself and one's reaction to volatility.**

The markets never sleep and as we are approaching book publication I wanted to update you on portfolio progress to June 1st, 2017. The TFSA is having a good year and is now up 5.7%. A couple of times through the bear market I promised to dig out of the hole without resorting to panicky changes and that's what we did. I hope this clearly demonstrates the point that the real risk resides in oneself rather than in the market. The RRSP slid marginally to being up 16.4%, mainly due to the Home Capital Group situation. This demonstrates the importance of controlling position size so that no one company can dramatically negatively effect the portfolio. The regular account continues to power forward and is now up 39.1%. That's pretty good!

Your next steps are up to you. As the old saying goes, "you can lead a horse to water, but you can't make them drink." I hope the book provided enough motivation and know-how to make you want to take a drink from the stock trough. **Start slow, build confidence and prosper**. Very few things can be guaranteed in life, but what can be guaranteed is if you "Take the Pay from an Hour a Day to Put Away" and invest it wisely, you will build significant wealth over time. For Canadian readers, should you wish to continue reading my work, please fill out the subscriber's agreement and mail or email you1st.stocks@gmail.com and check out www.you1stenterprises.com. Your Success Is Our Quest.

APPENDIX

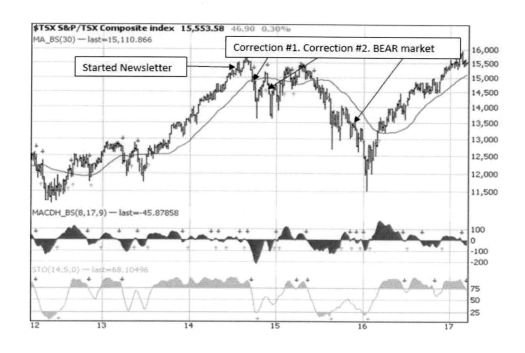

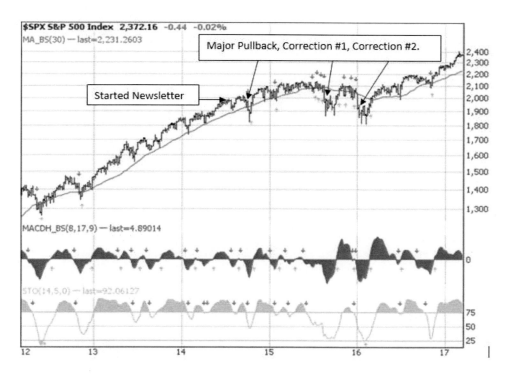

STOCKS for FUN and PROFIT: SUBSCRIBER'S AGREEMENT

You1st Enterprises Ltd. and Herman VanGenderen, as editor, will always endeavour to provide accurate and up-to-date information; however, financial markets are always changing, often rapidly. The subscriber hereby acknowledges this and shall not hold You1st Enterprises Ltd., Herman VanGenderen or any of its employees or agents liable for any reason.

You1st Enterprises Ltd., Herman VanGenderen as editor, employees or agents and the newsletter, *STOCKS for FUN and PROFIT* are advising generally and do not in any way purport to be tailoring their advice to the individual subscriber. The individual subscriber hereby acknowledges that they are taking responsibility for identifying their own needs, including the needs relative to consulting financial and tax professionals.

The subscriber also hereby agrees that they will NOT electronically forward or reproduce in any way, the contents of the newsletter without permission. As a subscriber you are paying good money for the newsletter, and only you and your spouse should benefit from it. The subscriber also recognizes the need for You1st Enterprises Ltd. to profit from the newsletter in order to continue providing the service.

The subscriber also hereby provides You1st Enterprises Ltd. permission to email.

You1st Enterprises Ltd. may, in its sole discretion, assign all of its rights and obligations under this agreement to an affiliated corporation.

Subscription Price: One year $500, two years $900, three years $1200 plus GST/HST. Please make cheques payable to You1st Enterprises Ltd. and mail to Herman VanGenderen, 45 Hampstead Manor NW, Calgary, AB T3A6A2.

The newsletter and other publications will contain the following disclaimer: The information presented has been obtained from sources believed to be reliable, and You1st Enterprises Ltd endeavours to present all information as accurately as possible. However, complete accuracy cannot be guaranteed. Opinions expressed reflect personal judgment, and are subject to change without notice. The publisher and its agents or employees shall not be held liable for any loss or damage that arises from negligence, misrepresentation or any act of omission of the publisher or its agents or employees. Trade in stocks and options carries substantial risk. Anyone considering such strategies recognizes this risk and must carefully consider their investments needs and their need to consult with financial and tax professionals. The writer is not a financial professional but rather a successful amateur. Writings should not be considered as advice, but rather in the context of what I have done myself to be successful. Future returns cannot be guaranteed. This report may not be reproduced or redistributed in whole or in part without the permission of You1st Enterprises Ltd.

I have read and understand this subscriber's agreement and hereby agree to honour it.

Full Name (please print) _____

Subscriber Signature _____ **Date** _____

Email _____

Address _____